Kaplan Publishing are constantly finding new ways to make a difference to your studies and our exciting online resources really do offer something different to students looking for exam success.

This book comes with free EN-gage online resources so that you can study anytime, anywhere.

Having purchased this book, you have access to the following online study materials:

CONTENT	ACCA (including FFA,FAB,FMA)		AAT		FIA (excluding FFA,FAB,FMA)	
	Text	Kit	Text	Kit	Text	Kit
iPaper version of the book	✓	✓	✓	✓	✓	✓
Interactive electronic version of the book	✓					
Fixed tests / progress tests with instant answers	✓		✓			
Mock assessments online			✓	✓		
Material updates	✓	✓	✓	✓	✓	✓
Latest official ACCA exam questions		✓				
Extra question assistance using the signpost icon*		✓				
Timed questions with an online tutor debrief using the clock icon*		✓				
Interim assessment including questions and answers		✓			✓	
Technical articles	✓	✓			✓	✓

* Excludes F1, F2, F3, FFA, FAB, FMA

How to access your online resources

Kaplan Financial students will already have a Kaplan EN-gage account and these extra resources will be available to you online. You do not need to register again, as this process was completed when you enrolled. If you are having problems accessing online materials, please ask your course administrator.

If you are already a registered Kaplan EN-gage user go to www.EN-gage.co.uk and log in. Select the 'add a book' feature and enter the ISBN number of this book and the unique pass key at the bottom of this card. Then click 'finished' or 'add another book'. You may add as many books as you have purchased from this screen.

If you purchased through Kaplan Flexible Learning or via the Kaplan Publishing website you will automatically receive an e-mail invitation to Kaplan EN·gage online. Please register your details using this email to gain access to your content. If you do not receive the e-mail or book content, please contact Kaplan Flexible Learning.

If you are a new Kaplan EN-gage user register at www.EN-gage.co.uk and click on the link contained in the email we sent you to activate your account. Then select the 'add a book' feature, enter the ISBN number of this book and the unique pass key at the bottom of this card. Then click 'finished' or 'add another book'.

Your Code and Information

This code can only be used once for the registration of one book online. This registration and your online content will expire when the final sittings for the examinations covered by this book have taken place. Please allow one hour from the time you submit your book details for us to process your request.

Please scratch the film to access your EN-gage code.

Please be aware that this code is case-sensitive and you will need to include the dashes within the passcode, but not when entering the ISBN. For further technical support, please visit www.EN-gage.co.uk

Professional Examinations

Paper P5

Advanced Performance Management

EXAM KIT

KAPLAN
PUBLISHING

PAPER P5 : ADVANCED PERFORMANCE MANAGEMENT

British Library Cataloguing-in-Publication Data

A catalogue record for this book is available from the British Library.

Published by:

Kaplan Publishing UK

Unit 2 The Business Centre

Molly Millar's Lane

Wokingham

Berkshire

RG41 2QZ

ISBN: 978-0-85732-688-1

© Kaplan Financial Limited, 2012

Printed and bound in Great Britain.

The text in this material and any others made available by any Kaplan Group company does not amount to advice on a particular matter and should not be taken as such. No reliance should be placed on the content as the basis for any investment or other decision or in connection with any advice given to third parties. Please consult your appropriate professional adviser as necessary. Kaplan Publishing Limited and all other Kaplan group companies expressly disclaim all liability to any person in respect of any losses or other claims, whether direct, indirect, incidental, consequential or otherwise arising in relation to the use of such materials.

All rights reserved. No part of this examination may be reproduced or transmitted in any form or by any means, electronic or mechanical, including photocopying, recording, or by any information storage and retrieval system, without prior permission from Kaplan Publishing.

Acknowledgements

The past ACCA examination questions are the copyright of the Association of Chartered Certified Accountants. The original answers to the questions from June 1994 onwards were produced by the examiners themselves and have been adapted by Kaplan Publishing.

We are grateful to the Chartered Institute of Management Accountants and the Institute of Chartered Accountants in England and Wales for permission to reproduce past examination questions. The answers have been prepared by Kaplan Publishing.

CONTENTS

	Page
Index to questions and answers	v
Analysis of past papers	xi
Exam technique	xiii
Paper specific information	xv
Kaplan's recommended revision approach	xix
Kaplan's detailed revision plan	xxi
Formulae and mathematical tables	xxix

Section

1	Practice questions – Section A	1
2	Practice questions – Section B	45
3	Answers to practice questions – Section A	111
4	Answers to practice questions – Section B	203

In addition to providing a wide ranging bank of real past exam questions, we have also included in this edition:

- An analysis of all of the recent examination papers.

- Paper specific information and advice on exam technique.

- Our recommended approach to make your revision for this particular subject as effective as possible.

    This includes step by step guidance on how best to use our Kaplan material (Complete text, pocket notes and exam kit) at this stage in your studies.

- Enhanced tutorial answers packed with specific key answer tips, technical tutorial notes and exam technique tips from our experienced tutors.

- Complementary online resources including full tutor debriefs and question assistance to point you in the right direction when you get stuck.

KAPLAN PUBLISHING

PAPER P5 : ADVANCED PERFORMANCE MANAGEMENT

June and December 2011 and 2012 – Real examination questions

The real June and December 2011 and 2012 exam questions with answers are available on Kaplan EN-gage at:

www.EN-gage.co.uk

You will find a wealth of other resources to help you with your studies on the following sites:
www.EN-gage.co.uk
www.accaglobal.com/students/

INDEX TO QUESTIONS AND ANSWERS

INTRODUCTION

Past exam questions have been modified (sometimes extensively) to reflect the current P5 syllabus.

KEY TO THE INDEX

PAPER ENHANCEMENTS

We have added the following enhancements to the answers in this exam kit:

Key answer tips

All answers include key answer tips to help your understanding of each question.

Tutorial note

All answers include more tutorial notes to explain some of the technical points in more detail.

Top tutor tips

For selected questions, we "walk through the answer" giving guidance on how to approach the questions with helpful 'tips from a top tutor', together with technical tutor notes.

These answers are indicated with the "footsteps" icon in the index.

PAPER P5 : ADVANCED PERFORMANCE MANAGEMENT

ONLINE ENHANCEMENTS

> *Timed question with Online tutor debrief*

For selected questions, we recommend that they are to be completed in full exam conditions (i.e. properly timed in a closed book environment).

In addition to the examiner's technical answer, enhanced with key answer tips and tutorial notes in this exam kit, online you can find an answer debrief by a top tutor that:

- works through the question in full
- points out how to approach the question
- how to ensure that the easy marks are obtained as quickly as possible, and
- emphasises how to tackle exam questions and exam technique.

These questions are indicated with the "clock" icon in the index.

> *Online question assistance*

Have you ever looked at a question and not know where to start, or got stuck part way through?

For selected questions, we have produced "Online question assistance" offering different levels of guidance, such as:

- ensuring that you understand the question requirements fully, highlighting key terms and the meaning of the verbs used
- how to read the question proactively, with knowledge of the requirements, to identify the topic areas covered
- assessing the detail content of the question body, pointing out key information and explaining why it is important
- help in devising a plan of attack

With this assistance, you should then be able to attempt your answer confident that you know what is expected of you.

These questions are indicated with the "signpost" icon in the index.

Online question enhancements and answer debriefs will be available on Kaplan EN-gage at:

www.EN-gage.co.uk

INDEX TO QUESTIONS AND ANSWERS

SECTION A TYPE QUESTIONS

		Page number		
		Question	Answer	Past exam
1	Quicklink	1	111	Jun 05 (A)
2	BSN	4	122	–
3	P Group	7	126	–
4	The NAW Group	11	131	Jun 04 (A)
5	Great Western Cake Company	13	137	Jun 06 (A)
6	Snowwell	15	142	Dec 03 (A)
7	Westamber	18	147	Pilot 07
8	The Geeland Bus Company (GBC)	20	150	Dec 07
9	Alpha Division	24	159	Dec 07
10	The Health & Fitness Group (HFG)	26	163	Jun 08
11	The Sentinel Company (TSC)	28	169	Dec 08
12	Royal Laurel Hospital (RLH)	31	174	Jun 09
13	The Benjamin Education College (BEC)	32	181	Dec 09
14	The RRR Group (RRR)	34	185	Dec 09
15	The Superior Business Consultancy (SBC)	37	188	Jun 10
16	The Equine Management Academy (EMA)	39	193	Jun 10
17	Film Productions Co (FP)	40	196	Dec 10
18	Robust Laptops Co (RL)	42	199	Dec 10

Note: (A) signifies that the question has been amended from the original

SECTION B TYPE QUESTIONS

STRATEGIC PLANNING AND CONTROL

		Page number		
		Question	Answer	Past exam
19	Virtual organisations	45	203	–
20	Universal University (UU)	45	205	Jun 09
21	Divisional actions	46	208	–
22	Diverse Holdings plc	47	210	Dec 05
23	Alternative budgeting	48	212	Jun 06
24	Performance management	49	214	Jun 06
25	Business process re-engineering	49	217	–
26	Budgeting	49	218	Pilot 07
27	The 'Care For Dogs Company' (CFD)	50	220	Dec 09
28	The Rubber Group (TRG)	50	222	Jun 08

KAPLAN PUBLISHING

PAPER P5 : ADVANCED PERFORMANCE MANAGEMENT

EXTERNAL INFLUENCES ON ORGANISATIONAL PERFORMANCE

		Page number		
		Question	Answer	Past exam
29	Boardman Foods (BF)	52	227	–
30	MTM Group	54	229	Nov 05
31	Social responsibility	54	231	–
32	Digwell Explorations	55	232	–
33	The Global Hotel Group	55	236	Jun 08
34	Franchising For You Ltd (F4U)	56	239	Jun 09
35	FGH Telecom (FGH)	57	242	Dec 10

PERFORMANCE MEASUREMENT SYSTEMS AND DESIGN

		Question	Answer	Past exam
36	Motor component manufacturer	59	245	Dec 02
37	Precision parts	59	247	–
38	Accounting systems	60	250	Jun 03
39	GMB Co	60	252	Dec 07
40	The Ornamental Company (TOC)	61	255	Dec 08
41	Report	63	259	Pilot 07
42	Environmental information	63	261	–

STRATEGIC PERFORMANCE MEASUREMENT

		Question	Answer	Past exam
43	HEG	63	262	Dec 07
44	The Motherhelp Company (TMC)	64	265	Dec 08
45	Statutory transport authority	65	269	–
46	Mission Statement	66	270	Dec 02
47	Project X	66	272	Jun 03
48	The Children's Toy Company (CTC)	67	276	Jun 08
49	Vision plc	69	278	Dec 06
50	Better Agriculture Group (BAG)	70	281	Dec 08
51	Unique Components Ltd	72	284	Pilot 07
52	SSA Group	73	286	Dec 09
53	Local government housing department	75	289	Jun 10
54	Pipe Dream	76	291	–
55	Universal Pottery Company (UPC)	76	293	–
56	Telecoms At Work (TAW)	77	297	Jun 08
57	Gibson & Chew	79	300	–
58	Equiguard	80	303	–
59	Business Solutions	82	307	Jun 02
60	Bettaserve	83	309	Pilot 07
61	Superior Software House (SSH)	84	311	Dec 08

INDEX TO QUESTIONS AND ANSWERS

PERFORMANCE EVALUATION AND CORPORATE FAILURE

		Page number		
		Question	*Answer*	*Past exam*
62	Royal Botanical Gardens	86	315	–
63	Specialist Clothing Company	87	318	*Jun 06*
64	BPC	88	321	*Dec 07*
65	Dental Health	89	323	*Jun 05*
66	BLA Ltd	91	326	*Dec 03*
67	Performance pyramid	93	330	*Jun 06 (A)*
68	The Success Education Centre (SEC)	94	334	*Pilot 07*
69	Cundy Aquatic Pursuits (CAP)	96	336	*Dec 09*
70	The Spare for Ships Company (SFS)	97	339	*Jun 10*
71	LOL Co	99	342	*Dec 10*
72	RM Batteries Co	100	345	*Dec 10*

CURRENT DEVELOPMENTS AND EMERGING ISSUES IN MANAGEMENT ACCOUNTING AND PERFORMANCE MANAGEMENT

73	Total Timber Group (TTG)	102	347	–
74	Public services	103	349	–
75	Shareholder value analysis	103	351	–
76	PD	104	353	–
77	Sports complex	104	355	–
78	BIOTEC	105	357	–
79	Bennett plc	107	360	*Dec 03*
80	The Better Electricals Group (BEG)	108	362	*Jun 10*

ANALYSIS OF PAST PAPERS

The table below summarises the key topics that have been tested in recent examinations to date.

	Pilot 07	Dec 07	Jun 08	Dec 08	Jun 09	Dec 09	Jun 10	Dec 10	Jun 11	Dec 11	Jun 12
CSFs		X				X		X			
KPIs						X		X		X	X
Mission Statements	X					X					
Gap analysis					X						
Benchmarking			X								X
Environmental issues			X	X		X					
Stakeholders									X		
PEST(EL)								X			
Porter's 5 forces		X									
Risk	X				X		X			X	
Ethics/CSR	X				X						
Budget calculations		X				X	X				
Budget discussion	X		X								
ABC/ABM/ABB		X			X		X	X			
Beyond budgeting	X					X		X			
Service companies	X				X		X	X			
Decision making systems									X		
Performance measurement systems						X				X	X
Information – EIS, etc								X	X	X	
Agency and expectancy theory					X						
Financial performance evaluation	X		X	X	X	X	X				
RI, ROI, EVA		X	X					X	X		
VBM								X			
BCG analysis									X		
Transfer pricing	X				X		X				
NFP organisations		X					X				
Non-financial performance (general)	X		X	X			X	X			X
Building block model			X			X			X		
Balanced scorecard					X		X		X		
Performance pyramid	X									X	
Performance prism											X
Corporate failure		X						X			
Quality			X	X	X		X			X	X
EMA									X		
League tables/targets				X							X
Reward systems										X	

KAPLAN PUBLISHING

EXAM TECHNIQUE

- Use the allocated **15 minutes reading and planning time** at the beginning of the exam:
    - read the questions and examination requirements carefully, and
    - begin planning your answers.

  See the Paper Specific Information for advice on how to use this time for this paper.

- **Divide the time** you spend on questions in proportion to the marks on offer:
    - there are 1.8 minutes available per mark in the examination
    - within that, try to allow time at the end of each question to review your answer and address any obvious issues

  Whatever happens, always keep your eye on the clock and **do not over run on any part of any question!**

- Spend the last **five minutes** of the examination:
    - reading through your answers, and
    - **making any additions or corrections.**

- If you **get completely stuck** with a question:
    - leave space in your answer book, and
    - **return to it later.**

- Stick to the question and **tailor your answer** to what you are asked.
    - pay particular attention to the verbs in the question.

- If you do not understand what a question is asking, **state your assumptions**.

  Even if you do not answer in precisely the way the examiner hoped, you should be given some credit, if your assumptions are reasonable.

- You should do everything you can to make things easy for the marker.

  The marker will find it easier to identify the points you have made if your **answers are legible**.

- **Written questions**:

  Your answer should have:
    - a clear structure
    - a brief introduction, a main section and a conclusion.

  Be concise.

  It is better to write a little about a lot of different points than a great deal about one or two points.

- **Computations**:

  It is essential to include all your workings in your answers.

  Many computational questions can be answered using a standard step by step approach.

  e.g. ABC computations, linear programming and variance calculations.

  Be sure you know these steps before the exam and practice answering a range of questions using the same step by step approach.

- **Reports, memos and other documents**:

  Some questions ask you to present your answer in the form of a report, a memo, a letter or other document.

  Make sure that you use the correct format – there could be easy marks to gain here.

PAPER P5 : ADVANCED PERFORMANCE MANAGEMENT

PAPER SPECIFIC INFORMATION

THE EXAM

FORMAT OF THE EXAM

	Number of marks
Section A: 1 compulsory question.	50
Section B: Choice of 2 from 3 questions worth 25 marks each.	50

There will be a mixture of written requirements and computational requirements.

Total time allowed: 3 hours plus 15 minutes reading and planning time.

Note that:

- All syllabus areas will be examined.
- The exam may contain one question from each syllabus area. However, some exam questions have examined more than one syllabus area in the same question, especially in section A.
- Questions will be based around a short scenario. It is important to refer back to this scenario when answering the question.
- Earlier knowledge from previous papers will be drawn on at times.

PASS MARK

The pass mark for all ACCA Qualification examination papers is 50%.

READING AND PLANNING TIME

Remember that all three hour paper based examinations have an additional 15 minutes reading and planning time.

ACCA GUIDANCE

ACCA guidance on the use of this time is as follows:

> This additional time is allowed at the beginning of the examination to allow candidates to read the questions and to begin planning their answers before they start to write in their answer books.
>
> This time should be used to ensure that all the information and, in particular, the exam requirements are properly read and understood.
>
> During this time, candidates may only annotate their question paper. They may not write anything in their answer booklets until told to do so by the invigilator.

PAPER P5 : ADVANCED PERFORMANCE MANAGEMENT

KAPLAN GUIDANCE

As all questions are compulsory, there are no decisions to be made about choice of questions, other than in which order you would like to tackle them.

Therefore, in relation to P5, we recommend that you take the following approach with your reading and planning time:

- **Skim through the whole paper**, assessing the level of difficulty of each question.

- **Write down** on the question paper next to the mark allocation **the amount of time you should spend on each part.** Do this for each part of every question.

- **Decide the order** in which you think you will attempt each question:

  This is a personal choice and you have time on the revision phase to try out different approaches, for example, if you sit mock exams.

  A common approach is to tackle the question you think is the easiest and you are most comfortable with first.

  Psychologists believe that you usually perform at your best on the second and third question you attempt, once you have settled into the exam, so not tackling the most difficult question first may be advisable.

  It is usual however that students tackle their least favourite topic and/or the most difficult question in their opinion last.

  Whatever you approach, you must make sure that you leave enough time to attempt all questions fully and be very strict with yourself in timing each question.

- **For each question** in turn, read the requirements and then the detail of the question carefully.

  Always read the requirement first as this enables you to **focus on the detail of the question with the specific task in mind**.

  For computational questions:

  Highlight key numbers / information and key words in the question, scribble notes to yourself on the question paper to remember key points in your answer.

  Jot down proformas required if applicable.

  For written questions:

  Take notice of the format required (e.g. letter, memo, notes) and identify the recipient of the answer. You need to do this to judge the level of financial sophistication required in your answer and whether the use of a formal reply or informal bullet points would be satisfactory.

  Plan your beginning, middle and end and the key areas to be addressed and your use of titles and sub-titles to enhance your answer.

  For all questions:

  Spot the easy marks to be gained in a question and parts which can be performed independently of the rest of the question. For example, a definition of a variance or an explanation of the steps carried out in target costing.

  Make sure that you do these parts first when you tackle the question.

PAPER SPECIFIC INFORMATION

> Don't go overboard in terms of planning time on any one question – you need a good measure of the whole paper and a plan for all of the questions at the end of the 15 minutes.
>
> By covering all questions you can often help yourself as you may find that facts in one question may remind you of things you should put into your answer relating to a different question.
>
> - With your plan of attack in mind, **start answering your chosen question** with your plan to hand, as soon as you are allowed to start.

Always keep your eye on the clock and do not over run on any part of any question!

DETAILED SYLLABUS

The detailed syllabus and study guide written by the ACCA can be found at:

www.accaglobal.com/students/

PAPER P5 : ADVANCED PERFORMANCE MANAGEMENT

KAPLAN'S RECOMMENDED REVISION APPROACH

QUESTION PRACTICE IS THE KEY TO SUCCESS

Success in professional examinations relies upon you acquiring a firm grasp of the required knowledge at the tuition phase. In order to be able to do the questions, knowledge is essential.

However, the difference between success and failure often hinges on your exam technique on the day and making the most of the revision phase of your studies.

The **Kaplan complete text** is the starting point, designed to provide the underpinning knowledge to tackle all questions. However, in the revision phase, pouring over text books is not the answer.

Kaplan Online fixed tests help you consolidate your knowledge and understanding and are a useful tool to check whether you can remember key topic areas.

Kaplan pocket notes are designed to help you quickly revise a topic area, however you then need to practice questions. There is a need to progress to full exam standard questions as soon as possible, and to tie your exam technique and technical knowledge together.

The importance of question practice cannot be over-emphasised.

The recommended approach below is designed by expert tutors in the field, in conjunction with their knowledge of the examiner and their recent real exams.

The approach taken for the fundamental papers is to revise by topic area. However, with the professional stage papers, a multi topic approach is required to answer the scenario based questions.

You need to practice as many questions as possible in the time you have left.

OUR AIM

Our aim is to get you to the stage where you can attempt exam standard questions confidently, to time, in a closed book environment, with no supplementary help (i.e. to simulate the real examination experience).

Practising your exam technique on real past examination questions, in timed conditions, is also vitally important for you to assess your progress and identify areas of weakness that may need more attention in the final run up to the examination.

In order to achieve this we recognise that initially you may feel the need to practice some questions with open book help and exceed the required time.

The approach below shows you which questions you should use to build up to coping with exam standard question practice, and references to the sources of information available should you need to revisit a topic area in more detail.

Remember that in the real examination, all you have to do is:

- attempt all questions required by the exam
- only spend the allotted time on each question, and
- get them at least 50% right!

Try and practice this approach on every question you attempt from now to the real exam.

PAPER P5 : ADVANCED PERFORMANCE MANAGEMENT

EXAMINER COMMENTS

We have included the examiners comments to the specific new syllabus examination questions in this kit for you to see the main pitfalls that students fall into with regard to technical content.

However, too many times in the general section of the report, the examiner comments that students had failed due to:

- "not answering the question"
- "a poor understanding of why something is done, not just how it is done"
- "simply writing out numbers from the question. Candidates must understand what the numbers tell them about business performance"
- "a lack of common business sense" and
- "ignoring clues in the question".

Good exam technique is vital.

THE KAPLAN PAPER P5 REVISION PLAN

Stage 1: Assess areas of strengths and weaknesses

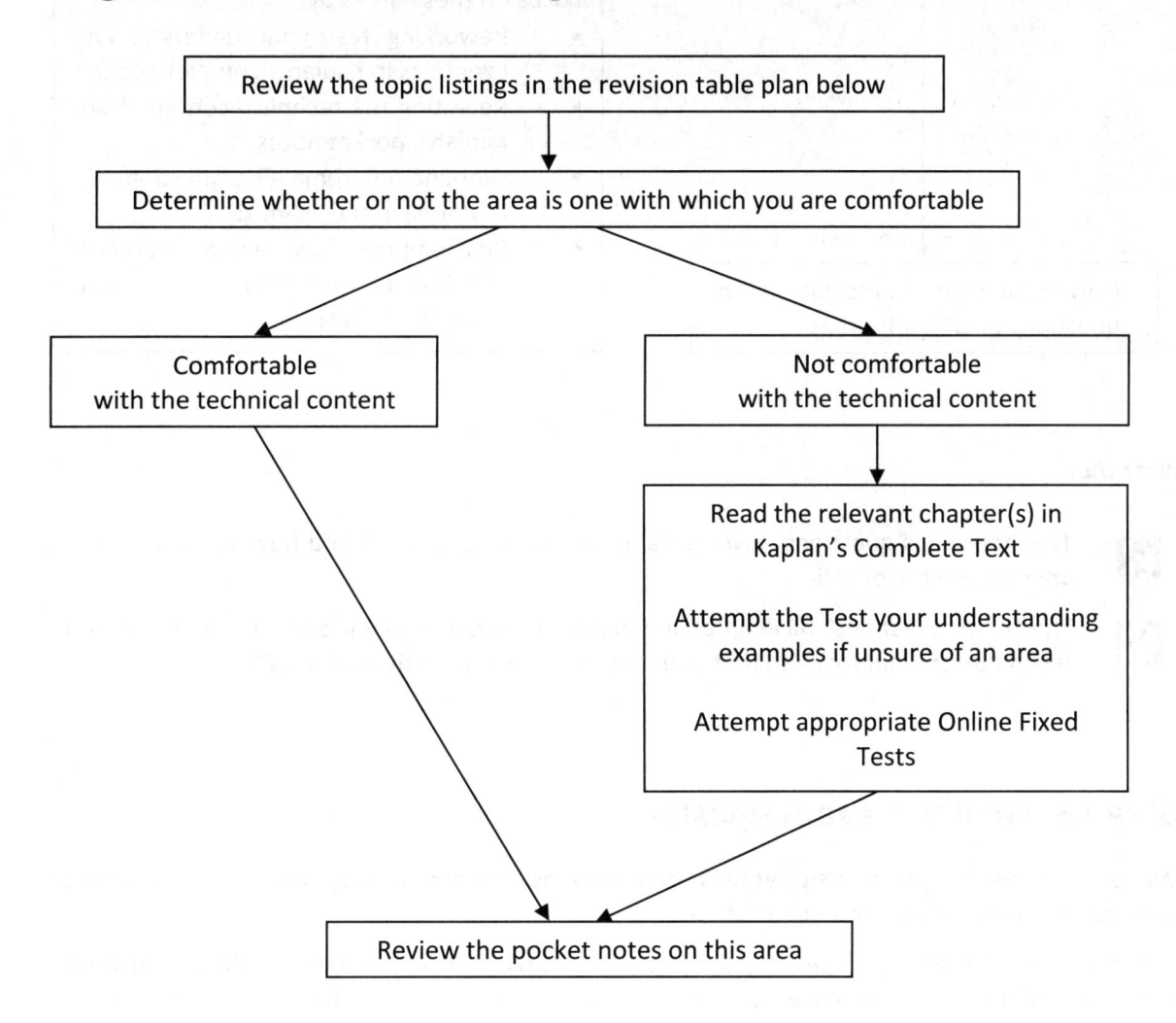

```
Review the topic listings in the revision table plan below
                            ↓
Determine whether or not the area is one with which you are comfortable
                    ↙                           ↘
    Comfortable                          Not comfortable
 with the technical content          with the technical content
                                              ↓
                                   Read the relevant chapter(s) in
                                       Kaplan's Complete Text

                                   Attempt the Test your understanding
                                     examples if unsure of an area

                                   Attempt appropriate Online Fixed
                                                Tests
                    ↘                           ↙
              Review the pocket notes on this area
```

Stage 2: Practice questions

Follow the order of revision of topics as recommended in the revision table plan below and attempt the questions in the order suggested.

Try to avoid referring to text books and notes and the model answer until you have completed your attempt.

Try to answer the question in the allotted time.

Review your attempt with the model answer and assess how much of the answer you achieved in the allocated exam time.

Fill in the self-assessment box below and decide on your best course of action.

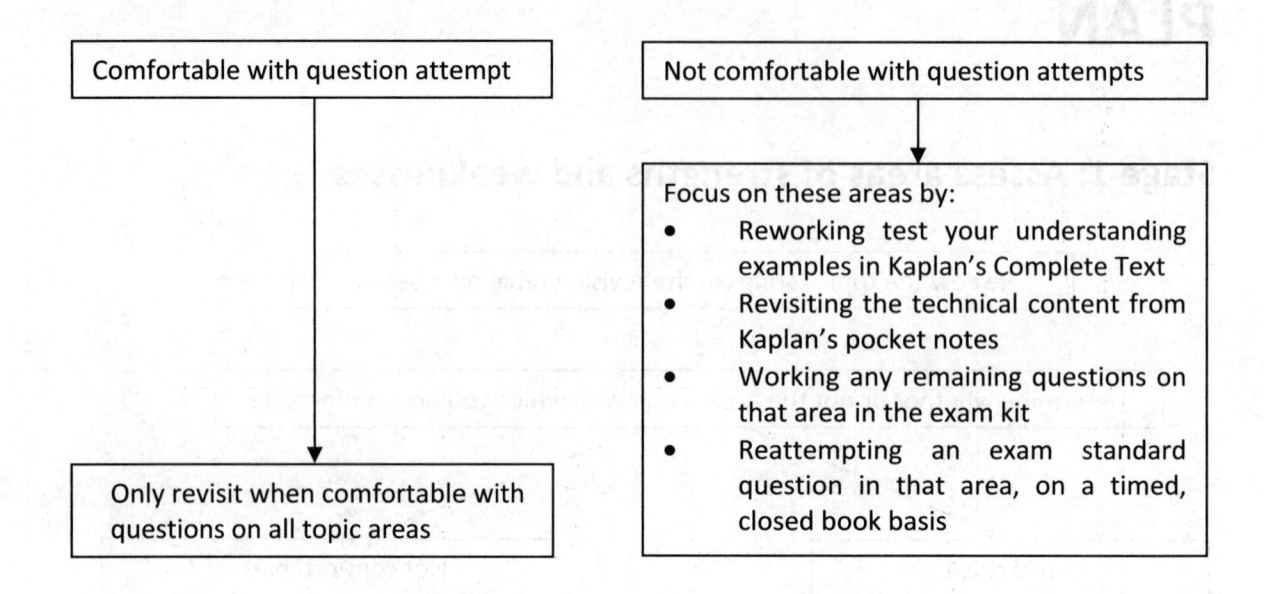

```
┌─────────────────────────────────────┐        ┌─────────────────────────────────────┐
│ Comfortable with question attempt   │        │ Not comfortable with question attempts │
└─────────────────────────────────────┘        └─────────────────────────────────────┘
                 │                                                │
                 │                                                ▼
                 │                              ┌─────────────────────────────────────┐
                 │                              │ Focus on these areas by:            │
                 │                              │  • Reworking test your understanding│
                 │                              │    examples in Kaplan's Complete Text│
                 │                              │  • Revisiting the technical content │
                 │                              │    from Kaplan's pocket notes       │
                 │                              │  • Working any remaining questions  │
                 │                              │    on that area in the exam kit     │
                 ▼                              │  • Reattempting an exam standard    │
┌─────────────────────────────────────┐         │    question in that area, on a timed,│
│ Only revisit when comfortable with  │         │    closed book basis                │
│ questions on all topic areas        │         └─────────────────────────────────────┘
└─────────────────────────────────────┘
```

Note that:

- The "footsteps questions" give guidance on exam techniques and how you should have approached the question.

- The "clock questions" have an online debrief where a tutor talks you through the exam technique and approach to that question and works the question in full.

Stage 3: Final pre-exam revision

We recommend that you **attempt at least one three hour mock examination** containing a set of previously unseen exam standard questions.

It is important that you get a feel for the breadth of coverage of a real exam without advanced knowledge of the topic areas covered – just as you will expect to see on the real exam day.

Ideally this mock should be sat in timed, closed book, real exam conditions and could be:

- a mock examination offered by your tuition provider, and/or

- the pilot paper in the back of this exam kit, and/or

- the last real examination paper (available shortly afterwards on Kaplan EN-gage with "enhanced walk through answers" and a full "tutor debrief").

THE DETAILED REVISION PLAN

Topic	Complete Text Chapter	Pocket note Chapter	Questions to attempt	Tutor guidance	Date attempted	Self assessment
Strategic planning and budgeting						
- Mission statements CSFs	1	1	Q17 Q27 Q43	Emphasise the importance of CSF's in planning as a method of performance management.		
- SWOT	1	1	Q22 Q19	Reminder of SWOT analysis and its importance.		
- Benchmarking	1	1	Q10(b) Q37(c)	This is a relatively straightforward technique but it is still important to practice at least one question to ensure you have the required knowledge.		
- Gap analysis	1	1	Q44 Q49	This is a very good question on establishing the strategic gap and how an organisation would attempt to close this gap.		
- Risk analysis	1	1	Q29 Q30	The calculations are important here but you must also be prepared to discuss the various methods of managing risk. Some of the terms, e.g. minimax regret, make this area appear difficult but the underlying concepts are straightforward. Also think about how the learning curve may affect decision making.		
- Stakeholders	2	2	Q32	Think about stakeholders and what do they want? How does Mendelow's matrix help to resolve conflict?		

PAPER P5 : ADVANCED PERFORMANCE MANAGEMENT

Topic	Complete Text Chapter	Pocket note Chapter	Questions to attempt	Tutor guidance	Date attempted	Self assessment
- Environmental	2	2	Q35 Q3 Q33	Think PESTLE!		
- Porter's 5 forces	2	2	Q64	An excellent question that will test your understanding of the five forces to an organisation looking at it from the performance angle.		
Budgeting						
- Various approaches	3	3	Q16 Q7	Do not overlook this area. Knowledge of the written areas of budgeting can help you to score relatively easy marks in the exam. Budgeting calculations should not cause you too many problems.		
- ABC / ABM	3	3	Q18 Q39 Q70	This is a key costing technique. Make sure that you can calculate the cost per unit using the five step approach. Be ready to explain the reasons for the development of ABC, the pros and cons of ABC and the implications of ABC.		
Changes in Business Structure						
- Porters value chain and BPR	4	4	Q25	Think about how organisations are facing changing business environments due to increasing competition, changes in technology and greater globalisation.		

Topic	Complete Text Chapter	Pocket note Chapter	Questions to attempt	Tutor guidance	Date attempted	Self assessment
The impact of Information Technology						
- MIS, EIS, DSS	5	5	Q17	Think about the link between performance management and MIS. In particular, what information needs does the organisation have, should they implement an EIS or a DSS, what are the implications of any plans for the company website?		
Financial performance						
- Operational and financial difficulties	7	7	Q8 Q68	Rather than focusing on achieving higher profit levels, companies are under increasing pressure to look at long-term value of the business.		
- Various financial performance calculations	7	7	Q10 Q69	Think about the importance of calculations such as working capital, gearing, liquidity, profit margin ratios, and EBITDA when assessing performance.		
- NPV & IRR	7	7	Q34 Q48	The challenge facing firms is how to adapt the NPV technique to set targets for managers and short-term performance management. It is also import to think of the effect of sensitivity to decision making.		
Divisional performance						
- ROI/RI	7	7	Q1 Q9 Q10	It is important that you can calculate the ROI and RI but you must also be able to discuss the pros and cons of each of these methods. Talk about the numerical measures of divisional performance – ROI & RI.		

PAPER P5 : ADVANCED PERFORMANCE MANAGEMENT

Topic	Complete Text Chapter	Pocket note Chapter	Questions to attempt	Tutor guidance	Date attempted	Self assessment
- Potential problems	7	7	Q21	Emphasise the potential for inappropriate investments decisions and ways to resolve the problem.		
- EVA	8	8	Q71 Q10	EVA™ is the financial performance measure that comes closer than any other to capturing the true *economic* profit of an organisation, and is the performance measure most directly linked to the creation of shareholder wealth over time.		
- Transfer pricing	8	8	Q50 Q51	The transfer price negotiated between the divisions, or imposed by head office, can have a profound, but perhaps arbitrary, effect on the reported performance and subsequent decisions made.		
- Ansoff & BCG	8	8	Q44 Q63	Where a planning gap exists, additional strategies are required. A company might make use of Ansoff's growth vector matrix which identifies various options that might be considered in order to close the planning gap. A company could use the Boston Consulting growth share matrix in order to classify its subsidiary companies in terms of their rate of market growth and relative market share.		

KAPLAN'S DETAILED REVISION PLAN

Topic	Complete Text Chapter	Pocket note Chapter	Questions to attempt	Tutor guidance	Date attempted	Self assessment
NFPIs						
- Not for profit organisations	9	9	Q45 Q53	Think about the problems and diversity of objectives and the different approaches to performance measurement in NFPs. How assessment can be achieved in a number of ways, including the use of VFM.		
- NFPIs, Balance scorecard, performance pyramid and building blocks	10	10	Q12 Q15 Q62 Q66	The aim of the balance scorecard, which is to enable the business to translate objectives into goals and performance measures. Refer to the issues involved in implementing the scorecard. Review the performance pyramid and Fitzgerald and Moon's building block model.		
Corporate failure						
- Z score & Argenti	10	10	Q72 Q6	Discuss corporate failure, assessing the likelihood and prediction models such as Altman's Z score and Argenti.		
Quality						
- Costs of quality	10	11	Q50 Q80	Ensure you understand the different definitions of quality and cost classification		
- Six sigma and DMAIC	10	11	Q55	Six sigma and DMAIC must be viewed as the most important aspects of quality within P5		
- TQM	10	11	Q54	Also make sure you know the basics of TQM		

PAPER P5 : ADVANCED PERFORMANCE MANAGEMENT

Topic	Complete Text Chapter	Pocket note Chapter	Questions to attempt	Tutor guidance	Date attempted	Self assessment
HR aspects						
- Recruitment, management and motivation	6	6	Q20	It is vital that managers are motivated to achieve the goals and KPIs of the organisation.		
- Assessment and appraisal	6	6	Q57	To ensure goal congruence it is essential that KPIS, CSFs and manager targets are linked.		
- Reward schemes	6	6	Q58	There is an ongoing debate surrounding the benefits of performance related pay and reward systems. Ensure you can discuss and apply these issues if required.		
PM developments						
- Kaizen, JIT, Target costing, social responsibility & EMA and performance prism.	11	11	Q78 Q75 Q77	Changes in the environment such as technology and globalisation have led to the application of various techniques such as kaizen costing, JIT, Target costing, EMA and the performance prism. This has changed the role of an accountant, how they report and analyse information.		

Note that not all of the questions in the kit are referred to in the programme above. We have recommended a large number of exam standard questions and successful completion of these should reassure you that you have a good grounding of all of the key topics and are well prepared for the exam.

The remaining questions are available in the kit for extra practice for those who require more questions on some areas.

FORMULAE AND MATHEMATICAL TABLES

FORMULAE

Learning curve

$Y = ax^b$

Where y = average cost per batch
          a = cost of first batch
          x = total number of batches produced
          b = learning factor (log LR/log 2)
         LR = the learning rate as a decimal

Demand curve

$P = a - bQ$

$b = \dfrac{\text{Change in price}}{\text{Change in quantity}}$

a = price when Q = 0

MATHEMATICAL TABLES

PRESENT VALUE TABLE

Present value of 1 i.e. $(1+r)^{-n}$ where r = discount rate, n = number of periods until payment

Periods (n)	\multicolumn{10}{c}{Discount rate (r)}	
	1%	2%	3%	4%	5%	6%	7%	8%	9%	10%	
1	0.990	0.980	0.971	0.962	0.952	0.943	0.935	0.926	0.917	0.909	1
2	0.980	0.961	0.943	0.925	0.907	0.890	0.873	0.857	0.842	0.826	2
3	0.971	0.942	0.915	0.889	0.864	0.840	0.816	0.794	0.772	0.751	3
4	0.961	0.924	0.888	0.855	0.823	0.792	0.763	0.735	0.708	0.683	4
5	0.951	0.906	0.863	0.822	0.784	0.747	0.713	0.681	0.650	0.621	5
6	0.942	0.888	0.837	0.790	0.746	0.705	0.666	0.630	0.596	0.564	6
7	0.933	0.871	0.813	0.760	0.711	0.665	0.623	0.583	0.547	0.513	7
8	0.923	0.853	0.789	0.731	0.677	0.627	0.582	0.540	0.502	0.467	8
9	0.914	0.837	0.766	0.703	0.645	0.592	0.544	0.500	0.460	0.424	9
10	0.905	0.820	0.744	0.676	0.614	0.558	0.508	0.463	0.422	0.386	10
11	0.896	0.804	0.722	0.650	0.585	0.527	0.475	0.429	0.388	0.350	11
12	0.887	0.788	0.701	0.625	0.557	0.497	0.444	0.397	0.356	0.319	12
13	0.879	0.773	0.681	0.601	0.530	0.469	0.415	0.368	0.326	0.290	13
14	0.870	0.758	0.661	0.577	0.505	0.442	0.388	0.340	0.299	0.263	14
15	0.861	0.743	0.642	0.555	0.481	0.417	0.362	0.315	0.275	0.239	15
(n)	11%	12%	13%	14%	15%	16%	17%	18%	19%	20%	
1	0.901	0.893	0.885	0.877	0.870	0.862	0.855	0.847	0.840	0.833	1
2	0.812	0.797	0.783	0.769	0.756	0.743	0.731	0.718	0.706	0.694	2
3	0.731	0.712	0.693	0.675	0.658	0.641	0.624	0.609	0.593	0.579	3
4	0.659	0.636	0.613	0.592	0.572	0.552	0.534	0.516	0.499	0.482	4
5	0.593	0.567	0.543	0.519	0.497	0.476	0.456	0.437	0.419	0.402	5
6	0.535	0.507	0.480	0.456	0.432	0.410	0.390	0.370	0.352	0.335	6
7	0.482	0.452	0.425	0.400	0.376	0.354	0.333	0.314	0.296	0.279	7
8	0.434	0.404	0.376	0.351	0.327	0.305	0.285	0.266	0.249	0.233	8
9	0.391	0.361	0.333	0.308	0.284	0.263	0.243	0.225	0.209	0.194	9
10	0.352	0.322	0.295	0.270	0.247	0.227	0.208	0.191	0.176	0.162	10
11	0.317	0.287	0.261	0.237	0.215	0.195	0.178	0.162	0.148	0.135	11
12	0.286	0.257	0.231	0.208	0.187	0.168	0.152	0.137	0.124	0.112	12
13	0.258	0.229	0.204	0.182	0.163	0.145	0.130	0.116	0.104	0.093	13
14	0.232	0.205	0.181	0.160	0.141	0.125	0.111	0.099	0.088	0.078	14
15	0.209	0.183	0.160	0.140	0.123	0.108	0.095	0.084	0.074	0.065	15

FORMULAE AND MATHEMATICAL TABLES

ANNUITY TABLE

Present value of an annuity of 1 i.e. $\dfrac{1-(1+r)^{-n}}{r}$ where r = discount rate, n = number of periods

Periods (n)	1%	2%	3%	4%	5%	6%	7%	8%	9%	10%	
1	0.990	0.980	0.971	0.962	0.952	0.943	0.935	0.926	0.917	0.909	1
2	1.970	1.942	1.913	1.886	1.859	1.833	1.808	1.783	1.759	1.736	2
3	2.941	2.884	20829	2.775	2.723	2.673	2.624	2.577	2.531	2.487	3
4	3.902	3.808	3.717	3.630	3.546	3.465	3.387	3.312	3.240	3.170	4
5	4.853	4.713	4.580	4.452	4.329	4.212	4.100	3.993	3.890	3.791	5
6	5.795	5.601	5.417	5.242	5.076	4.917	4.767	4.623	4.486	4.355	6
7	6.728	6.472	6.230	6.002	5.786	5.582	5.389	5.206	5.033	4.868	7
8	7.652	7.325	7.020	6.733	6.463	6.210	5.971	5.747	5.535	5.335	8
9	8.566	8.162	7.786	7.435	7.108	6.802	6.515	6.247	5.995	5.759	9
10	9.471	8.983	8.530	8.111	7.722	7.360	7.024	6.710	6.418	6.145	10
11	10.37	9.787	9.253	8.760	8.306	7.887	7.499	7.139	6.805	6.495	11
12	11.26	10.58	9.954	9.385	8.863	8.384	7.943	7.536	7.161	6.814	12
13	12.13	11.35	10.63	9.986	9.394	8.853	8.358	7.904	7.487	7.103	13
14	13.00	12.11	11.30	10.56	9.899	9.295	8.745	8.244	7.786	7.367	14
15	13.87	12.85	11.94	11.12	10.38	9.712	9.108	8.559	8.061	7.606	15

(n)	11%	12%	13%	14%	15%	16%	17%	18%	19%	20%	
1	0.901	0.893	0.885	0.877	0.870	0.862	0.855	0.847	0.840	0.833	1
2	1.713	1.690	1.668	1.647	1.626	1.605	1.585	1.566	1.547	1.528	2
3	2.444	2.402	2.361	2.322	2.283	2.246	2.210	2.174	2.140	2.106	3
4	3.102	3.037	2.974	2.914	2.855	2.798	2.743	2.690	2.639	2.589	4
5	3.696	3.605	3.517	3.433	3.352	3.274	3.199	3.127	3.058	2.991	5
6	4.231	4.111	3.998	3.889	3.784	3.685	3.589	3.498	3.410	3.326	6
7	4.712	4.564	4.423	4.288	4.160	4.039	3.922	3.812	3.706	3.605	7
8	5.146	4.968	4.799	4.639	4.487	4.344	4.207	4.078	3.954	3.837	8
9	5.537	5.328	5.132	4.946	4.772	4.607	4.451	4.303	4.163	4.031	9
10	5.889	5.650	5.426	5.216	5.019	4.833	4.659	4.494	4.339	4.192	10
11	6.207	5.938	5.687	5.453	5.234	5.029	4.836	4.656	4.486	4.327	11
12	6.492	6.194	5.918	5.660	5.421	5.197	4.988	4.793	4.611	4.439	12
13	6.750	6.424	6.122	5.842	5.583	5.342	5.118	4.910	4.715	4.533	13
14	6.982	6.628	6.302	6.002	5.724	5.468	5.229	5.008	4.802	4.611	14
15	7.191	6.811	6.462	6.142	5.847	5.575	5.324	5.092	4.876	4.675	15

Section 1

PRACTICE QUESTIONS – SECTION A

1 QUICKLINK LTD (JUN 05 – AMENDED) *Walk in the footsteps of a top tutor*

Quicklink Ltd operates in the distribution and haulage industry and has achieved significant growth since its formation in 1997. Its main activities comprise the door-to-door delivery of mail, parcels and industrial machinery.

The information contained in notes (i–vii) below relates to Quicklink Ltd in respect of the year ended 31 May 2005 and changes planned in the year ending 31 May 2006.

(i) Contracted clients were charged at the following rates during the year ended 31 May 2005: Mail $6 per delivery, Parcels $10 per delivery and Machinery $200 per delivery.

(ii) Rates for non-contract clients during each of the years ended 31 May 2005 and year ending 31 May 2006, were/are based upon the contracted client rates per delivery plus an additional percentage fee per delivery charged to non-contract clients as follows:

Activity	Additional Fee
Mail	40%
Parcel	20%
Machinery	50%

(iii) On 1 June 2003, Quicklink Ltd entered into a fixed price contract for the provision of fuel for its delivery vehicles for the three-year period ending 31 May 2006. For the year ending 31 May 2006 fuel costs will be as follows:

(a) $0.10 per kilometre in respect of the delivery of mail and parcels

(b) $0.50 per kilometre in respect of the delivery of industrial machinery.

Each vehicle owned by Quicklink Ltd is in use for 340 days per annum.

(iv) Employee salaries were paid throughout the year ended 31 May 2005 at a rate of $26,400 per employee, per annum.

(v) Sundry operating costs (excluding fuel and salaries) of Quicklink Ltd amounted to $3,000,000 during the year ended 31 May 2005.

(vi) The board of directors expect that for the year ending 31 May 2006 the following will apply:

(a) contract rates of Quicklink Ltd business will increase by 5%

(b) sales volumes are expected to remain at the same level as in the year ended 31 May 2005

(c) salaries and other operating expenses will increase by 4%.

(vii) The board of directors agreed to purchase Celer Transport, an unincorporated business, which was founded in December 2001. The purchase took effect on 1 June 2005. Celer Transport has main activities comprising the delivery of mail, parcels and processed food. The managing director of Quicklink Ltd has expressed his view that 'the acquisition of the Celer Transport business would constitute a good strategic move even though it is expected to make a loss of $50,000 during the year ending 31 May 2006'.

The information contained in notes (viii–xii) below relates to the business of Celer Transport in respect of the year ending 31 May 2006:

(viii) A distinctive competence of the Celer Transport business relates to its success in winning contracts with major food producers. Each contract is for a fixed term of three years and all contracts were renewed on 1 June 2005.

Contract values per annum are as follows:

Number of contracts	Value per contract ($)
4	225,000
6	150,000
9	100,000

(ix) (1) The sales volume of mail and parcel deliveries to Celer Transport clients is expected to increase by 10% per annum with effect from 1 June 2005. It is intended to use the client billing rates of Quicklink Ltd that were in application during the year ended 31 May 2005 as the basis of charging for mail and parcel deliveries to Celer Transport clients during the year ending 31 May 2006. This is due to the fact that Quicklink Ltd had higher client billing rates than Celer Transport and the board of directors recognised that it would have been difficult to adopt company-wide billing rates with effect from 1 June 2005.

(2) During the year ended 31 May 2005 the billing rates of Celer Transport in respect of contract and non-contract mail and parcel deliveries were 90% of the level of the rates charged by Quicklink Ltd.

(x) Fuel requirements for the Celer Transport business activities are forecast to cost $0.12 per kilometre for mail and parcel deliveries and $0.60 per kilometre for deliveries of processed food. The fuel required for Celer Transport business during the year ending 31 May 2006 cannot be provided under the current agreement entered into by Quicklink Ltd as detailed in note (iii). Each Celer Transport vehicle is in use for 340 days per annum.

(xi) All Celer Transport employees will be paid on the same basis as Quicklink Ltd employees.

(xii) Sundry operating costs (excluding fuel and salaries) of the Celer Transport business will amount to $1,990,340.

Other information:

(xiii) During the year ended 31 May 2005 the number of employees was as follows:

	Quicklink Ltd		Celer Transport	
Activity type	Mail and parcels	Machinery	Mail and parcels	Processed food
Number of Employees	50	20	20	20

The number of employees is forecast to remain unchanged during the year ending 31 May 2006.

(xiv) Quicklink Ltd implemented a new call management system for customer enquiries/orders which became fully operational with effect from 1 June 2004.

(xv) The Managing Director of Quicklink Ltd recently attended a seminar on Total Quality Management (TQM) and is firmly of the opinion that the adoption of a TQM philosophy would benefit the company.

Other actual operating statistics for the year ended 31 May 2005 are contained in tables 1, 2 and 3 below. Target statistics are shown in bold type.

Table 1

	Quicklink Ltd			Celer Transport		
	Mail	Parcels	Machinery	Mail	Parcels	Processed food
Number of deliveries	468,000	234,000	35,700	120,000	75,000	32,500
Contract deliveries (%)	60	60	90	30	30	100
Number of on-time deliveries	465,660	232,830	35,700	99,900	60,000	31,525
Mix of business deliveries:						
Same day delivery	93,600	46,800	35,700	90,000	56,250	32,500
Next day delivery	374,400	187,200	–	30,000	18,750	–
On-time delivery target (%)	99	99	99	95	95	100
Number of lost items	–	–	–	120	25	–

Table 2

	Quicklink Ltd		Celer Transport	
Vehicle type	Mail and parcels	Machinery	Mail and parcels	Processed food
Average kilometres per vehicle per day	300	400	300	300
Number of vehicles	55	21	22	22

Note: The statistics in Table 2 are expected to remain unchanged during the year ending 31 May 2006.

Table 3

	Quicklink Ltd	Celer Transport
Target time period for answering telephone calls	20 seconds	30 seconds
Number of telephone calls received	1,650,000	600,000
Number of telephone calls answered within target time period	1,633,500	540,000
Number of abandoned telephone calls	–	12,000

Required:

Write a report to the Managing Director of Quicklink including the following:

(a) Prepare, in columnar format, the budgeted income statements for the year ending 31 May 2006 of:

    (i) Quicklink Ltd;

    (ii) Celer Transport; and

    (iii) The combined entity. **(18 marks)**

(b) Comment (with relevant calculations) on the performance of the business of Quicklink Ltd and Celer Transport during the year ended 31 May 2005 and, insofar as the information permits, its projected performance for the year ending 31 May 2006. Your answer should specifically consider:

(i) Revenue generation per vehicle

(ii) Vehicle utilisation and delivery mix

(iii) Service quality. **(14 marks)**

(c) Explain why the Managing Director of Quicklink Ltd might consider the acquisition of the Celer Transport business to be a 'good strategic move' insofar as may be determined from the information provided. **(8 marks)**

(d) Discuss the main benefits that might accrue from the successful implementation of a Total Quality Management programme by the management of the combined entity. **(6 marks)**

Professional marks will be awarded in for appropriateness of format, style and structure of the report. **(4 marks)**

(Total: 50 marks)

2 BSN

Introduction

BSN is a public service radio and television broadcasting organisation. Its Board of Directors stated in its latest annual report that the main objectives of the organisation are to:

- remain a public service broadcaster
- provide a comprehensive range of distinctive programmes and give excellence in providing a public broadcasting service
- make and broadcast television and radio programmes which inform, educate and entertain.

BSN is mainly funded through television licence fees, which are paid by the residents of the country in which it is based. The television signal is currently broadcast through transmitters located on land rather than via satellite. The Board of Directors is held responsible by the government for ensuring that best value is obtained by the licence-fee payer.

Competition

The main competition for BSN comes from commercial broadcasters who are funded through advertising revenue. Some of these broadcasters use earth-bound transmission media for both television and radio programmes, and others transmit via satellite. BSN has achieved an improvement in its market share of the viewing the viewing and listening audience in recent years despite this competition. One of the most distinguished services provided by BSN is its world radio service, which is renowned for its unbiased and uncensored news broadcasts relating to national and international events. None of its competitors is able to provide a parallel service of the same quality and reputation.

Accountability and editorial policy

BSN is accountable through its Board of Directors to the licence-fee payers and to the government.

It regularly consults with representatives of its audiences for both television and radio programmes and has established independent panels of viewers and listeners to review and advise on programmes.

In terms of editorial policy the Board of Directors tries to ensure that there is as little interference as possible on the creativity of programme makers. Nevertheless, the Board aims to ensure that programmes are fair, accurate and impartial, and meet the highest standards of good taste and decency.

New developments

Recently, BSN has introduced a 24-hour television news service. In addition, the organisation has entered a joint venture with a television subscription channel provider which allows the subscriber to access television programmes at any time to suit themselves rather than when they are broadcast. The additional income earned through subscriptions to this facility is re-invested by BSN in its main public service. Another potential development is the connection of the television to the telecommunications network which would allow greater efficiency in the delivery of programmes.

Financial efficiency

The Board of Directors has entered a four-year licence-fee agreement with the government. The terms of this are that the licence fee will increase at a compound rate of 2% per annum both this year and next year. The licence fee will then remain at this level for the remaining two years of the agreement.

The total licence fee income received in the last financial year was $2,147 million. The Board of Directors expects the number of licences sold to remain at the same level as last year for the full four-year period.

The Board of Directors is proud that BSN exceeded the efficiency savings target set by the government by 2% in each of the last three years. Over this period, BSN has out-sourced its financial processing functions and sold its transmission service to an independent company, which has guaranteed the maintenance of a high-quality service at a reduced cost. The Board of Directors has placed much emphasis on the elimination of duplication of effort and reduction in waste from surplus capacity or over-staffing. An internal market has been introduced into BSN with programme-makers given the freedom to buy from producers who may be employed by the organisation or who may be external and completely independent of it. The savings achieved have been re-invested in programmes and services.

Despite these efficiency measures, BSN has experienced a steady average compound rate of growth of 3.7% in its expenditure over the last five years, and this is expected to continue at the same level over the next four-year period.

The following estimated levels of income and expenditure for the four-year period of the licence fee agreement are as follows:

	Income $ million	Expenditure $ million
Year 1	2,190	2,114
Year 2	2,234	2,192
Year 3	2,234	2,273
Year 4	2,234	2,357

Future targets and developments

The government has congratulated the Board of Directors on its record of achieving efficiency savings and has set a Return on Capital Employed (ROCE) target of 6% per annum.

Its current ROCE is 9%, which has been calculated as follows:

$$\frac{\text{Excess of income over expenditure} \times 100}{\text{Average capital employed}} = \frac{\$108 \text{ million}}{\$1,195 \text{ million}}$$

with average capital employed here equalling $\frac{\$1,250m + \$1,140m}{2}$

It is assumed that the value of capital employed by BSN will change only by adjustments in its operating reserve.

There has been continuing debate on the funding mechanism used for BSN through the licence fee. Some members of the government have questioned the fairness of this. They argue that commercial broadcasters cannot rely on a regular and guaranteed source of income and that the licence itself is a form of tax giving no discretion to the fee payer. One suggestion being considered by the government to reduce BSN's dependence on the licence fee is to separate the radio and television services. The radio services may then be financed by advertising revenue but would remain within the overall group alongside the television service. The rationale for this is that the licence fee is charged only on television receivers and therefore BSN does not obtain any direct income to support its radio services.

Financial extracts

Extracts from BSN's accounts reveal an increase in the overall surplus transferred to the operating reserve in the last financial year. Comparative extracts from the accounts over the last two years are as follows:

	Last year $ million	Previous year $ million
Income and expenditure account		
Excess of income over expenditure	108	82
Statement of financial position		
Total assets less current liabilities	1,355	1,240
Long-term creditors and provisions	105	100
	1,250	1,140
represented by:		
Capital reserve	700	698
Operating reserve	550	442
	1,250	1,140

BSN's total expenditure in the last financial year was $2,039 million, compared with $1,700 million five years ago. The breakdown of these costs in the last financial year was as follows:

	Last year $ million
Broadcast expenditure:	
Television services	1,265
Radio services	423
Non-broadcast expenditure	351
	2,039

Required:

Write a report to the Board of Directors of BSN addressing the following:

(a) BSN's major stakeholders are the public, the government, its employees and management.

    (i) Outline the main risk areas that will concern each stakeholder group.

    (ii) Explain how the Board of Directors can obtain the views of BSN's major stakeholders in determining the future strategic development of the organisation. **(12 marks)**

(b) (i) Calculate BSN's ROCE for each of the four years of the licence fee agreement.

    (ii) In the light of your findings, discuss what action BSN's management could take. **(15 marks)**

(c) Discuss the implications for BSN's objectives if the television and radio services are separated. **(10 marks)**

(d) Explain what financial and non-financial information should be provided to the Board of Directors of BSN on the performance of the radio subsidiary following its separation from the television service. **(9 marks)**

Professional marks will be awarded in for appropriateness of format, style and structure of the report. **(4 marks)**

(Total: 50 marks)

3 P GROUP

Background

The corporate history of the P Group (P) stretches back 30 years. During that time, P has developed internationally and now trades in many diverse areas. Fifteen years ago, the company launched P Airlines, which has proved to be one of its most successful business ventures. Five years ago, the company established P Rail and obtained franchises for running rail services in its home country. However, P Rail has not achieved the success that P had intended and is frequently publicly criticised for providing services which do not run on time.

The Group has a distinctive brand name which was established when P's charismatic founder and Chairman launched the first business venture. The majority of the citizens in its home country have heard of the brand which has over time been applied to many diverse areas of business. The Chairman believes the reputation of the brand name places a heavy burden of responsibility on P not to disappoint its customers. The Chairman himself has impressed his own personality on P by pursuing personal publicity in business ventures and becoming involved in high-profile and sometimes dangerous 'leisure' activities.

P has achieved a reputation for entering markets which are dominated by major companies, and has been successful in taking business from some major competitors by exposing their consistently poor service and complacency.

The principal business approach which has been adopted is that of 'brand stretching' across different products and services. Each company within the group runs its own affairs but they are all encouraged to help each other resolve their particular problems in a kind of family spirit.

Key strategic factors

The Chairman has stated that P is in business 'to be different' and that the P brand name should be clearly associated with this.

It is considered essential by the Directors that any products or services incorporated within the brand must help to build its good reputation, provide an opportunity to add value, and yield an appropriate trade-off between risk and rewards.

The Chairman considers that there are a number of key factors which have contributed to the success of P. The brand name is associated with being the consumer's champion, and has been very successful in delivering what the Chairman refers to as a 'sense of excitement' in most ventures to which it has been applied. In addition, the business contacts which have been established are important and he recognises that his own personality attracts customers and venture partners. P also encourages talented staff within the group to interact with each other in order to solve problems. The management style of P is therefore seen as a major contributory factor in its corporate success. Much weight is placed on its corporate image. The Chairman explains that the quality of a customer's experience when coming into contact with P is the most important item in determining its success.

Management style

The Directors agree that the first priority in being able to achieve success is for P to ensure that the Group employs personnel of the best quality and calibre. Their simple philosophy is that motivated staff lead to satisfied customers which results in repeat and new business, and provides benefit to the shareholders.

P has a flat management structure with few authority levels within the hierarchy. The Chairman himself is committed to providing good communication channels within and outside the group. He believes very firmly that managers within the organisation must be prepared to listen both to the customers and also the staff.

Financial performance

The business approach which has been developed is that the brand name is provided by P with a cash injection from a joint venture partner. This has generally proved to be a very successful formula although this has not been the case with the latest venture into the domestic railway market. The Directors consider that the performance of P Rail will improve following a programme to upgrade the infrastructure inherited from the previous nationalised rail network.

Comparative financial information relating to P Airlines and P Rail for the last two years at 31 December is as follows:

	20X3 $m	20X4 $m
Turnover		
Airlines	570	678
Rail	410	423
Pre-tax profit		
Airlines	60	80
Rail	30	32
Capital employed		
Airlines	750	790
Rail	530	640

Other performance indicators

The following information is provided relating to P's airline and rail businesses:

Airline	20X3	20X4
Number of passengers carried	1.2 million	1.4 million
Passenger miles travelled	3,000 million	3,300 million
Ratio of cabin staff to passengers (excluding aircrew, i.e. pilots and navigators):		
Economy class	1 to 10	1 to 12
Business and first class	1 to 4	1 to 5
Number of airline routes flown	40	44

- P Airlines sells economy, business and first-class seats to passengers. The prices reflect the level of comfort and service. For example, first-class seats cost double the price of business class seats and ten times the price of economy seats.

- Airline passenger numbers are expected to increase by 3% in the next two years in the long-distance economy-class market from which P attracts most of its customers.

- There is an increasing level of alliances emerging among airlines whereby each carries the other's passengers as well as its own on designated routes. P is engaged in such alliances for two of its routes.

- A general survey of satisfaction among airline passengers carried out by independent representatives from the travel industry in P's home country ranks P as being within the top three for most services.

Rail	20X3	20X4
Number of passengers carried	4.5 million	4.3 million
Passenger miles travelled	160 million	150 million
Ratio of customer attendants to passengers:		
Standard class	1 to 100	1 to 120
First class	1 to 20	1 to 25
Number of routes travelled	25	25

- P Rail sells standard and first-class seats to its passengers. The first-class seat is priced at about double that of a standard priced seat.

- An increase of 5% in total rail passengers is expected over the next four years.

- P operates the railway services under a franchise agreement, which is due for renewal in five years' time.

- The government has established a Railway Regulatory Authority to monitor the quality of the services provided by the P Group and other railway franchisees, and is constantly increasing pressure on the franchisees to improve their services.

- A general survey of passenger satisfaction carried out by the Railway Regulatory Authority was highly critical of P's services with regard to its record relating to punctuality and service on its trains.

Future development

P has enjoyed considerable success in its ventures within its domestic market. However, the Directors believe there is much opportunity to develop the brand name within the emerging highly populated retail markets elsewhere in the world where currently it is relatively unknown.

The other development that the Board want to address is the increasing importance of green and environmental issues to customers, Governments and potential investors. While P's record in these respects is not inferior to that of competitors, P does not have a focussed approach to defending and improving its green credentials. One director has suggested that P should investigate the implementation of environmental management accounting (EMA).

Required:

Write a report to the Board of Directors of P Group addressing the following issues:

(a) Discuss the importance of the external forces which P faces in its worldwide business development. (10 marks)

(b) With reference to the comparative financial and other performance indicators, evaluate the performance of the P Airlines and P Rail companies. Recommend ways in which they may increase their individual contribution to the future development of the Group. (15 marks)

(c) Explain the main factors which have contributed to P's commercial success so far. Comment on the Chairman's personal responsibilities to the Group's shareholders, employees, joint venture partners and customers. (10 marks)

(d) (i) Discuss the importance of EMA to P (4 marks)

    (ii) Explain, giving examples, how EMA could be applied to P. (7 marks)

Professional marks for the format, style and structure of the report. (4 marks)

(Total: 50 marks)

PRACTICE QUESTIONS – SECTION A : SECTION 1

4   THE NAW GROUP (JUN 04 – AMENDED)

The NAW Group manufactures healthcare products which it markets both under its own brand and in unbranded packs. The group has adopted a divisional structure. Division O, which is based in a country called Homeland, manufactures three pharmaceutical products for sale in the domestic market. Budgeted information in respect of Division O for the year ending 31 May 2005 is as follows:

Sales information:

Product		Painfree	Digestisalve	Awaysafe
Sales packs (000's)	NAW Brand	5,000	5,000	15,000
	Unbranded	15,000	20,000	–
Selling price per pack ($)	NAW Brand	2.40	4.80	8.00
	Unbranded	1.20	3.60	–

Cost of sales information:

Variable manufacturing costs per pack:	*Material and conversion costs* $	*Packaging costs.* $
'Painfree'		
NAW Brand	0.85	0.15
Unbranded	0.85	0.05
'Digestisalve'		
NAW Brand	1.85	0.25
Unbranded	1.85	0.15
'Awaysafe'		
NAW Brand	2.80	0.40

Other relevant information is as follows:

(1) Each of the three products is only sold in tablet form in a single pack-size which contains 12 tablets. During the year to 31 May 2005 it is estimated that a maximum of 780 million tablets could be manufactured. All three products are manufactured by the same process therefore management have the flexibility to alter the product mix. Management expect that sales volume will increase by 10% in the year ending 31 May 2006.

(2) Advertising expenditure has been committed to under a fixed term contract with a leading consultancy and is therefore regarded as a fixed cost by management. Advertising expenditure in respect of the turnover of branded products in the year ending 31 May 2005 is apportioned as follows:

Product:	Advertising expenditure as a % of turnover
Painfree	5%
Digestisalve	10%
Awaysafe	12%

(3) The average capital employed in the year to 31 May 2005 is estimated to be $120 million. The company's cost of capital is 10%.

(4) The management of the NAW Group use both Return on Investment (ROI) and Residual Income (RI) to assess divisional performance.

(5) Budgeted fixed overheads (excluding advertising) for Division O during the year ended 31 May 2005 amount to $81,558,000.

(6) There is no planned change in manufacturing capacity between the years ended 31 May 2005 and 31 May 2006.

(7) Ignore taxation for all calculations other than those in part (c).

Required:

Write a report to the Directors of The NAW Group addressing the following issues:

(a) (i) **Prepare a statement of budgeted profit in respect of Division O for the year ended 31 May 2005.**

   Your answer should show the annual budgeted contribution of each branded and unbranded product. Calculate BOTH the residual income (RI) and Return on Investment (ROI) for Division O. (7 marks)

   (ii) **Discuss the factors, other than profit maximisation, that the management of the NAW Group ought to consider when deciding upon the product mix strategy for the year ending 31 May 2006.** (5 marks)

   (iii) **Suggest THREE reasons why the management of the NAW Group may have chosen to use Residual Income (RI) in addition to Return on Investment (ROI) in order to assess divisional performance.** (3 marks)

Division L of the NAW Group is based in Farland. The management of Division L purchases products from various sources, including other divisions of the group, for subsequent resale. The manager of Division L has requested two alternative quotations from Division O in respect of the year ended 31 May 2005:

Quotation 1 – Purchasing five million packs of 'Awaysafe'.

Quotation 2 – Purchasing nine million packs of 'Awaysafe'.

The management of the NAW Group has made a decision that a minimum of 15 million packs of 'Awaysafe' must be reserved for Homeland customers in order to ensure that customer demand can be satisfied and the product's competitive position is further established in the Homeland market.

The management of the NAW Group is willing, if necessary, to reduce the budgeted sales quantities of other products in order to satisfy the requirements of Division L. They wish, however, to minimise the loss of contribution to the group.

The management of Division L is aware of the availability of another product that competes with 'Awaysafe' which could be purchased at a local currency price that is equivalent to $5.50 per pack. The NAW Group's policy is that all divisions are allowed the autonomy to set transfer prices and purchase from whatever sources they choose. The management of Division O intend to use market price less 30% as the basis for each of the quotations.

(b) (i) **From the viewpoint of the NAW Group, comment on the appropriateness of the decision by the management of Division O to use an adjusted market price as a basis for the preparation of Quotations 1 and 2, and the implications of the likely decision by the management of Division L.** (5 marks)

(ii) Recommend the prices that should be quoted by Division O for 'Awaysafe', in respect of Quotations 1 and 2, which will ensure that the profitability of the NAW group as a whole is not adversely affected by the decision of the management of Division L. **(5 marks)**

(iii) Discuss the proposition that transfer prices should be based on opportunity costs. **(4 marks)**

(c) (i) After much internal discussion concerning Quotation 2 by the management of the NAW Group, Division O is not prepared to supply nine million packs of 'Awaysafe' to Division L at a price lower than market price less 30%. All profits earned in Farland are subject to taxation at a rate of 20%. Division O pays tax in Homeland at a rate of 40% on all profits.

Advise the management of the NAW Group whether the management of Division L should be directed to purchase 'Awaysafe' from Division O, or purchase a similar product from a local supplier. Supporting calculations should be provided. **(6 marks)**

(ii) Identify and comment on the major issues that can arise with regard to transfer pricing in a multinational organisation. **(5 marks)**

(d) Evaluate the extent to which the management of the NAW Group could make use of the product life cycle model in the determination of its product pricing strategy.

(6 marks)

Professional marks for the format, style and structure of the report. **(4 marks)**

(Total: 50 marks)

5 GREAT WESTERN CAKE COMPANY (JUN 06 – AMENDED)

The Great Western Cake Company (GWCC) is a well-established manufacturer of specialist flour confectionery products, including cakes. GWCC sells its products to national supermarket chains. The company's success during recent years is largely attributable to its ability to develop innovative products which appeal to the food selectors within national supermarket chains.

The marketing department of Superstores plc, a national supermarket chain has asked GWCC to manufacture a cake known as the 'Mighty Ben'. Mighty Ben is a character who has recently appeared in a film which was broadcast around the world. The cake is expected to have a minimum market life of one year although the marketing department consider that this might extend to eighteen months.

The management accountant of GWCC has collated the following estimated information in respect of the Mighty Ben cake:

(1) Superstores plc has decided on a launch price of $20.25 for the Mighty Ben cake and it is expected that this price will be maintained for the duration of the product's life. Superstores plc will apply a 35% mark-up on the purchase price of each cake from GWCC.

(2) Sales of the Mighty Ben cake are expected to be 100,000 units per month during the first twelve months. Thereafter sales of the Mighty Ben cake are expected to decrease by 10,000 units in each subsequent month.

(3) Due to the relatively short shelf-life of the Mighty Ben cake, management has decided to manufacture the cakes on a 'just-in-time' basis for delivery in accordance with agreed schedules. The cakes will be manufactured in batches of 1,000. Direct materials input into the baking process will cost $7,000 per batch for each of the first three months' production. The material cost of the next three months' production is expected to be 95% of the cost of the first three months' production. All batches manufactured thereafter will cost 90% of the cost of the second three months' production.

(4) Packaging costs will amount to $0.75 per cake. The original costs of the artwork and design of the packaging will amount to $24,000. Superstores plc will reimburse GWCC $8,000 in the event that the product is withdrawn from sale after twelve months.

(5) The design of the Mighty Ben cake is such that it is required to be hand-finished. A 75% learning curve will apply to the total labour time requirement until the end of month five. Thereafter a steady state will apply with labour time required per batch stabilising at that of the final batch in month five.

The labour requirement for the first batch of Mighty Ben cakes to be manufactured is expected to be 6,000 hours at $10 per hour.

(6) A royalty of 5% of sales revenue (subject to a maximum royalty of $1.1 million) will be payable by GWCC to the owners of the Mighty Ben copyright.

(7) Variable overheads are estimated at $3.50 per direct labour hour.

(8) The manufacture of the Mighty Ben cake will increase fixed overheads by $75,000 per month.

(9) In order to provide a production facility dedicated to the Mighty Ben cake, an investment of $1,900,000 will be required and this will be fully depreciated over twelve months.

(10) The directors of GWCC require an average annual return of 35% on their investment over 12 months and 18 months.

(11) Ignore taxation and the present value of cash flows.

Note: Learning curve formula:

$y = ax^b$

where:

   y = average cost per batch

   a = the cost of the initial batch

   x = the total number of batches

   b = learning index (= –0.415 for 75% learning rate)

Required:

Write a report to the Directors of GWCC addressing the following issues:

(a) **Prepare detailed calculations to show whether the manufacture of Mighty Ben cakes will provide the required rate of return for GWCC over periods of twelve months and eighteen months.** **(20 marks)**

(b) (i) Advise the directors of GWCC on specific actions which may be considered in order to improve the estimated return on their investment of $1,900,000.
(8 marks)

(ii) Briefly discuss TWO factors which could reduce the rate of return earned by the investment as per the results in part (a).
(4 marks)

(c) Explain the term 'target costing' and how it may be applied by GWCC. Briefly discuss any potential limitations in its application.
(8 marks)

(d) Identify and explain TWO key performance indicators that would be used by Superstores plc to monitor the production of Mighty Ben cakes.
(6 marks)

Professional marks for the format, style and structure of the report. (4 marks)

(Total: 50 marks)

6 SNOWWELL (DEC 03 – AMENDED)

Assume that 'now' is December 20X3.

The managing director of Snowwell plc has received an unsolicited letter from a reputable organisation specialising in the prediction of corporate failure, which suggests that Snowwell has been identified as a probable failing company. The organisation has offered to supply details of the full report on Snowwell for $100,000.

Given the collapse of many companies' share prices during the last few years, the managing director of Snowwell is concerned that if the contents of the report become public knowledge, Snowwell's share price could also fall.

He has also read about various models which use combinations of financial ratios to attempt to predict corporate failure, including a leading business school's S_0 model (developed in 20X1) which produces a score based upon the following equation:

$S_0 = 3.5S_1 + 1.8S_2 + 0.25S_3 + 0.69S_4$

where:

S_1 = Earnings before interest and tax/market value of equity

S_2 = Working capital/medium and long term capital employed

S_3 = Market value of equity/market value of debt

S_4 = The present value to infinity of current operating free cash flow/turnover

According to the S_0 system, a company scoring less than 1 has a high probability of failure; a score of 1 – 2 suggests remedial action is necessary to improve corporate financial performance; and a score of over 2 means that a company has a high probability of survival for at least three years, which is the maximum claimed prediction period for the model.

The latest summarised accounts of Snowwell plc are shown over the page:

Income statement for the years ending

	31 March 20X3 $ million	31 March 20X2 $ million
Sales revenue	620	580
Earnings before interest and tax	43	52
Interest	20	18
Profit before tax	23	34
Taxation	7	10
Available to shareholders	16	24
Dividend	17	17
Retained earnings	(1)	7

Statements of financial position (Balance sheets) as at

	31 March 20X3		31 March 20X2	
	$ million	$ million	$ million	$ million
Non-current assets				
Land and buildings (net)		211		196
Other fixed assets (net)		247		235
		458		431
Current assets				
Inventory	156		127	
Receivables	32		34	
Cash	5		3	
		193		164
Total assets		651		595
Ordinary shares (50 pence par)		75		75
Reserves		117		118
Shareholders' funds		192		193
Non-current liabilities				
14% loan stock redeemable December 20X6 ($100 par)		150		150
Floating rate bank term loans		94		64
		244		214

Current liabilities

Payables	196	166
Dividend	12	12
Taxation	7	10
	215	188
Total equity and liabilities	651	595

Additional information:

(i) The share price of Snowwell plc is currently $2.32.

(ii) The current redemption yield on loan stock of similar risk to that of Snowwell is 8%, which is also the current interest rate of the floating rate term loan.

(iii) Snowwell needs to invest approximately $35 million per year to maintain operations at current levels.

(iv) Tax allowable depreciation in 20X3 was $38 million.

(v) Snowwell's cost of equity is estimated to be 12%.

(vi) Corporate tax is at the rate of 30% per year.

(vii) The average gearing of Snowwell's industry is 50% (measured by the market value of medium and long-term debt related to the market value of equity).

(viii) Snowwell's turnover is mostly retail sales of high quality jewellery and watches.

Required:

Write a report to the Directors of Snowwell including the following issues:

(a) A discussion of the nature of corporate failure prediction models and how they can be used in the process of identifying potentially failing companies. (12 marks)

(b) An estimate of the S_0 score for Snowwell plc. (11 marks)

(c) A discussion of the significance of this score for Snowwell plc. (4 marks)

(d) A discussion of alternative ways of assessing whether or not Snowwell plc is likely to experience financial distress and/or corporate failure. (8 marks)

(e) Recommendations as to whether or not Snowwell should take any action based upon your findings above and any other relevant information or analysis. (7 marks)

(f) A discussion as to whether or not Snowwell should purchase the full report for $100,000. (4 marks)

Professional marks for the format, style and structure of the report. (4 marks)

(Total: 50 marks)

7 WESTAMBER (PILOT 07) — Walk in the footsteps of a top tutor

The Westamber Hospital ('Westamber'), which is partially government-funded, specialises in the provision of ear, nose and throat operations for patients in Zonderland. Its mission statement states that the hospital 'is committed to providing high quality healthcare to all patients'. Westamber provides treatment to private fee-paying patients as well as to patients who are funded by the government.

Relevant operating data for Westamber for the year ended 30 June 2006 is as follows:

(1) The budgeted mix of operations

Type of operation	% of total operations
Ear	30
Nose	30
Throat	40

(2) Fees (budget and actual) payable to Westamber in respect of each patient who received treatment from the hospital are as follows:

Type of operation:	Fee payable by private patients ($)	Fee payable by government ($)
Ear	3,000	2,000
Nose	4,000	3,000
Throat	5,000	4,000

It was budgeted that 50% of patients (for each type of operation) would have the cost of their operations funded by the government because under existing legislation they earned what the government defined as a low income.

(3) Budgeted costs for the year based on 100% capacity utilization.

	$000	Variable cost (%)	Fixed cost (%)
Surgical	35,400	25	75
Nursing	8,000	30	70
Depreciation	1,700	–	100
Administration	3,250	–	100
Sundry	5,750	20	80

Variable surgical costs include a total amount of $1,000,000 in respect of operations undertaken on an emergency basis.

(4) Actual costs incurred during the year

	Variable costs ($000)	Fixed costs ($000)
Surgical	8,284	26,550
Nursing	2,224	5,600
Depreciation		1,700
Administration		3,412
Sundry	1,116	4,912

Note:

(i) $800,000 of the variable surgical costs related to the provision of emergency operations.

(ii) The proportion of emergency operations as a percentage of total operations was as per budget.

(5) Westamber had no loan finance during the year.

(6) A recently qualified accountant employed by Westamber has stated that 'it is obvious that the mix of government to private patients mix is the key determinant of profitability. Next year it looks as if demand for total operations will exceed our available capacity and therefore we should give priority to private fee-paying patients as we receive more fees from them for each type of operation. It is as simple as that since there aren't any ethical issues to be considered'.

(7) Other statistics relating to Westamber (all stated on an ACTUAL basis):

Capacity utilisation (%):	80%
Patient mix (%) for each type of operation:	
Government-funded patients	75%
Privately-funded patients	25%
Operation mix (%):	
Ear	35%
Nose	30%
Throat	35%

Eastgreen Hospital ('Eastgreen'), is a privately owned hospital which also specialises in the provision of ear, nose and throat operations. All of its patients are responsible for the payment of their own fees. Eastgreen does not undertake operations on an emergency basis.

The summary income statement for Eastgreen on an actual basis was as follows:

	$000
Fee income	36,000
Costs:	
Surgery & nursing	25,000
Depreciation	3,400
Loan interest	500
Administration and sundry	5,100
Total costs	34,000
Net profit	2,000

(i) Eastgreen operates comparable accounting policies to those of Westamber.

(ii) The income of Eastgreen is derived from the provision of an annual healthcare scheme. Each patient pays $100 per month under a fixed term contract of three years. All contracts were renewed on 1 July 2005. There were 30,000 contracts in existence throughout the year. *Note:* Contracts can only be entered into on 1 July in each year.

Each hospital is comprised of 15 wards, each of which can accommodate eight patients. The average patient stay in both hospitals was three days. Each hospital is open for 365 days per annum.

Required:

(a) Prepare a statement, in columnar format, which shows comparable actual and budgeted results for Westamber for the year ended 30 June 2006. **(14 marks)**
(Including 2 professional marks)

(b) Explain FOUR reasons why it may be inappropriate to make a direct comparison of the financial performance of the Westamber and Eastgreen hospitals on the basis of the information provided. **(6 marks)**

(c) Using only information contained in the question make THREE adjustments to the income statements you have prepared in your answer to (a) that you consider would assist in the development of a more appropriate comparison of the financial performance of Westamber and Eastgreen hospitals. **(6 marks)**

(d) Discuss the statement of Westamber's recently qualified accountant including comments on the ethical implications of the statement. **(3 marks)**

(e) Excluding the number of complaints by patients, state FOUR performance measures that may be used in order to assess the surgical quality provided by a hospital indicating how each measure may be assessed. **(6 marks)**

(Total: 35 marks)

8 THE GEELAND BUS COMPANY (GBC) (DEC 07)

Walk in the footsteps of a top tutor

The Geeland Bus Company (GBC) is a partly government-funded organisation which provides transport services to the population of Geeland, a country which is divided into four regions i.e. Northern, Eastern, Southern and Western. The Western region differs from the Northern, Eastern and Southern regions in that it is a rural area with a low population.

The Terrific Transport Company (TTC) is a privately owned organisation which also provides transport services to the population of Geeland. All TTC buses are luxuriously fitted; each passenger has their own television and all buses have on-board catering facilities which serve a variety of drinks and snacks. The costs of these luxuries are included in fares charged by TTC.

Both GBC and TTC operate from premises in the Northern region. GBC operates a bus service to and from the Eastern, Southern and Western regions as well as a 'Hopper' service which takes passengers around all regions, other than the Western region, within Geeland. TTC also operates a bus service to and from the Eastern and Southern regions of Geeland as well as a Hopper service. TTC does not operate a service to and from the Western region.

PRACTICE QUESTIONS – SECTION A : SECTION 1

The following information is available:

(1) A summary of the financial performance of GBC and TTC for the years ended 30 November 2006 and 2007 is as follows:

Revenue:

	GBC			TTC		
	2006 Actual $000	2007 Actual $000	2007 Budget $000	2006 Actual $000	2007 Actual $000	2007 Budget $000
Eastern	*1,689,600	1,536,000	1,843,200	1,566,720	2,088,960	1,958,400
Southern	2,457,600	*2,304,000	1,843,200	1,566,720	*2,088,960	1,958,400
Western	256,000	230,400	614,400	–	–	–
Hopper	1,267,200	1,152,000	1,382,400	1,175,040	1,566,720	*1,468,800
Total revenue	5,670,400	5,222,400	5,683,200	4,308,480	5,744,640	5,385,600

Costs:

	GBC			TTC		
	2006 Actual $000	2007 Actual $000	2007 Budget $000	2006 Actual $000	2007 Actual $000	2007 Budget $000
Variable costs						
Eastern		*806,400			544,000	
Southern		967,680			*652,800	
Western		268,800				
Hopper		604,800			408,000	
Total variable costs	2,521,600	2,647,680	2,550,000	1,528,380	1,604,800	1,600,000
Salaries	1,225,000	1,275,000	1,250,000	1,240,000	1,250,000	1,250,000
Repairs and maintenance	100,000	160,000	120,000	40,000	40,000	42,000
Depreciation	70,000	70,000	70,000	250,000	250,000	250,000
Other operating costs	240,000	253,000	240,000	280,000	300,000	320,000
Loan interest	0	0	0	100,000	100,000	100,000
Total costs	4,156,600	4,405,680	4,230,000	3,438,380	3,544,800	3,562,000
Net profit	1,513,800	816,720	1,453,200	870,100	2,199,840	1,823,600

(2) The actual data categorised by route activity for the year ended 30 November 2007:

Route	Eastern		Southern		Western		Hopper	
Company	GBC	TTC	GBC	TTC	GBC	TTC	GBC	TTC
Number of buses operated per route	6	4	6	4	2	–	3	2
Number of journeys per bus per route, per day	2	2	2	2	1	–	1	1
Route length (km) per return journey	100	100	120	120	200	–	300	300
Capacity utilisation per bus (%)	60	80	75	80	30	–	60	80
Fare per passenger per journey ($)	10	12	10	12	20	–	30	36

(3) Each company operates for 365 days per year. Each GBC bus is in operation for 320 days of the year, whereas each TTC bus is in operation for 340 days of the year. The remaining days are taken up with planned maintenance work on the buses.

(4) Fares charged by GBC and TTC have not increased since 1 December 2005.

(5) GBC provides free transport for senior citizens on the Eastern, Western and Hopper routes. Free transport for senior citizens does not apply to the Southern route. Where applicable, capacity utilisation includes non fare-paying passengers. TTC does not provide any free transport.

(6) All buses operated by each company had a maximum capacity of 80 seats.

(7) Actual average variable costs of operating the bus service during the year ended 30 November 2007 amounted to $2.10 per km for GBC and $2.00 per km for TTC. The difference was solely attributable to the fact that GBC uses fuel which is more environmentally-friendly and, therefore, more costly than the fuel used by TTC.

(8) The written down values of non-current assets are as follows:

	2006	2007
	$000	$000
Premises:		
GBC	300	270
TTC	900	810
Vehicles:		
GBC	400	360
TTC	1,600	1,440

Note: There have been no additions or disposals of non-current assets since 1 December 2005 as per budget.

(9) The average number of fare-paying passengers per bus during the years ended 30 November 2006 and 30 November 2007 was as follows:

Number of fare-paying passengers per bus:

	2006		2007	
	GBC	*TTC*	*GBC*	*TTC*
Route:				
Eastern	44	48	40	64
Southern	64	48	60	64
Western	20	–	18	–
Hopper	44	48	40	64

The same number of non fare-paying senior citizens travelled on GBC buses during the year ended 30 November 2006 as during the year ended 30 November 2007.

(10) Budgeted occupancy rates for all buses on all routes in operation, for the year ended 30 November 2007, were as follows:

Company	Budgeted occupancy rate for fare-paying passengers (%)
GBC	60
TTC	75

(11) Only the variable costs of operating the bus services (as per note 7) would be avoided if a route was to be discontinued since all other costs are fixed.

(12) At a meeting of the board of directors held during 2007, the managing director of GBC stated that: 'on no account shall we discontinue the operation of our Western route'.

Required:

(a) Prepare a report on the operating performance and financial performance of GBC and TTC for the years ended 30 November 2006 and 2007. As part of your report, you should include an appendix showing detailed workings of how each of the six figures marked with an asterisk (*) in note 1 has been calculated. (23 marks)

Note: 6 marks are available in respect of the six figures marked with an asterisk (*). 17 marks are available for other calculations and discussion.

(b) Explain THREE problems in undertaking a performance comparison of GBC and TTC and also explain THREE items of additional information that would be of assistance in assessing the operating and financial performance of GBC and TTC. (6 marks)

(c) Critically discuss the statement (in note 12) of the managing director of GBC and suggest how the company could calculate the value of the service provision to the population of the Western region. (6 marks)

(Total: 35 marks)

PAPER P5 : ADVANCED PERFORMANCE MANAGEMENT

9 ALPHA DIVISION (DEC 07)

Alpha Division, which is part of the Delta Group, is considering an investment opportunity to which the following estimated information relates:

(1) An initial investment of $45m in equipment at the beginning of year 1 will be depreciated on a straight-line basis over a three-year period with a nil residual value at the end of year 3.

(2) Net operating cash inflows in each of years 1 to 3 will be $12.5m, $18.5m and $27m respectively.

(3) The management accountant of Alpha Division has estimated that the NPV of the investment would be $1.937m using a cost of capital of 10%.

(4) A bonus scheme which is based on short-term performance evaluation is in operation in all divisions within the Delta Group.

Required:

(a) (i) **Calculate the residual income of the proposed investment and comment briefly (using ONLY the above information) on the values obtained in reconciling the short-term and long-term decision views likely to be adopted by divisional management regarding the viability of the proposed investment.**
 (6 marks)

(ii) A possible analysis of divisional profit measurement at Alpha Division might be as follows:

	$m
Sales revenue	xxx
Less: variable costs	xxx
1 Variable short run contribution margin	xxx
Less: controllable fixed costs	xxx
2 Controllable profit	xxx
Less: non-controllable avoidable costs	xxx
3 Divisional profit	xxx

Required:

Discuss the relevance of each of the divisional profit measures 1, 2 and 3 in the above analysis as an acceptable measure of divisional management performance and/or divisional economic performance at Alpha Division.

You should use appropriate items from the following list relating to Alpha Division in order to illustrate your discussion:

(i) Sales to customers external to the Delta Group

(ii) Inter-divisional transfers to other divisions within the Delta Group at adjusted market price

(iii) Labour costs or equipment rental costs that are fixed in the short term

(iv) Depreciation of non-current assets at Alpha Division

(v) Head office finance and legal staff costs for services provided to Alpha Division.
(8 marks)

(b) Summary financial information for the Gamma Group (which is not connected with the Delta Group) is as follows:

Income statements/financial information:

	2006 $m	2007 $m
Revenue	400	450
Profit before tax	96	117
Income tax expense	(29)	(35)
Profit for the period	67	82
Dividends	(23)	(27)
Retained earnings	44	55

Statements of financial position (Balance Sheets):

	2006 $m	2007 $m
Non-current assets	160	180
Current assets	180	215
	340	395
Financed by:		
Total equity	270	325
Long-term debt	70	70
	340	395

Other information is as follows:

(1) Capital employed at the end of 2005 amounted to $279m.

(2) The Gamma Group had non-capitalised leases valued at $16m in each of the years 2005 to 2007 which were not subject to amortisation.

(3) Amortisation of goodwill amounted to $5m per year in both 2006 and 2007. The amount of goodwill written off against reserves on acquisitions in years prior to 2006 amounted to $45m.

(4) The Group's pre-tax cost of debt was estimated to be 10%.

(5) The Group's cost of equity was estimated to be 16% in 2006 and 18% in 2007.

(6) The target capital structure is 50% equity, 50% debt.

(7) The rate of taxation is 30% in both 2006 and 2007.

(8) Economic depreciation amounted to $40m in 2006 and $45m in 2007. These amounts were equal to the depreciation used for tax purposes and depreciation charged in the income statements.

(9) Interest payable amounted to $6m per year in both 2006 and 2007.

(10) Other non-cash expenses amounted to $12m per year in both 2006 and 2007.

Required:

(i) Stating clearly any assumptions that you make, estimate the Economic Value Added (EVA™) of the Gamma Group for both 2006 and 2007 and comment briefly on the performance of the Group. **(8 marks)**

(ii) Briefly discuss THREE disadvantages of using EVA™ in the measurement of financial performance. **(3 marks)**

(Total: 25 marks)

10 THE HEALTH AND FITNESS GROUP (HFG) (JUN 08)

Timed question with Online tutor debrief

The Health and Fitness Group (HFG), which is privately owned, operates three centres in the country of Mayland.

Each centre offers dietary plans and fitness programmes to clients under the supervision of dieticians and fitness trainers. Residential accommodation is also available at each centre. The centres are located in the towns of Ayetown, Beetown and Ceetown.

The following information is available:

(1) Summary financial data for HFG in respect of the year ended 31 May 2008.

	Ayetown $000	Beetown $000	Ceetown $000	Total $000
Revenue:				
Fees received	1,800	2,100	4,500	8,400
Variable costs	(468)	(567)	(1,395)	(2,430)
Contribution	1,332	1,533	3,105	5,970
Fixed costs	(936)	(1,092)	(2,402)	(4,430)
Operating profit	396	441	703	1,540
Interest costs on long-term debt at 10%				(180)
Profit before tax				1,360
Income tax expense				(408)
Profit for the year				952
Average book values for 2008:				
Assets				
Non-current assets	1,000	2,500	3,300	6,800
Current assets	800	900	1,000	2,700
Total assets	1,800	3,400	4,300	9,500

Equity and liabilities:				
Share capital				2,500
Retained earnings				4,400
Total equity				**6,900**
Non-current liabilities				
Long-term borrowings				1,800
Total non-current liabilities				**1,800**
Current liabilities	80	240	480	800
Total current liabilities	**80**	**240**	**480**	**800**
Total liabilities				**2,600**
Total equity and liabilities				**9,500**

(2) HFG defines Residual Income (RI) for each centre as operating profit minus a required rate of return of 12% of the total assets of each centre.

(3) At present HFG does not allocate the long-term borrowings of the group to the three separate centres.

(4) Each centre faces similar risks.

(5) Tax is payable at a rate of 30%.

(6) The market value of the equity capital of HFG is $9 million. The cost of equity of HFG is 15%.

(7) The market value of the long-term borrowings of HFG is equal to the book value.

(8) The directors are concerned about the return on investment (ROI) generated by the Beetown centre and they are considering using sensitivity analysis in order to show how a target ROI of 20% might be achieved.

(9) The marketing director stated at a recent board meeting that 'The Group's success depends on the quality of service provided to our clients. In my opinion, we need only to concern ourselves with the number of complaints received from clients during each period as this is the most important performance measure for our business. The number of complaints received from clients is a perfect performance measure. As long as the number of complaints received from clients is not increasing from period to period, then we can be confident about our future prospects'.

Required:

(a) The directors of HFG have asked you, as management accountant, to prepare a report providing them with explanations as to the following:

(i) Which of the three centres is the most 'successful'? Your report should include a commentary on return on investment (ROI), residual income (RI), and economic value added (EVA) as measures of financial performance. Detailed calculations regarding each of these three measures must be included as part of your report;

Note: A maximum of seven marks is available for detailed calculations.

(14 marks)

(ii) The percentage change in revenue, total costs and net assets during the year ended 31 May 2008 that would have been required in order to have achieved a target ROI of 20% by the Beetown centre. Your answer should consider each of these three variables in isolation. State any assumptions that you make. **(6 marks)**

(iii) Whether or not you agree with the statement of the marketing director in note (9) above. **(5 marks)**

Professional marks for appropriateness of format, style and structure of the report.
(4 marks)

(b) The Superior Fitness Co (SFC), which is well established in Mayland, operates nine centres. Each of SFC's centres is similar in size to those of HFG. SFC also provides dietary plans and fitness programmes to its clients. The directors of HFG have decided that they wish to benchmark the performance of HFG with that of SFC.

Required:

Discuss the problems that the directors of HFG might experience in their wish to benchmark the performance of HFG with the performance of SFC, and recommend how such problems might be successfully addressed. **(7 marks)**

(Total: 36 marks)

11 THE SENTINEL COMPANY (TSC) (DEC 08)

Timed question with Online tutor debrief

The Sentinel Company (TSC) offers a range of door-to-door express delivery services. The company operates using a network of depots and distribution centres throughout the country of Nickland. The following information is available:

(1) Each depot is solely responsible for all customers within a specified area. It collects goods from customers within its own area for delivery both within the specific area covered by the depot and elsewhere in Nickland.

(2) Collections made by a depot for delivery outside its own area are forwarded to the depots from which the deliveries will be made to the customers.

(3) Each depot must therefore integrate its deliveries to customers to include:

(i) goods that it has collected within its own area; and

(ii) goods that are transferred to it from depots within other areas for delivery to customers in its area.

(4) Each depot earns revenue based on the invoiced value of all consignments collected from customers in its area, regardless of the location of the ultimate distribution depot.

(5) Depot costs comprise all of its own operating costs plus an allocated share of all company costs including centralised administration services and distribution centre costs.

(6) Bonuses for the management team and all employees at each depot are payable quarterly. The bonus is based on the achievement of a series of target values by each depot.

(7) Internal benchmarking is used at TSC in order to provide sets of absolute standards that all depots are expected to attain.

(8) (a) The Appendix shows the target values and the actual values achieved for each of a sample group of four depots situated in Donatellotown (D), Leonardotown (L), Michaelangelotown (M), and Raphaeltown (R).

(b) The target values focus on three areas:

(i) depot revenue and profitability;

(ii) customer care and service delivery; and

(iii) credit control and administrative efficiency.

(c) The bonus is based on a points system, which is also used as a guide to the operational effectiveness at each depot. One point is allocated where the target value for each item in the Appendix is either achieved or exceeded, and a zero score where the target is not achieved.

APPENDIX

Target and actual value statistics for Donatellotown (D), Leonardotown (L), Michaelangelotown (M), and Raphaeltown (R) for the Year ended 31 October 2008

Revenue and Profit Statistics:

	Revenue (1)		Profit (2)	
	Target	Actual	Target	Actual
	$m	$m	$m	$m
Company overall	200	240	30	32
Selected depots:				
D	16	15	2.4	2.3
L	14	18	2.1	2.4
M	12	14	1.8	2.2
R	18	22	2.7	2.8

Note: For the purpose of calculation of each depot's points it is essential that actual profit as a percentage of actual revenue must exceed the target profit (%).

Customer Care & Service Delivery Statistics:

		Actual			
Selected Depots:	Target	D	L	M	R
	%	%	%	%	%
Measure (% of total):					
(3) Late collection of consignments	2.0	1.9	2.1	1.8	2.4
(4) Misdirected consignments	4.0	4.2	3.9	3.3	5.1
(5) Delayed response to complaints	1.0	0.7	0.9	0.8	1.2
(6) Delays due to vehicle breakdown	1.0	1.1	1.4	0.3	2.0
Measure (% of revenue):	Target	D	L	M	R
(7) Lost items	1.0	0.6	0.9	0.8	1.9
(8) Damaged items	2.0	1.5	2.4	1.5	1.8

Credit Control & Administration Efficiency Statistics:

	Target	Actual D	L	M	R
(9) Average debtor weeks	5.5	5.8	4.9	5.1	6.2
(10) Debtors in excess of 60 days (% of total)	5%	?	?	?	?
(11) Invoice queries (% of total)	5%	1.1%	1.4%	0.8%	2.7%
(12) Credit notes as a % of revenue	0.5%	?	?	?	?

Other information:

	D	L	M	R
	$000	$000	$000	$000
Aged Debtor analysis (extract):				
Less than 30 days	1,300	1,500	1,180	2,000
31–60 days	321	133	153	552
Value of credit notes raised during the period ($000)	45	36	28	132

Note: TSC operates all year round.

Required:

(a) Prepare a report for the directors of TSC which:

 (i) contains a summary table which shows the points gained (or forfeited) by each depot. The points table should facilitate the ranking of each depot against the others for each of the 12 measures provided in the Appendix.
 (9 marks)

 (ii) evaluates the relative performance of the four depots as indicated by the analysis in the summary table prepared in (i); **(5 marks)**

 (iii) assesses TSC in terms of financial performance, competitiveness, service quality, resource utilisation, flexibility and innovation and discusses the interrelationships between these terms, incorporating examples from within TSC; and **(10 marks)**

 (iv) critiques the performance measurement system at TSC. **(5 marks)**

Note: Requirement (a) includes 4 professional marks.

A central feature of the performance measurement system at TSC is the widespread use of league tables that display each depot's performance relative to one another.

Required:

(b) Evaluate the potential benefits and problems associated with the use of 'league tables' as a means of measuring performance. **(6 marks)**

(Total: 35 marks)

12 ROYAL LAUREL HOSPITAL (RLH) (JUN 09)

The Royal Laurel Hospital (RLH) and The King Hardy Hospital (KHH) are government funded institutions which are managed by the Glasburgh Trust. The following information is available for the year ended 31 May 2009.

	RLH Actual	RLH Budget	KHH Actual
Total inpatients	37,000	36,500	40,000
Number of inpatients waiting >5 weeks for admission	3,330	365	320
Number of inpatients waiting >11 weeks for admission	740	0	0
Total outpatients	44,000	43,800	44,000
Number of outpatients waiting >5 weeks for treatment	4,400	2,190	352
Number of outpatients waiting >11 weeks for treatment	1,320	438	220
Number of outpatients waiting >13 weeks for treatment	220	0	0
Achievement (%) of target maximum waiting time of 2 weeks for admission to rapid access chest pains clinic	70	98	100
Number of emergency admissions	300	400	300
Number of 12 hour 'trolley' waits for emergency admissions	4	0	0
Achievement (%) of target of 4 hours or less time spent in accident and Emergency ward	96	98	100
Number of complaints received	1,620	803	420
Number of complaints responded to within 25 days	1,539	803	416
Number of deaths (all inpatients)	600	730	800
Infection control – number of instances of infections reported	2	6	0
Number of drug administration errors	80	100	20
Number of staff shortages	80	60	20
Staff productivity measure (number of patient days per staff member)	8·4	7·4	9·2
Number of times of Government or agency staff usage	80	60	20
Bed occupancy (number of inpatient bed days)	138,750	146,000	134,320
Theatre utilisation (%)	?	?	?
% of inpatients requiring a single operation	80%	80%	80%
Number of operations performed	29,008	?	31,840
Revenue from clinical and non-clinical activities ($m)	54·2	55·2	60·2
Medical staff costs ($m)	22·3	22·2	19·6
Other staff costs ($m)	5·5	5·5	4·0
Income and expenditure surplus margin	(1·0)	0·0	4·0
Number of days cash in hand	31	30	35

Additional information:

(1) Both hospitals were in operation for 365 days during the year

(2) Each hospital has 42 wards, each of which accommodates 10 beds

(3) RLH budgeted that each inpatient would require a stay of four days and nights in hospital.

(4) Each hospital has ten operating theatres in each of which an average of nine operations per day were undertaken. (5) No outpatient required an operation during the year.

(6) The management of the trust uses a 'balanced scorecard' approach in order to assess the performance of each hospital. Their balanced scorecard has four dimensions which are as follows:

(i) Access to services

(ii) Clinical

(iii) Efficiency

(iv) Financial management.

Required:

Prepare a report to the management of the Glasburgh Trust which:

(a) critically assesses, on the basis of the above information, the performance of both hospitals for the year ended 31 May 2009. You should use the four dimensions to perform your assessment as per note (6) above; **(20 marks)**

(b) evaluates the balanced scorecard used by the Glasburgh Trust and provides recommendations which would improve its usefulness as a performance measurement tool. **(11 marks)**

4 professional marks will be awarded in question 1 for the appropriateness of the format and presentation of the report and the quality of its content. **(4 marks)**

(Total: 35 marks)

13 THE BENJAMIN EDUCATION COLLEGE (BEC) (DEC 09)

The Benjamin Education College (BEC), which is partially government funded, is a well-established provider of professional courses for students of accounting, law and marketing in the country of Brightland.

Its mission statement states that the college 'is committed to providing high quality education to all students'. BEC provides education to private fee-paying students as well as to students who are funded by the government.

The Jackson Business Centre (JBC) which commenced trading during 2004 is also a provider of professional courses for students of accounting, law and marketing in the country of Brightland. It is a privately owned college and all its students are responsible for the payment of their own fees.

Relevant operating data for BEC and JBC for the year ended 30 November 2009 are as follows:

(1) Both BEC and JBC offer a range of courses in accounting, law and marketing on a twice per annum basis.

(2) Fees (budget and actual) payable to BEC and JBC in respect of each student who enrolled for a course

	BEC Privately funded students	BEC Government funded students	JBC Privately funded students
Course type:	$	$	$
Accounting	1,200	900	1,000
Law	1,000	750	1,200
Marketing	800	600	1,200

(3) Salary costs per staff member were payable as follows:

	BEC Budget $	BEC Actual $	JBC Actual $
Lecturer	50,000	52,000	55,000
Administrative	20,000	20,800	22,000

(4) Budgeted costs for the year based on 8,000 students per annum for BEC were as follows:

	$	Variable cost (%)	Fixed cost (%)
Tuition materials	720,000	100	–
Catering	100,000	80	20
Cleaning	40,000	25	75
Other operating costs	600,000	20	80
Depreciation	40,000	–	100

Variable costs vary according to the number of students attending courses at BEC.

(5) Actual costs (other than salary costs) incurred during the year:

	BEC $	JBC $
Tuition materials	741,600	730,000
Catering	95,680	110,000
Cleaning	40,950	40,000
Other operating costs (including costs of freelance staff)	646,800	645,000
Depreciation	40,000	60,000

(6) The management of JBC is considering introducing on-line tuition support by its lecturing staff.

(7) Both BEC and JBC operated a policy which aimed to employ 60 lecturers throughout the year.

(8) The appendix below shows budget and actual statistics for BEC and actual statistics for JBC.

APPENDIX

Sundry statistics for the year ended 30 November 2009

	BEC Budget	BEC Actual	JBC Actual
Number of students:			
Accounting	3,600	3,800	4,000
Law	1,500	1,400	1,560
Marketing	1,800	2,000	2,000
Student mix (%) for each course type:			
Privately funded	80	70	100
Government funded	20	30	

	BEC Budget	BEC Actual	JBC Actual
Number of enquiries received:			
Accounting	4,800	4,750	5,000
Law	2,000	2,800	2,000
Marketing	2,400	2,500	2,400
Number of lecturers employed throughout the year	60	60	60
Number of lecturers recruited during the year:			
Accounting	2	6	1
Law	1	3	–
Marketing	1	3	–
Number of admin. staff employed throughout the year	10	10	8
Number of administrative staff recruited during the year	2	8	–
Number of times freelance lecturing staff were used	–	–	20
Number of new courses under development	–	–	4

Required:

The senior management team of BEC has asked you, as management accountant, to prepare a report providing them with the following:

(i) A statement which shows actual and budgeted income statements of BEC and an actual income statement for JBC in respect of the year ended 30 November 2009 on a comparable basis; **(10 marks)**

(ii) An assessment of the performance of BEC and JBC using both financial and non-financial measures based on the information contained in the question. You should identify other measures of performance which you consider relevant to BEC; **(10 marks)**

(iii) A discussion of the issues that might restrict the extent to which a performance measurement system is accepted and supported by management and employees; **(6 marks)**

Professional marks will be awarded in question 1 for appropriateness of format, style and structure of the report. **(4 marks)**

(Total: 30 marks)

14 THE RRR GROUP (RRR) (DEC 09)

The RRR Group (RRR) provides roof repair, refurbishment and renewal services to individual customers on a nationwide basis. RRR operates a large number of regional divisions, each of which offers a similar range of services.

RRR expects divisional management to prepare its own annual budget by focusing on the achievement of a net profit figure set at group level. This budget is currently used for planning and reporting.

Table A shows actual results for Alpha division for the years ending 30 November 2008 and 30 November 2009, together with data representing an average of a number of similar competitor company divisions.

RRR has given Alpha division a budgeted profit requirement of $20m for the year to 30 November 2010. The management of Alpha division has prepared the strategy shown in Table B as the framework for the achievement of the budget profit requirement for the year to 30 November 2010.

RRR plc has, however, decided that in line with current 'beyond budgeting' philosophy, each division should follow a number of adaptive processes including the following:

(1) Setting 'stretch goals' aimed at relative improvement and avoiding dysfunctional decision-making.

(2) Evaluation and rewards at each division based on relative improvement contracts (with hindsight).

(3) Action planning that focuses on a strategy to achieve continuous value creation for the group.

As an incentive to the overall achievement of goals and the creation of 'value', a set of KPIs (key performance indicators) will be introduced in 2010 and used on the basis of the data in Table C.

Divisional staff will be paid a bonus as a percentage of salary based on the overall weighted percentage score deduced from the analysis as per Table C.

TABLE A

Summary of financial and other operating information

	Alpha division 2009 $m	Alpha division 2008 $m	Competitor divisions 2009 $m
Sales revenue	90.0	80.0	85.0
Less Costs:			
Cost of sales (note 1)	60.0	50.0	
Marketing	8.5	8.0	
Staff training	4.0	4.0	
Remedial work on orders (note 2)	0.8	0.5	
Customer enquiry costs (note 3)	1.5	1.4	
Customer complaint related costs (note 4)	0.2	0.1	
Total costs	75.0	64.0	69.5
Net profit	15.0	16.0	15.5
Number of:			
Customer enquiries	15,000	16,000	
Customer orders placed	10,000	8,800	
Orders placed requiring remedial work	300	440	
Customer complaints	100	132	

Note 1: Includes materials, wages/salaries, vehicle and machine costs, etc

Note 2: Following inspection by surveyors after work implemented

Note 3: Initial survey and site analysis

Note 4: Investigation & action on complaints.

TABLE B

Proposed strategy for Alpha division for year to 30 November 2010

It is estimated that the budgeted profit requirement of $20m will be achieved as a consequence of the following:

- The number of orders received and processed will be 11,000 (with average price levels remaining as per 2009 actual price levels) from an initial total of 15,500 customer enquiries
- The marketing cost allowance would be reduced to $7.2m
- The training cost allowance would be reduced to $3m
- Cost of sales ($) will rise by 10% from the 2009 actual total to allow for the combined effect of volume and price changes
- Remedial work on orders will total $1m for material, labour and overhead costs
- Initial survey and analysis costs on customer enquiries will remain at the 2009 average cost per enquiry
- Customer complaint related costs are expected to rise to $0.25m.

TABLE C

Staff bonus calculation for the year ended 30 November 2009 using Key Performance Indicators (KPIs) based on relative contract factors

KPI	Weighting Factor (A)	KPI Total Score % (B)* (see below for basis)	Weighted Score % (A) × (B)
Revenue 2009 versus previous year	0.15		
Revenue 2009 versus competitor	0.20		
Profit 2009 versus previous year	0.15		
Profit 2009 versus competitor	0.20		
Quality items 2009 versus previous year:			
No. of orders requiring remedial work	0.075		
No. of complaints investigated	0.075		
% of enquiries converted into orders	0.15		
Total	1.000	Bonus (%) =	?

(B)* – each KPI score value is positive (+) where the 2009 value shows an improvement over the previous year OR negative (–) where the 2009 value shows poorer performance than in the previous year.

Each KPI score value is the % increase (+) or decrease (–) in 2009 as appropriate.

Required:

(a) Evaluate the extent to which the budget of Alpha division for the year ending 30 November 2010 is achievable and consistent with the 'beyond budgeting' philosophy detailed above.

Note: Your answer should include specific examples from the data contained in the question to illustrate your discussion. **(14 marks)**

(b) (i) Apply the KPI performance appraisal process shown and explained in Table C, using actual data for 2008 and 2009 in order to show the bonus (as a % of salary) that would have been achieved by Alpha division for the year ending 30 November 2009; **(12 marks)**

(ii) Discuss potential benefits that may be derived from the application of the KPI appraisal and bonus approach, both for Alpha division and throughout the RRR Group. **(4 marks)**

(Total: 30 marks)

15 THE SUPERIOR BUSINESS CONSULTANCY (SBC) (JUN 10)

The Superior Business Consultancy (SBC) which is based in Jayland provides clients with consultancy services in Advertising, Recruitment and IT Support. SBC commenced trading on 1 July 2003 and has grown steadily since then.

The following information, together with that contained in the appendix, is available:

(1) Three types of consultants are employed by SBC on a full-time basis. These are:

Advertising consultants who provide advice regarding advertising and promotional activities

Recruitment consultants who provide advice regarding recruitment and selection of staff, and

IT consultants who provide advice regarding the selection of business software and technical support.

(2) During the year ended 31 May 2010, each full-time consultant was budgeted to work on 200 days. All consultations undertaken by consultants of SBC had a duration of one day.

(3) During their 200 working days per annum, full-time consultants undertake some consultations on a 'no-fee' basis. Such consultations are regarded as Business Development Activity (BDA) by the management of SBC.

(4) SBC also engages the services of subcontract consultants who provide clients with consultancy services in the categories of Advertising, Recruitment and IT Support. All of the subcontract consultants have worked for SBC for at least three years.

(5) During recent years the directors of SBC have become increasingly concerned that SBC's systems are inadequate for the measurement of performance. This concern was further increased after they each read a book entitled '*How to improve business performance* measurement' which was written by Ino Itall, a business analyst of worldwide repute.

APPENDIX

SBC – Relevant actual and forecast statistics

	2010 Actual	2011 Forecast	2012 Forecast
Number of full-time consultants by category:			
Advertising	20	20	20
Recruitment	30	25	20
IT Support	50	50	50
Salaries per full-time consultant ($):			
Advertising	40,000	40,800	40,800
Recruitment	35,000	35,700	35,700
IT Support	30,000	30,600	30,600
Number of chargeable consultations (total demand):			
Advertising	4,200	4,100	4,000
Recruitment	6,250	5,750	5,000
IT Support	10,250	10,500	10,000
Per cent of chargeable days spent on Business Development Activity (%):			
Advertising	7	8	10
Recruitment	22	22	25
IT Support	12	13	14
Cost per consultation undertaken by subcontract consultants ($):			
Advertising	300		
Recruitment	220		
IT Support	200		
Other operating costs ($000):			
Full-time consultants	1,075	1,050	1,270
Subcontract consultants	125	270	182

Required:

Prepare a report for the directors of SBC which:

(i) discusses the importance of non-financial performance indicators (NFPIs) and evaluates, giving examples, how a 'balanced scorecard' approach may be used to improve performance within SBC; **(13 marks)**

(ii) contains a calculation of the actual average cost per chargeable consultation for both full-time consultants and separately for subcontract consultants in respect of each of the three categories of consultancy services during the year ended 31 May 2010; **(7 marks)**

(iii) suggests reasons for the trends shown by the figures contained in the appendix; **(5 marks)**

(iv) discusses the potential benefits and potential problems which might arise as a consequence of employing subcontract consultants within SBC. **(6 marks)**

Professional marks will be for appropriateness of format, style and structure of the report. **(4 marks)**

(Total: 35 marks)

16 THE EQUINE MANAGEMENT ACADEMY (EMA) (JUN 10)

The Equine Management Academy (EMA) which was founded in 1990 is a privately owned organisation located in Hartland, a developing country which has a large agricultural sector and where much transportation is provided by horses. EMA operates an Equine College which provides a range of undergraduate and postgraduate courses for students who wish to pursue a career in one of the following disciplines:

- Equine (Horse) Surgery
- Equine Dentistry, and
- Equine Business Management.

The Equine College which has a maximum capacity of 1,200 students per annum is currently the only equine college in Hartland.

The following information is available:

(1) A total of 1,200 students attended the Equine College during the year ended 31 May 2010. Student mix and fees paid were as per the following table:

Student category	% of total number of students	Fee ($) per student, per annum
Surgery	30	12,000
Dentistry	25	10,000
Business Management	45	6,000

(2) Total operating costs (all fixed) during the year amounted to $6,500,000.

(3) Operating costs of the Equine College are expected to increase by 4% during the year ending 31 May 2011. This led to a decision by the management to increase the fees of all students by 5% with effect from 1 June 2010. The management expect the number of students and the mix of students during the year ending 31 May 2011 to remain unchanged from those of the year ended 31 May 2010.

(4) EMA also operates a Riding School at which 240 horses are stabled. The Riding School is open for business on 360 days per annum. Each horse is available for four horse-riding lessons per day other than on the 40 days per annum that each horse is rested, i.e. not available for the provision of riding lessons. During the year ended 31 May 2010, the Riding School operated at 80% of full capacity.

(5) Horse-riding lessons are provided for riders in three different skill categories. These are 'Beginner', 'Competent' and 'Advanced'.

During the year ended 31 May 2010, the fee per riding lesson was as follows:

Skill category of horse rider	Lesson mix	Fee ($) per lesson
Beginner	50%	15
Competent	25%	30
Advanced	25%	50

(6) Total operating costs of the Riding School (all fixed) amounted to $5,750,000 during the year ended 31 May 2010.

(7) It is anticipated that the operating costs of the Riding School will increase by 6% in the year ending 31 May 2011. The management have decided to increase the charge per lesson, in respect of 'Competent' and 'Advanced' riders by 10% with effect from 1 June 2010. There will be no increase in the charge per lesson for 'Beginner' riders.

(8) The lesson mix and capacity utilisation of the Riding School will remain the same during the year ending 31 May 2011.

Required:

(a) Prepare a statement showing the budgeted net profit or loss for the year ending 31 May 2011. **(7 marks)**

Some time ago the government of Hartland, which actively promotes environmental initiatives, announced its intention to open an academy comprising an equine college and riding school. The management of EMA are uncertain of the impact that this will have on the budgeted number of students and riders during the year ending 31 May 2011, although they consider that due to the excellent reputation of the instructors at the riding school capacity utilisation could remain unchanged, or even increase, in spite of the opening of the government funded academy. Current estimates of the number of students entering the academy and the average capacity utilisation of the riding school are as follows:

	Equine College		Riding School	
	Student Fees	Probability	Capacity utilisation	Probability
No change		0.20	90%	0.10
Decrease by 10%		0.60	80%	0.60
Decrease by 20%		0.20	70%	0.30

Required:

(b) (i) Prepare a summary table which shows the possible net profit or loss outcomes, and the combined probability of each potential outcome for the year ending 31 May 2011. The table should also show the expected value of net profit or loss for the year; **(9 marks)**

(ii) Comment briefly on the use of expected values by the management of EMA; **(3 marks)**

(iii) Suggest three reasons why the government of Hartland might have decided to open an academy comprising an equine college and a riding school. **(6 marks)**

(Total: 25 marks)

17 FILM PRODUCTIONS CO (FP) (DEC 10)

Film Productions Co (FP) is a small international company producing films for cinema release and also for sale on DVD or to television companies. FP deals with all areas of the production from casting, directing and managing the artists to negotiating distribution deals with cinema chains and TV channels. The industry is driven by the tastes of its films' audience, which when accurately predicted can lead to high levels of profitability on a successful film.

The company's stated mission is to 'produce fantastic films that have mass appeal'. The company makes around $200 million of sales each year equally split between a share of cinema takings, DVD sales and TV rights. FP has released 32 films in the past five years. Each film costs an average of $18 million and takes 12 months to produce from initial commissioning through to the final version. Production control is important in order to hit certain key holiday periods for releasing films at the cinema or on DVD.

The company's films have been moderately successful in winning industry awards although FP has never won any major award. Its aims have been primarily commercial with artistic considerations secondary.

The company uses a top-down approach to strategy development with objectives leading to critical success factors (CSFs) which must then be measured using performance indicators. Currently, the company has identified a number of critical success factors. The two most important of these are viewed as:

(i)   improve audience satisfaction

(ii)   strengthen profitability in operations

At the request of the board, the chief executive officer (CEO) has been reviewing this system in particular the role of CSFs. Generally, the CEO is worried that the ones chosen so far fail to capture all the factors affecting the business and wants to understand all possible sources for CSFs and what it means to categorise them into monitoring and building factors.

These CSFs will need to be measured and there must be systems in place to perform that role. The existing information system of the company is based on a fairly basic accounting package. However, the CEO has been considering greater investment in these systems and making more use of the company's website in both driving forward the business' links to its audience and in collecting data on them.

The CEO is planning a report to the board of Film Productions and has asked you to help by drafting certain sections of this report.

Required:

You are required to draft the sections of the CEO's report answering the following questions:

(a)   Explain the difference between the following two types of CSF: monitoring and building, using examples appropriate to FP. **(4 marks)**

(b)   Identify information that FP could use to set its CSFs and explain how it could be used giving two examples that would be appropriate to FP. **(6 marks)**

(c)   For each of the two critical success factors given in the question, identify two performance indicators (PIs) that could support measurement of their achievement and explain why each PI is relevant to the CSF. **(10 marks)**

(d)   Discuss the implications of your chosen PIs for the design and use of the company's website, its management information system and its executive information system. **(9 marks)**

Professional marks will be awarded for appropriateness of style and structure of the answer. **(2 marks)**

(Total: 31 marks)

18 ROBUST LAPTOPS CO (RL) (DEC 10)

Robust Laptops Co (RL) make laptop computers for use in dangerous environments. The company's main customers are organisations like oil companies and the military that require a laptop that can survive rough handling in transport to a site and can be made to their unique requirements.

The company started as a basic laptop manufacturer but its competitors grew much larger and RL had to find a niche market where its small size would not hinder its ability to compete. It is now considered one of the best quality producers in this sector.

RL had the same finance director for many years who preferred to develop its systems organically. However, due to fall in profitability, a new chief executive officer (CEO) has been appointed who wishes to review RL's financial control systems in order to get better information with which to tackle the profit issue.

The CEO wants to begin by thinking about the pricing of the laptops to ensure that selling expensive products at the wrong price is not compromising profit margins. The laptops are individually specified by customers for each order and pricing has been on a production cost plus basis with a mark-up of 45%. The company uses an absorption costing system based on labour hours in order to calculate the production cost per unit.

The main control system used within the company is the annual budget. It is set before the start of the financial year and variances are monitored and acted upon by line managers. The CEO has been reading about major companies that have stopped using budgets and wants to know how such a radical move works and why a company might take such a step. He has been worried by moves by competitors into RL's market with impressive new products. This has created unrest among the staff at RL with two experienced managers leaving the company.

Financial and other information for Robust Laptops

Robust Laptops

Data for the year ended 30 September 2010

			Total
Volume (units)		23,800	
			$000
Direct variable costs			40,650
	Material		
	Labour		3,879
	Packaging and transport		2,118
	Subtotal		46,647
Overhead costs	Customer service		7,735
	Purchasing and receiving		2,451
	Inventory management		1,467
	Administration of production		2,537
	Subtotal		14,190
	Total		60,837

Labour time per unit	3 hours	
Data collected for the year:		
No of minutes on calls to customer	899,600	
No of purchase orders raised	21,400	
No of components used in production	618,800	

Order 11784

Units ordered	16	
Direct costs for this order:		$
Material		27,328
Labour		2,608
Packaging and transport		1,424
Other activities relating to this order:		
No of minutes on calls to customer	1,104	
No of purchase orders raised	64	
No of components used in production	512	
Administration of production (absorbed as general overhead)	3 Labour hrs per unit	

Required:

Write a report to the CEO to include:

(a) An evaluation of the current method of costing against an Activity Based Costing (ABC) system. You should provide illustrative calculations using the information provided on costs for 2010 and Order 11784. Briefly state what action management might take in the light of your results with respect to this order. **(15 marks)**

(b) An explanation of the operation of a beyond budgeting approach and an evaluation of the potential of such a change at RL. **(10 marks)**

Professional marks will be awarded in for appropriateness of format, style and structure of the report. **(4 marks)**

(Total: 29 marks)

Section 2

PRACTICE QUESTIONS – SECTION B

STRATEGIC PLANNING AND CONTROL

19 VIRTUAL ORGANISATIONS

For an organisation to successfully achieve its strategies it will need to give adequate consideration to both structure and support systems. Similarly, it should consider the issue of relationship management, as all organisations are reliant on relationships with others. In varying degrees, organisations explore their boundaries of responsibility with others and many have taken the decision to outsource activities, some to the extent that they operate as 'networked organisations'.

The term 'virtual organisations' has been used to describe an extreme form of networked organisation that has minimal owned resources and activities. Here the emphasis is almost solely upon partnership and collaboration rather than permanent staff, physical sites and formal structures. Critics feel that such organisations are unable to operate beyond the short term, citing as evidence the number of so-called 'dot com' companies that have gone out of business.

Required:

(a) Discuss the key strategic issues that will lead to potential strategic strengths or weaknesses for a virtual networked organisation. **(13 marks)**

(b) Discuss the benefits and difficulties of conducting an environmental analysis in an organisation that is highly networked. **(12 marks)**

(Total: 25 marks)

20 UNIVERSAL UNIVERSITY (UU) (JUN 09)

(a) The senior management of Universal University (UU) intend to develop both quantitative and qualitative measures of performance in relation to lecturing staff.

As part of UU's mission to provide 'quality education' to its students, lecturers are encouraged to apply their skill and judgement in the creation, delivery and assessment aspects of the learning process.

Academic staff are organised on a departmental basis. Each department is expected to achieve and improve on targets in the achievement of its role.

As part of their development both personally and as departmental members, staff are encouraged to participate fully in research publication, new course design and innovation in teaching and learning methods.

Academic staff have differing views on whether action on their part in pursuing aspects of such goals is compatible with their personal goals.

Required:

Using the above scenario, discuss in relation to the lecturing staff within (UU) each of the following:

(i) The application of Agency Theory to staff, in their role as agents and provide examples of the observability of their role in relation to outcomes and effort;

(ii) The application of Expectancy Theory with specific reference to the relationship between:

- strength of motivation to do (X);
- strength of preference for outcome (Y);
- expectation that doing (X) will result in (Y). **(12 marks)**

(b) 'Hard Accountability' is deemed to apply to lecturing staff in each of three specific areas as follows:

(i) accounting for the numbers;

(ii) ensuring the numbers are accounted for;

(iii) being held accountable for events and circumstances leading to the numbers.

Required:

Describe how each of the areas (b)(i) to (iii) may be applied at UU and critically evaluate this approach to performance measurement in the context of the scenario described above. **(8 marks)**

(Total: 20 marks)

21 DIVISIONAL ACTIONS

Within a large group, divisional managers are paid a bonus which can represent a large proportion of their annual earnings. The bonus is paid when the budgeted divisional profit for the financial year is achieved or exceeded.

Meetings of divisional boards are held monthly and attended by the senior management of the division, and senior members of group management.

With the end of the financial year approaching, there had been discussions in all divisional board meetings of forecast profit for the year, and whether budgeted profit would be achieved. In three board meetings, for divisions that were having difficulty in achieving budgeted profits, the following divisional actions had been discussed. In each case, the amounts involved would have been material in determining whether the division would achieve its budget:

- **Division A** had severely cut spending on training, and postponed routine re-painting of premises.

- **Division B** had re-negotiated a contract for consultancy services. It was in the process of installing Total Quality Management (TQM) systems, and had originally agreed to pay progress payments to the consultants, and had budgeted to make these payments. It had re-negotiated that the consultancy would invoice the division with the total cost only when the work was completed in the next financial year.

- **Division C** had persuaded some major customers to take early delivery, in the current financial year, of products originally ordered for delivery early in the next financial year. This would ensure virtually nil inventory at year end.

Required:

Discuss the financial accounting, budgeting, ethical and motivational issues which arise from these divisional actions.

Comment on whether any group management action is necessary. (20 marks)

22 DIVERSE HOLDINGS PLC (DEC 05)

Diverse Holdings Plc has five wholly-owned subsidiary companies. These are:

(i) Organic Foods Ltd (OFL) which is involved in the production and sale of organically grown fruit and vegetables. OFL has built up a very good reputation as a supplier of quality produce.

(ii) Haul-Trans Ltd (HTL) which was acquired on 1 December 20X5 and is involved in transporting a range of products on behalf of third parties.

(iii) Kitchen Appliances Ltd (KAL) which is involved in the manufacture and sale of small, manually-operated kitchen appliances. KAL has recently suffered from squeezed margins as a consequence of competition from low cost imports.

(iv) Paper Supplies Ltd (PSL) which manufactures and sells a narrow range of stationery products to two distributors.

(v) Office Products Ltd (OPL) which manufactures and sells computer workstations with unique design features which are highly regarded by health and safety experts.

The management accountant of Diverse Holdings Plc has gathered the following actual and forecast information relating to the five subsidiaries:

	Year ending 30 November				
	20X3 Actual	20X4 Actual	20X5 Actual	20X6 Forecast	20X7 Forecast
(OFL)					
Market size ($m)	100.0	120.0	150.0	180.0	225.0
Turnover ($m)	5.0	8.0	10.0	13.5	18.0
Operating Profit ($m)	1.0	1.8	2.5	3.0	3.6
(HTL)					
Market size ($m)	Unknown	Unknown	Unknown	Unknown	Unknown
Turnover ($m)	40.0	40.0	41.0	42.0	42.0
Operating Profit ($m)	4.0	4.0	4.0	5.0	5.6
(KAL)					
Market size ($m)	252.0	250.0	245.0	242.0	240.0
Turnover ($m)	37.5	37.5	35.5	32.0	29.0
Operating Profit/(loss) ($m)	1.5	1.1	0.7	0.3	(0.2)
(PSL)					
Market size ($m)	60.0	65.0	70.0	77.0	84.0
Turnover ($m)	2.0	2.0	2.0	2.0	2.1
Operating Profit ($m)	0.6	0.6	0.6	0.5	0.5
(OPL)					
Market size ($m)	200.0	220.0	240.0	260.0	280.0
Turnover ($m)	15.0	16.0	16.5	17.0	17.5
Operating Profit ($m)	1.50	1.60	1.65	1.70	1.75

The management accountant has also collated the following information relating to the market share held at 30 November 20X5 by the market leader in those markets in which each subsidiary operates:

Subsidiary	Market	Market share (%) held by market leader
Organic Foods Ltd	Food production	6.66
Haul-Trans Ltd	Transport	Unknown
Kitchen Appliances Ltd	Kitchen appliances	16
Paper Supplies Ltd	Stationery	35
Office Products Ltd	Workstations	25

The management has decided not to undertake any further acquisitions during the next two years due to a shortage of funds.

Required:

(a) Identify and comment on FOUR advantages that may be gained as a result of the adoption of a formal system of strategic planning. **(4 marks)**

(b) Explain how the use of SWOT a1nalysis may be of assistance to the management of Diverse Holdings Plc. **(3 marks)**

(c) (i) Using ONLY the above information, assess the competitive position of Diverse Holdings Plc. **(7 marks)**

(ii) Explain THREE strategies that might be adopted in order to improve the future prospects of Diverse Holdings Plc. **(6 marks)**

(Total: 20 marks)

23 ALTERNATIVE BUDGETING (JUN 06)

Better budgeting in recent years may have been seen as a movement from 'incremental budgeting' to alternative budgeting approaches.

However, academic studies (e.g. Beyond Budgeting – Hope & Fraser) argue that the annual budget model may be seen as (i) having a number of inherent weaknesses and (ii) acting as a barrier to the effective implementation of alternative models for use in the accomplishment of strategic change.

Required:

(a) Identify and comment on FIVE inherent weaknesses of the annual budget model irrespective of the budgeting approach that is applied. **(8 marks)**

(b) Discuss ways in which the traditional budgeting process may be seen as a barrier to the achievement of the aims of EACH of the following models for the implementation of strategic change:

   (i) benchmarking;

   (ii) balanced scorecard; and

   (iii) activity-based models. **(12 marks)**

(Total: 20 marks)

24 PERFORMANCE MANAGEMENT (JUN 06)

A management accounting focus for performance management in an organisation may incorporate the following:

(1) The determination and quantification of **objectives** and **strategies.**

(2) The measurement of the **results** of the strategies implemented and of the achievement of the results through a **number of determinants.**

(3) The application of **business change techniques**, in the improvement of those determinants.

Required:

(a) Discuss the meaning and inter-relationship of the terms (shown in bold type) in the above statement. Your answer should incorporate examples that may be used to illustrate each term in BOTH profit-seeking organisations and not-for-profit organisations in order to highlight any differences between the two types of organisation. **(14 marks)**

(b) Provide an example that illustrates a structured application of the terms contained in the above statement in respect of a profit-seeking organisation OR a not-for-profit organisation of your own choice. **(6 marks)**

(Total: 20 marks)

25 BUSINESS PROCESS RE-ENGINEERING

Business process re-engineering (BPR) has been promoted as a major management technique, but it is also criticised as little more than cost reduction.

Required:

(a) Briefly explain business process re-engineering. **(4 marks)**

(b) Explain the contribution the management accountant should make to the planning and implementation of a business process re-engineering programme. **(8 marks)**

(c) Explain the main advantages and criticisms of business process re-engineering programmes. **(8 marks)**

(Total: 20 marks)

26 BUDGETING (PILOT 07)

Budgeting may be viewed as a relevant technique in facilitating the assessment of business performance from initial planning to actual results. It will be necessary, however, to consider how to overcome factors that may limit its effectiveness.

Required:

(a) Critically discuss the arguments for the use of budgeting in the implementation of FOUR aspects of the performance cycle. **(8 marks)**

(b) Highlight THREE advantages that may be claimed for the use of activity based budgeting rather than a traditional incremental budgeting system. **(6 marks)**

(c) Suggest FOUR reasons why advocates of a 'Beyond Budgeting' philosophy may not regard a major annual budget preparation exercise as an effective use of resources. **(6 marks)**

(Total: 20 marks)

PAPER P5 : ADVANCED PERFORMANCE MANAGEMENT

27 THE 'CARE FOR DOGS COMPANY' (CFD) (DEC 09)

The 'Care For Dogs Company' (CFD) is a very profitable organisation which was established in 1998. CFD offers accommodation, care and supervision for pet dogs owned by inhabitants of Barkland.

CFD provides temporary accommodation for dogs whose owners are unable to care for them due to holidays, work commitments, illness etc. As part of the service offered to dog owners, CFD collects and returns dogs at the beginning and end of all dog stays.

When CFD was formed, the directors created a mission statement which was 'to provide very high value for money to all of our clients'.

The directors have always attempted to manage CFD in a socially responsible manner. Indeed, they are now considering the creation of a 'Dog Sanctuary' for homeless dogs which would involve an allocation of 20% of the total accommodation available for dogs to the Dog Sanctuary. The Dog Sanctuary would accommodate homeless dogs until such time as a new owner was found for them. CFD would not receive any revenue whatsoever in respect of any homeless dog.

Required:

(a) (i) Discuss the purpose, potential benefits and potential problems of mission statements; **(8 marks)**

(ii) Advise the directors of CFD regarding the appropriateness of its mission statement. **(3 marks)**

(b) Explain the term 'critical success factor' and discuss THREE critical success factors for CFD clearly highlighting a key performance indicator for each critical success factor. **(6 marks)**

(c) Excluding the number of complaints by clients, identify and briefly explain THREE quantitative non-financial performance measures that could be used to assess the 'quality of service' provided by CFD. **(3 marks)**

(Total: 20 marks)

28 THE RUBBER GROUP (TRG) (JUN 08)

The Rubber Group (TRG) manufactures and sells a number of rubber-based products. Its strategic focus is channelled through profit centres which sell products transferred from production divisions that are operated as cost centres.

The profit centres are the primary value-adding part of the business, where commercial profit centre managers are responsible for the generation of a contribution margin sufficient to earn the target return of TRG. The target return is calculated after allowing for the sum of the agreed budgeted cost of production at production divisions, plus the cost of marketing, selling and distribution costs and central services costs.

The Bettamould Division is part of TRG and manufactures moulded products that it transfers to profit centres at an agreed cost per tonne. The agreed cost per tonne is set following discussion between management of the Bettamould Division and senior management of TRG.

The following information relates to the agreed budget for the Bettamould Division for the year ending 30 June 2009:

(1) The budgeted output of moulded products to be transferred to profit centres is 100,000 tonnes. The budgeted transfer cost has been agreed on a two-part basis as follows:

   (i) A standard variable cost of $200 per tonne of moulded products;

   (ii) A lump sum annual charge of $50,000,000 in respect of fixed costs, which is charged to profit centres, at $500 per tonne of moulded products.

(2) Budgeted standard variable costs (as quoted in 1 above) have been set after incorporating each of the following:

   (i) A provision in respect of processing losses amounting to 15% of material inputs. Materials are sourced on a JIT basis from chosen suppliers who have been used for some years. It is felt that the 15% level of losses is necessary because the ageing of the machinery will lead to a reduction in the efficiency of output levels.

   (ii) A provision in respect of machine idle time amounting to 5%. This is incorporated into variable machine costs. The idle time allowance is held at the 5% level partly through elements of 'real-time' maintenance undertaken by the machine operating teams as part of their job specification.

(3) Quality checks are carried out on a daily basis on 25% of throughput tonnes of moulded products.

(4) All employees and management have contracts based on fixed annual salary agreements. In addition, a bonus of 5% of salary is payable as long as the budgeted output of 100,000 tonnes has been achieved;

(5) Additional information relating to the points in (2) above (but NOT included in the budget for the year ending 30 June 2009) is as follows:

   (i) There is evidence that materials of an equivalent specification could be sourced for 40% of the annual requirement at the Bettamould Division, from another division within TRG which has spare capacity.

   (ii) There is evidence that a move to machine maintenance being outsourced from a specialist company could help reduce machine idle time and hence allow the possibility of annual output in excess of 100,000 tonnes of moulded products.

   (iii) It is thought that the current level of quality checks (25% of throughput on a daily basis) is vital, although current evidence shows that some competitor companies are able to achieve consistent acceptable quality with a quality check level of only 10% of throughput on a daily basis.

The directors of TRG have decided to investigate claims relating to the use of budgeting within organisations which have featured in recent literature. A summary of relevant points from the literature is contained in the following statement:

'The use of budgets as part of a 'performance contract' between an organisation and its managers may be seen as a practice that causes management action which might lead to the following problems:

(a) Meeting only the lowest targets

(b) Using more resources than necessary

(c) Making the bonus – whatever it takes

(d) Competing against other divisions, business units and departments

(e) Ensuring that what is in the budget is spent

(f) Providing inaccurate forecasts

(g) Meeting the target, but not beating it

(h) Avoiding risks.'

Required:

(a) Explain the nature of SIX of the eight problems listed above relating to the use of budgeting; **(12 marks)**

(b) Illustrate each of the problems chosen in (a) using the data from the Bettamould division/TRG scenario; and **(6 marks)**

(c) Suggest ways in which each of the problems chosen in (a) above may be overcome. **(6 marks)**

One professional mark is also available. **(Total: 25 marks)**

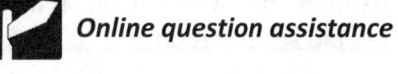

Online question assistance

EXTERNAL INFLUENCES ON ORGANISATIONAL PERFORMANCE

29 BOARDMAN FOODS (BF)

Boardman Foods (BF) produces frozen ready meals for the catering market. Its Greenlight Division is developing a growing range of meals containing less fat, salt and sugar designed to meet the 'green traffic light' standard for food labelling, allowing outlets such as pubs and canteens to market them as a healthy option. After early successes, the next phase of the project is the roll out of the full product range in their national market, and the introduction of the bestselling items across Europe.

BF has already invested heavily in the development of the new range and the finance manager has requested an analysis of the risks involved in this next phase, before further funds are committed.

The finance manager has received reports that one of the division's production lines has had an on-going problem with poorly packaged meals and she is concerned that the cause is a maintenance fault that could affect other lines and ultimately impact the campaigns' success. Previous findings suggest that 3% of the time lines are not properly maintained. When properly maintained, 95% meals are packaged correctly compared to only 30% of meals when they are maintained poorly. These results have been tabulated below.

Machine maintenance	Good		Poor	
	97%		3%	
Food packaging	Correct	Faulty	Correct	Faulty
	95%	5%	30%	70%

Preliminary investigations of the production line show that on the day of testing the first meal produced was correctly packaged.

Marketing research suggests that success in the national market depends on two key factors, the level of advertising spending and the speed of economic growth over the next six months.

With high marketing spend, net returns are predicted to be $15,000, $48,000 and $92,000 depending on whether the recovery is slow, moderate or rapid respectively. With medium marketing spend predicted returns are $30,000, $43,000 and $77,000 respectively and low marketing investment would lead to respective predicted returns of $22,000, $44,000 and $51,000. Data from previous periods, show that in 58% of the periods under review growth was slow, 26% of the time it was moderate, and it was rapid 16% of the time.

However, treasury forecasts are available which predict the expected rate of growth for the next six months and BF are considering whether to use them to determine which marketing campaign to follow. Unfortunately treasury forecasts are not wholly reliable.

The two key uncertainties affecting the success of the European launch are the strength of the euro against the dollar and the likelihood of the European Parliament backing the revised traffic light system currently before it for consideration.

The expected results for the next six months have been assessed as follows:

Euro dollar exchange rate / Parliament decision	Euro strong	Euro average	Euro weak
Favourable	$16,000	$25,000	$55,000
Uncertain	($2,000)	$8,000	$15,000
Rejected	($35,000)	($12,000)	$5,000

The probability of a strong, average or weak euro has been assessed as 0.4, 0.5 and 0.1 respectively. The Parliamentary decision is assessed as having probabilities of favourable 0.15, uncertain 0.3 and rejected 0.55.

In order to fund the Greenlight divisional expansion, BF will need to liquidate one of its portfolios of financial assets in one month. The financial director knows from experience that although the expected value of the portfolio in a month is $480,000, it has a monthly standard deviation of $47,000.

Required:

(a) What is the probability that the Beta unit production line is properly maintained, given the first meal off the line was correctly packaged? (5 marks)

(b) Advise the finance manager on the level of marketing spend would be recommended for the national campaign using expected values and assuming no growth forecasts are taken into account. Comment on any weakness in this approach. (5 marks)

(c) What would be the value to BF of obtaining a treasury forecast on economic growth, assuming such forecasts to be perfect? (5 marks)

(d) What is the probability that the European campaign will make a loss and what is the likelihood of it earning results in excess of $15,000? (5 marks)

(e) Using a 95% confidence level, identify the value at risk of BF's asset portfolio and explain the significance of your answer to BF (5 marks)

(Total: 25 marks)

Note: From the normal distribution tables, 1.65 is the normal distribution value for a one-tailed 5% probability level.

30 MTM GROUP (NOV 05)

The MTM Group (MTM) is a major tobacco products manufacturer. As a global organisation, MTM has production facilities on every continent, and a highly sophisticated distribution network. MTM uses a 'rational planning model' to produce a strategic plan for each country in which it operates. The plan states any assumptions about the business environment in that country, then forecasts retail price levels, the market size and market share of MTM for each of the next five years. This plan is then used as a basis for next year's budget for that country. The budget is fixed at the beginning of the year, and used for control and reporting for the year.

The directors of MTM are currently formulating the organisation's strategy relating to a small Asian country (referred to as the SAC) where the government is known to be considering the introduction of a ban on all tobacco advertising. At present, the probability of such legislation has been estimated at 40%, and the marketing department has estimated that the effect of the ban would be to reduce MTM's profits in the SAC by 20%.

Such a reduction would be significant enough to threaten the viability of MTM's operations in the SAC. The marketing manager has therefore suggested that the strategic plan should assume an 8% reduction in profits from the SAC (40% × 20%).

Required:

(a) Discuss the limitations of the use of the expected values technique in the context of a single strategic decision such as this. **(7 marks)**

(b) Recommend how the planning processes of MTM, for the SAC, should be modified to take account of the possible new legislation. **(13 marks)**

(Total: 20 marks)

31 SOCIAL RESPONSIBILITY

An increasing number of companies have expressed their willingness to consider their wider social responsibilities. This often involves them in voluntarily undertaking extra responsibilities and costs, for example:

- In order to reduce pollution, they may decide to treat waste products to a higher standard than required by legislation.
- They may decline to trade with countries whose governments they find objectionable.
- They may pay wages above minimum levels.

Required:

(a) Discuss:

   (i) whether the pursuit of a policy of social responsibility necessarily involves a conflict with the objective of shareholder wealth-maximisation;

   (ii) the extent to which the existence of a conflict between a company's objectives is acceptable. **(8 marks)**

(b) Discuss the extent to which it is feasible for a company to 'operationalise' its social responsibility aspirations, that is, whether it is possible to bring these considerations to strategic decision making in a programmed or systematic way. **(7 marks)**

(c) Discuss whether it is feasible for companies to include the requirements of their stakeholders when they seek to recognise their wider social responsibilities.

(5 marks)

(Total: 20 marks)

32 DIGWELL EXPLORATIONS

Eastborough is a large region with a rugged, beautiful coastline where rare birds have recently settled on undisturbed cliffs. Since mining ceased 150 years ago, its main industries have been agriculture and fishing. However, today, many communities in Eastborough suffer high unemployment. Government initiatives for regeneration through tourism have met with little success as the area has poor road networks, unsightly derelict buildings and dirty beaches.

Digwell Explorations, a listed company, has a reputation for maximising shareholder returns and has discovered substantial tin reserves in Eastborough. With new technology, mining could be profitable, provide jobs and boost the economy. A number of interest and pressure groups have, however, been vocal in opposing the scheme.

Digwell Explorations, after much lobbying, has just received government permission to undertake mining. It could face difficulties in proceeding because of the likely activity of a group called the Eastborough Protection Alliance. This group includes wildlife protection representatives, villagers worried about the potential increase in traffic congestion and noise, environmentalists, and anti-capitalism groups.

Required:

(a) Discuss the ethical issues that should have been considered by the government when granting permission for mining to go ahead. Explain the conflicts between the main stakeholder groups. **(12 marks)**

(b) By use of some (mapping) framework, analyse how the interest and power of pressure and stakeholder groups can be understood. Based on this analysis, identify how Digwell Explorations might respond to these groups. **(13 marks)**

(Total: 25 marks)

33 THE GLOBAL HOTEL GROUP (JUN 08)

The Global Hotel Group (GHG) operates hotels in most of the developed countries throughout the world. The directors of GHG are committed to a policy of achieving 'growth' in terms of geographical coverage and are now considering building and operating another hotel in Tomorrowland. Tomorrowland is a developing country which is situated 3,000 kilometres from the country in which GHG's nearest hotel is located.

The managing director of GHG recently attended a seminar on 'the use of strategic and economic information in planning organisational performance'.

He has called a board meeting to discuss the strategic and economic factors which should be considered before a decision is made to build the hotel in Tomorrowland.

Required:

(a) Discuss the strategic and economic factors which should be considered before a decision is made to build the hotel. **(14 marks)**

(b) GHG has always used local labour to build and subsequently operate hotels. The directors of GHG are again considering employing a local workforce not only to build the hotel but also to operate it on a daily basis.

Required:

Explain TWO ways in which the possibility of cultural differences might impact on the performance of a local workforce in building and operating a hotel in Tomorrowland. **(6 marks)**

(Total: 20 marks)

34 FRANCHISING FOR YOU LTD (F4U) (JUN 09)

Franchising For You Ltd (F4U) markets a range of franchises which it makes available to its customers, the franchisees. F4U supplies the franchisee with information of the mode of operation, detailed operation schedules and back-up advice (by telephone, internet) and undertakes national advertising. Each franchisee must arrange for its own premises, equipment and undertake local marketing.

F4U is considering the introduction of a Dance and Drama franchise which would have an expected life of six years. From this project, the only income F4U will receive from franchisees comes from the initial franchise fee.

The following estimates have been made relating to the cash outflows and inflows for F4U in order that F4U can evaluate the financial viability of the Dance and Drama franchise proposal:

(1) Initial investment of $6m. This will include a substantial element relating to the 'intellectual capital' requirement of the proposal.

(2) Development/improvement costs of $1m per year at the end of each of years two and three.

(3) 300 franchises will be sold each year at a fee of $20,000 per franchisee.

(4) Variable costs, payable in full on the issue of each franchise, are estimated at $6,000 per franchise.

(5) Directly attributable fixed costs of $0.6m per year in each of years one to six. No further fixed costs will be payable by F4U after this period.

(6) Corporation tax at the rate of 30%, payable in the year in which cash flow occurs. Tax allowances are not available on the initial investment or development/improvement costs payable by F4U.

(7) All cash flows are stated in current prices and with the exception of the initial investment will occur at the end of each year.

(8) The money cost of capital is 15.44%. Annual inflation during the period is estimated at 4%.

Required:

(a) Calculate the net present value (NPV) of the Dance and Drama franchise proposal and recommend whether it should be undertaken by F4U. **(6 marks)**

(b) Discuss the elements to be considered as 'intellectual capital' and issues associated with its valuation for inclusion in the initial investment of $6m. **(6 marks)**

(c) **Discuss ways in which reliance solely on financial performance measures can detract from the effectiveness of the performance management system within an organisation.** **(6 marks)**

F4U has identified key variables as follows:

(1) The number of franchises taken up each year. It is estimated that a flexible pricing policy will result in the following outcomes:

Fee per franchise $	Number of franchises sold each year
22,000	270
20,000	300
18,000	355

(2) The variable cost per franchise may be $7,000, $6,000 or $5,000.

The NINE possible outcomes of a spreadsheet model used in calculating the NPV and incorporating the variables 1 and 2 above, have been identified as follows:

Payoff Matrix: NPV values

		Fee per franchise ($000)		
		18	20	22
Variable cost	5	4,348,226	4,007,630	4,274,183
Per franchise	6	3,296,822	3,119,120	3,474,524
($000)	7	2,245,419	2,230,610	2,674,865

Required:

(d) State the franchise fee pricing strategy ($ per franchise) which will result from the operation of each of the following decision rules:

(i) Maximax;

(ii) Maximin;

(iii) Minimax regret.

Your answer should explain the basis of operation of each of the three decision rules. **(7 marks)**

(Total: 25 marks)

35 FGH TELECOM (FGH) (DEC 10)

FGH Telecom (FGH) is one of the largest providers of mobile and fixed line telecommunications in Ostland. The company has recently been reviewing its corporate objectives in the light of its changed business environment. The major new addition to the strategic objectives is under the heading: 'Building a more environmentally friendly business for the future'. It has been recognised that the company needs to make a contribution to ensuring sustainable development in Ostland and reducing its environmental footprint. Consequently, it adopted a goal that, by 2017, it would have reduced its environmental impact by 60% (compared to year 2001).

The reasons for the board's concern are that the telecommunications sector is competitive and the economic environment is increasingly harsh with the markets for debt and equities being particularly poor. On environmental issues, the government and public are calling for change from the business community. It appears that increased regulation and legislation will appear to encourage business towards better performance. The board have recognised that there are threats and opportunities from these trends. It wants to ensure that it is monitoring these factors and so it has asked for an analysis of the business environment with suggestions for performance measurement.

Additionally, the company has a large number of employees working across its network. Therefore, there are large demands for business travel. FGH runs a large fleet of commercial vehicles in order to service its network along with a company car scheme for its managers. The manager in charge of the company's travel budget is reviewing data on carbon dioxide emissions to assess FGH's recent performance.

Recent initiatives within the company to reduce emissions have included:

(a) the introduction in 2010 of a homeworking scheme for employees in order to reduce the amount of commuting to and from their offices and

(b) a drive to increase the use of teleconferencing facilities by employees.

Data on FGH Telecom:

Carbon Dioxide emissions Measured in millions of kgs	Base year 2001	2009	2010
Commercial Fleet Diesel	105.4	77.7	70.1
Commercial Fleet Petrol	11.6	0.4	0.0
Company Car Diesel	15.1	14.5	12.0
Company Car Petrol	10.3	3.8	2.2
Other road travel (Diesel)	0.5	1.6	1.1
Other road travel (Petrol)	3.1	0.5	0.3
Rail travel	9.2	9.6	3.4
Air Travel (short haul)	5.0	4.4	3.1
Air Travel (long haul)	5.1	7.1	5.4
Hire Cars (Diesel)	0.6	1.8	2.9
Hire Cars (Petrol)	6.7	6.1	6.1
Total	172.6	127.5	106.6

Required:

(a) Perform an analysis of FGH's business environment to identify factors which will affect its environmental strategy. For each of these factors, suggest performance indicators which will allow FGH to monitor its progress. **(8 marks)**

(b) Evaluate the data given on carbon dioxide emissions using suitable indicators. Identify trends from within the data and comment on whether the company's behaviour is consistent with meeting its targets. **(9 marks)**

(c) Suggest further data that the company could collect in order to improve its analysis and explain how this data could be used to measure the effectiveness of the reduction initiatives mentioned. **(3 marks)**

(Total: 20 marks)

PERFORMANCE MEASUREMENT SYSTEMS AND DESIGN

36   MOTOR COMPONENT MANUFACTURER (DEC 02)

You are responsible for managing the preparation of all revenue and cost budgets for a motor component manufacturer. You are aware that the external environment has a significant impact on the business activity and financial performance of your company and that the current information systems are underdeveloped and ineffective in this respect.

Required:

(a)   Identify which aspects of the external environment you are likely to consider and give reasons for your choice. **(10 marks)**

(b)   Identify where you might find the relevant sources of information.. **(5 marks)**

(c)   Suggest how an external environment information system could be introduced into your company. **(5 marks)**

(Total: 20 marks)

37   PRECISION PARTS

You have recently been appointed to lead the management accounting department of W Ltd, which is a small engineering company engaged in the manufacture of precision parts. The market in which the company sells its products is small and W Ltd faces severe competition. Due to the production facilities available, the company is able to undertake only small-scale engineering work. Large-scale engineering jobs are turned away as the company does not possess the manufacturing facilities to undertake them. At best, it can act only as agent for another contractor to do the work.

The board of W Ltd is aware that the volume of work which is being turned away is increasing. This is particularly frustrating as the company is unable to utilise its capacity to the fullest extent all the time. W Ltd has achieved a steady increase in profit over the last few years. Nevertheless, the board of the company believes that it could increase profitability still further by expanding and thus being able to carry out the larger scale work which is currently being turned away.

Budgetary control and standard costing information has, for many years, been provided as the sole output of the management accounting department. The previous management accountant prided himself on the punctuality and comprehensiveness of the reports produced. Each job is priced by adding a percentage to its total cost calculated in accordance with the company's standard costing procedures. The annual cost budget is split into monthly parts and flexed to take account of a particular period's actual production. Monthly cost variances – comprising those for direct materials, direct labour, variable and fixed production overheads – are produced and provided to the relevant manager. In addition, sales price and volume variances are produced by the management accounting department each period.

The company does not have a marketing department although new customers are obtained from advertising within professional engineering journals and by attendance at trade shows. At one such recent trade show, the managing director was introduced to the concept of benchmarking. He believes that there may be advantages in W Ltd undertaking benchmarking.

Required:

(a) In consideration of the need for the board of W Ltd to be provided with information which assists its strategic decision making, comment critically on the management accounting reports currently provided. **(5 marks)**

(b) State and justify what changes you, as management accountant, would make in providing information which facilitates strategic planning in the company.

Within your answer, describe what financial and non-financial information you would supply which is different from that already provided. **(10 marks)**

(c) Explain the concept of benchmarking and suggest how it might be applied to information for strategic planning in W Ltd. **(5 marks)**

(Total: 20 marks)

38 ACCOUNTING SYSTEMS (JUN 03)

'A competent management accounting system should endeavour to enhance the performance of a company. It should, in particular, consider the behavioural consequences of the system.'

Required:

(a) Explain why it is necessary when designing a management accounting system to consider the behavioural consequences of its application. **(5 marks)**

(b) Explain the potential behavioural issues that may arise in the application of performance monitoring, budgeting and transfer pricing and suggest how problems may be overcome. **(15 marks)**

(Total: 20 marks)

39 GMB CO (DEC 07)

GMB Co designs, produces and sells a number of products. Functions are recognised from design through to the distribution of products. Within each function, a number of activities may be distinguished and a principal driver identified for each activity.

Each sales order will normally comprise a number of batches of any one of a range of products. The company is active in promoting, where possible, a product focus for design, dedicated production lines and product marketing. It also recognises that a considerable level of expenditure will relate to supporting the overall business operation.

It is known that many costs may initially be recognised at the unit, batch, product sustaining (order) or business/facility sustaining (overall) levels. A list of expense items relating to Order Number 377 of product Zeta is shown below.

The methods of calculating the values for Order Number 377 shown below are given in brackets alongside each expense item. These methods also indicate whether the expense items should be regarded as product unit, batch, product sustaining (order) or business/facility sustaining (overall) level costs. The expense items are not listed in any particular sequence. Each expense item should be adjusted to reflect its total cost for Order Number 377.

Order Number 377 comprises 5,000 units of product Zeta. The order will be provided in batches of 1,000 product units.

Order Number 377

	$
Production scheduling (rate per hour × hours per batch)	60,000
Direct material cost (per unit material specification)	180
Selling – batch expediting (at rate per batch)	60,000
Engineering design & support (rate per hour × hours per order)	350,000
Direct labour cost (rate per hour × hours per unit)	150
Machine set-up (rate per set-up × number of set-ups per batch)	34,000
Production line maintenance (rate per hour × hours per order)	1,100,000
Business/facility sustaining cost (at 30% of all other costs)	1,500,000
Marketing (rate per visit to client × number of visits per order)	200,000
Distribution (tonne miles × rate per tonne mile per batch)	12,000
Power cost (rate per Kilowatt hour × Kilowatts per unit)	120
Design work (rate per hour × hours per batch)	30,000
Administration – invoicing and accounting (at rate per batch)	24,000

Required:

(a) Prepare a statement of total cost for Order Number 377, which analyses the expense items into sections for each of four levels, with sub-totals for each level where appropriate. The four levels are:

   (i) Unit-based costs;

   (ii) Batch-related costs;

   (iii) Product sustaining (order level) costs; and

   (iv) Business/facility sustaining (overall level) costs. **(5 marks)**

(b) Identify and discuss the appropriateness of the cost drivers of any TWO expense values in EACH of levels (i) to (iii) above and ONE value that relates to level (iv).

In addition, suggest a likely cause of the cost driver for any ONE value in EACH of levels (i) to (iii), and comment on possible benefits from the identification of the cause of each cost driver. **(10 marks)**

(c) Discuss the practical problems that may be encountered in the implementation of an activity-based system of product cost management. **(5 marks)**

(Total: 20 marks)

Online question assistance

40 THE ORNAMENTAL COMPANY (TOC) (DEC 08)

The Ornamental Company (TOC) makes and sells a range of ornamental products in Baseland. TOC employs experienced sculptors who have an excellent reputation for producing high-quality products. TOC has been approached by The Superior Garden Group (SGG) and asked to make two products. The two products are a water fountain known as 'The Fountain' and a large garden gnome known as 'The Goblin'.

The management accountant of TOC has estimated the variable costs per unit of The Fountain and The Goblin as being $622.50 and $103.75 respectively. She based her calculations on the following information:

(1) Product data

	The Fountain	The Goblin	Other products
Production/sales (units)	2,000	4,000	16,000
	$000	$000	$000
Total direct material costs	450	150	1,200
Total direct labour cost	300	100	1,200

(2) Total variable overheads for TOC will amount to $2,400,000 of which 30% relates to the procurement, warehousing and use of direct materials. All other variable overheads are direct labour related.

(3) TOC currently absorbs variable overheads into product units using company-wide percentages on total direct material cost and total direct labour cost.

(4) SGG is willing to purchase The Fountain at $750 per unit and The Goblin at $150 per unit.

(5) TOC will not undertake any work which does not yield an estimated contribution to sales ratio of 28%.

(6) The directors of TOC are considering switching to an activity-based costing system and recently appointed a firm of management consultants to undertake a detailed review of existing operations. As part of that review, the management consultants concluded that estimated relevant cost drivers for material and labour related overhead costs attributable to The Fountain and The Goblin are as follows:

	The Fountain	The Goblin	Other products
Direct material related overheads:			
The cost driver is the volume of raw materials held to facilitate production of each product.			
Material proportions per product unit:	4	7	4
Direct labour related overheads:			
The cost driver is the number of labour operations performed.			
Labour operations per product unit:	6	5	4

Required:

(a) Calculate variable cost per unit of both products using an activity-based costing approach. **(8 marks)**

(b) Using the unit cost information available and your calculations in (a), prepare a financial analysis of the decision strategy which TOC may implement with regard to the manufacture of each product. **(6 marks)**

(c) Critically discuss the adoption of activity-based management (ABM) in companies such as TOC. **(6 marks)**

(Total: 20 marks)

PRACTICE QUESTIONS – SECTION B : SECTION 2

41 REPORT (PILOT 07)

Your manager has asked for some help in preparing a report entitled 'How to design an effective management information system'. The report should incorporate references to specific environment(s)/organisation type(s) and examples of the management accounting tools that would be of use.

Required:

Prepare a draft report as requested by your manager. (20 marks)

42 ENVIRONMENTAL INFORMATION

Management accounting practice has traditionally focused on techniques to assist organisational decision-making and cost control. In concentrating on the internal environment, the management accounting function has been criticised for not addressing the needs of senior management to enable effective strategic planning. In particular, the criticism has focused on inadequate provision of information which analyses the organisation's exposure to environmental change and its progress towards the achievement of corporate objectives.

Required:

Explain how strategic management accounting can provide information which meets the requirements of senior managers in seeking to realise corporate objectives. (20 marks)

STRATEGIC PERFORMANCE MEASUREMENT

43 HEG (DEC 07) *Walk in the footsteps of a top tutor*

The directors of The Healthy Eating Group (HEG), a successful restaurant chain, which commenced trading in 1998, have decided to enter the sandwich market in Homeland, its country of operation. It has set up a separate operation under the name of Healthy Sandwiches Co (HSC). A management team for HSC has been recruited via a recruitment consultancy which specialises in food sector appointments. Homeland has very high unemployment and the vast majority of its workforce has no experience in a food manufacturing environment. HSC will commence trading on 1 January 2008.

The following information is available:

(1) HSC has agreed to make and supply sandwiches to agreed recipes for the Superior Food Group (SFG) which owns a chain of supermarkets in all towns and cities within Homeland. SFG insists that it selects the suppliers of the ingredients that are used in making the sandwiches it sells and therefore HSC would be unable to reduce the costs of the ingredients used in the sandwiches. HSC will be the sole supplier for SFG.

(2) The number of sandwiches sold per year in Homeland is 625 million. SFG has a market share of 4%.

(3) The average selling price of all sandwiches sold by SFG is $2.40. SFG wishes to make a mark-up of 33⅓% on all sandwiches sold. 90% of all sandwiches sold by SFG are sold before 2 pm each day. The majority of the remaining 10% are sold after 8 pm. It is the intention that all sandwiches are sold on the day that they are delivered into SFG's supermarkets.

(4) The finance director of HSC has estimated that the average cost of ingredients per sandwich is $0.70. All sandwiches are made by hand.

(5) Packaging and labelling costs amount to $0.15 per sandwich.

(6) Fixed overheads have been estimated to amount to $5,401,000 per annum. Note that fixed overheads include all wages and salaries costs as all employees are subject to fixed term employment contracts.

(7) Distribution costs are expected to amount to 8% of HSC's revenue.

(8) The finance director of HSC has stated that he believes the target sales margin of 32% can be achieved, although he is concerned about the effect that an increase in the cost of all ingredients would have on the forecast profits (assuming that all other revenue/cost data remains unchanged).

(9) The existing management information system of HEG was purchased at the time that HEG commenced trading. The directors are now considering investing in an enterprise resource planning system (ERPS).

Required:

(a) Using only the above information, show how the finance director of HSC reached his conclusion regarding the expected sales margin and also state whether he was correct to be concerned about an increase in the price of ingredients. **(5 marks)**

(b) Explain FIVE critical success factors to the performance of HSC on which the directors must focus if HSC is to achieve success in its marketplace. **(10 marks)**

(c) Explain how the introduction of an ERPS could impact on the role of management accountants. **(5 marks)**

(Total: 20 marks)

44 THE MOTHERHELP COMPANY (TMC) (DEC 08)

The Motherhelp Company (TMC), which is based in Happyland, manufactures and markets disposable nappies for babies and infant children. Disposable nappies are made of super-absorbent chemicals, paper pulp and plastics.

TMC has been very successful since its formation in 1996. It has established a very strong brand name and its products are sold by all leading pharmacies and supermarkets in Happyland. TMC has a strong organisational culture with high levels of employee motivation and satisfaction throughout the organisation.

Available information regarding the disposable nappy market size and TMC's revenue is as follows:

	Actual 2005 $m	Actual 2006 $m	Actual 2007 $m	Actual 2008 $m	Forecast 2009 $m	Forecast 2010 $m
Market size	2,726	2,807	2,920	3,095	3,249	3,347
Revenue	354	421	526	681	715	736

The marketing director of TMC has obtained information that the birth-rate in Happyland is projected to fall after 2010. However, the number of years over which the projected fall might take place cannot be forecast with any degree of certainty.

The directors of TMC are most concerned that in spite of the growth achieved during recent years, there remains a projected 'planning gap' at the end of 2012.

In view of this fact the directors of TMC are considering the acquisition of The Comfy Baby Company (CBC), a competitor, which had revenue of $155m during 2008 from sales of its disposable nappies. None of the directors of TMC have any previous experience of such an acquisition. The directors of TMC have heard that CBC has experienced workplace culture based problems during recent years.

The government of Happyland has recently issued a green paper, designed to encourage discussion and potentially pave the way for legislation, concerning the environment in which they stated their concerns about companies such as TMC whose entire revenues derive from sales of non-biodegradable products.

Required:

(a) Using the above information, explain the term 'planning gap' and discuss other suitable alternative strategies to closing the planning gap which the directors of TMC might have considered prior to giving consideration to the purchase of CBC.

(5 marks)

(b) Analyse THREE potential problems, based solely on the information provided above, that TMC might encounter in the acquisition of CBC. (5 marks)

(c) Explain the reasons for the concerns of the government of Happyland with companies such as TMC and advise the directors of a strategy that might be considered in order to avoid being subject to any forthcoming legislation concerning the environment. (5 marks)

(d) Evaluate the circumstances in which a government can act as an aid to business performance. (5 marks)

(Total: 20 marks)

45 STATUTORY TRANSPORT AUTHORITY

A statutory transport authority is committed to the provision of rural passenger transport services in an area between two large cities. It has received applications from operators as follows:

(a) M Ltd offers to operate a limited stop service between the two main cities in the authority's area. Buses would be timed at hourly intervals from 7 am until 9 pm on condition that the authority would authorise no other operator to service this route or any part of it. M Ltd also requires that district councils would grant the required permission to allow on-board catering.

(b) N Ltd is willing to operate 'social-service' vehicles for disabled passengers and others between the urban areas. Services would operate half-hourly from 6.30 am until 10.30 pm at a cost to the authority of $4,000 per week for the service. All fares would go to the authority. It is estimated that total fare income could eventually amount to $2,400 per week but would initially be between $800 and $1,500 per week. Six months' notice of termination would be required from the authority or the operator, should it be found that some other service is more appropriate to travellers' needs.

(c) O Ltd proposes to operate dial-a-bus rural services (a service by which intending passengers can telephone for a bus). Travellers from within the rural area between the two cities would be able to make use of these out-of-town services to and from either centre at reasonable cost. The authority would need to subsidise the cost of this service by regular weekly payments of $3,000 and all fare income would be retained by O Ltd.

Required:

(a) Discuss the criteria which should be applied to evaluate the three proposals, taking account of the authority's need to seek out the best value-for-money. **(10 marks)**

(b) Discuss how such an authority can quantify the value of a social service such as a public passenger transport facility to a community. **(5 marks)**

(c) Describe and assess other sources of funding that might become available for the successful operation of a rural passenger transport facility other than revenue earned from passenger fares and public funds. **(5 marks)**

(Total: 20 marks)

46 MISSION STATEMENT (DEC 02)

(a) Explain the role and content of a Mission Statement. **(5 marks)**

(b) Explain how a Mission Statement could contribute towards the planning and performance measurement process. **(9 marks)**

(c) Identify the potential problems arising from using a Mission Statement to manage performance. **(6 marks)**

(Total: 20 marks)

47 PROJECT X (JUN 03)

A large conglomerate with diverse business activities is currently considering whether it should commence Project X and has gathered the following data:

Project X Data

(1) An initial investment of $54 million will be required on 1 January year 1. The project has a three year life with a nil residual value. Depreciation is calculated on a straight line basis.

(2) The project is expected to generate annual revenue flows of $80m in year 1, $90m in year 2 and $100m in year 3. These values may vary by ±5%.

(3) The incremental costs will be $50m in year 1, $60m in year 2 and $70m in year 3. These may vary by ±10%.

(4) The most likely cost of capital is 10%. This may vary from 8% to 13% for the life of the project.

Additional information:

Assume that all cash flows other than the initial investment take place at the end of each year. Use the written down value of the asset at the start of each year to represent the value of the asset for the year. Ignore taxation.

Required:

(a) Prepare two tables showing net profit, residual income and return on investment for each year of the project and also net present value (NPV) for:

    (i) The best outcome

    (ii) The worst outcome. **(8 marks)**

(b) Explain the distinctive features of Residual Income, Return on Investment and Net Present Value in measuring financial performance.

Your answer should include a critique of the strengths and weaknesses of each measure. **(8 marks)**

(c) What broader issues are likely to be considered when deciding whether the company should proceed with a particular project? **(4 marks)**

(Total: 20 marks)

48 THE CHILDRENS TOY COMPANY (CTC) (JUN 08)

> *Timed question with Online tutor debrief*

The Childrens Toy Company (CTC) manufactures electrically-operated toy versions of animals. The activities of CTC are confined to the country of Stableland, which has a zero-inflation economy. The government of Stableland has granted tax-exempt status to CTC since it provides goods or services exclusively for children. However, no tax allowances are available on investments made by CTC.

CTC has a total production capacity of 400,000 units which cannot be exceeded. The products to be manufactured together with forecast sales volumes are as follows:

Product	Forecast sales units (000)			
	2008	2009	2010	2011
Bruno the Bear	180	120	100	60
Kong the Ape	150	48	24	0
Leo the Lion	60	72	76	30

Other relevant information relating to the products is as follows:

(1) Selling prices per unit and contribution to sales ratios (%) for 2008 and 2009:

	Selling price per unit ($)	Contribution to sales ratio (%)
Product:		
Bruno	40	70
Kong	50	65
Leo	60	60

(2) Product-specific fixed overheads:

	2008 $000	2009 $000
Bruno	3,800	2,400
Kong	2,400	1,340
Leo	2,040	2,100

(3) The company's other fixed overheads are estimated at $1.65 million per annum.

Required:

(a) (i) Prepare a statement of product profitability for each of years 2008 and 2009 which also shows the net profit or loss of CTC. **(4 marks)**

 (ii) Comment on the figures in the statement prepared in (a)(i) above. **(4 marks)**

(b) The marketing director of CTC has suggested the introduction of a new toy 'Nellie the Elephant' for which the following estimated information is available:

 (1) Sales volumes and selling prices per unit

Year ending, 31 May	2009	2010	2011
Sales units (000)	80	180	100
Selling price per unit ($)	50	50	50

 (2) Nellie will generate a contribution to sales ratio of 50% throughout the three year period.

 (3) Product specific fixed overheads during the year ending 31 May 2009 are estimated to be $1.6 million. It is anticipated that these fixed overheads would decrease by 10% per annum during each of the years ending 31 May 2010 and 31 May 2011.

 (4) Capital investment amounting to $3.9 million would be required in June 2008. The investment would have no residual value at 31 May 2011.

 (5) Additional working capital of $500,000 would be required in June 2008. A further $200,000 would be required on 31 May 2009. These amounts would be recovered in full at the end of the three year period.

 (6) The cost of capital is expected to be 12% per annum.

 Assume all cash flows (other than where stated) arise at the end of the year.

 Required:

 (i) Determine whether the new product is viable purely on financial grounds. **(4 marks)**

 (ii) Calculate the minimum target contribution to sales ratio (%) at which 'Nellie the Elephant' will be financially viable, assuming that all other data remain unchanged. **(4 marks)**

 (iii) Identify and discuss an alternative strategy that may assist in improving the performance of CTC with effect from 1 May 2009 (where only the products in (a) and (b) above are available for manufacture). **(4 marks)**

 (Total: 20 marks)

49 VISION PLC (DEC 06)

Vision plc is a reputable manufacturer of a specialist range of optical and photographic equipment. At present, marketing activities are confined to its home market in Blinkland. The directors wish to achieve a net profit per annum of $150 million by the year ending 30 November 2009. The following information is available:

Note 1:

The most recent forecast covering the three year period ending 30 November 2009, based on sales of products which were in existence at 1 December 2006 to existing customers, is as follows:

Year ending 30 November:	2007	2008	2009
	$m	$m	$m
Turnover	100.0	105.0	110.0
Net Profit	40.0	42.0	44.0

Note 2:

Vision plc manufactures a range of products within its three divisions, as follows:

Division	Description
Astronomy	This division manufactures telescopic equipment which is sold via mail order to private individuals.
Medical	This division manufactures microscopes and associated equipment which are sold to hospitals and schools in Blinkland.
Outdoor pursuits	This division manufactures a range of cameras and binoculars which are sold via mail order to private individuals.

Note 3:

The following became effective on 1 December 2006:

(i) The company created a new division called the Oceanic division which manufactures cameras suitable for underwater use. These are sold to clubs and societies that engage in scuba diving activities. Sales revenue is forecast to be $5 million in the first year of operation with an anticipated doubling of sales volume during each of the next two years of operation.

Variable costs are forecast at 40% of sales revenue in the first year of operation and are expected to reduce to 35% and 30% during each of the next two years respectively. Fixed overheads are forecast at $1 million in the first year of operation and are expected to increase by 10% per annum during each of the next two years.

(ii) The company purchased the 'Sound and vision' chain of camera shops comprising a total of 30 retail outlets within Blinkland. Each of the 20 'out of town' outlets is forecast to make a profit of $750,000 and each of the 10 city outlets is forecast to make a profit of $1 million during the year ending 30 November 2007. It is anticipated that profits of 'out of town' and city outlets will increase by 8% and 4% per annum respectively during each of the next two years.

(iii) The company purchased Racquets Ltd, a well-established manufacturer of tennis, badminton and squash racquets. Racquets Ltd made a profit of $15 million during the year ended 30 November 2006 and profit is expected to increase by $1 million per annum during each of the next three years.

(iv) A new camera known as the 'Birdcam-V' was launched. This camera will allow bird-watching activities to take place during the night, irrespective of prevailing noise and weather conditions. The Birdcam-V is the only camera on the market which has special 'noise and weather' filtering capabilities and has an expected life of three years.

The marketing director has estimated that at a selling price of $600 per unit, a total of 85,000 units per annum would be sold during the year ending 30 November 2007 and that each increase or decrease in the selling price of $10 will cause quantity demanded to decrease or increase by 1,000 units. This information implies that:

The demand function is $P = 1,450 - 0.01q$, giving marginal revenue of $MR = 1,450 - 0.02q$

Where P is the price per unit in $ and q is the quantity demanded.

The variable cost per unit is expected to remain constant at $180. Development costs amounting to $45,967,500 are to be written off evenly over the expected life of the Birdcam-V. The directors of Vision plc have agreed to adopt the combination of selling price and output that will maximise profit earned from sales of the Birdcam–V.

Required:

(a) Calculate the 'profit gap' that is forecast to exist at 30 November 2009. **(10 marks)**

(b) (i) Explain how the use of Ansoff's product-market matrix might assist the management of Vision plc to reduce the profit-gap that is forecast to exist at 30 November 2009. **(3 marks)**

(ii) Explain how the existing product range and the actions per Note 3 would feature in Ansoff's product-market matrix. **(7 marks)**

(Total: 20 marks)

50 BETTER AGRICULTURE GROUP (BAG) (DEC 08)

The Better Agriculture Group (BAG), which has a divisional structure, produces a range of products for the farming industry. Divisions B and C are two of its divisions. Division B sells a fertiliser product (BF) to customers external to BAG. Division C produces a chemical (CC) which it could transfer to Division B for use in the manufacture of its product BF. However, Division C could also sell some of its output of chemical CC to external customers of BAG.

An independent external supplier to The Better Agriculture Group has offered to supply Division B with a chemical which is equivalent to component CC. The independent supplier has a maximum spare capacity of 60,000 kilograms of the chemical which it is willing to make available (in total or in part) to Division B at a special price of $55 per kilogram.

Forecast information for the forthcoming period is as follows:

Division B:

Production and sales of 360,000 litres of BF at a selling price of $120 per litre.

Variable conversion costs of BF will amount to $15 per litre.

Fixed costs are estimated at $18,000,000.

Chemical (CC) is used at the rate of 1 kilogram of CC per 4 litres of product BF.

Division C:

Total production capacity of 100,000 kilograms of chemical CC.

Variable costs will be $50 per kilogram of CC.

Fixed costs are estimated at $2,000,000.

Market research suggests that external customers of BAG are willing to take up sales of 40,000 kilograms of CC at a price of $105 per kilogram. The remaining 60,000 kilograms of CC could be transferred to Division B for use in product BF. Currently no other market external to BAG is available for the 60,000 kilograms of CC.

Required:

(a) (i) State the price/prices per kilogram at which Division C should offer to transfer chemical CC to Division B in order that the maximisation of BAG profit would occur if Division B management implement rational sourcing decisions based on purely financial grounds.

Note: You should explain the basis on which Division B would make its decision using the information available, incorporating details of all relevant calculations. **(6 marks)**

(ii) Division C is considering a decision to lower its selling price to customers external to the group to $95 per kilogram. If implemented, this decision is expected to increase sales to external customers to 70,000 kilograms.

Required:

For BOTH the current selling price of CC of $105 per kilogram and the proposed selling price of $95 per kilogram, prepare a detailed analysis of revenue, costs and net profits of BAG.

Note: In addition, comment on other considerations that should be taken into account before this selling price change is implemented. **(6 marks)**

(b) The management of Division C has identified the need to achieve cost savings in order to become more competitive. They have decided that an analysis and investigation of quality costs into four sub-categories will provide a focus for performance measurement and improvement.

Required:

Identify the FOUR sub-categories into which quality costs can be analysed and provide examples (which must relate to Division C) of each of the four sub-categories of quality cost that can be investigated in order that overall cost savings might be achieved and hence the performance improved. **(8 marks)**

(Total: 20 marks)

Online question assistance

51 UNIQUE COMPONENTS LTD (PILOT 07)

(a) The Creative Division (CD) of Unique Components Ltd produces wooden components that it both sells to external customers and transfers to other divisions within its own group of companies. The production involves the preparation of timber, cutting the timber into shapes and the assembly of the shapes into components.

The total component cost for component A has been estimated as $41.21 per unit. Selling prices to external customers have been set by adding a mark-up of 35% to total estimated component cost.

Required:

Discuss the application and acceptability of each of the following transfer price bases at which component A may be offered by CD to other divisions within the same group of companies:

(i) External selling price and adjusted selling price;

(ii) Marginal cost marginal cost plus an annual lump sum; and

(iii) Dual pricing.

Your answer should incorporate illustrative values ($) for each transfer price using data provided above and additional data of your choice. **(10 marks)**

(b) A redesign of component A is being considered that is likely to result in changes in the quantity of timber and number of cuts, in the shaping process that will be required. A data-table analysis has been prepared to monitor the effect on unit cost for component A of a range of values for such changes. In addition, a set of subjective probabilities have been assigned to the likelihood of (i) the timber required and (ii) the number of cuts required, being at the levels shown in the data-table analysis.

A matrix has been constructed showing the combined probability for each possible combination of changes of timber and number of cuts. The data-table analysis and combined probability matrix are as follows:

Data-table of values of total component cost for component A per unit ($) for a range of values of number of cuts in shaping and timber required (square metres).

Timber (square metres)	Number of cuts				
	25	30	35	40	50
0.8	47.15	47.69	48.15	48.55	49.21
0.7	43.50	44.04	44.50	44.90	45.56
0.6	39.81	40.34	40.81	41.21	41.87
0.5	36.07	36.61	37.07	37.47	38.13
0.4	32.28	32.81	33.28	33.68	34.34

Combined probability matrix showing combined probability values for a range of values of number of cuts in shaping and timber required (square metres).

Timber
(square metres)   Number of cuts

		25	30	35	40	50
	Prob.	0.2	0.3	0.3	0.1	0.1
0.8	0.1	0.02	0.03	0.03	0.01	0.01
0.7	0.2	0.04	0.06	0.06	0.02	0.02
0.6	0.2	0.04	0.06	0.06	0.02	0.02
0.5	0.4	0.08	0.12	0.12	0.04	0.04
0.4	0.1	0.02	0.03	0.03	0.01	0.01

Note: The expected value of unit cost, based on above data-table and combined probability matrix is $39.84.

You may assume that management attitudes vary as follows:

(i) Some of the management team are in favour of change provided that a reduction of at least 12% from the existing total unit cost is achieved;

(ii) Others in the management team are not in favour of change if it might lead to an increase in total unit cost from the current level of $41.21; and

(iii) The remainder of the management team are of the view that they are willing to consider the re-design change if the expected value (EV) solution is less than the current value of total unit cost.

Required:

Discuss the impact of the possible changes in the quantity of timber and number of cuts in the Shaping process caused by the re-design of component A on the total cost per unit of component A.

You should incorporate an analysis of statistics from the data-table and probability information contained in the model into your discussion with specific reference to the impact of management attitude to risk when deciding whether or not to change from the existing quantity of timber and number of cuts for component A.

(10 marks)

(Total: 20 marks)

52 SSA GROUP (DEC 09)

You are the management accountant of the SSA Group which manufactures an innovative range of products to provide support for injuries to various joints in the body. The group has adopted a divisional structure. Each division is encouraged to maximise its reported profit.

Division A, which is based in a country called Nearland, manufactures joint-support appliances which incorporate a 'one size fits all people' feature. A different appliance is manufactured for each of knee, ankle, elbow and wrist joints.

Budget information in respect of Division A for the year ended 31 December 2010 is as follows:

Support appliance	Knee	Ankle	Elbow	Wrist
Sales units (000's)	20	50	20	60
Selling price per unit ($)	24	15	18	9
Total variable cost of sales ($000)	200	350	160	240

Each of the four support products uses the same quantity of manufacturing capacity. This gives Division A management the flexibility to alter the product mix as desired. During the year to 31 December 2010 it is estimated that a maximum of 160,000 support products could be manufactured.

The following information relates to Division B which is also part of the SSA group and is based in Distantland:

(1) Division B purchases products from various sources, including from other divisions in SSA group, for subsequent resale to customers.

(2) The management of Division B has requested two alternative quotations from Division A in respect of the year ended 31 December 2010 as follows:

Quotation 1 – Purchase of 10,000 ankle supports.

Quotation 2 – Purchase of 18,000 ankle supports.

The management of the SSA Group has decided that a minimum of 50,000 ankle supports must be reserved for customers in Nearland in order to ensure that customer demand can be satisfied and the product's competitive position is maintained in the Nearland market.

The management of the SSA Group is willing, if necessary, to reduce the budgeted sales quantities of other types of joint support in order to satisfy the requirements of Division B for ankle supports. They wish, however, to minimise the loss of contribution to the Group.

The management of Division B is aware of another joint support product, which is produced in Distantland, that competes with the Division A version of the ankle support and which could be purchased at a local currency price that is equivalent to $9 per support. SSA Group policy is that all divisions are allowed autonomy to set transfer prices and purchase from whatever sources they choose. The management of Division A intends to use market price less 30% as the basis for each of quotations 1 and 2.

Required:

(a) (i) The management of the SSA Group have asked you to advise them regarding the appropriateness of the decision by the management of Division A to use an adjusted market price as the basis for the preparation of each quotation and the implications of the likely sourcing decision by the management of Division B.

Your answer should cite relevant quantitative data and incorporate your recommendation of the prices that should be quoted by Division A for the ankle supports in respect of quotations 1 and 2, that will ensure that the profitability of SSA Group as a whole is not adversely affected by the decision of the management of Division B. **(8 marks)**

(ii) Advise the management of Divisions A and B regarding the basis of transfer pricing which should be employed in order to ensure that the profit of the SSA Group is maximised. **(4 marks)**

(b) After considerable internal discussion concerning Quotation 2 by the management of SSA Group, Division A is not prepared to supply 18,000 ankle supports to Division B at any price lower than 30% below market price. All profits in Distantland are subject to taxation at a rate of 20%. Division A pays tax in Nearland at a rate of 40% on all profits.

Advise the management of SSA Group whether the management of Division B should be directed to purchase the ankle supports from Division A, or to purchase a similar product from a local supplier in Distantland. Supporting calculations should be provided. (8 marks)

(Total: 20 marks)

53 LOCAL GOVERNMENT HOUSING DEPARTMENT (JUN 10)

A local government housing department (LGHD) has funds which it is proposing to spend on the upgrading of air conditioning systems in its housing inventory.

It is intended that the upgrading should enhance the quality of living for the occupants of the houses.

Preferred contractors will be identified to carry out the work involved in the upgrading of the air conditioning systems, with each contractor being responsible for upgrading of the systems in a proportion of the houses. Contractors will also be required to provide a maintenance and operational advice service during the first two years of operation of the upgraded systems.

Prior to a decision to implement the proposal, LGHD has decided that it should carry out a value for money (VFM) audit.

You have been given the task of preparing a report for LGHD, to help ensure that it can make an informed decision concerning the proposal.

Required:

Prepare a detailed analysis which will form the basis for the preparation of the final report. The analysis should include a clear explanation of the meaning and relevance of each of (i) to (iii) below:

(i) **Value for Money (VFM) audit (including references to the roles of principal and agent).** (6 marks)

(ii) **Economy, efficiency and effectiveness as part of the VFM audit.** (6 marks)

(iii) **The extent (if any) to which each of intangibility, heterogeneity, simultaneity and perishability may be seen to relate to the decision concerning the proposal, and any problems that may occur.** (8 marks)

Note: Your analysis should incorporate specific references to examples relating to the upgrading proposal.

(Total: 20 marks)

PAPER P5 : ADVANCED PERFORMANCE MANAGEMENT

54 PIPE DREAM

Pipe Dream manufactures a wide range of pipes and tubes. The company has recently appointed a new chief executive who has announced his intention to convert Pipe Dream into a world class company. After several months in the job, he has succeeded in converting his management team to his point of view. He has argued that although the company's operations appear to be fairly efficient, there are many areas in which improvements need to be made.

A major planning meeting has been called, to discuss the steps that might be needed to introduce Total Quality Management (TQM) concepts into the company.

Required:

Prepare a discussion paper for the meeting in which you:

(a) describe the main features of TQM (6 marks)

(b) recommend an approach for introducing TQM into the company, and the problems you would expect to encounter (9 marks)

(c) justify the use of TQM for a company whose products do not need to be manufactured to the very highest level of precision. (5 marks)

(Total: 20 marks)

55 UNIVERSAL POTTERY COMPANY (UPC)

The country of Europia has an extensive historical and industrial heritage. It has many tourist sites (such as castles, palaces, temples, houses and factories) which attract visitors from home and abroad. Most of these tourist sites have gift shops where visitors can buy mementos and souvenirs of their visit. These souvenirs often include cups, saucers, plates and other items which feature a printed image of the particular tourist site.

The Universal Pottery Company (UPC) is the main supplier of these pottery souvenir items to the tourist trade. It produces the items in its potteries and then applies the appropriate image using specialised image printing machines. UPC also supplies other organisations that require personalised products. For example, it recently won the right to produce souvenirs for the Eurasian Games, which are being held in Europia in two years time. UPC currently ships about 250,000 items of pottery out of its factory every month. Most of these items are shipped in relatively small packages. All collections from the factory and deliveries to customers are made by a nationwide courier company.

In the last two years there has been a noticeable increase in the number of complaints about the quality of these items. The complaints, from gift shop owners, concentrate on two main issues:

(i) The physical condition of goods when they arrive at the gift shop. Initial evidence suggests that 'a significant number of products are now arriving broken, chipped or cracked'. These items are unusable and they have to be returned to UPC. UPC management are convinced that the increased breakages are due to packers not following the correct packing method.

(ii) Incorrect alignment of the image of the tourist site on the selected item. For example, a recent batch of 100 cups for Carish Castle included 10 cups where the image of the castle sloped significantly from left to right. These were returned by the customer and destroyed by UPC.

The image problem was investigated in more depth and it was discovered that approximately 500 items were delivered every month with misaligned images. Each item costs, on average, $20 to produce.

As a result of these complaints, UPC appointed a small quality inspection team who were asked to inspect one in every 20 packages for correct packaging and correct image alignment. However, although some problems have been found, a significant number of defective products have still been delivered to customers. A director of UPC used this evidence to support his assertion that the 'quality inspection team is just not working'.

The payment system for packers has also been such an issue. It was established ten years ago as an attempt to boost productivity. Packers receive a bonus for packing more than a target number of packages per hour. Hence, packers are more concerned with the speed of packing rather than its quality.

Finally, there is also evidence that to achieve agreed customer deadlines, certain managers have asked the quality inspection team to overlook defective items so that order deadlines could be met.

The company has decided to review the quality issue again. The director who claimed that the quality inspection team is not working has suggested using a Six Sigma approach to the company's quality problems.

Required:

(a) Analyse the current and potential role of quality, quality control and quality assurance at UPC. **(15 marks)**

(b) Examine how adopting a Six Sigma approach would help address the quality problems at UPC. **(10 marks)**

(Total: 25 marks)

56 TELECOMS AT WORK (TAW) (JUN 08)

Timed question with Online tutor debrief

Telecoms At Work (TAW) manufactures and markets office communications systems. During the year ended 31 May 2008 TAW made an operating profit of $30 million on sales of $360 million. However, the directors are concerned that products do not conform to the required level of quality and TAW is therefore not fulfilling its full potential in terms of turnover and profits achieved.

The following information is available in respect of the year ended 31 May 2008:

(1) Production data:

Units manufactured and sold	18,000
Units requiring rework	2,100
Units requiring warranty repair service	2,700
Design engineering hours	48,000
Process engineering hours	54,000
Inspection hours (manufacturing)	288,000

PAPER P5 : ADVANCED PERFORMANCE MANAGEMENT

(2) Cost data:

	$
Design engineering per hour	96
Process engineering per hour	70
Inspection per hour (manufacturing)	50
Rework per communication system reworked (manufacturing)	4,800
Customer support per repaired unit (marketing)	240
Transportation costs per repaired unit (distribution)	280
Warranty repairs per repaired unit (customer service)	4,600

(3) Staff training costs amounted to $180,000 and additional product testing costs of $72,000.

(4) The marketing director has estimated that sales of 1,800 units were lost as a result of public knowledge of poor quality at TAW. The average contribution per communication system is estimated at $7,200.

Required:

(a) **Prepare a cost analysis which shows actual prevention costs, appraisal costs, internal failure costs, and external failure costs for the year ended 31 May 2008. Your statement should show each cost heading as a % of turnover and clearly show the total cost of quality. Comment briefly on the inclusion of opportunity costs in such an analysis.** (11 marks)

(b) A detailed analysis has revealed that the casings in which the communications systems are housed are often subject to mishandling in transit to TAW's manufacturing premises.

The directors are considering two alternative solutions proposed by the design engineering team which are aimed at reducing the quality problems that are currently being experienced. These are as follows:

Option 1 – Increase the number of immediate physical inspections of the casings when they are received from the supplier. This will require an additional 10,000 inspection hours.

Option 2 – Redesign and strengthen the casings and the containers used to transport them to better withstand mishandling during transportation. Redesign will require an additional 2,000 hours of design engineering and an additional 5,000 hours of process engineering.

Internal failure costs of rework for each reworked communication system are as follows:

	$
Variable costs (including direct materials, direct labour rework and supplies)	1,920
Allocated fixed costs (equipment, space and allocated overhead)	2,880
Total costs (as per note 2 on cost data)	4,800

The directors of TAW believe that, even if it is able to achieve improvements in quality, it will be unable to save any of the fixed costs of internal and external failure.

If TAW chooses to inspect the casings more carefully, it expects to eliminate re-work on 720 communication systems whereas if it redesigns the casings it expects to eliminate rework on 960 communication systems.

If incoming casings are inspected more carefully, TAW estimates that 600 fewer communication systems will require warranty repair and that it will be able to sell an additional 300 communication systems. If the casing is redesigned, the directors estimate that 840 fewer communication systems will require warranty repair and that an additional 360 communication systems will be sold.

External failure costs of repair for each repaired communication system are as follows:

	Variable costs $	Fixed costs $	Total costs $
Customer support costs	96	144	240
Transportation costs	210	70	280
Warranty repair costs	1,700	2,900	4,600

Required:

Prepare an estimate of the financial consequences of each option and advise the directors of TAW which option should be chosen. (9 marks)

(Total: 20 marks)

57 GIBSON & CHEW

Gibson & Chew (G&C) is a certified accountancy practice specialising in medium-sized company audits, venture finance and taxation planning. G&C comprise six partners, eight managers, three other qualified staff, 15 accounting technicians and trainees and 20 office support staff. The senior and founding partners are David Gibson and Charles Chew. Gibson manages the audit part of the practice while Chew manages the special finance and taxation part. The workloads in the two areas are broadly equal.

G&C have a first class professional reputation and the practice has, over the 10 years since its formation, grown steadily on the strength of its technical excellence. G&C prides itself on being a good employer. It pays staff market salary rates or above, provides a pleasant office working environment and supports its junior staff by paying their fees for professional training.

Two years ago the two senior partners designed and implemented a staff appraisal scheme to assist in the process of staff development and staff performance reviews. The system has been based around an annual appraisal interview conducted by either David Gibson or Charles Chew. All staff have since been appraised once, the last few employees having just been appraised by the partners. The time delay in seeing all staff has posed some problems as the senior partners had also intended to use the appraisal interview as the basis to agree the annual bonus.

Partners', managers' and support staff's views on the appraisal scheme have been very mixed. Some informal comments have been so negative as to cause the two senior partners to question whether the scheme should be abandoned altogether. Charles Chew and David Gibson have decided to list their feelings about the scheme and its operation:

'The appraisal scheme has taken up far more of our time than we first thought.'

'Appraisal interviews have been very difficult to fit into our busy schedule.'

'We have had to see staff at random, as and when the appraisal interview could be organised.'

'Some staff seem to see the interview as an opportunity to complain or ask for things.'

'Some staff just sit there and do not contribute anything to the interview.'

'It is difficult to think of having to start again with the second round of interviews so soon after finishing the first.'

'We have doubts whether the scheme has improved partnership performance in terms of client service, productivity and overall fee income.'

'We know for a fact that some of the problems in performance that we pointed out to staff during their appraisal interview have been totally ignored.'

Required:

(a) Explain the function, operation and potential benefits of staff appraisal schemes.

(9 marks)

(b) Comment on the apparent appraisal problems experienced at Gibson & Chew and suggest how a successful appraisal scheme could be organised and operated so as to address these problems.

(11 marks)

(Total: 20 marks)

58 EQUIGUARD

Equiguard offers warranties for electrical and electronic equipment to both business and household customers. For a fixed annual fee the company will provide a free fault diagnosis and repair service for equipment covered by the warranty. A warranty lasts for one year and customers are invited to renew their warranty one month before it expires. Equiguard employs 340 full-time engineers around the country to undertake these repairs. It costs about $6,000 to train a newly recruited engineer.

When equipment breaks down the customer telephones a support help line number where their problem is dealt with by a customer support clerk. This clerk has access to the work schedules of the engineers and an appointment is made for a visit from an engineer at the earliest possible time convenient to the customer. When the engineer makes the visit, faults with equipment are diagnosed and are fixed free of charge under the terms of the warranty.

Equiguard is extremely concerned about the relatively high labour turnover of its engineers and has commissioned a report to investigate the situation. Some of the findings of the report are summarised in the following table (Table 1). It compares Equiguard with two of its main competitors.

Table 1

Company	Labour turnover*	Average salary ($)	Profit sharing scheme	Average days holiday/ year	Performance related pay	Average spend per year per engineer ($)
Equiguard	12%	24,000	No	20	No	1,000
Safequipe	8%	23,000	Yes	23	Yes	1,500
Guarantor	7%	22,500	Yes	25	Yes	1,250

* Labour turnover is the number of engineers leaving in the last year as a percentage of the number of engineers employed at the beginning of the year

An exit survey of engineers leaving the company recorded the following comments:

(1) 'There is no point in doing a good job, because you get paid no more than doing an ordinary one. Average work is tolerated here.'

(2) 'This is the first place I have worked where learning new skills is not encouraged. There is no incentive to improve yourself. The company seems to believe that employees who gain new skills will inevitably leave, so they discourage learning.'

(3) 'The real problem is that the pay structure does not differentiate between good, average and poor performers. This is really de-motivating.'

The HR director of Equiguard is anxious to address the high turnover issue and believes that quantitative measurement of employee performance is essential in a re-structured reward management scheme. He has suggested that the company should introduce two new performance related pay measures. The first is a team based bonus based on the average time it takes for the company to respond to a repair request. He proposes that this should be based on the time taken between the customer request for a repair being logged and the date of the engineer attending to fix the problem. He argues that customers value quick response times and so the shorter this time the greater the bonus should be for the whole team.

In addition, he proposes an individual bonus. This will be based on the average time taken for an engineer to fix a reported fault once they have arrived. This is the average time taken for the engineer to repair the fault from the start time of the job to its completion. He argues that the company values quick repair time as this increases business efficiency and so the quicker the fix the greater the bonus should be for the individual.

Required:

(a) Assess the deficiencies of Equiguard's current rewards management scheme.

(12 marks)

(b) Analyse the limitations of the proposed performance measures suggested by the HR director.

(8 marks)

(Total: 20 marks)

PAPER P5 : ADVANCED PERFORMANCE MANAGEMENT

59 BUSINESS SOLUTIONS (JUN 02)

Business Solutions is a firm of management consultants which experienced considerable business growth during the last decade. By 2000 the firm's senior managers were beginning to experience difficulties in managing the business.

During 2001 the firm was reorganised and a regional divisional structure was introduced with individual profit targets being set for each of the semi-autonomous profit centres. Although North division has its own customer base that is distinct from that of its sister division South, it does occasionally call upon the services of a South consultant to assist with its projects. North has to pay a cross charge to South per consulting day. The amount of the charge is determined by HQ. North is free to choose whether it employs a South consultant or subcontracts the project to an external consultant. The manager of North division believes that the quality of the external consultant and the one from South division are identical and on this basis will always employ the one who is prepared to work for the lower fee.

The following information is also available:

- North division is very busy and it charges its clients $1,200 per consulting day
- North division pays its external consultant $500 per consulting day
- The variable cost per internal consulting day is $100.

Required:

(a) Determine a possible optimal daily cross charge that should be paid by North for the services of a consultant from South in the scenarios outlined below. The charges that you select must induce both divisional managers to arrive at the same decision independently. Explain how you have determined your cross charges and state any assumptions that you think necessary.

Scenario (i)

South division has spare consulting capacity.

Scenario (ii)

South division is fully occupied earning fees of $400 per consulting day.

Scenario (iii)

South division is fully occupied earning fees of $700 per consulting day. (10 marks)

(b) Identify the possible factors that may have prompted the senior management to introduce a divisional structure in 2001 and suggest some potential problems that may arise. (10 marks)

(c) Senior management are also considering the use of additional indicators to assist in managing the performance of the divisions. Identify three possible indicators, giving reasons for your choice. (5 marks)

(Total: 25 marks)

60 BETTASERVE (PILOT 07)

Bettaserve Limited has identified and defined a market in which it wishes to operate. This will provide a 'gold standard' focus for an existing range of services. Bettaserve plc has identified a number of key competitors and intends to focus on close co-operation with its customers in providing services to meet their specific design and quality requirements. Efforts will be made to improve the effectiveness of all aspects of the cycle from service design to after-sales service to customers. This will require inputs from a number of departments in the achievement of the specific goals of the 'gold standard' range of services. Efforts will be made to improve productivity in conjunction with increased flexibility of methods.

An analysis of financial and non-financial data relating to the 'gold standard' proposal for each of the years 2007, 2008 and 2009 is shown below.

Required:

(a) Prepare an analysis (both quantitative and discursive) of the 'gold standard' proposal for the period 2007 to 2009. You should use the information provided in the question, together with the data in Schedule 1 below. Your analysis should include the following:

  (i) A definition of corporate 'vision or mission' and consideration of how the proposal may be seen as identifying and illustrating a specific sub-set of this 'vision or mission'. **(5 marks)**

  (ii) Discussion and, where possible, quantification of the proposal in both marketing and financial terms. **(5 marks)**

  (iii) Discussion of the external effectiveness of the proposal in the context of ways in which each of Quality and Delivery are expected to affect customer satisfaction and hence the marketing of the product. **(5 marks)**

  (iv) Discussion of the internal efficiency of the proposal in the context of ways in which the management of each of Cycle Time and Waste are expected to affect productivity and hence the financial aspects of the proposal. **(5 marks)**

Schedule 1

'Gold Standard' proposal – estimated statistics

	2007	2008	2009
Total market size ($m)	240	250	260
Bettaserve plc – sales ($m)	30	36	40
Bettaserve plc – total costs ($m)	28.2	25.448	25.1
Bettaserve plc – sundry statistics:			
Services achieving design quality standards (%) and accepted without further rectification	95	97	98
Rectification claims from customers ($m)	0.9	0.54	0.2
Cost of after sales rectification service ($m)	3	2.5	2
Sales meeting planned completion dates (%)	90	95	99
Average cycle time: (customer enquiry to service finalisation) (weeks)	6	5.5	5
Service enquiries not taken up by customers (% of enquiries)	7.50	5.00	2.50
Idle capacity of service personnel (%)	10	6	2

Analysis of total cost:	$000	$000	$000
target cost – variable	12,000	14,400	16,000
target cost – fixed	4,000	4,000	5,000
internal failure costs	3,200	1,840	1,050
external failure costs	4,000	2,208	1,050
appraisal costs	1,000	1,000	1,000
prevention costs	4,000	2,000	1,000
Total cost	28.200	25,448	25,100

(b) Discuss the links, both vertical and horizontal, of the performance measures investigated in (a). The discussion should include comment on the hierarchy and inter-relationships between the measures, including internal and external aspects of the expected trends in performance.

(Note: A diagram may be used to illustrate the links, together with relevant discussion). **(5 marks)**

(Total: 25 marks)

61 SUPERIOR SOFTWARE HOUSE (SSH) (DEC 08)

The Superior Software House (SSH) commenced trading on 1 December 2002 in the country of Bonlandia. SSH develops bespoke software packages on behalf of clients. When requested to do so, SSH also provides training to clients' staff in the use of these software packages.

On 1 December 2006, the directors of SSH established a similar semi-autonomous operation in Karendia. All software packages are produced in Bonlandia and transferred to Karendia at cost plus attributable overheads i.e. there is no mark-up on the software packages transferred from Bonlandia to Karendia.

Karendia is a country in which the structure of industry has changed during recent years. There has been a major shift from traditional manufacturing businesses to service orientated businesses which place a far greater emphasis upon the use of business software.

The operational managers in both Bonlandia and Karendia have no control over company policies in respect of acquisitions and financing.

The operational manager of Bonlandia receives a bonus of 40% of his basic salary for meeting all client delivery deadlines in respect of Karendia. At a recent meeting he instructed his staff to 'install client software by the due date and we'll worry about fixing any software problems after it's been installed. After all, we always fix software problems eventually'.

He also stated that 'it is of vital importance that we grow our revenues in Karendia as quickly as possible. Our clients in Karendia might complain but they have spent a lot of money on our software products and will not be able to go to any of our competitors once we have installed our software as all their businesses would suffer huge disruption'.

Financial data (all stated on an actual basis) in respect of the two divisions for the two years ended 30 November 2007 and 2008 are shown below:

Summary Income Statements:

	Bonlandia 2008 $000	Karendia 2008 $000	Combined 2008 $000	Bonlandia 2007 $000	Karendia 2007 $000	Combined 2007 $000
Revenue	14,600	2,800	17,400	14,000	2,000	16,000
Salaries	4,340	1,248	5,588	4,000	1,200	5,200
Software and consumables	2,040	486	2,526	2,000	450	2,450
Other operating costs	2,880	654	3,534	2,800	600	3,400
	9,260	2,388	11,648	8,800	2,250	11,050
Marketing	2,392	600	2,992	2,100	400	2,500
Interest (Group)			850			900
Depreciation and amortisation	400	160	560	400	100	500
	2,792	760	4,402	2,500	500	3,900
Total costs	12,052	3,148	16,050	11,300	2,750	14,950
Profit/(loss) for the period	2,548	(348)	1,350	2,700	(750)	1,050

Statements of financial position:

	Bonlandia 2008 $000	Karendia 2008 $000	Combined 2008 $000	Bonlandia 2007 $000	Karendia 2007 $000	Combined 2007 $000
Assets						
Non-current assets	9,000	1,600	10,600	8,000	1,000	9,000
Current assets	4,550	1,000	5,550	5,000	800	5,800
Total assets	13,550	2,600	16,150	13,000	1,800	14,800
Equity and liabilities						
Share capital and reserves			9,150			7,800
Non-current liabilities						
Long-term borrowings (Group)			4,000			4,500
Current liabilities	2,400	600	3,000	2,000	500	2,500
Total equity and liabilities			16,150			14,800

PAPER P5 : ADVANCED PERFORMANCE MANAGEMENT

Required:

(a) Assess the financial performance of SSH and its operations in Bonlandia and Karendia during the years ended 30 November 2007 and 2008.

Note: You should highlight additional information that would be required in order to provide a more comprehensive assessment of the financial performance of each operation. **(14 marks)**

(b) Discuss the statements of the operational manager of Bonlandia and assess their implications for SSH. **(4 marks)**

(c) Assess the likely criteria which would need to be satisfied for software to be regarded as 'quality software'. **(4 marks)**

(d) Suggest a set of SIX performance measures which the directors of SSH could use in order to assess the quality of service provided to its clients. **(3 marks)**

(Total: 25 marks)

PERFORMANCE EVALUATION AND CORPORATE FAILURE

62 ROYAL BOTANICAL GARDENS

The Royal Botanical Gardens has been established for more than 120 years and has the following mission statement:

'The Royal Botanical Gardens belongs to the Nation. Our mission is to increase knowledge and appreciation of plants, their importance and their conservation, by managing and displaying living and preserved collections and through botanical and horticultural research.'

Located toward the edge of the city, the Gardens are regularly visited throughout the year by many local families and are an internationally well-known tourist attraction. Despite charging admission it is one the top five visitor attractions in the country. Every year it answers many thousands of enquiries from Universities and research establishments, including pharmaceutical companies from all over the world and charges for advice and access to its collection. Enquiries can range from access to the plant collection for horticultural work, seeds for propagation or samples for chemical analysis to seek novel pharmaceutical compounds for commercial exploitation. It receives an annual grant in aid from Central Government, which is fixed once every five years. The grant in aid is due for review in three years' time.

The Finance Director has decided that, to strengthen its case when meeting the Government representatives to negotiate the grant, the Management Board should be able to present a balanced scorecard demonstrating the performance of the Gardens. He has asked you, the Senior Management Accountant, to assist him in taking this idea forward. Many members of the board, which consists of eminent scientists, are unfamiliar with the concept of a balanced scorecard.

Required:

(a) Prepare a briefing For the benefit of the Management Board, on the concept of a balanced scorecard, which also analyses its usefulness for The Royal Botanical Gardens. **(10 marks)**

(b) Discuss the process you would employ to develop a suitable balanced scorecard for The Royal Botanical Gardens and give examples of measures that would be incorporated within it. **(15 marks)**

(Total: 25 marks)

63 SPECIALIST CLOTHING COMPANY (JUN 06)

The Specialist Clothing Company Ltd (SCC Ltd) is a manufacturer of a wide range of clothing. Its operations are organised into five divisions which are as follows:

(i) Fashion

(ii) Industrial

(iii) Leisure

(iv) Children

(v) Footwear

The Fashion division manufactures a narrow range of high quality clothing which is sold to a leading retail store which has branches in every major city in its country of operation. The products have very short life cycles.

The Industrial division manufactures a wide range of clothing which has been designed for use in industrial environments. In an attempt to increase sales volumes, SCC Ltd introduced the sale of these products via mail order with effect from 1 June 2005.

The Leisure division manufactures a narrow range of clothing designed for outdoor pursuits such as mountaineering and sky diving, which it markets under its own, well-established 'Elite' brand label.

The Children division manufactures a range of school and casual wear which is sold to leading retail stores.

The Footwear division manufactures a narrow range of footwear.

The management accountant of SCC Ltd has gathered the following actual and forecast information relating to the five divisions:

Year ending 31 May	2004 Actual	2005 Actual	2006 Actual	2007 Forecast	2008 Forecast
Fashion					
Market size ($m)	200.0	240.0	280.0	305.0	350.0
Sales revenue ($m)	10.0	14.4	22.4	30.5	35.0
Industrial					
Market size ($m)	150.0	158.0	166.0	174.0	182.0
Sales revenue ($m)	15.0	15.1	15.2	15.3	15.4
Leisure					
Market size ($m)	20.0	20.5	21.0	21.5	21.8
Sales revenue ($m)	13.6	14.2	14.7	15.0	15.2

PAPER P5 : ADVANCED PERFORMANCE MANAGEMENT

Year ending 31 May	2004 Actual	2005 Actual	2006 Actual	2007 Forecast	2008 Forecast
Children					
Market size ($m)	60.0	70.0	80.0	90.0	100.0
Sales revenue ($m)	2.0	2.1	2.2	2.3	2.4
Footwear					
Market size ($m)	20.0	20.2	20.4	20.6	21.0
Sales revenue ($m)	0.50	0.52	0.54	0.52	0.50

The management accountant has also collated the following information relating to the market share held at 31 May 2006 by the market leader or nearest competitor in the markets in which each division operates:

Division	(%) Market share held by market leader/nearest competitor
Fashion	18
Industrial	15
Leisure	70
Children	28
Footwear	33

Required:

(a) Use the Boston Consulting Group matrix in order to assess the competitive position of SCC Ltd. **(10 marks)**

(b) Advise the management of SCC Ltd of THREE strategies that should be considered in order to improve the future performance of SCC Ltd. **(6 marks)**

(c) Discuss TWO limitations of the Boston Consulting Group matrix as a strategic planning tool. **(4 marks)**

(Total: 20 marks)

64 BPC (DEC 07)

The directors of Blaina Packaging Co (BPC), a well-established manufacturer of cardboard boxes, are currently considering whether to enter the cardboard tube market. Cardboard tubes are purchased by customers whose products are wound around tubes of various sizes ranging from large tubes on which carpets are wound, to small tubes around which films and paper products are wound. The cardboard tubes are usually purchased in very large quantities by customers. On average, the cardboard tubes comprise between 1% and 2% of the total cost of the customers' finished product.

The directors have gathered the following information:

(1) The cardboard tubes are manufactured on machines which vary in size and speed. The lowest cost machine is priced at $30,000 and requires only one operative for its operation. A one-day training course is required in order that an unskilled person can then operate such a machine in an efficient and effective manner.

(2) The cardboard tubes are made from specially formulated paper which, at times during recent years, has been in short supply.

(3) At present, four major manufacturers of cardboard tubes have an aggregate market share of 80%. The current market leader has a 26% market share. The market shares of the other three major manufacturers, one of which is JOL Co, are equal in size. The product ranges offered by the four major manufacturers are similar in terms of size and quality. The market has grown by 2% per annum during recent years.

(4) A recent report on the activities of a foreign-based multinational company revealed that consideration was being given to expanding operations in their packaging division overseas. The division possesses large-scale automated machinery for the manufacture of cardboard tubes of any size.

(5) Another company, Plastic Tubes Co (PTC) produces a narrow, but increasing, range of plastic tubes which are capable of housing small products such as film and paper-based products. At present, these tubes are on average 30% more expensive than the equivalent sized cardboard tubes sold in the marketplace.

Required:

(a) **Using Porter's five forces model, assess the attractiveness of the option to enter the market for cardboard tubes as a performance improvement strategy for BPC.**

(10 marks)

JOL Co was the market leader with a share of 30% three years ago. The managing director of JOL Co stated at a recent meeting of the board of directors that: 'our loss of market share during the last three years might lead to the end of JOL Co as an organisation and therefore we must address this issue immediately'.

Required:

(b) **Discuss the statement of the managing director of JOL Co and discuss six performance indicators, other than decreasing market share, which might indicate that JOL Co might fail as a corporate entity.**

(10 marks)

(Total: 20 marks)

65 DENTAL HEALTH (JUN 05)

The Dental Health Partnership was established in 20X0 and provides dentistry and other related services to the population of Blaintopia, a country in which the public health service is partially funded by the Government.

Additional information relating to the Dental Health Partnership for the year ended 31 May 20X5 is as follows:

(1) The partnership was open for five days per week during 48 weeks of the year.

(2) Each dentist treated 20 patients per day. The maximum number of patients that could have been treated by a dentist on any working day was 24 patients.

(3) (i) The partnership received a payment from the government each time any patient was consulted as shown in the following table:

Category of treatment	Payments from Government ($)
No treatment required	12
Minor treatment	50
Major treatment	100

(ii) In addition, adult patients paid a fee for each consultation which was equal to the amount of the payment shown per category of treatment in the above table. Children and Senior Citizens were not required to pay a fee for any dental consultations.

(4) The partnership received an annual fee of $20,800 from a well-known manufacturer of dental products under a fixed-term contract of three years' duration. The contract commenced on 1 June 20X4 and relates to the promotion of the products of the manufacturer.

(5) The total of material and consumable costs (which are 100% variable) during the year ended 31 May 20X5 amounted to $446,400.

(6) Staff costs were paid as follows:

Category of Employee	Salary per annum, per employee ($s)
Dentist	60,000
Dental Assistant	20,000
Administrator	16,000

Note: A fixed bonus payment amounting to 4% of their basic salary was paid to each Dental Assistant and Administrator.

(7) Establishment costs and other operating costs amounted to $85,000 and $75,775 respectively for the year ended 31 May 20X5.

(8) All costs other than materials and consumables costs incurred by the Dental Health Partnership are subject to contracts and are therefore to be treated as fixed costs.

(9) A table of non-financial information relating to the Dental Health Partnership for the year ended 31 May 20X5 is as follows:

Number of Dentists:	6
Dental Assistants	7
Administrators	2
Patient 'Mix' (%):	
Adults	50%
Children	40%
Senior Citizens	10%
Mix of patient appointments (%):	
No treatment required	70%
Minor treatment	20%
Major treatment	10%

Required:

(a) Prepare a summary Profit and Loss Account of the Dental Health Partnership for the year ended 31 May 20X5 and calculate the percentage of maximum capacity that was required to be utilised in order to break even in the year ended 31 May 20X5. **(12 marks)**

(b) Discuss FOUR factors that distinguish service from manufacturing organisations and explain how each of these factors relates to the services provided by the Dental Health Partnership. **(5 marks)**

(c) Excluding the number of complaints by patients, identify and briefly explain THREE quantitative non-financial performance measures that could be used to assess the 'quality of service' provided by the Dental Health Partnership. **(3 marks)**

(Total: 20 marks)

66 BLA LTD (DEC 03)

Assume that the date is December 20X3.

BLA Ltd is a design consultancy that provides advice to clients regarding property maintenance and improvements. Three types of consultant are employed by BLA Ltd. These are:

(1) Architectural consultants who provide advice with regard to exterior building improvements.

(2) Interior design consultants who provide advice regarding interior design, and

(3) Landscape consultants who provide advice regarding landscaping of properties and garden design improvements.

BLA Ltd does not undertake building work on behalf of its clients and will only recommend contractors that undertake the three types of work when requested to do so by its clients. The following information is relevant:

(i) Each consultation, other than those detailed in notes (iv) and (v), is charged at a rate of $150 per consultation.

(ii) The consultants are each paid a fixed annual salary of $45,000. In addition they receive a bonus of 40% of the fee income generated in excess of budget. The bonus is shared equally among the consultants employed by BLA Ltd on 31 October in the year to which the bonus relates.

(iii) Other operating expenses (excluding the salaries of the consultants) were budgeted at $2,550,000 for the year to 31 October 20X3.
The actual amount incurred in respect of the year to 31 October 20X3 was $2,805,000, which excludes payments to subcontractors per note (vii) below.

(iv) In an attempt to gain new business, consultants may undertake consultations on a 'no-fee' basis. Such consultations are regarded as Business Development Activity by the management of BLA Ltd.

(v) Consultants will sometimes undertake remedial consultations with clients who experience problems at the time when work commences on each client's site. Remedial consultations are also provided on a non-chargeable, i.e. 'no fee' basis.

(vi) In November 20X2, BLA Ltd purchased 'state of the art' business software for use by its consultants in simulating design improvements. The software was used throughout the year by consultants who specialise in landscape and garden design. It is now planned to introduce the use of the software by the other categories of consultant within BLA Ltd.

(vii) BLA Ltd has a policy of maintaining staff at a level of 45 consultants on an ongoing basis, irrespective of fluctuations in the level of demand. Also, BLA Ltd has retained links with retired consultants and will occasionally subcontract work to them at a cost of $150 per consultation, if current full-time consultants within a particular category are fully utilised. During the year ended 31 October 20X3 subcontractors only undertook non chargeable client consultations.

BLA Ltd

Sundry statistics for year ended 31 October 20X3

	Budget	Actual
Number of consultants by category:		
Exterior design	18	15
Interior design	18	18
Landscape and garden design	9	12
Total client enquiries:		
New business	67,500	84,000
Repeat business	32,400	28,000
Number of chargeable client consultations:		
New business	24,300	22,400
Repeat business	16,200	19,600
Mix of chargeable client consultations:		
Exterior design	16,200	13,830
Interior design	16,200	17,226
Landscape and garden design	8,100	10,944
Number of non-chargeable client consultations undertaken by BLA consultants		
Number of business development consultations	1,035	1,200
Number of remedial consultation	45	405
Number of non-chargeable client consultations undertaken by subcontractors		120
Other statistics:		
Number of complaints	324	630

Required:

(a) Fitzgerald and Moon have suggested that business performance should be measured in a number of ways.

Using FIVE different performance indicators and the quantitative data contained above, comment on the performance of BLA Ltd. **(15 marks)**

(b) Briefly discuss THREE factors that should be considered in the determination of expected standards in a performance measurement system. **(5 marks)**

(Total: 20 marks)

PRACTICE QUESTIONS – SECTION B : SECTION 2

67 PERFORMANCE PYRAMID (JUN 06 – AMENDED)

(a) 'EAJ', which commenced trading on 1 June 20X3, is a business services group whose consultants implement three types of application software packages designed to meet the accounting, distribution and manufacturing requirements of its clients. Each consultant specialises in the implementation of one type of application software i.e. accounting, distribution or manufacturing. EAJ does not sell application software packages. EAJ implements application software packages but clients are responsible for purchasing the packages.

At a recent CPD course the Finance Director learnt about the performance pyramid and wishes to use the perspectives as part of the performance management system within IAJ.

The following information relates to the year ended 31 May 20X6:

(1) Each consultation, other than those detailed in notes (4) and (5), is charged at a rate of $700 per day for new clients and $550 per day for existing clients. Consultants are budgeted to work for 240 days per year.

(2) The consultants are each paid a fixed annual salary of $50,000. In addition they receive a bonus of 40% of the net value of the fee income generated in excess of budget minus the revenue foregone as a consequence of undertaking remedial consultations (per notes 5 and 8) based on a 'notional' rate of $700 per consultant day. The bonus is shared equally among the consultants employed by EAJ on 31 May in the year to which the bonus relates.

(3) Other operating expenses (excluding the salaries of the consultants) were budgeted at $3,600,000. The actual amount incurred was $4,500,000.

(4) In an attempt to gain new business, consultants may undertake consultations on a 'no-fee' basis. Such consultations are regarded as business development activity by the management of EAJ. Each of these consultations is budgeted to take one consultant day.

(5) Consultants will sometimes undertake remedial consultations with new clients who experience problems with regard to implementation.

Remedial consultations are also provided on a non-chargeable, i.e. 'no fee' basis. Each of these consultations requires two consultant days.

(6) Since its formation EAJ has had a policy of maintaining staff at a level of 100 consultants on an ongoing basis, irrespective of fluctuations in the level of demand.

(7) EAJ has a help desk which provides support to its client base.

(8) Sundry statistics for the year ended 31 May 20X6 together with other statistics for the previous two years are as follows:

	Budget	Actual
Number of consultants by category:		
Accounting	40	40
Distribution	30	25
Manufacturing	30	35
Total client enquiries (in days):		
New clients	12,000	15,000
Existing clients	25,200	24,500

	Budget	Actual
*Number of **chargeable** client days:*		
New clients	4,200	4,500
Existing clients	12,600	14,700
*Mix of **chargeable** client days:*		
Accounting	6,720	8,480
Distribution	5,040	4,000
Manufacturing	5,040	6,720

Other statistics (all stated on an ACTUAL basis) relating to the years ended 31 May 20X4–20X6 are as follows:

	2004	2005	2006
Number of clients	320	500	700
Number of client complaints:	160	225	280
Number of on-time implementations (%)	92%	96%	99%
Implementation time per application (days)	3.0	2.5	2.0
Number of accounts in dispute	20	15	10
% of support desk calls resolved	85%	95%	99%
Chargeable client days	16,800	18,000	19,200
Number of business development consultations	100	200	300
Number of remedial consultations (New clients)	310	380	450
Turnover ($000)	4,000	7,500	?
Net profit ($000)	600	900	?

Required:

Using the above information, analyse and discuss the performance of EAJ for the year ended 31 May 20X6 under the following headings:

(i) financial performance and competitiveness;

(ii) external effectiveness;

(iii) internal efficiency. **(15 marks)**

(b) Discuss the limitations of performance management which is based purely on quantitative information. Identify issues which an organisation needs to consider when working with qualitative information. **(10 marks)**

(Total: 25 marks)

68 THE SUCCESS EDUCATION CENTRE (SEC) (PILOT 07)

The Success Education Centre (SEC), which commenced trading in 2003, provides tuition for students preparing for accountancy examinations in Homeland. In 2005, SEC established a similar semi-autonomous operation in the neighbouring country of Awayland. Divisional managers have no control over acquisition and financing policy with regard to operations under their control.

Financial data (all stated on an actual basis) in respect of the two divisions for the two years ended 30 November 2006 and 2007 is as follows:

Income statement

	2006			2007		
	Homeland	Awayland	Combined	Homeland	Awayland	Combined
	$000	$000	$000	$000	$000	$000
Revenue	4,500	1,000	5,500	5,000	1,300	6,300
Salaries	1,500	600	2,100	1,575	630	2,205
Tuition materials & consumables	500	150	650	510	155	665
Other operating costs	1,000	300	1,300	1,040	300	1,340
	3,000	1,050	4,050	3,125	1,085	4,210
Marketing	250	75	325	300	100	400
Interest (Group)			150			125
Depreciation and amortisation	350	50	400	350	100	450
	600	125	875	650	200	975
	3,600	1,175	4,925	3,775	1,285	5,185
Profit	900	(175)	575	1,225	15	1,115

Summary Statements of Financial Position	2006			2007		
Non-current Assets	2,750	250	3,000	2,750	500	3,250
Net Current Assets	750	150	900	1,315	200	1,515
	3,500	400	3,900	4,065	700	4,765
10% Loan stock			1,500			1,250
			2,400			3,515
Capital and Reserves			2,400			3,515

Required:

(a) Provide an assessment of the financial performance of SEC and of the respective contributions of the operations in Homeland and Awayland during the two years ended 30 November 2007. **(8 marks)**

(b) Discuss FOUR items of additional information that would be required in order to provide a more comprehensive assessment of the financial performance of each operation. **(4 marks)**

(c) Discuss FOUR factors that should be taken into consideration when assessing the comparative financial performance of the two operations. **(4 marks)**

(d) Discuss FOUR advantages of using Earnings Before Interest, Taxation, Depreciation and Amortisation (EBITDA) as a measure of financial performance. **(4 marks)**

(Total: 20 marks)

69 CUNDY AQUATIC PURSUITS (CAP) (DEC 09)

Cundy Aquatic Pursuits (CAP) was founded in 1978 by its managing director, Jody Cundy. CAP owns and operates a chain of Aqua Parks in the country of Lizland. Each Aqua Park has a number of large indoor and outdoor swimming pools together with a range of attractions such as water-slides, toboggan runs and surfing rides.

Jody Cundy firmly believes that growth in the number of Aqua Parks is the key to success for CAP, and therefore CAP pursued organic growth which has been financed from retained profits and public share issues. At present, Jody Cundy owns 55% of the ordinary share capital of CAP. Jody has stated on many occasions that 'I always want to control this business'.

The following information is available:

Year ended 30 November	2006	2007	2008	2009
Revenue ($m)	330	320	308	280
Operating costs	270	264	256	240
Profit before tax ($m)	60	56	52	40
Number of Aqua Parks	56	58	60	62

Summary Income Statement for year ended 30 November 2009

	$m
Revenue	280
Operating costs	240
Profit before tax	40
Taxation	(10)
Profit after tax	30

Summary Statement of Financial Position at 30 November 2009

		$m
Non-current assets		220
Net current assets		30
		250
9% Redeemable preference shares (2010)	(100)	
		150

Financed by:	$m
Ordinary shares $1	28
Retained profits	122
	150

Other information:

(1) Jody Cundy considers that it is becoming more and more difficult to earn profits in Lizland and is considering a proposal to expand operations into the country of Robland. CAP would begin construction of forty new Aqua Parks within Robland, on 1 December 2009. Each Aqua Park will require a capital outlay of $3 million.

(2) Robland is a country which is 3,200 kilometres from Lizland. A market research study commissioned by Jody Cundy indicated 'reasonable' future prospects for Robland. During recent years Robland has experienced some significant variations in its currency, the 'Rob'.

(3) CAP's price earnings ratio at the end of 2009 was 10 compared to an industry average of 12.

(4) Dividends were paid during the year ended 30 November 2009 as follows:

	$m
Preference	9
Ordinary	14

(5) Net current assets at 30 November 2009 were as follows:

	$m
Inventories	30
Trade and other receivables	5
Bank	10
Trade and other payables	(15)
	30

(6) No provision has been made for redemption of the preference shares which are redeemable at a premium of 10% on 30 November 2010.

(7) Revenue during the year ended 30 November 2005 amounted to $325 million.

Required:

(a) Evaluate the financial performance of CAP. (6 marks)

(b) Discuss the principal financial, economic and social considerations that should be considered by Jody Cundy prior to a decision to proceed with the proposed expansion into Robland. (14 marks)

(Total: 20 marks)

70 THE SPARE FOR SHIPS COMPANY (SFS) (JUN 10)

The Spare for Ships Company (SFS) has a specialist machining facility which serves the shipbuilding components market. The current job-costing system has two categories of direct cost (direct materials and direct manufacturing labour) and a single indirect cost pool (manufacturing overhead which is allocated on the basis of direct labour hours). The indirect cost allocation rate of the existing job-costing system is $120 per direct manufacturing labour-hour.

Recently, the Visibility Consultancy Partnership (VCP) proposed the use of an activity-based approach to redefine the job-costing system of SFS. VCP made a recommendation to retain the two direct cost categories. However, VCP further recommended the replacement of the single indirect-cost pool with five indirect-cost pools.

Each of the five indirect-cost pools represents an activity area at the manufacturing premises of SFS. Each activity area has its own supervisor who is responsible for his/her operating budget.

Relevant data are as follows:

Activity area	Cost driver used as allocation base	Cost allocation rate ($)
Materials handling	Number of components	0.50
Lathe work	Number of cuts	0.70
Milling	Number of machine hours	24.00
Grinding	Number of components	1.50
Inspection	Number of units inspected	20.00

SFS has recently invested in 'state of the art' IT systems which have the capability to automatically collate all of the data necessary for budgeting in each of the five activity areas.

The management accountant of SFS calculated the manufacturing cost per unit of two representative jobs under the two costing systems as follows:

	Job order 973	Job order 974
	$	$
Current costing system	1,172.00	620.00
Activity-based costing system	1,612.00	588.89

Required:

(a) (i) Compare the cost figures per unit for Job order 973 and Job order 974 calculated by the management accountant and explain the reasons for, and potential consequences of, the differences in the job cost estimates produced under the two costing systems; **(8 marks)**

(ii) Explain two potential problems that SFS might have experienced in the successful implementation of an activity-based costing system using its recently acquired 'state of the art' IT systems. **(4 marks)**

(b) The application of Activity Based Management (ABM) requires that the management of SFS focus on each of the following:

(i) Operational ABM;

(ii) Strategic ABM;

(iii) The implicit value of an activity'.

Required:

Critically appraise the above statement and explain the risks attaching to the use of ABM. **(8 marks)**

(Total: 20 marks)

71 LOL CO (DEC 10)

LOL Co is a chain of shops selling cards and gifts throughout its country. It has been listed on the stock exchange for 10 years and enjoys a fairly high profile in the retail sector of the national economy. You have been asked by the chief executive officer (CEO) to advise the company on value-based management (VBM), as a different approach to performance management. The CEO has read about this method as a way of focusing on shareholder interests and in the current tough economic climate, she thinks that it may be a useful development for LOL.

The company has traditionally used earnings per share (EPS) growth and share price in order to assess performance. The changes being proposed are considered significant and the CEO wants to be briefed on the implications of the new analysis and also how to convince both the board and the major investors of the benefits.

Financial data for LOL

	2009 $m	2010 $m
Profit before interest and tax	50.7	43.5
Interest paid	4.0	7.8
Profit after interest and tax	35.0	26.8
Average number of shares in issue (millions)	160	160

Capital employed at the end of the year was (in $m)

2008	99.2
2009	104.1
2010	97.8

LOL aims for a capital structure of 50:50 debt to equity.

Costs of capital were

	2009	2010
Equity	12.70%	15.30%
Debt (post-tax cost)	4.20%	3.90%

Corporation tax is at the rate of 25%.

Stock market information

	2009	2010
Stock market all-share index	2,225.4	1,448.9
Retailing sector index	1,225.6	907.1
LOL (average share price) ($)	12.20	10.70

Required:

(a) Explain to the CEO what value-based management involves and how it can be used to focus the company on shareholder interests. **(4 marks)**

(b) Perform an assessment of the financial performance of LOL using Economic Value Added (EVA™) and evaluate your results compared with those of earnings per share (EPS) growth and share price performance. You should state any assumptions made. **(12 marks)**

(c) Evaluate VBM measures against traditional profit based measures of performance.

(4 marks)

(Total: 20 marks)

72 RM BATTERIES CO (DEC 10)

RM Batteries Co (RMB) is a manufacturer of battery packs. It has expanded rapidly in the last few years under the leadership of its autocratic chairman and chief executive officer, John Smith. Smith is relentlessly optimistic. He likes to get his own way and demands absolute loyalty from all his colleagues.

The company has developed a major new product over the last three years which has necessitated a large investment in new equipment. Smith has stated that this more efficient battery is critical to the future of the business as the company operates in a sector where customers expect constant innovation from their suppliers.

However, the recent share price performance has caused concern at board level and there has been comment in the financial press about the increased gearing and the strain that this expansion is putting on the company. The average share price has been $1.56 (2008), $1.67 (2009) and $1.34 (2010). There are 450 million shares in issue.

A relevant Z-score model for the industry sector is:

$Z = 1.2X1 + 1.4X2 + 3.3X3 + 0.6X4 + X5$

Where

X1 is working capital/total assets (WC/TA);

X2 is retained earnings reserve/total assets (RE/TA);

X3 is Profit before interest and tax/total assets (PBIT/TA);

X4 is market value of equity/total long-term debt (Mve/total long-term debt); and

X5 is Revenue/total assets (Revenue/TA).

A score of more than 3 is considered safe and at below 1.8, the company is at risk of failure in the next two years.

The company's recent financial performance is summarised below:

Summary income statements

	2008 $m	2009 $m	2010 $m
Revenue	1,460	1,560	1,915
Operating Costs	1,153	1,279	1,724
Operating profit	307	281	191
Interest	35	74	95
Profit before tax	272	207	96
Tax	87	66	31
Profit for the period	185	141	65

Statements of Financial Position

	2008 $m	2009 $m	2010 $m
Assets			
Non-current assets	1,120	1,778	2,115
Current Assets	235	285	341
Total Assets	1,355	2,063	2,456
Equity and Liabilities			
Share capital	230	230	230
Retained earnings reserve	204	344	410
Long-term borrowings	465	991	1,261
Current liabilities	456	498	555
Total equity and liabilities	1,355	2,063	2,456

A junior analyst in the company has correctly prepared a spreadsheet calculating the Z-score as follows:

		2008	2009	2010
Share price ($)		1.56	1.67	1.34
No of shares (millions)		450	450	450
Market value of Equity ($M)		702	752	603
x1	WC/TA	−0.163	−0.103	−0.087
x2	RE/TA	0.151	0.167	0.167
x3	PBIT/TA	0.227	0.136	0.078
x4	Mve/Total long-term debt	1.510	0.758	0.478
x5	Revenue/TA	1.077	0.756	0.780
	Z	2.746	1.770	1.452
Gearing [debt/equity]		107%	173%	197%

Required:

(a) Discuss the strengths and weaknesses of quantitative and qualitative models for predicting corporate failure. **(6 marks)**

(b) Comment on the results in the junior analyst's spreadsheet. **(5 marks)**

(c) Identify the qualitative problems that are apparent in the company's structure and performance and explain why these are relevant to possible failure. **(5 marks)**

(d) Critically assess the results of your analysis in parts (b) and (c) alongside details of RMB's recent financial performance and suggest additional data that should be acquired and how it could be used to assess RMB's financial health. **(4 marks)**

(Total: 20 marks)

CURRENT DEVELOPMENTS AND EMERGING ISSUES IN MANAGEMENT ACCOUNTING AND PERFORMANCE MANAGEMENT

73 TOTAL TIMBER GROUP (TTG)

Total Timber Group (TTG) runs both a national chain of timber suppliers, selling to both trade and DIY customers, and a large scale manufacturing business specialising in the production of wooden construction items from roof trusses to window frames.

The firm has been in business for over twenty years, but in the last few years has noted a marked increase in the number of customer queries about TTY's environmental policies, not just from the retail DIY market but from large corporate construction clients. The board of TTG is aware that it is not just a response to high profile campaigns targeting the logging of vulnerable rainforests, but part of a greater level of environmental awareness and the general trend towards greener consumption.

TTG has always considered itself to be an environmentally responsible company as it purchases all its timber from legal sources and is committed to only using wood from well-managed and sustainable forests. However, the non-executive directors on the board have suggested that a system of environmental management accounting be introduced in order to improve their environmental credentials. The executive team are dubious about the benefits and believe they are already fulfilling their environmental responsibilities.

Required:

Describe the purpose of environmental management accounting (EMA) and explain how using it would benefit TTG. Your answer should include a discussion of the aspects of business costs considered by EMA and the accounting techniques used in its application. You should ensure that your answer is relevant to TTG. **(20 marks)**

PRACTICE QUESTIONS – SECTION B : SECTION 2

74 PUBLIC SERVICES

A mixed economy operates a range of public services including Fire, Police, Education and Health. The services are provided on a regional basis but are funded from central government taxation. The government is endeavouring to improve the 'overall performance' of the services and is considering a range of issues surrounding this objective.

Required:

(a) Explain the term 'overall performance' in respect of public services and suggest a structured approach to its assessment.

Your answer should be from a generic point of view and references to particular services should be used only for illustrative purposes. **(10 marks)**

(b) Explain the particular problems that are likely to occur in attempting to monitor the performance of a public service that would not arise when assessing private sector activities. **(6 marks)**

(c) Suggest ways in which the problems that you have highlighted in answering section (b) may be managed or overcome. **(4 marks)**

(Total: 20 marks)

75 SHAREHOLDER VALUE ANALYSIS

The chairman of your group, which is large and diversified, has expressed concern at the inadequacies of the present voluminous monthly reporting package. He acknowledges that it compares actual and forecast results for all operations with the budget, and that it contains extensive reporting of non-financial indicators of customer satisfaction and quality, and of factory performance towards attaining JIT (just-in-time manufacturing) and TQM (total quality management). However, he regards much of this as operational detail, and considers that the Board should place more emphasis on the shareholders' interests. This would be in accord with the declared group aim of maximising shareholder value in the long run. As part of a response to the chairman's concerns, the finance director has asked you to prepare a report on certain aspects of the problem.

Required:

(a) Explain what is meant by shareholder value, and how it can be assessed; and

(6 marks)

(b) Explain what measure, or measures, of divisional performance would enable the management of a diversified group to assess divisional performance against the group objective of maximising shareholder value. Include in your report appropriate commentary on the role of non-financial indicators, and a possible approach to changing the reporting to the Board which will reflect different perspectives of performance. **(14 marks)**

(Total: 20 marks)

PAPER P5 : ADVANCED PERFORMANCE MANAGEMENT

76 PD

PD manufactures a range of hygiene products. The company is well established and has an international reputation for high quality. Its main objective is to increase shareholder value. Achieving this objective is becoming more difficult because of increasing pressure from competitors in its home and overseas markets and the concentrated efforts of environmental groups. PD has received regular public criticism from environmental pressure groups in respect of its use of non-renewable natural resources, its volumes of waste products and levels of emissions of pollution into the atmosphere. The levels of the atmospheric emissions are only just within legal limits.

Required:

(a) The CEO of PD is looking for ways of improving the performance management system of the company and has read about the Performance Prism approach.

Suggest how PD could use the Performance Prism to assist in the design of a new performance management system. **(12 marks)**

(b) In the light of the pressure from environmental groups, explain the contribution which environmental management accounting could make to the management of PD. **(8 marks)**

(Total: 20 marks)

77 SPORTS COMPLEX

A sports complex includes an ice rink and a swimming pool in its facilities. The ice rink is used for skating and for curling, which became more popular after the 20X8 Winter Olympics. The swimming pool is used for leisure purposes and as a venue for swimming competitions. The sports complex management is concerned at falling profit levels which are due to falling revenue and rising costs.

A proposal to change, and hence improve, the method used for heating the water in the swimming pool is currently being investigated as part of a quality improvement programme. A survey of the complex to check energy usage has been carried out at a cost of $30,000. This has shown that the heat removed from the ice rink (to keep the ice temperature regulated to the required level for good ice conditions) could be used to heat the swimming pool. At present the heat removed in the regulation of ice temperature is not utilised and is simply vented into the atmosphere outside the complex.

The following additional information is available:

(i) The expected costs for the ice rink heat extraction for the year ended 31 May 20X9 are $120,000. It is estimated that, due to rising prices, this cost will increase by 10% during the year to 31 May 20Y0. Heat extracted totalled 500,000 units of heat during the year to 31 May 20X9 and this figure is expected to apply for the year to 31 May 20Y0.

(ii) The water in the swimming pool is currently heated by a separate system which is also used for a range of other heating purposes in the sports complex. In the year ended 31 May 20X9, the swimming pool share of the system had operating costs of $150,000 and used 200,000 units of heat. This was made up of 70% variable avoidable cost and 30% which is a share of general fixed overhead. On average all such costs will increase by 10% through price changes in the year to 31 May 20Y0.

(iii) In order to utilise the heat extracted from the ice rink for heating the water in the swimming pool, equipment would need to be hired at a cost of $75,000 per annum. This equipment would be supervised by an employee who is currently paid a salary of $15,000 for another post in the year ended 31 May 20X9 and who would be retiring if not given this new role. His salary for the year to 31 May 20Y0 would be $17,500. His previous post would not be filled on his retirement. It is anticipated that this system would help to improve the ice quality on the rink.

(iv) Only part of the heat extracted from the ice rink could be recovered for use in heating the water in the swimming pool using the new equipment. The current most likely estimate of the recovery level is 25% of the heat extracted from the ice rink.

If the quantity of heat available were insufficient for the heating of the swimming pool, any balance could continue to be obtained from the existing system.

Required:

(a) Prepare an analysis for the year to 31 May 20Y0 to show whether the sports complex should proceed with the heat recovery proposal on financial grounds where a 25% level of recovery applies. Explain any assumptions made and give reasons for the figures used in or omitted from your calculations. (10 marks)

(b) Calculate the percentage level of heat recovery from the ice rink at which the sports complex management would be indifferent to the proposed changes on financial grounds for the year ended 31 May 20Y0. (7 marks)

(c) In response to public concerns the sports complex management are considering the environmental benefits of the proposal in addition to the above analysis. Explain why organisations are beginning to consider environmental issues as part of decision making and how this can be done through the use of environmental management accounting (8 marks)

(Total: 25 marks)

78 BIOTEC

Background

Set up 30 years ago, BIOTEC is a government-funded public-sector organisation involved with biotechnology research and employs 300 staff. The research covers a wide range of fields including weapons research and medical research but the bulk of projects are focussed on food and drink related problems, such as developing crops that have higher yields and greater resistance to disease.

While there have been highly publicised problems in the past, such as the protests against new GM-crops, BIOTEC staff have generated many breakthroughs that have been successful both practically and commercially. Where developments show commercial promise, other government departments take over responsibility for patenting the innovations and managing any subsequent commercial exploitation. This can include selling licences to private sector companies or developing the product themselves. Some of these innovations have been extremely successful and generated significant revenues.

Financial control

Since inception BIOTEC has been managed as a cost centre. It currently has over a hundred research projects, each of which is also treated as a cost unit in its own right. Each year the Director of BIOTEC agrees an overall cost and funding budget with the government minister responsible. BIOTEC receives no income other than through this budget which for 20X1/20X2 has been agreed to be $30 million.

If a deficit or a surplus arises by the year end, then this is not carried forward to the next year. BIOTEC has normally had a deficit for the period and in 20X0/20X1 there was an over spend of $5 million.

Partly due to its history of being a government research laboratory, BIOTEC does not have a detailed management accounting function and there is no formal system in place for forecasting spending. However, the Director knows approximately, on a monthly basis, the total spending that has taken place within BIOTEC. Furthermore BIOTEC has no record of its capital equipment as this is purchased, on its behalf, by a central government ministry and, therefore, appears in that ministry's accounts.

BIOTEC does not pay any of the costs associated with subsequent patenting and commercial exploitation of ideas, consistent with the fact that it does not receive any subsequent revenues generated.

Staffing issues

Three years ago a third of BIOTEC staff were recognised as world leaders in their specific research areas. That figure has now dropped to around a quarter. Unfortunately, in some cases, when such experts produced an innovation with commercial potential, they moved to a much better paid position in the private sector, sometimes in the middle of a research project. However, other BIOTEC staff are long-serving employees but there are many who have not yet produced any significant research breakthroughs. The director is worried about this ongoing erosion of BIOTEC's core competencies.

Recent meeting

In the context of an ongoing economic recession and cuts in government spending, the Director of BIOTEC has had a meeting with the government minister responsible where the following issues were discussed:

(i) From the next financial year BIOTEC will "not be allowed to run at a deficit" but will be allowed to carry forward and use any surplus.

(ii) While BIOTEC has been spared funding cuts for the next year, the minister also revealed plans to introduce league tables to compare the performance of similar such research departments to assist funding decisions. While the criteria for these league tables have yet to be confirmed, it is likely that return on investment (ROI) will be the main measure, along with other financial and non-financial performance indicators.

(iii) At the very least the director has been encouraged to introduce better financial control.

Required:

(a) **Discuss the role of financial performance measurement and control in BIOTEC, taking particular account of the problems facing the organisation** (15 marks)

(b) **Evaluate the usefulness of government league tables in the context given.**

(10 marks)

(Total: 25 marks)

79 BENNETT PLC (DEC 03)

The directors of Bennett plc are evaluating a proposal to enter the market for a single product which has an estimated life cycle of four years. The company has recently paid $200,000 to a market research consultancy for work done in respect of the proposal.

The market researchers estimated that the total market size would be as follows:

Year	Units
1	1,000,000
2	1,600,000
3	1,200,000
4	500,000

The Marketing Director has estimated that sales volume amounting to 5% of the total market size can be achieved in year 1 if a selling price of $80 per unit is maintained throughout the year. The board of directors are in agreement that they wish to maintain a 5% share by volume, of the total market size in each of years 2–4.

The Finance Director has gathered relevant information and prepared the following evaluation relating to the proposed manufacture and sale of the new product:

	Year 0	Year 1	Year 2	Year 3	Year 4	Year 5	NPV	IRR
Sales unit		50,000	80,000	60,000	25,000			
Selling price per unit ($'s)		80	74	78	85			
Cost/residual value	–2,700					750		
Working capital	–800				800			
Sales revenue		4,000	5,920	4,680	2,125			
Advertising costs	–1,200	–800	–400	–200				
Variable costs ($35/unit)		–1,750	–2,800	–2,100	–875			
Attributable fixed costs		–700	–700	–700	–700			
Net cash flow	–4,700	750	2,020	1,680	1,350	750		
Discount factor at 14%	1.000	0.877	0.769	0.675	0.592	0.519		
Discounted cash flow	–4,700	658	1,533	1,134	799	389		
NPV at 14%							–187	
Discount factor at 12%	1.000	0.893	0.797	0.712	0.636	0.567		
Discounted cash flow	–4,700	670	1,610	1,196	859	425		
NPV at 12%							60	
IRR =								12.5

The Finance Director uses a cost of capital of 14% to evaluate all such proposals.

Required:

(a) Using the above information, critically assess the evaluation prepared by the Finance Director. **(10 marks)**

(b) Describe the use of target costing and explain how it could be of assistance to Bennett plc following a decision by the directors to manufacture the product. Your answer should include a flow diagram to illustrate a target costing cycle. **(10 marks)**

(Total: 20 marks)

80 THE BETTER ELECTRICALS GROUP (BEG) (JUN 10)

The Better Electricals Group (BEG) which commenced trading during 2002 manufactures a range of high quality electrical appliances such as kettles, toasters and steam irons for domestic use which it sells to electrical stores in Voltland.

The directors consider that the existing product range could be extended to include industrial sized products such as high volume water boilers, high volume toasters and large steam irons for the hotel and catering industry.

They recently commissioned a highly reputable market research organisation to undertake a market analysis which identified a number of significant competitors within the hotel and catering industry.

At a recent meeting of the board of directors, the marketing director proposed that BEG should make an application to gain 'platinum status' quality certification in respect of their industrial products from the Hotel and Catering Institute of Voltland in order to gain a strong competitive position. He then stressed the need to focus on increasing the effectiveness of all operations from product design to the provision of after sales services.

An analysis of financial and non-financial data relating to the application for 'platinum status' for each of the years 2011, 2012 and 2013 is contained in the appendix.

The managing director of BEG recently returned from a seminar, the subject of which was 'The Use of Cost Targets'. She then requested the management accountant of BEG to prepare a statement of total costs for the application for platinum status for each of years 2011, 2012 and 2013. She further asked that the statement detailed manufacturing cost targets and the costs of quality.

The management accountant produced the following statement of manufacturing cost targets and the costs of quality:

	2011 Forecast $m	2012 Forecast $m	2013 Forecast $m
Variable manufacturing costs	8,400	10,500	12,600
Fixed manufacturing costs	3,000	3,400	3,400
Prevention costs	4,200	2,100	1,320
Appraisal costs	800	700	700
Internal failure costs	2,500	1,800	1,200
External failure costs	3,100	2,000	980
Total costs	22,000	20,500	20,200

APPENDIX

'PLATINUM STATUS' QUALITY CERTIFICATION APPLICATION – RELEVANT STATISTICS

	2011 Forecast	2012 Forecast	2013 Forecast
Total market size ($m)	300	320	340
BEG – sales ($m)	24	30	36
BEG – total costs ($m)	22	20.5	20.2
BEG – sundry statistics:			
% of products achieving design quality standards and accepted without further rectification	92	95	99
Rectification claims from customers ($m)	0.96	0.75	0.1
Cost of after sales rectification service ($m)	1.8	1.05	0.8
% of sales meeting planned delivery dates	88.5	95.5	99.5
Average cycle time: (customer enquiry to product delivery) (days)	49	45	40
Product enquiries not taken up by customers (% of enquiries)	10.5	6	3
Idle capacity of manufacturing staff (%)	12	6	1.5

Required:

(a) Explain how the use of cost targets could be of assistance to BEG with regard to their application for platinum status. Your answer must include commentary on the items contained in the statement of manufacturing cost targets and the costs of quality prepared by the management accountant. **(8 marks)**

(b) Assess the forecasted performance of BEG for the period 2011 to 2013 with reference to the application for 'platinum status' quality certification under the following headings:

   (i) Financial performance and marketing;

   (ii) External effectiveness; and

   (iii) Internal efficiency. **(12 marks)**

(Total: 20 marks)

Section 3

ANSWERS TO PRACTICE QUESTIONS – SECTION A

KEY POINTS FOR EACH QUESTION ARE HIGHLIGHTED

1   QUICKLINK LTD (JUN 05 – AMENDED)   *Walk in the footsteps of a top tutor*

> **Key answer tips**
>
> The first part of the question (requirements (a) and (b)) invites candidates to apply a range of accounting and management technique to a practical business situation. Comparison is invited of two businesses in the transport sector, starting with the preparation of budgets for the two entities and extending to the development of appropriate performance indicators. This addresses the core concept underpinning performance evaluation – that performance is a relative thing and can only be understood in the context of a comparison of likes.
>
> The second part of the question (requirements (c) and (d)) invites discussion on the merits of a business acquisition and the adoption of TQM.

ANSWER 1 – INCORPORATING THE OFFICIAL ACCA EXAMINER'S SOLUTION

REPORT

To: Managing Director, Quicklink

From: A Accountant

Date: 9 December 2005

Subject: Plans for 2006

Introduction

This report addresses the following issues:

Firstly, the projected income statements for 2006 are prepared. Next the projected performance of Quicklink and Celer Transport, a potential acquisition target are compared. Thirdly the strategic arguments for the acquisition are outlined and finally the main benefits that might accrue from the successful implementation of a Total Quality Management programme are discussed.

(a)

Quicklink Ltd
Budgeted Income Statements for the year ending 31 May 2006

	Quicklink Ltd $	Celer Transport $	Combined $
Revenue:			
Contract clients:			
Mail	1,769,040	237,600	2,006,040
Parcels	1,474,200	247,500	1,721,700
Machinery/processed food	6,747,300	2,700,000	9,447,300
	9,990,540	3,185,100	13,175,640
Non-contract clients:			
Mail	1,651,104	776,160	2,427,264
Parcels	1,179,360	693,000	1,872,360
Machinery/processed food	1,124,550	–	1,124,550
	3,955,014	1,469,160	5,424,174
Total revenue	13,945,554	4,654,260	18,599,814
Operating costs:			
Fuel	1,989,000	1,615,680	3,604,680
Salaries	1,921,920	1,098,240	3,020,160
Sundry operating costs	3,120,000	1,990,340	5,110,340
Total operating costs	7,030,920	4,704,260	11,735,180
Net profit	6,914,634	(50,000)	6,864,634

Workings:

(W1) Sales Revenue:

Quicklink Ltd

Contract clients:	Total number of deliveries	Contract deliveries (%)	Number of contract deliveries	Fee per delivery	Total ($)
Mail	468,000	60	280,800	$6.30 ($6 × 1.05)	1,769,040
Parcels	234,000	60	140,400	$10.50 ($10 × 1.05)	1,474,200
Machinery	35,700	90	32,130	$210 ($200 × 1.05)	6,747,300

Non-contract clients:	Total number of deliveries	Non-contract deliveries (%)	Number of non-contract deliveries	Fee per delivery	Total ($)
Mail	468,000	40	187,200	$8.82 ($6 ×1.05 × 140%)	1,651,104
Parcels	234,000	40	93,600	$12.60 ($10 ×1.05 × 120%)	1,179,360
Machinery	35,700	10	3,570	$315 ($200 × 1.05 × 150%)	1,124,500

Celer Transport

Contract clients:	Total number of deliveries	Contract deliveries (%)	Number of contract deliveries	Fee per delivery	Total ($)
Mail	132,000 (120,000 × 110%)	30	39,600	$6	237,600
Parcels	82,500 (75,000 × 110%)	30	24,750	$10	247,500
Processed food	32,500	100	32,500		2,700,000

4 × $225,000 + 6 × $150,000 + 9 × $100,000 = $2,700,000

Non-contract clients:	Total number of deliveries	Non-contract deliveries (%)	Number of non-contract deliveries	Fee per delivery	Total ($)
Mail	132,000 (120,000 × 110%)	70	92,400	$8.40 ($6 × 140%)	777,160
Parcels	82,500 (75,000 × 110%)	70	57,750	$12.00 ($10 × 20%)	693,000

(W2) Fuel costs:

Quicklink Ltd	Number of vehicles	Days in use	Average kilometres per vehicle per day	Cost per kilometre	Cost ($)
Mail and parcels	55	340	300	$0.10	561,000
Machinery	21	340	400	$0.50	1,428,000
					1,989,000

Celer Transport	Number of vehicles	Days in use	Average kilometres per vehicle per day	Cost per kilometre	Cost ($)
Mail and parcels	22	340	300	$0.12	269,280
Machinery	22	340	300	$0.60	1,346,400
					1,615,680

(W3) Salaries

	Number of employees	Salary per annum	Cost ($)
Quicklink Ltd	70	$27,456 ($26,400 ×104%)	1,921,920
Celer Transport	40	$27,456 ($26,400 ×104%)	1,098,240

(W4) Sundry operating costs

		Cost ($)
Quicklink Ltd	($3,000,000 × 104%)	3,120,000
Celer Transport	Per question	1,990,340

(b) The businesses of Quicklink Ltd and Celer Transport are engaged in the same industry and are therefore broadly comparable.

Each business has its own 'distinctive competence' which in the case of Quicklink Ltd is the delivery of industrial machinery whilst Celer Transport has developed a specialism in the delivery of processed food.

Relevant operating statistics are as follows:

	Quicklink Ltd 2005 Actual	Quicklink Ltd 2006 Forecast	Celer Transport 2005 Actual	Celer Transport 2006 Forecast
Revenue per vehicle (per annum):				
Mail and parcels	$105,172	$110,431	$72,679	$88,830
Machinery/processed food	$357,000	$374,850	$122,727	$122,727
Vehicle in-use %	93	93	93	93
Deliveries per vehicle (per annum):				
Mail and parcels	12,764	12,764	8,864	9,750
Machinery/processed food	1,700	1,700	1,477	1,477
Delivery mix (mail/parcels):				
Same day	20%		75%	
	80%		25%	
On-time deliveries (%):				
Mail and parcels	99.5%	99%	82%	95%
Machinery/processed food	100.0%	99%	97%	100%
Number of lost items		–		145
% of telephone calls answered within target time	99%		90%	
% of telephone calls abandoned	0%		2.00%	

The number of mail and parcel deliveries per vehicle, per annum, made by Quicklink Ltd during the year ended 31 May 2005 was 44% higher than those made by Celer Transport which explains the higher budgeted revenues per Quicklink vehicle engaged in the delivery of mail and parcels for the year ending 31 May 2006. The revenue generation per vehicle shows that the budgeted average revenue generated vehicle used in the delivery of mail and parcels in respect of the year ending 31 May 2006 amounts to $110,431 and $88,830 in respect of Quicklink Ltd and Celer Transport respectively. However, this difference will reduce in the year ending 31 May 2006 due to the projected growth in sales volumes of the Celer Transport business. The average mail/parcels delivery of mail/parcels per vehicle of the Quicklink Ltd part of the business is budgeted at 12,764 which is still 30.91% higher than that of the Celer Transport business.

As far as specialist activities are concerned, Quicklink Ltd is budgeted to generate average revenues per vehicle amounting to $374,850 whilst Celer Transport is budgeted to earn an average of $122,727 from each of the vehicles engaged in delivery of processed food. It is noticeable that all contracts with major food producers were renewed on 1 June 2005 and it would appear that there were no increases in the annual value of the contracts with major food producers.

This might have been the result of a strategic decision by the management of the combined entity in order to secure the future of this part of the business which had been built up previously by the management of Celer Transport.

Each vehicle owned by Quicklink Ltd and Celer Transport is in use for 340 days during each year, which based on a 365 day year would give an in use % of 93%. This appears acceptable given the need for routine maintenance and repairs due to wear and tear.

During the year ended 31 May 2005 the number of on-time deliveries of mail and parcel and industrial machinery deliveries were 99.5% and 100% respectively. This compares with ratios of 82% and 97% in respect of mail and parcel and processed food deliveries made by Celer Transport. In this critical area it is worth noting that Quicklink Ltd achieved their higher on-time delivery target of 99% in respect of each activity whereas Celer Transport were unable to do so. Moreover, it is worth noting that Celer Transport missed their target time for delivery of food products on 975 occasions throughout the year 31 May 2005 and this might well cause a high level of customer dissatisfaction and even result in lost business.

It is interesting to note that, whilst the businesses operate in the same industry, they have a rather different delivery mix in terms of same day/next day demands by clients. Same day deliveries only comprise 20% of the business of Quicklink Ltd whereas they comprise 75% of the business of Celer Transport.

This may explain why the delivery performance of Celer Transport with regard to mail and parcel deliveries was not as good as that of Quicklink Ltd.

The fact that 120 items of mail and 25 parcels were lost by the Celer Transport business is most disturbing and could prove damaging as the safe delivery of such items is the very substance of the business and would almost certainly have resulted in a loss of customer goodwill. This is an issue which must be addressed as a matter of urgency.

The introduction of the call management system by Quicklink Ltd on 1 June 2004 is now proving its worth with 99% of calls answered within the target time of 20 seconds. This compares favourably with the Celer Transport business in which only 90% of a much smaller volume of calls were answered within a longer target time of 30 seconds. Future performance in this area will improve if the call management system is applied to the Celer Transport business. In particular, it is likely that the number of abandoned calls will be reduced and enhance the 'image' of the Celer Transport business.

Workings: **Revenue generation per vehicle:**

Quicklink Ltd	2006	2005
Mail and parcels:	$	$
Contract mail	1,769,040	
Contract parcels	1,474,200	
Non-contract mail	1,651,104	
Non-contract parcels	1,179,360	
Total	6,073,704	
Number of vehicles	55	
Revenue per vehicle	$110,431	= $105,172 (110,431/1.05)
Machinery:	$	$
Contract	6,747,300	
Non-contract	1,124,550	
Total	7,871,850	
Number of vehicles	21	
Revenue per vehicle	$374,850	= $357,000 (374,850/1.05)

Celer Transport	2006	2005
Mail and parcels:	$	$
Contract mail	237,600	
Contract parcels	247,500	
Non-contract mail	776,160	
Non-contract parcels	693,000	
Total	1,954,260	
Number of vehicles	22	
Revenue per vehicle	$88,830	= $72,679 (88,830/1.10 × 90%)
Processed food:	2,700,000	2,700,000
Number of vehicles	22	
Revenue per vehicle	$122,757	$122,757 (no change in contract values)

Deliveries per vehicle:	Quicklink Ltd		Celer Transport	
	2005 Actual	2006 Forecast	2005 Actual	2006 Forecast
Mail and parcel deliveries:				
Number of deliveries	702,000	702,000	195,000	214,500
	(468,000 + 234,000)			(195,000 × 110%)
Number of vehicles	55	55	22	22
Deliveries per vehicle	12,764	12,764	8,864	9,750
Machinery/processed food deliveries:				
Number of deliveries	35,700	35,700	32,500	32,500
Number of vehicles	21	21	22	22
Deliveries per vehicle	1,700	1,700	1,477	1,477

(c) The managing director of Quicklink Ltd might consider 'the acquisition of the Celer Transport business to be a good strategic move' for the following reasons:

- The acquisition of the Celer Transport business would enable a rapid expansion of the business, whereas to grow organically in a competitive industry requires a much longer timescale and would be more difficult to achieve.

- Since the business operates both mail and parcel deliveries there is the potential for synergies to be taken advantage of in terms of route scheduling as well as the opportunities to take advantage of the complementary mix of same day/next day business that are distinctive features of the separate businesses.

- The fact that each of the Quicklink Ltd and Celer Transport businesses has a distinctive competence in terms of the delivery of machinery and food products respectively helps to reduce the threat to future income streams.

- The combination of the Quicklink Ltd and Celer Transport business might well present opportunities to take advantage of economies of scale. There would undoubtedly be scope for savings in establishment costs, staff costs, communication costs etc.

- It is quite possible that the fuel costs per kilometre of the Celer Transport business during the year ended 31 May 2006, which are 20% higher than those of Quicklink Ltd has, may have reduced profitability by $269,280. Hence the Celer Transport business would have been budgeted to make a profit of $219,280 as opposed to a loss of $50,000 (Note 1), had its fuel been provided under the terms of the contract with the supplier of fuel to Quicklink Ltd.

Note 1:

	$	$
Loss per part 1(a)		(50,000)
Potential saving in fuel costs:		
Actual expenditure by Celer Transport business:		
340 × 300 × 22 × ($0.12 + $0.60)=	1,615,680	
Expenditure at contract rates:		
340 × 300 × 22 × ($0.10 + $0.50) =	1,346,400	
Potential saving in fuel costs		269,280
Potential net profit		219,280

Note: The above calculation assumes that the cost per kilometre of a vehicle used in the delivery of processed food would be the same as that of a vehicle used in the delivery of industrial machinery.

(d) The benefits that might accrue from the successful implementation of a Total quality management programme by the management of the combined entity include the following:

- There will be an increased awareness of all personnel within Quicklink Ltd of the need to establish a 'quality culture' within the company which will provide a basis of improved performance throughout the organisation.

- The successful adoption of a TQM philosophy would ensure that there is a real commitment to 'continuous improvement' in all processes.

- It would place a greater focus on customer satisfaction since at the heart of any TQM programme is a deep-seated commitment to the satisfaction of every customer.

PAPER P5 : ADVANCED PERFORMANCE MANAGEMENT

- There would be a greater emphasis upon teamwork which would be used in a number of forms e.g. quality circles which could be established with a view to improving performance within every area of the business. The fostering of team spirit will also improve communication within Quicklink Ltd.

- A major characteristic of a TQM programme is process-redesign which is used to simplify processes, systems, procedures and the organisation itself. In this respect the adoption of a TQM philosophy will be invaluable since the integration of the Quicklink Ltd and Celer Transport businesses will require, of necessity, a detailed review of those processes currently employed.

- The adoption of a TQM philosophy will necessitate the monitoring of quality costs in order to measure whether the objective of continuous improvement is being achieved. In this respect, the aim will be to eliminate internal failure costs such as late deliveries and lost items which are clearly detrimental to a business which operates in the transport and haulage industry.

ANSWER 2 – Tackling the calculations – walk in the footsteps of a top tutor

Start by calculating Quicklink delivery numbers for contract and non contract work.

Quicklink Ltd

2005		Workings	Mail	Parcels	Machinery	Total
No' of deliveries	1		468,000	234,000	35,700	
Contract %	2		60%	60%	90%	
No' Contract deliveries	3	1 × 2	280,800	140,400	32,130	
No' non contract deliveries	4	1 – 3	187,200	93,600	3,570	

Now adjust the contract client rates for the non contract work.

Contract clients rates per delivery $	5	Given	6.00	10.00	200.00	
Non contract clients rate premium over contract	6		40%	20%	50%	
Non contract clients rates		Need for Celer	8.40	12.00	300.00	

ANSWERS TO PRACTICE QUESTIONS – SECTION A : SECTION 3

> Bring down the number of deliveries as per 2005 but change the contract and non contract rates as below:

2006			Mail	Parcels	Machinery	Total
No' Contract deliveries	8	stay same	280,800	140,400	32,130	
No' Non contract deliveries	10	stay same	187,200	93,600	3,570	
Contract clients rates per delivery in 2006 $	7	incr by 5%	6.30	10.50	210.00	
Non contract clients rates per delivery in 2006 $	9	answer to 7 increase by premium in 6	8.82	12.60	315.00	

> Multiply the number of deliveries by the new rates calculated to get to total revenue.

		Mail	Parcels	Machinery	Total
Sales revenue contract	7 * 8	1,769,040	1,474,200	6,747,300	9,990,540
Sales revenue non contract	9 * 10	1,651,104	1,179,360	1,124,550	3,955,014
Total revenue					**13,945,554**

> We now need to calculate the costs, let's start with fuel. We need to calculate the number of KM travelled each year and multiply by the cost per Km.

		Mail & Parcels	Machines		
Fuel for delivery vehicles					
$ per km y/e 31 May 2006	15	0.10	0.50		
No' days vehicles in use	11	340	340		
Average Km per vehicle per day	12	300	400		
No'. of vehicles	13	55	21		
No' Km travelled each year	14	11 × 12 × 13 5,610,000	2,856,000		8,466,000
Total Fuel cost		14*15 561,000	1,428,000		**1,989,000**

KAPLAN PUBLISHING

PAPER P5 : ADVANCED PERFORMANCE MANAGEMENT

> *Increase the number of employees and employee salary as 26,400 by 4% in 2006.*

<u>Employee salaries</u>

2005 per employee $	Incr. by 4% in 2006	26,400	26,400		
No' employees – 2005	unchanged in 2006	50	20		
2006 per employee $	Incr by 4%	27,456	27,456		
Total salary costs		1,372,800	549,120		**1,921,920**

> *Sundry costs are given as 3 million and that they will also increase by 4%.*

<u>Sundry Operating costs</u>

Total in year ended 31/05/2005		3,000,000
Total Sundry in year ended 31/05/2006	Incr. by 4% in 2006	**3,120,000**
	Profit	**6,914,634**

Celer Transport

> *Start with calculating delivery numbers for contract and non contract work as below:*

2005		**Workings**	Mail	Parcels	Machinery	Total
No' of deliveries	1		120,000	75,000	32,500	
Contract %	2		30%	30%	100%	
No' Contract deliveries	3	1 × 2	36,000	22,500	32,500	
No' Non contract deliveries	4	1 – 3	84,000	52,500	0	

> *Now adjust the contract client rates for the non contract work:*

Quicklink contract clients rates per delivery in 2005 $	5	Given	6.00	10.00	200.00
Celer contract clients rates per delivery in 2005 $	6	90% of Quicklink contract client rates	5.40	9.00	180.00

120

KAPLAN PUBLISHING

ANSWERS TO PRACTICE QUESTIONS – SECTION A : SECTION 3

Quicklink non contract clients rates per delivery in '05 $		Fee + additional premium	8.40	12.00	300.00
			(6*1.4)	(10*1.2)	(200*1.5)
2006					
No' Contract deliveries	8	increase no' contract deliveries by 10%	39,600	24,750	
No' Non contract deliveries	10	incr no' non contract deliveries by 10%	92,400	57,750	
Contract clients rates per delivery in 2006 $	7	Increase by 5% = *1.05	6.00	10.00	
Non contract clients rates per delivery in 2006 $	9	7 multiply by answer in (1+6)	8.40	12.00	

👣 *Multiply the number of deliveries by the new rates calculated to get to total revenue.*

		Mail	Parcels	Machinery	Total
Sales revenue – contract	7 * 8	237,600	247,500	2,700,000	3,185,100
Sales revenue – non contract	9 * 10	776,160	693,000		1,469,160
Total revenue					**4,654,260**

👣 *We now need to calculate the costs, let's start with fuel. We need to calculate the number of KM travelled each year and multiply by the cost per Km.*

			Mail & Parcels	Proc food	**Total**
Fuel for delivery vehicles					
$ per Km y/e 31 May 2006	15		0.12	0.60	
No' days vehicles in use	11		340	340	
Average Km per vehicle per day	12		300	300	
No. of vehicles	13		22	22	
No' Km travelled each year	14	11 × 12 × 13	2,244,000	2,244,000	4,488,000
Total Fuel cost		14*15	269,280	1,346,400	**1,615,680**

KAPLAN PUBLISHING

PAPER P5 : ADVANCED PERFORMANCE MANAGEMENT

> We are given the number of employees and employee salary as 26,400 and are told it will increase by 4% in 2006.

Employee salaries

2005 per employee $	Incr. by 4% in 2006	26,400	26,400	
No' employees – 2005	unchanged in 2006	20	20	
2006 per employee $	Incr by 4%	27,456	27,456	
Total salary costs		549,120	549,120	**1,098,240**

> We are given sundry costs, then deduct all costs from revenue to get profit/loss.

Sundry Operating costs

Total sundry costs	1,990,340
	(50,000)
	Loss

2 BSN

Key answer tips

Ensure you answer the question set. You are NOT required to give a description of any strategic planning tool, nor a detailed description of the stakeholder groups, nor financial and non-financial information relating to the television service division.

REPORT

To: Board of Directors, BSN

From: A Accountant

Date: Today

Subject: Future targets and developments

Introduction

This report covers the following areas:

Firstly it considers the concerns of stakeholders and how to determine those concerns.

Secondly it analyses the likelihood of BSN meeting Government expectations and how the Directors can close the expected "gap".

Thirdly it discusses the implications for BSN's objectives if the television and radio services are separated and finally it explains what information should be provided to the Board on the performance of the radio subsidiary following its separation from the television service.

Stakeholder concerns

(a) (i) The key risk concerns of stakeholders are likely to be as follows:

The **general public** will be most concerned about the possible fall in the quality and breadth of programming should the television and radio services be separated and funded differently. For example, the need to attract advertising may force the world service radio programme to dumb down its content and will certainly interrupt the flow of news and comment.

The **Government** is concerned with ensuring that best value is obtained for the licence-fee payer. This is translated firstly into cost efficiency and ROCE targets. The main risk, therefore, would be if these targets were not met as the Government would feel they need to intervene to address any problems to avoid bad publicity with the electorate. In addition the Government is trying to reduce the financial burden on licence fee payers via a new funding model and the key risk would thus be a failure of this model.

Employees will see the main risk as the possibility that cost and efficiency saving may impact jobs and/or artistic freedom. In the case of the latter, they may feel under pressure to make more commercial content to attract advertising.

Management, especially the Board of Directors, will be most concerned with the risk that they fail to get an acceptable balance of the different objectives – for example, on the one hand giving creative freedom to programme makers but trying to cut costs and hit ROCE targets.

(ii) BSN is a public sector organisation providing radio and television broadcasting services. Its main stakeholders are the government, the public, employees and management. Like other 'not for profit' organisations no one stakeholder group dominates, so the directors of BSN need to consult with all its stakeholders to determine its future development. The following ways of communicating with stakeholders can be used:

- The present system of using independent panels of viewers and listeners should continue. Checks should be carried out to verify the independence of panel members and to ensure they are representative of the views of the general public.

- Questionnaires can be sent out to licences to obtain feedback on their views of BSN and the services it provides.

- Feedback on individual programmes can be obtained from members of the public by asking for their comments and providing internal addresses and telephone numbers.

- Members of the government can be consulted by using formal committees and working parties, and setting up informal discussion procedures.

- The directors should establish formal and informal communication procedures with employees and management. Many methods can be used including working parties, work groups, committees and staff suggestion schemes.

Meeting the Government target for ROCE

(b) (i) BSN's ROCE for the four years of the licence fee agreement is calculated as follows:

$m	Year			
	1	2	3	4
Income	2,190	2,234	2,234	2,234
Expenditure	(2,114)	(2,192)	(2,273)	(2,357)
Surplus/(deficit)	76	42	(39)	(123)
Capital employed				
Bal b/f	1,250	1,326	1,368	1,329
Surplus/(deficit)	76	42	(39)	(123)
Bal c/f	1,326	1,368	1,329	1,206
Average capital Employed	1,288	1,347	1,348.5	1,267.5

	1	2	3	4
ROCE	76/1,288	42/1,347	(39)/1348.5	(123)/1,267.5
	= 5.9%	= 3.1%	= (2.9%)	= (9.7%)

The government has set a target ROCE of 6%. In years 2, 3 and 4 BSN will fail to reach this target. A planning gap is opening and will need to be closed.

(ii) BSN's management will need to take action to achieve the target ROCE of 6% by finding ways of closing the planning gap. The options available are as follows:

Increase revenue

The government has stipulated that no further increase in the licence fee can be allowed. Other ways of obtaining revenue should be considered, such as:

- advertising
- obtaining sponsorship of programmes
- selling programmes to other broadcasting companies
- copyright fees charged to video recording companies.

Cost reduction

BSN should investigate ways of reducing costs without compromising programme and service quality. The best way to achieve this would be to find further ways of increasing efficiency. The directors have a good track record over the last three years of initiating improvements to efficiency within BSN.

Reduction in capital employed

BSN's management should investigate ways of reducing the organisation's capital employed. The need to maintain quality might make this difficult.

ANSWERS TO PRACTICE QUESTIONS – SECTION A : SECTION 3

Using other performance measures

The management of BSN should try to persuade the government to use other performance indicators to assess its performance as the ROCE ignores many factors such as providing a world service, which generates no income, and public satisfaction.

Separating the television and radio services

(c) At present, users of the radio service do not pay a licence fee and are subsidised by television licence payers. Separating the television and radio services will result in major changes occurring including:

- Separate charges can be made for using the television and radio services. Making a separate charge to radio users will be difficult to apply unless radio owners are registered. Registering radio owners will be costly and will meet with opposition from the public. A one-off charge added to the selling price of a new radio might be practical.

- BSN could turn its radio division into a commercial radio station raising revenue from advertising and merchandising. The objective of public service broadcasting will have to be changed. To maximise income BSN will then have to maximise audiences by supplying popular programmes so the objectives of providing programmes that inform, educate and entertain will also have to be changed.

- Each division will have to pay for itself. The radio division will have to set new performance criteria for each service provided. Unless the government pays for loss-making services, such as the world service, they will have to be discontinued.

- The perceived quality of programmes by many current radio listeners will be seen to deteriorate if BSN adopts a populist approach to its radio division.

Before a decision is made to separate the services BSN's managers should consult with stakeholder groups and consider the long-term implications.

(d) The following information should be provided to BSN's directors relating to the radio division following its separation from the television service:

Financial information

- Budgets should be produced for the division. Actual results should be compared with the budgeted figures and variances reported.

- Costs should be analysed by programme and operation. This will enable the directors to see where costs are being incurred.

- Analysis of revenue by source. It is important that the directors know the amount and source of revenue.

- For decision making purposes, the contribution earned by each programme should be repeated.

- The net present value of each capital investment project being planned for the division should be reported before a decision to proceed is made.

PAPER P5 : ADVANCED PERFORMANCE MANAGEMENT

Non-financial information

- Reports should be produced giving the number of listeners analysed by programme, day and time.
- The radio services market share should be reported together with competitors' market share.
- Feedback should be obtained on listener satisfaction and reported.
- An analysis of listeners as a proportion of the total population in each area would also be useful information.
- The management accountant should play an important role in providing this information.

3 P GROUP

> **Key answer tips**
>
> A sound answer can be based on standard models and concepts. Part (a) can be answered by using Porter's Five Forces Model – but you must use the scenario. In Part (b) ensure that you use financial and other performance indicators in your evaluation of the performance of each company. In Part (c) remember to consider each stakeholder referred to in the question, i.e. shareholders, employees, joint venture partners and customers. As always, apply the theories to the situation given. In part (d) the key is application to the scenario rather than reproducing learnt notes.

REPORT

To: Board of Directors, P Group

From: A Accountant

Date: Today

Subject: Future strategy and developments

Introduction

This report covers the following areas:

Firstly it examines the importance of the key external factors that influence P.

Secondly it analyses the performance of the two main aspects of P's business with recommendation on improving performance.

Thirdly it explains the main factors that have contributed to P's commercial success so far and comments on the role of the Chairman going forwards.

Finally it considers the role of EMA within P.

External factors

(a) If a business is to be successful it must not only establish but also maintain competitive advantage. During the last 30 years the P Group has developed internationally and has a trading presence in many diverse areas. This inevitably means that the company is likely to encounter many external forces which will make it much more difficult for P Group to meet its objective of not disappointing customers with any of the products and services provided.

The external forces, to which P Group is subject in developing its business, can be analysed using Michael Porter's 'Five Forces Model':

Power of the buyers

Management must have knowledge of the needs of their customers and also information about the conditions that subsist in the different markets in which they have a presence. Such information assumes critical importance if P Group is to be successful in different sectors. The conditions in the market places will invariably differ, and thus if P Group is to be successful then due consideration should be given to the political, legal and social environments which exist within each market place. It is possible that the buyers may benefit from the entry of the P Group, as it is likely that the existing suppliers may have become too self-satisfied, however this situation could well change and become a threat to the P Group.

Power of suppliers

The management of P Group must be certain that there are available suppliers who can provide them with the materials and services needed. The quality and reliability of suppliers could potentially become a major issue; hence managers should take steps to ensure that supplies of materials, services and appropriately skilled personnel can be obtained.

Competitors

In attempting to enter new markets, P Group will be faced with competitors who are already established and have acquired market knowledge. It will be difficult to compete effectively in these markets and thus it is essential that P Group acquired skilled managers in order to improve the likelihood of attaining the objectives of the organisation.

Availability of substitutes

P Group is involved in different businesses and it is probable that the tastes and life style of customers within each business will differ. It is therefore essential that products and services of the P Group are adapted to meet the requirements of different types of customer. By the same token, it is essential that such differences are incorporated into the strategic and marketing plans of the organisation.

If P Group is to be successful it is vital that its product and service offerings represent 'value for money' and satisfies the needs of its customers.

Entry barriers

The structure and business conditions may vary considerably within each industry, and information should be obtained in order for P Group to be able to operate in an effective manner. If the management of P Group are able to introduce new ventures which are innovative and 'exciting' within particular industries, then it is possible that they are simultaneously creating barriers to entry to those industries.

Each time P Group mounts a challenge to major companies it will probably require the commitment of significant resources. It is therefore of paramount importance that the external forces be evaluated prior to any major decisions are made.

Performance Appraisal

(b) During 20X4, the turnover of the Airline business increased by almost 19%, whilst the turnover of the rail business only increased by just over 3%. There were marked differences in the performance of these respective divisions of the P Group:

Airline	20X3 %	20X4 %
Pre-tax Profit as percentage of Turnover	10.5	11.8
Return on Capital Employed	8.0	10.1
Turnover/Capital employed	76.0	85.8

Rail	20X3 %	20X4 %
Pre-tax Profit as percentage of Turnover	7.3	7.6
Return on Capital Employed	5.7	5.0
Turnover/Capital employed	77.4	66.1

P Airlines

A comparison of the results of the two years reveals that no significant change has occurred in any of the ratios, however some of the trends may become significant in the future. The profitability of the Airline division has improved and the ROCE has increased by over 2%. However, the ROCE of the Rail division has declined and this will surely cause anxiety within the management team.

As regards the Airline division, management need to review the current strategy to ensure that the company is able to cope with the competition and the problems faced by those companies within this volatile industry that is subject to international influences. The company should undertake a review of its cost structure and its selling prices as it is vital that these aspects are closely monitored in order to ensure that the Airline division does not become uncompetitive. The development of overseas business should be given serious consideration, as this is critical to the development of those organisations within the airline industry.

Whilst airline traffic in terms of passengers, passenger miles travelled and the number of routes flown have increased, it is possible that the management of the P Group should consider investing additional funds to ensure that these favourable trends continue. P Group should take steps to ensure that they benefit from the 3% projected growth in the long-distance economy market from which P attracts most of its customers.

In order to ensure that the customers are given good service it may be necessary to improve the ratio of cabin staff to passengers in both the economy class. P Group must take steps to ensure that the good reputation it has earned and which has become a source of competitive advantage is not lost, hence it is essential to ensure that service levels provided to passengers are maintained and preferably enhanced.

A review of all routes and alliances with other airlines should be undertaken in order to ensure that P Group is operating efficiently and effectively. It is possible that expanding into too many routes could cause fragmentation and this could be injurious to the overall success of organisation. P Group should ascertain the profitability attached to each route and try to focus upon the most profitable routes.

It is likely that price competition may become fierce as competitors attempt to take market share from P Group. It is necessary for the Airline division to protect its strength in the economy class markets where by the customers are very aware of prices charged by P Group and its competitors.

P Rail

A comparison of the two years shows that the profitability of the division is static and this makes it essential for management to review its strategic options.

Perhaps ways could be devised that may permit management to increase the level of fares currently being charged, decrease operating costs and reduce the level of capital employed. Of paramount importance is the need for management to successfully address the operating problems which have precipitated a loss of customer confidence. If such problems persist it is quite possible that these could have a seriously detrimental effect on every division of the P Group.

Punctuality is probably the most significant issue that needs to be addressed. The management of P Group should give consideration to the fact that the reduction in the number of attendants could be impacting adversely upon customers' perception of the service being offered.

Passenger traffic has decreased in terms of both the number of passengers and the passenger miles travelled and management should attempt to ascertain the reason for this as soon as possible. There has been a significant fall in the turnover to capital employed ratio and a solution to this problem will be required if the objectives of the organisation are to be met.

Unless P Group is able to improve the services it offers, it may not be able to take full advantage of the projected growth of the market over the next four years.

The Regulator poses another threat that the management of the P Group need to address. The loss of the franchise would be a major problem for the organisation. The results of the passenger survey were not good and thus it is vital that punctuality and the services provided improve quickly. The reduction in the number of attendants should be investigated as this could well be a partial cause of customer dissatisfaction.

The role of the Chairman

(c) The personality and charisma of the chairman is an important factor as regards the success of P Group. The activities of P Group are kept in the public eye via his dominant personality and activities, which generate 'personal publicity'. However, these personal attributes do not guarantee long-term company prosperity, since the organisation must satisfy the expectations of their customers if it is to be a successful business.

Other important strategic factors are:

- the development of a culture which enables employee to interact successfully and to contribute fully towards the overall organisational aims and objectives
- the association of the brand with high levels of customer value
- the importance that is attached to the creation and maintenance of a progressive corporate image
- the concern of the Chairman to be 'exciting' and the relaxed management style may increase and sustain the level of motivation of the employees of the organisation.

The Chairman dominates P Group and should consider the interests of all stakeholders. The shareholders, the participants in any management buy-out and any joint venture partners have expectations of returns on their investments. The Chairman, together with other members of the board of directors, need to ensure that these stakeholders are satisfied. The Chairman should also be aware that employees will identify with him and that he must help provide an environment wherein they can develop and realise their full potential thereby benefiting not only themselves but also P Group.

Whilst the customers will be aware of the public activities of the Chairman, management need to ensure that the quality of the products and services offered to the customers satisfy their expectations.

The fact that the Chairman deliberately keeps himself in the public spotlight raises his profile as Chairman of P Group. Each stakeholder group must remain convinced as to his ability to satisfy their expectations.

Environmental Management Accounting

(d) (i) EMA is likely to be highly important to P for the following reasons:

- Air travel is frequently criticised for its impact on global warming via exhaust emissions and its use of oil. Companies with poor green credentials will be criticised even more.

- Rail travel on the other hand is portrayed as a more environmentally-friendly alternative to people driving their cars to work. To reinforce (defend) this image it is vital that train operators are as environmentally friendly as possible.

EMA can play a crucial role in both of these areas.

(ii) The first aspect of EMA that would be of value to P is in helping them to define, identify and hopefully control environmental costs.

EMA breaks down environmental costs into four areas:

Conventional costs such as buying fuel. P will already be recording spending in these areas, but may not be thinking about the environmental impact of inefficiencies in their use.

Hidden costs – these costs will be captured within the management accounts but then tend to become lost in general overheads – this would include items such as other energy and water usage and waste disposal all of which have significant environmental impacts.

Contingent or future costs – these may include later management of environmental damage caused by accidents. More tricky would be identifying the knock-on impact of the release of greenhouse gasses on global warming, for example.

Image and relationship costs – P are becoming more aware of the importance to their clients and therefore to their brand of their environmental credentials. Improving the environmental impact of their entire operations will provide them with a valuable marketing tool.

The next benefit of EMA is in providing accounting techniques which will assist P in identifying the actual environmental costs they are incurring.

Activity based costing (ABC) could be used to allocate environmental costs to the main cost drivers of those costs, in this case plane and train journeys, although a cost per air (rail) mile or per passenger air (rail) mile is likely to be more useful. Targets could be set to reduce these going forwards. Some airlines give customers the opportunity to invest in offset schemes, such as planting trees to offset the greenhouse gasses released during their flight.

ANSWERS TO PRACTICE QUESTIONS – SECTION A : SECTION 3

Lifecycle costing involves considering the costs associated with a product over its entire lifecycle. This could be applied to aircraft and trains to take into account the environmental implications of construction, operation and decommissioning.

Total quality management approach would help P group to focus on the importance of improving every aspect of their business, and applied to environmental failure – as measured by the accounting techniques described above – it could produce significant gains in their environmental performance.

(*Note:* As P group is not a manufacturer, Input/output analysis is less likely to be useful.)

4 THE NAW GROUP (JUN 04 – AMENDED)

> **Key answer tips**
>
> This question asks for a number of different calculations – however it is important to give sufficient attention to the non-financial aspects of the issues as well.

REPORT

To: Board of Directors, P Group
From: A N Accountant
Date: Today
Subject: 2006 Product mix strategy

Introduction

This report starts by setting out the budget for Division O, the main factors that influence product mix and why NAW group uses both ROI and RI in divisional appraisal. It then examines the particular problems that arise from transfer pricing by looking at the recent quotations division O has been asked to prepare for Division L.

(a) (i) NAW Group:

Statement of Budgeted Profit for the year to 31 May 2005 – Division O

Product	Painfree Branded	Painfree Unbranded	Digestisalve Branded	Digestisalve Unbranded	Awaysafe Branded	Total
Sales-packs (000)	5,000	15,000	5,000	20,000	15,000	60,000
Selling price ($)	2.40	1.20	4.80	3.60	8.00	
	$000	$000	$000	$000	$000	$000
Sales revenue	12,000	18,000	24,000	72,000	120,000	246,000
Cost of sales:						
Material/conv costs	4,250	12,750	9,250	37,000	42,000	105,250
Packaging costs	750	750	1,250	3,000	6,000	11,750
Total variable costs	5,000	13,500	10,500	40,000	48,000	117,000
Contribution	7,000	4,500	13,500	32,000	72,000	129,000

KAPLAN PUBLISHING

Fixed costs:	
Fixed overheads	81,558
Advertising and promotion costs	17,400
Net profit	30,042
Net profit	30,042
Required return (10%)	12,000
Residual Income (RI)	18,042
Invested capital ($000)	120,000
Return on Investment (ROI)	25.04%

(ii) During the years ended 31 May 2005 and 2006, manufacturing capacity is restricted to 780,000,000 tablets. Since the tablets are only sold in one pack size that contains 12 tablets, enough tablets could be produced to satisfy a sales demand of up to 65,000,000 packs during each year. Forecast demand for the year ended 31 May 2005 is 60,000,000 packs. Division O has spare capacity equivalent to 5,000,000 packs of tablets. However, forecast sales demand for the year ended 31 May 2006 is 10% higher than that of the previous year (i.e. 60,000,000 × 110%) = 66,000,000 packs. Therefore demand is forecast to be in excess of available capacity by 1,000,000 packs, which is likely to prove costly to the NAW group not only in terms of contribution foregone but also in terms of potential loss of customer goodwill. It is clearly essential that management attention should be focused on the identification and removal of the limiting factor/(s) that would otherwise prevent Division O meeting forecast demand during the year ending 31 May 2006.

Management should also give consideration to qualitative factors that may be affected by the product-mix decision. For example, customers may be affected by the decision to manufacture one product as opposed to another. The management of the NAW Group need to consider the extent to which their customers will be affected by any decision which alters the availability of the finished product.

For example, a decision to increase the output of 'Awaysafe' and reduce the output of 'Painfree' could result in customers who previously purchased both branded and unbranded versions of 'Painfree' and/or 'Digestisalve' finding an alternative supplier who is able to supply a substitute product in both branded and unbranded (generic) variants.

Management will need to assess the market position of each product before making a decision regarding product-mix. This might involve a reduction in short-term profitability in order to gain in the longer-term.

Suppliers also require consideration since they will be affected by any changes to the product mix that necessitate different ingredients and revisions to delivery schedules. Further negotiations will almost inevitably be required.

Management should also consider the likely response of competitors as any decision to change a production specification, such as for example the introduction of a new tablet format, will affect competitors who will then consider their response.

It is quite conceivable that a change in production as a result of product-mix considerations might well result in a changed demand for individual resources, which in turn could impact upon resource availability.

(iii) The use of Residual Income helps to overcome many of the disadvantages of Return on Investment. In particular, it reduces the temptation on the part of management to reject projects with returns greater than the hurdle rate required by the group (10%), but acceptance of which would cause a lowering in the division's current level of return on investment (25.04%). Thus, any project that generates a positive residual income enhances corporate performance. Consequently the use of Residual Income is more consistent than ROI with the objective of maximisation of the total profitability of the NAW Group. Thus, RI could also be used as a basis for management incentive schemes. A further advantage of the RI approach lies in the fact that it is possible to apply different cost of capital percentage rates to investments that have different levels of risk. Also, the use of the RI approach serves to provide a focus on the cost of funds to divisional managers.

(b) (i) As regards Quotation 1 in respect of the year ending 31 May 2005, the manager of Division L would purchase from a local supplier in order to increase the profitability of his/or her division. An internal transfer price of $5.60 ($8.00 less 30%) would appear unattractive in comparison with a locally available price of $5.50. Since the NAW Group measures divisional performance via the use of ROCE and RI, it follows that the manager of Division L will consider the maximisation of profit (via lowering of purchase costs) to be of critical importance. The cost to the group will be $11,500,000. This is due to the fact that Division O could potentially have supplied these 5,000,000 units at a marginal cost of $3.20= $16,000,000, however an external supplier would be paid $27,500,000 for the required 5,000,000 packs of an equivalent product.

As regards Quotation 2 in respect of the year ending 31 May 2005, the manager of Division L would again purchase from a local supplier in order to increase the profitability of his/or her division. Division O could potentially have supplied these 9,000,000 units at a marginal cost of $3.20= $28,800,000 although sales of 4,000,000 packs of another product (unbranded 'Painfree' has the lowest contribution of $0.30 per pack) would need to be foregone, resulting in an additional cost to the group of $1,200,000.

Since an external supplier would be paid $49,500,000 for the required 9,000,000 packs of an equivalent product, the cost to the group would be $19,500,000 ($49,500,000 – $28,800,000 – $1,200,000).

(ii) In order for the profitability of the NAW group not to suffer during the year ended 31 May 2005, the following prices should be charged in respect of each quotation:

Quotation 1

5,000,000 packs should be offered for transfer at $3.20, which is the marginal cost of production. It is also the opportunity cost to Division O, since there is enough spare capacity within Division O to meet the quotation quantity. Thus the quoted price should be $16,000,000.

Quotation 2

Since 9,000,000 packs of 'Awaysafe' are required, then 5,000,000 of these can be satisfied by using the spare capacity that is available within Division O.

Since management of the NAW Group have decided that 15,000,000 packs of 'Awaysafe' must be available for purchase within the UK, then in order to meet the requirement of Quotation 2, management should forego sales of 4,000,000 packs of unbranded 'Painfree' which is the product with the lowest contribution. ($0.30 per unit). Thus the quoted price should be $30,000,000 which is comprised as follows:

	$
Variable costs of manufacturing 9,000,000 packs of 'Awaysafe' at $3.20 per pack	28,800,000
Contribution foregone on 4,000,000 packs of unbranded 'Painfree' at $0.30	1,200,000
Quoted Price	30,000,000

(iii) The 'ideal' transfer price should reflect the opportunity cost of sale to the supplying division and the opportunity cost of purchase to the buying division. Thus the general rule put forward is that the transfer price per unit should be the standard variable costs of the producing division plus the opportunity cost to the company as a whole of supplying the unit internally. The use of opportunity cost as a basis for transfer pricing would necessitate consideration of any alternative use that could be made of the capacity within the supplying division. The supplying division would be indifferent as whether its output was sold internally or externally. The purchasing division would choose on the basis of whether the external purchase price was lower than the internal transfer price and this would require that full information is available about the opportunity cost to the group of internal supply, in order to ensure that the correct purchase decision is made from a group perspective. A significant problem lies in the fact that full information about opportunity costs may not be easily obtainable in practice. A further consideration lies in the fact that the imposition of a transfer price may undermine divisional authority.

(c) (i) If Division L buys from a local supplier, the financial implications for the NAW Group are as follows:

		$
Division O sales:		
15,000,000 packs of 'Painfree' at Contribution of $0.30 per pack =		4,500,000
Taxation at 40% thereon		1,800,000
After tax benefit of sales		2,700,000
Division L purchases:		
9 million packs of 'Awaysafe' at Cost of $5.50 per pack		49,500,000
Taxation benefit at 20% thereon		9,900,000
After tax cost of purchases		39,600,000
Net cost to NAW Group	$2,700,000 less $39,600,000	36,900,000

If Division L buys internally from Division O the financial implications for the NAW Group are as follows:

		$
Division O sales:		
External:		
11 million packs of 'Painfree'	at Contribution of $0.30 per pack =	3,300,000
9 million packs of 'Awaysafe' to Division O	at Contribution of $2.40 per pack =	21,600,000
		24,900,000
Sales b/f		24,900,000
Taxation at 40% thereon		9,960,000
After tax benefit of sales		14,940,000
Division L purchases:		
9 million packs of 'Awaysafe'	at Cost of $5.60 per pack	50,400,000
Taxation benefit at 20% thereon		10,080,000
After tax cost of purchases		40,320,000
Net cost to NAW Group	$14,940,000 less $40,320,000	25,380,000

The NAW Group will be $36,900,000 – $25,380,000 = $11,520,000 better off if Division L purchases product 'Awaysafe' from Division O, as opposed to purchasing an equivalent product from a local supplier. Notwithstanding the fact that the wealth of the NAW Group is enhanced by the decision, there is also the fact that it makes good commercial sense to promote the 'Awaysafe' brand in the international arena.

(ii) When determining transfer prices the management of the NAW Group should consider the following issues:

Taxation – In a large number of multinational organisations the issues relating to taxation take precedence over other transfer pricing issues and significant amounts of management time are spent attempting to determine the transfer prices that will minimise tax paid on a global basis. Transfer prices should be set in a way that minimises the taxation payable by the organisation as a whole. Management should be cognisant of the fact that anti-avoidance legislation exists to prevent companies using transfer policies to divert profits to subsidiaries/divisions based abroad.

Import duties/tariffs – can prove problematic. Again, whilst it is desirable that transfer prices be kept as low as possible in order to minimise the payment of duty in countries that impose import tariffs based on the 'value' of incoming goods, it should be borne in mind that governments are mindful of such practices and may invoke similar policies to that of anti-avoidance legislation.

Currency fluctuations – can also prove problematic as they give rise to exchange risk.

Many international organisations attempt to reduce their exposure to exchange risk by paying early or late to 'profit' from the anticipated movements in exchange. Whilst the management of NAW Group should give careful consideration regarding which currencies to invoice in and which currencies to settle invoices etc, management should avoid the temptation to use transfer prices as a means of moving funds from a weaker currency into a stronger currency.

Repatriation of funds – must be considered when dealing with countries, which have a high inflation rate or stringent foreign exchange regulations. It is imperative that transfer prices are only set after giving due consideration to which countries and in what currencies cash balances should be maintained.

(d) The product life cycle depicts the movements of a product through the four phases of introduction, growth, maturity and finally decline. The returns that the management of NAW Group will expect from each of its product will be dependent on where that product is in its life cycle. By giving due consideration to the life cycle of the different products, the management of NAW Group will gain a better understanding of the likely demand for its products.

This will be a significant aid in the formulation and development of a marketing plan and provide the basis for the allocation of available resources such as the advertising and promotional budget which in the year ending 31 May 2005 is forecasted to amount to $17,400,000 (7% of total turnover). Hence various aspects relating to how a product is managed relate to management's perception of its current position in the life cycle. The use of the product life cycle would encourage the management of NAW Group to look beyond the current level of returns when deciding upon investment strategy. The use of the model would enable management to evaluate investment in products on a 'whole life basis'. Use of the model might not only enable management to assess whether revenues were likely to grow or not, but might also enable them to gauge the amount of future investment needed.

The specific implications of the product life cycle for the management of the NAW Group are dependent upon the stage within the product life cycle that a product is in, and the nature of the pricing decision being made.

In the pre-launch stage management will be concerned with the establishment of price objectives. This will necessitate the identification and analysis of the various influences upon price such as product specifications, supply forecast levels of demand and legal and environmental constraints.

In the introduction phase management will consider whether to employ skimming or penetration pricing policies depending on their desired objectives and their assessment of market characteristics. At this stage the management of the NAW Group should consider the trade discount structure that they wish to be employed and develop special offers to encourage the adoption of the new product.

In the growth phase management should use price as a means to combat competition and attempt to maximise the benefit to be derived from economies of scale whilst improving the perceptions of price and value of the product.

In the maturity phase management should use price in order to protect the market position of the product. Consideration should be given to identifying alternative distribution channels which may offer the opportunity to charge higher prices.

When a product reaches the decline phase management should use price in order to maximise potential profits, even if this involves a diminution in market share.

ANSWERS TO PRACTICE QUESTIONS – SECTION A : SECTION 3

Clearly, it is important that the performance measures used to assess each product take account of the stage that each respective product is at in its life cycle. Traditional performance measures such as profit and return on capital employed are most suited to products in the mature and decline stages where management focus is upon the use of scarce resources and the maximisation of cash flows. During the introduction and growth phases the factors that need to be controlled are those related to the product gaining market success since these will ultimately determine its future financial value.

The management of NAW Group will be unable to forecast the precise shape or duration of a product's life cycle from the model. Hence, whilst useful as a descriptive model the plc has no predictive value. Since the management of the NAW Group only have access to past sales data they would also find it difficult to locate the position of a product on the life cycle. For example, if sales revenues grew during each of the past four years it would still be impossible to discern whether the product was in the early, mid or late growth stages. Likewise a dip in sales may not signal entry into the decline stage but may be attributable to short term economic recession.

5 GREAT WESTERN CAKE COMPANY (JUN 06 – AMENDED)

Key answer tips

As always with the longer questions in exams at this level, this question draws on a wide range of syllabus topics, including some studied for underpinning papers. But it is structured in a manner such that imperfect understanding of one topic need not prevent the candidate from achieving a good mark overall. Answering requirement (a) involves the ability to undertake a detailed manipulation of the learning curve model. But, the answering of requirements (b) on project management and (c) on target costing are almost independent of the answer offered to (a). The key to part (d) is to look at the KPIs from the customer's perspective.

REPORT

To: Board of Directors, GWCC

From: A N Accountant

Date: Today

Subject: The Mighty Ben cake proposal

Introduction

This report examines the Mighty Ben cake proposal. Firstly it examines the likely return over 12 and 18 months. Secondly it considers how the return could be improved. Thirdly it examines the role of target costing in the context of the high customer power of Superstores plc and finally it looks at the KPIs that are likely to be most important for Superstores plc.

(a) **Project return**

		12 months	18 months
Sales units	(Working 1)	1,200,000	1,590,000
		$	$
Sales revenue	(Working 1)	18,000,000	23,850,000
Costs:			
Direct Materials	(Working 2)	7,686,000	10,020,150
Packaging	(Working 3)	916,000	1,216,500
Direct Labour	(Working 4)	4,140,155	5,179,115
Royalties	(Working 5)	900,000	1,100,000
Variable overheads	(Working 6)	1,449,054	1,812,690
Fixed overheads		900,000	1,350,000
Total costs		15,991,209	20,678,455
Profit		2,008,791	3,171,545
Less:			
Cost of investment		1,900,000	1,900,000
Projected return:		108,791	1,271,545
Average annual projected return		108,791	847,697
			(2/3)
Average annual rate of return		5.73%	44.62%
Required average annual rate of return:		35%	35%

The required average annual rate of return (35%) will be achieved over an eighteen month period (projected = 44.62%) but will not be achieved in the event that the product is withdrawn from the market after a period of twelve months (projected = 5.73%).

Workings:

(1) Sales units are 100,000 units per month for months 1–12 inclusive. Thereafter sales units fall by 10,000 each month.

Thus sales units in months 13–18 are as follows:

Month No.	Sales (units)	12 months	18 months
13	90,000		
14	80,000		
15	70,000		
16	60,000		
17	50,000		
18	40,000		
Total months (13–18)	390,000	1,200,000	1,590,000

Selling price per cake = $20.25 × (100/135)		$15	$15
Sales revenue =		$18,000,000	$23,850,000

(2) Direct materials:

Months	Batches	$
1–3	300 × 7,000	2,100,000
4–6	300 × 6,650	1,995,000
7–12	600 × 5,985	3,591,000
Cost for 12 months		7,686,000
13–18	390 × 5,985	2,334,150
Cost for 18 months		10,020,150

(3) Packaging costs:

Months 1–12

	$
Unit costs = $0.75 × 1,200,000 =	900,000
Design and artwork costs:	
$24,000 less refund of $8,000 =	16,000
	916,000

Months 1–18

	$
Unit costs = $0.75 × 1,590,000 =	1,192,500
Design and artwork costs =	24,000
	1,216,500

(4) Direct Labour:

For months (1–5 inclusive) $y = ax^b = 60,000 \times 500^{-0.415} = \$4,550.71$

Therefore the total cost = $4,550.71 × 500 = $2,275,355

All batches after the first 500 batches will have the labour cost of the 500th batch.

For 499 batches $y = ax^b = 60,000 \times 499^{-0.415} = \$4,554.49$

Therefore the total cost = $4,554.49 × 499 = $2,272,691

The cost of the 500th batch is $2,275,355 − $2,272,691 = $2,664

The total cost for 12 months is $2,275,355 + (700 × $2,664) = $4,140,155

The total cost for 18 months is $4,140,155 + (390 × $2,664) = $5,179,115

(5) Royalties

Months 1–12: 5% × $18,000,000 = $900,000

Months 1–18: 5% × $23,850,000 = $1,192,500 (subject to a max of $1.1m)

(6) Variable overheads amount to $3.50 per hour i.e. 35% of direct labour.

PAPER P5 : ADVANCED PERFORMANCE MANAGEMENT

(b) **Improving the expected return**

(i) The directors of GWCC might consider any of the following actions to improve the return on the investment:

- Attempt to raise the selling price of the Mighty Ben cake to Superstores plc. Much will depend on the nature of the relationship in terms of mutuality of trust and co-operation between the parties. If Superstores plc are insistent on a launch price of $20.25 and a mark-up of 35% on its purchase price from GWCC then this is likely to be unsuccessful.

- Attempt to reduce the material losses in the first 600 batches of production via improved process control.

- Attempt to negotiate a retrospective rebate based on volumes of packaging purchased.

- Improve the rate of learning of the hand-skilled cake decorators via a more intensive training programme and/or altering the flow of production.

- Undertake a thorough review of all variable overhead costs which have been absorbed on the basis of direct labour hours. It might well be the case that labour is not the only 'cost driver' in which case variable overheads might be overstated.

- Undertake a thorough review of all fixed overheads to ensure that they are specific to the production of the Mighty Ben cake.

- Adopt a 'value engineering' approach in order to identify 'non value added' features/aspects of the product or processes used to produce it. This would have to be done in conjunction with Superstores plc, but might end in a 'win-win' scenario.

- Ensure that all overhead expenditure will be incurred in the most 'economic' manner.

(ii) Two factors which might reduce the return earned by the investment are as follows:

Poor product quality

The very nature of the product requires that it is of the highest quality i.e. the cakes are made for human consumption. Bad publicity via a 'product recall' could potentially have a catastrophic effect on the total sales to Superstores plc over the eighteen month period.

The popularity of the Mighty Ben character

There is always the risk that the popularity of the character upon which the product is based will diminish with a resultant impact on sales volumes achieved. In this regard it would be advisable to attempt to negotiate with Superstores plc in order to minimise potential future losses.

(c) **The role of target costing**

Target costing should be viewed as an integral part of a strategic profit management system. The initial consideration in target costing is the determination of an estimate of the selling price for a new product which will enable a firm to capture its required share of the market. In this particular example, Superstores plc, which on the face of it looks a powerful commercial organisation, wishes to apply a 35% mark-up on the purchase price of each cake from GWCC.

Since Superstores plc has already decided on a launch price of $20.25 then it follows that the maximum selling price that can be charged by GWCC is (100/135) × $20.25 which is $15.00.

This is clearly a situation which lends itself to the application of target costing/pricing techniques as in essence GWCC can see the extent to which they fall short of the required level of return with regard to a contract with Superstores plc which ends after twelve months. Thus it is necessary to reduce the total costs by $556,029 to this figure in order to achieve the desired level of profit, having regard to the rate of return required on new capital investment. The deduction of required profit from the proposed selling price will produce a target price that must be met in order to ensure that the desired rate of return is obtained. Thus the main theme that underpins target costing can be seen to be 'what should a product cost in order to achieve the desired level of return'.

Target costing will necessitate comparison of current estimated cost levels against the target level which must be achieved if the desired levels of profitability, and hence return on investment, are to be achieved.

Thus where a gap exists between the current estimated cost levels and the target cost, it is essential that this gap be closed.

The Directors of GWCC plc should be aware of the fact that it is far easier to 'design out' cost during the pre-production phase than to 'control out' cost during the production phase. Thus cost reduction at this stage of a product's life cycle is of critical significance to business success.

A number of techniques may be employed in order to help in the achievement and maintenance of the desired level of target cost. Attention should be focussed upon the identification of value added and non-value added activities with the aim of the elimination of the latter. The product should be developed in an atmosphere of 'continuous improvement'. In this regard, total quality techniques such as the use of Quality circles may be used in attempting to find ways of achieving reductions in product cost.

Value engineering techniques can be used to evaluate necessary product features such as the quality of materials used.

It is essential that a collaborative approach is taken by the management of GWCC and that all interested parties such as suppliers and customers are closely involved in order to engineer product enhancements at reduced cost.

The degree of success that will be achieved by GWCC via the application of target costing principles will be very much dependent on the extent of 'flexibility' in variable costs. Also the accuracy of information gathered by GWCC will assume critical importance because the use of inaccurate information will produce calculated 'cost gaps' which are meaningless and render the application of target costing principles of little value.

(d) **KPIs of relevance to Superstores plc**

Two KPIs of relevance to Superstores plc are as follows:

- Number of stockouts – this is especially relevant given GWCC is expected to supply on a just in time basis, so any delivery or production issues could have a major impact on Superstores.

PAPER P5 : ADVANCED PERFORMANCE MANAGEMENT

- The number of rejects as part of a process of quality control – for example Superstore managers may wish to examine the quality of the hand finishing. Quality is important as Superstores may be concerned that GWCC may seek to save costs and quality may suffer as a result.

Note: There are a number of issues that would not qualify as relevant KPIS here:

- Superstores will have enough customer power to ensure that GWCC sticks to the agreed price so this will not be an issue.
- Superstores will be unconcerned with whether or not GWCC achieves its target cost

6 SNOWWELL (DEC 03 – AMENDED)

Key answer tips

This question uses a fictitious corporate failure prediction model to test your understanding of the principles behind techniques that might be used to attempt to forecast corporate failure, how to estimate free cash flow, and what actions should be taken, if any, as a result of information provided and calculated regarding a company's financial health. It also requires a discussion of the weaknesses of such methods and the other issues which need to be considering in assessing the likelihood of failure. Part (e) examines understanding of factors that might influence the expenditure of $100,000 on a report, including the possible effect of market efficiency on this decision, drawing on your understanding of financial management from previous studies.

REPORT

To: Board of Directors, Snowwell

From: A N Accountant

Date: Today

Subject: Corporate failure

Introduction

This report examines Snowwell and its risk of corporate failure. The report starts with a general discussion of corporate failure models, then calculates an S_0 score for Snowwell, followed by a discussion of the usefulness of such a score and possible alternative methods of analysis. Finally it considers what action should be taken by Snowwell, including whether or not to buy a full report from external consultants.

(a) **Corporate failure prediction models**

Some of the numerous models developed have been quantitative and some qualitative.

Quantitative models

Most quantitative models have been based on the analysis of key financial ratios, which have been weighted and combined to give an overall score. The best known example of this is the Z score.

The approach to quantifying likelihood varies between models. Some models have incorporated trend analysis, and some research has also attempted to take account of variations by industry. Other models have included a range of different variables, such as:

- Macroeconomic variables
- The quality of management of the company
- The growth phase of the firm
- The quality of the company's assets.

There are a number of limitations of the Z score and other similar quantitative failure prediction models:

- The score estimated is a snapshot – it gives an indication of the situation at a given point in time but does not determine whether the situation is improving or deteriorating. Further analysis is needed to fully understand the situation.
- Scores are only good predictors in the short-term
- Some scoring systems tend to rate companies low and are likely to classify distressed firms as actually failing.

Qualitative models

Other models have attempted to use qualitative information, by assigning scores to particular qualitative risk factors. Most qualitative methods are based on the use of scoring systems to weight factors which have been seen to be important in cases of corporate failure. Some models make extensive use of information technology and systems such as neural networks and expert systems which model human learning and decision-making processes.

Use is made of sets of rules based on the attributes of failing firms and systems have been developed which are capable of handling multiple criteria.

However these models also have limitations, as results from such systems are only as good as the information which is input to them, and this information and the decision rules are based on the subjective judgment of experts – the models are therefore not completely objective.

Both qualitative and quantitative models range in complexity. However research into their effectiveness has not shown that the more complicated models predict failure more accurately, and simple approaches like the Z score, which is based on applying different weightings to five ratios to arrive at a single score, remains in common use as a predictor.

Used in isolation, these models cannot give a completely reliable prediction and should only be seen as an indicator of whether further investigations should be undertaken to build up a complete picture of the company's state of health.

(b) **Current S_0 score**

The current S_0 score may be estimated as follows:

			Weighted score	See working:
S_1	$3.5 \times (43/348)$	=	0.432	W1
S_2	$1.8 \times (193 - 215)/436$	=	(0.091)	W2
S_3	$0.25 \times (348/267)$	=	0.326	W1, W3
S_4	$0.69 \times (336/620)$	=	0.374	W4
Total S_0 score			**1.041**	

Workings:

(W1) Total market value of equity

$2.32 × 150 million shares = $348 million.

(W2) Medium and long-term capital employed (assumed to be book values)

	$m
Shareholders' funds	192
14% loan stock	150
Floating rate bank loans	94
	436

(W3) Market value of debt

The market value of the loan stock is not given in the question. Given a current redemption yield of 8%, the market value of 14% loan stock with three years remaining to maturity and redemption is estimated to be:

Years		Cash flow $	Discount factor at 8%	Present value $
1–3	Interest	14	2.577	36.08
3	Redemption	100	0.794	79.40
				115.48

Tutorial note

The redemption yield is a gross yield, ignoring taxation.

Total market value of loan stock = $150 million nominal value × 1.1548 = $173.22 million.

Total market value of debt is therefore $173.22 million + $94 million = $267.22 million, say $267 million.

(W4) Present value to infinity of current operating free cash flow

Current operating free cash flow may be estimated as follows:

	$ million
Profit before tax	23
Add:	
Depreciation	38
After-tax cost of interest (20 × 0.70)	14
	75
Subtract:	
Tax	(7)
Increase in working capital ((22) – (24))	(2)
Replacement investment	(35)
Free cash flow	31

Note: Other definitions of free cash flow are possible, including adjustments for the change in loans and disposal of assets.

Weighted average cost of capital:

The pre-tax cost of debt is 8%, therefore the after-tax cost of debt is:

8 (1 – 0.30)% = 5.6%.

	Market value $m		Cost	$m
Equity	348	**(W1)**	12.0%	41.760
Debt	267	**(W3)**	5.6%	14.952
	615			56.712

WACC = (56.712/615) = 0.922 or 9.22%.

Present value to infinity of free cash flow: $31 million/0.0922 = $336 million.

(c) **Significance of the S_0 score**

The S_0 model suggests that a score of 1.04 is just above the level of probable failure, and at the low end of the remedial action range. However, this model is unlikely to be useful in predicting the probability of failure of Snowwell plc because:

- The model was produced in 20X1 and might not still be relevant in 20X3.
- Models predicting corporate failure are usually tailored to specific industries and specific size of companies. This general model might not be applicable to Snowwell.
- There is no evidence about the predictive ability of the model.
- Models which are based upon accounting ratios suffer the same weaknesses as the accounting systems on which they are based.
- No matter what such models predict, managers may be able to take remedial action that will prevent corporate failure.

(d) **Alternative assessment methods**

Other ways by which corporate financial distress or failure might be predicted include:

- Analysis of the company accounts to identify problems relating to key ratios such as liquidity, debt cover and profitability
- Other information in the published accounts, such as:
    - very large increases in intangible fixed assets
    - a worsening cash and cash equivalents position shown by the
    - cash flow statement
    - very large contingent liabilities
    - important post-balance sheet events
- Information in the chairman's report and the directors' report (including warnings, evasions, changes in the composition of the board since last year)
- Information in the press (about the industry, the company or its competitors)
- Information about environmental or external matters such as changes in the market for the company's products or services.

- Alternative models predicting failure such as those of Argenti, Marais and Beaver, or use of profit and logic analysis.
- Macro events affecting the company, including inflation and foreign exchange rates.
- Comment by company directors (e.g. profit warnings), analysts and newspapers.
- Audit reports – if accurate!
- Credit ratings produced by specialist agencies and banks.

(e) **Recommendations**

Snowwell is not recommended to take any action based solely upon the S_0 model. Any recommendation would be assisted by additional financial analysis, especially of growth trends and ratios.

Selected ratios and growth trends:

	% growth	
Sales revenue	6.9	
Non-current assets	6.3	
Inventory	22.8	
Payables	18.1	
Receivables	(5.9)	

	20X3	20X2
Current ratio	0.90	0.87
Quick ratio	0.17	0.20

Gearing (market value of medium- and long-term debt/ market value of equity) = 276/348 = 77%.

Interest cover = 43/20 = 2.15 times.

The current and quick ratios are low, but probably not unusually low for a retailer.

Gearing at 77% is significantly higher than the industry average and might be a cause for concern, and interest cover at 2.15 is quite low.

The immediate problem is that inventory has increased much more than sales revenue, leading to a similar increase in payables. Snowwell's managers should urgently review the company's inventory levels. Reducing inventory would release cash flow and might allow gearing to be reduced. Consideration might also be given to reducing the level of dividends paid, unless profits are expected to increase in 20X4.

(f) **Purchasing the full report**

The organisation providing the forecast is considered to be reputable and is likely to have tailored the forecast to Snowwell using analysis which has been specifically related to Snowwell's size and industry. If Snowwell could not easily replicate the analysis itself, and if the forecasting company has a good track record of predicting failure it might be worth purchasing the forecast. However, if the market in which Snowwell operates is considered to be efficient, then market analysts will already be aware of the publicly available information used in the model, and this should already have been incorporated in the share price of 232 pence. A price of this level does not suggest that investors feel that the company is likely to fail in the near future.

If the market is not considered to be efficient, and/or the forecasting technique is believed to be superior, and to convey significant new information, then Snowwell might have a reason to purchase. In such circumstances a purchase might be conditional upon the information not being released to any third parties, although if relevant information was then to be withheld by Snowwell's managers this might not be considered to be ethical, and acting in the best interests of all stakeholders.

7 WESTAMBER (PILOT 07) — *Walk in the footsteps of a top tutor*

(a) Westamber Hospital

Income statement for the year ended 30 June 2006

	Budget $000	Actual $000
Revenue:		
Private patients:		
Ear	5,256	3,066
Nose	7,008	3,504
Throat	11,680	5,110
	23,944	11,680
Government patients:		
Ear	3,504	6,132
Nose	5,256	7,884
Throat	9,344	12,264
	18,104	26,280
Total revenue	**42,048**	**37,960**
Variable costs:		
Surgery	7,080	8,284
Nursing	1,920	2,224
Sundry	920	1,116
Total variable costs	9,920	11624
Contribution	**32,128**	**26,336**
Fixed costs:		
Surgery	26,550	26,550
Nursing	5,600	5,600
Depreciation	1,700	1,700
Administration	3,250	3,412
Sundry	4,600	4,912
Total fixed costs	41,700	42,174
Net Loss	**(9,572)**	**(15,838)**

(b) (i) The hospitals have differing objectives. Eastgreen is a profit-seeking organisation whereas Westamber is, in part, a not-for-profit organisation.

(ii) The hospitals have different fee structures. Westamber undertakes the treatment of government-funded patients and receives a lower fee in respect of such operations.

(iii) The level of operating costs differs as evidenced by the fact that annual depreciation in Eastgreen is 100% greater than Westamber.

(iv) Eastgreen is partially funded by loan finance as evidenced by the $500,000 of loan interest charged to its profit and loss account during the year whereas Westamber hasn't any loan finance in its capital structure.

N.B: Other reasonable explanations would be acceptable.

(c) Adjustments:

	Westamber 2007 Budget $000	Westamber 2007 Actual $000	Eastgreen 2007 Actual $000
Original Profit /(Loss)	(9,572)	(15,838)	2,000
Attributable income – subsidised operations	5,840	8,760	
Cost of emergency operations	1,000	800	
Loan interest adjustment			500
Operating profit / (loss) after adjustments	(2,732)	(6,278)	2,500

Note:

Attributable income (budget) = (Number of government funded patients = (14,600 × 80%) = 11,680 × 50% = 5,840 × $1,000 = $5,840,000.

Attributable income (actual) = (Number of government funded patients = 14,600 × 80%) = 11,680 × 75% = 8,760 × $1,000 = $8,760,000.

(d) The statement of the recently qualified accountant is correct insofar as the fees received from private paying patients are higher than those received in respect of government funded patients. However, there is an ethical issue in that government funded patients require medical treatment and that fact should always be considered especially since Westamber is a government-funded hospital. The mission statement of the hospital states that it 'is committed to providing high quality healthcare to all patients' and therefore it should not give priority treatment to private fee-paying patients.

(e) The following performance measures could be used to assess the quality of service provided by the management of either hospital:

(i) The time spent waiting for non-emergency operations which could be measured by reference to the time elapsed from the date when an operation was deemed necessary until it was actually performed;

(ii) The number of successful operations as a percentage of total operations performed which could be measured by the number of remedial operations undertaken;

ANSWERS TO PRACTICE QUESTIONS – SECTION A : SECTION 3

(iii) The percentage of total operations performed in accordance with agreed schedules which could be measured by reference to agreed operation schedules;

(iv) The standards of cleanliness and hygiene maintained which could be measured by observation;

(v) The staff: patient ratio which could be measured by reference to personnel and patient records; and (vi) The responsiveness of staff to requests of patients which could be measured via a patient survey.

NB: Only four performance measures were required and alternative appropriate performance measures would be acceptable.

WESTAMBER — Guided walkthrough

The question gives fees charged but does not directly give you patient numbers.

We are told that each hospital has 15 wards, each accommodating 8 patients, with an average stay of 3 days. The hospital is open 365 days a year.

15*8*365 = 43,800 divide this by the 3 days that each patient stays for their operation equals 14,600. Now take 14,600 * 80% actual utilisation to get total number as 11,680.

Now split out the total patients 11,680 into the % split of operations and then again into the private and government patients.

Total operations	**Budget**	**Actual**	**Budget**	**Actual**
Ear	30%	35%	3,504	4,088
Nose	30%	30%	3,504	3,504
Throat	40%	35%	4,672	4,088
			11,680	11,680
Total Private patients	50%	25%		
Ear			1,752	1,022
Nose			1,752	876
Throat			2,336	1,022
			5,840	2,920
Total Govt patients	50%	75%		
Ear			1,752	3,066
Nose			1,752	2,628
Throat			2,336	3,066
			5,840	8,760

Then multiply the no. of patients as above by the fees charged by type of patient.

Total Revenue Private patients $000		**Budget**	**Actual**
Ear	Budget Fee $3,000	5,256	3,066
Nose	Budget Fee $4,000	7,008	3,504
Throat	Budget Fee $5,000	11,680	5,110
		23,944	11,680

PAPER P5 : ADVANCED PERFORMANCE MANAGEMENT

Total Revenue Govt patients $000

Ear	Budget Fee $2,000	3,504	6,132
Nose	Budget Fee $3,000	5,256	7,884
Throat	Budget Fee $4,000	9,344	12,264
		18,104	26,280
TOTAL REVENUE		**42,048**	**37,960**

Next we need to calculate the budgeted cost for comparison with the actual costs given.

COSTS

100% capacity	$000 Budget	% Variable	% Fixed	$000 Variable	$000 Fixed	$000 Fixed
Surgical	35,400	25%	75%	8,850	26,550	26,550
Nursing	8,000	30%	70%	2,400	5,600	5,600
Depreciation	1,700		100%	0	1,700	1,700
Admin	3,250		100%	0	3,250	3,412
Sundry	5,750	20%	80%	1,150	4,600	4,912
					41,700	42,174

80% capacity				$000 Variable @80%	$000 Variable	$000 Variable
Surgical				7,080	7,080	8,284
Nursing				1,920	1,920	2,224
Depreciation				0	0	0
Admin				0	0	0
Sundry				920	920	1,116
					9,920	11,624
TOTAL COST					**51,620**	**53,798**
NET (LOSS)				**(9,572)**	**(15,838)**	

8   THE GEELAND BUS COMPANY (GBC) (DEC 07)

Walk in the footsteps of a top tutor

Key answer tips

The question tests your ability to produce a report with an appendix showing detailed workings of how each of the six figures marked with an asterisk have been calculated. Within the report you are requested to explain why it is difficult to compare the two organisations and to recommend information that would aid comparison. This could be answered first but must relate to the information within the scenario. The final part of the question requires thought and application to the scenario.

ANSWERS TO PRACTICE QUESTIONS – SECTION A : SECTION 3

ANSWER 1 – OFFICIAL ACCA EXAMINER'S SOLUTION

(a) **Operating performance**

Bus occupancy is the critical operating statistic in assessing the operating performance of GBC and TTC since it is the number of fare-paying passengers which drives the revenue generation of each organisation. Indeed, passenger fares constitute the only source of income of each of the respective organisations.

Actual and budgeted levels of total bus occupancy (fare-paying and non fare-paying passengers) achieved/to be achieved were as follows:

	GBC			TTC		
Year	2006	2007	2007	2006	2007	2007
% occupancy	(W2)	(actual)	(budget)		(actual)	(budget)
Route						
Eastern	65	60	60	60	80	75
Southern	80	75	60	60	80	75
Western	32.5	30	60	–	–	–
Hopper	65	60	60	60	80	75

However, GBC provides free transport for passengers on its Eastern, Western and Hopper routes and the % occupancy of fare-paying passengers only is as follows:

Year	2006	2007
	% occupancy	% occupancy
Route		
Eastern	55	50
Southern	80	75
Western	25	22.5
Hopper	55	50

Hence it can be seen that GBC's bus actual occupancy has fallen from the levels achieved during the previous year. On the other hand, TTC has achieved average increases of 20% with regard to all three routes it operated and also exceeded a more demanding budget of 75% average bus occupancy with regard to each route.

It is quite conceivable that TTC has gained business at the expense of GBC by virtue of the fact that it provides a higher quality of service for which customers are willing to pay the average 20% premium charged by TTC. The fact that TTC operates fewer vehicles than GBC together with its higher depreciation charge in respect of vehicles suggests that the fleet of buses operated by TTC is newer than that of GBC.

It is interesting to note that, on average each GBC bus was in operation for 320 days whereas each TTC bus was in operation for 340 days. This might well be indicative of the fact that the fleet of buses operated by GBC is much older than that of TTC, a fact seemingly supported by the much higher repairs and maintenance costs incurred by GBC.

PAPER P5 : ADVANCED PERFORMANCE MANAGEMENT

Financial performance

	2006 GBC Actual	2007 GBC Actual	2007 GBC Budget	2006 TTC Actual	2007 TTC Actual	2007 TTC Budget
Turnover($)	5,670,400	5,222,400	5,683,200	4,308,480	5,744,640	5,385,600
Net profit ($)	1,513,800	816,720	1,453,200	870,100	2,199,840	1,823,600
Assets (nbv) ($)	700,000	630,000	630,000	2,500,000	2,250,000	2,250,000
Profit/Assets (%)	216.3	129.64	230.7	34.8	97.8	81.0
Profit/Sales (%)	26.7	15.64	25.6	20.2	38.3	33.9

GBC had a much poorer year in 2007 than it had anticipated. It made a profit of $816,720 which is a reduction of $697,080 (46%) from that of the previous year. During the previous year GBC had made a profit of $1,513,800. GBC had budgeted for a fall in profit of $60,600 ($1,513,800 – $1,453,200) but such a large deviation from plan would certainly alarm its stakeholders. By contrast, TTC has had an excellent year in 2007 achieving a net profit amounting to $2,199,840 which is more than 2.5 times the level of profit achieved in 2006 ($870,100). TTC also exceeded its budgeted profit by $376,240 (20.6%).

Revenues from fares within GBC during 2007 have fallen by $448,000 (7.9%) from the previous year, whereas revenue from fares within TTC during 2007 have increased by $1,436,160 (33.33%) over the previous year's level.

Variable costs per mile are 10 cents per bus mile higher in GBC than they are in TTC. The fact that GBC has opted to use environmentally friendly fuel in its vehicles is evidence of its concern for society. The use of environmentally friendly fuel caused increases in average variable costs amounting to $126,080 (1,260,800 × ($2.10 – $2)) during 2007.

Fixed costs during 2006 within GBC were above budget with salaries, repairs and maintenance, and other operating expenses exceeding budgeted levels by $25,000, $40,000 and $13,000 respectively and were $50,000, $60,000 and $13,000 above the levels incurred during 2006. By contrast, TTC salaries were as per budget whilst repairs and maintenance and other operating expenses were $2,000 and $20,000 below budgeted levels. Salaries increased by $10,000 whilst other operating costs by $20,000 over the previous year's levels. Repairs and maintenance costs remained at $40,000, the same level as incurred during 2006.

Workings:

(W1) Calculation of figures marked with an asterisk(*):

	Buses per route	Journeys per Route	Days in operation	Fare-paying passenger	Fare per passenger ($)	$
GBC East revenue (06)	6	2	320	44	10	= 1,689,600
GBC South revenue (07)	6	2	320	60	10	= 2,304,000
TTC South revenue (07)	4	2	340	64	12	= 2,088,960
TTC Hopper budgeted revenue (07)	2	1	340	60	36	= 1,468,800

	Buses / route	Days	Km	Journeys	Cost ($)	
GBC Eastern variable costs (07)	6	320	100	2	2.1	= 806,400
TTC Southern variable costs (07)	4	340	120	2	2	= 652,800

ANSWERS TO PRACTICE QUESTIONS – SECTION A : SECTION 3

(W2) **GBC – Level of total occupancy:**

Route	No. of fare-paying passengers	No. of non fare-paying passengers	Total	Occupancy %
Eastern	44	8	52	65
Southern	64	0	64	80
Western	20	6	26	32.5
Hopper	44	8	52	65

(b) The relative performance of GBC and TTC is difficult to assess due to the following:

(i) They would appear to have differing objectives. GBC provides free transport for senior citizens and charges lower fares than TTC. GBC also uses environmentally friendly fuel. Each of these factors inhibits a direct comparison of the two organisations.

(ii) The organisations are funded differently. It is evident that TTC uses loan finance to fund operations which gives rise to interest charges which are not incurred by GBC. On the other hand GBC is funded by the government.

(iii) TTC has higher fixed asset values which precipitate much higher depreciation charges.

(iv) There is also a lack of non-financial performance indicators such as the number of on-time arrivals, number of accidents, complaints re passenger dissatisfaction, staff turnover, adherence to relevant legislation, convenience of pick-up/drop-off points etc.

The following items of additional information would assist in assessing the financial and operating performance of the two companies:

(1) The number of staff employed by each organisation would assist in the assessment of the financial and operating performance. Ratios such as revenue generated per employee and operating costs per employee might provide useful comparators of financial and operating efficiency.

(2) Safety and accident records of each organisation would give an indication of the reliability and safety afforded to passengers by each organisation. Passenger safety is of paramount importance to all passenger transport businesses.

(3) Records of late/cancelled buses together with the number of complaints received from the passengers would provide an indication of the efficiency of the service provided by each organisation.

(4) The accessibility of the services, location of pick-up/drop-off points would provide an indication of the flexibility of service delivery provided by each organisation.

(5) The comfort, cleanliness and age of the respective bus fleets would provide a further indication of the level of service quality provided by each organisation.

(6) The fuel emission levels of the buses operated by each organisation would provide an indication of the extent of their 'social responsibility'.

Notes:

(i) Only three items of additional information were required.

(ii) Alternative relevant discussion and examples would be acceptable.

(c) It would appear that in operating a bus service to the Western region of Geeland that GBC is fulfilling a social objective since a contribution loss amounting to $38,400 ($230,400 – $268,800) was made as a consequence of operating the route to the Western region during 2007. As an organisation which is partially funded by the government it is highly probable that GBC has objectives which differ from those of TTC which is a profit-seeking organisation.

The value of a social service such as the provision of public transport can be quantified, albeit, in non-financial times. It is possible to apply quantitative measures to the bus service itself, the most obvious ones being the number of passengers carried and the number of passenger miles travelled.

The cost of the provision of alternative transport to the Western region might also enable a value to be placed on the current service by GBC.

It might be possible to estimate quantitatively some of the social benefits resulting from the provision of the transport facility to and from the Western region. For example, GBC could undertake a survey of the population of the Western region in order to help estimate the extent to which rural depopulation would otherwise have occurred had the transport facility not been made.

The application of the technique of cost-benefit analysis makes it possible to estimate money values for non-monetary benefits. Social benefits can therefore be expressed in financial terms. It is highly probable that the fact that the Western region is served by GBC will increase the attractiveness of living in a rural area, which may in turn precipitate an increase in property values in the Western region and the financial benefit could be expressed in terms of the aggregate increase in property values in the region as a whole.

	Marking scheme		
			Marks
(a)	Operating performance	– calculations	3
		– comments	6
	Financial performance	– calculations	11
		– comments	6
	Professional marks		4
			23
(b)	Comments (on merit):		
	Problems 3 × 1		3
	Items of information 3 × 1		3
			6
(c)	Comments (on merit):		
	Reasons		4
	Value		4
			6
Total			35

ANSWERS TO PRACTICE QUESTIONS – SECTION A : **SECTION 3**

> **Examiner's comments**
>
> A large number of candidates produced good answers to each part of question 1 and consequently achieving a high mark. However, it was noticeable that there were significant variations in the quality of candidates' answers to this question. Most candidates managed to score well in part (a), although a number of candidates ignored the requirement to include an appendix to the report showing detailed workings of how each of the six figures marked with an asterisk in note 1 had been calculated. Indeed, many candidates simply reproduced the performance data provided in note (1) of the question.
>
> In general, answers to part (b) were good although a number of candidates provided poor examples of additional information that would be of assistance in assessing the financial and operating performance of GBC and TTC.
>
> The quality of answers to part (c) varied significantly. A large number of candidates achieved very high marks. However, it was disappointing to observe the significant number of candidates who made no attempt whatsoever to provide an answer to part (c) which potentially was worth six marks. It was noticeable that virtually all candidates who attempted this part of the question received some credit.

ANSWER 2 – *Walk in the footsteps of a top tutor*

With a large scenario question like this one you need to read the requirements and scenario very carefully. It is very easy to miss very important information and to get tied down with the lengthy calculations.

> *Start with the easy marks first – part (b).*

Part (b) may be answered without completing the calculations in part (a). It asks for three problems with undertaking a performance comparison of the two companies and for three items of additional information that would assist the comparison.

Start by looking at the way in which the organisations are operated and how they are financed.

For example some key differences between the two bus companies are:

- *GBC is partly government funded, whilst TTC is privately owned.*
- *TTC has loan interest to pay, GBC does not.*
- *GBC covers all four regions, whilst TTC covers three.*
- *GBC gives free transport to senior citizens.*
- *GBC uses environmentally friendly fuel.*
- *TTC buses are luxuriously fitted.*
- *GBC has much lower value assets with lower depreciation.*
- *GBC operates for 320 days whilst TTC operates for 340.*

(These few points may indicate older buses, needing more maintenance.)

KAPLAN PUBLISHING

PAPER P5 : ADVANCED PERFORMANCE MANAGEMENT

Examples of some additional information that may help comparison:

- *How much is the funding from the government for GBC.*
- *What is the funding for? Does the government provide the funding as GBC gives free transport to senior citizens? Or perhaps it is because they use low emission fuel?*
- *How many people are employed by each organisation with % cost and revenue generated per employee?*
- *The age of the buses and how well they are maintained and cleaned.*
- *The accessibility of the buses, pick up and drop off points. Especially for GBC in the western area.*

> *Now for the tough bit – part (a).*

Part (a) requires a report on the operating and financial performance of GBC and TTC and an explanation of how 6 highlighted figures have been calculated.

In order to work out the revenue figures we need to know how the revenue is generated. Start with the number of buses that are in use and how many journeys they make and for how many days in a year. Multiply this figure by the number of fee paying passengers.

To calculate variable cost, take the number of buses that are in use and how many journeys they make and for how many days in a year. Multiply this figure by the number of miles and variable cost per mile.

The next part of the question is split between financial and operational performance.

To calculate percentage movements take the movement from one year to the next (change) and divide by the starting position figure.

To analyse the financial performance is easier as the figures are all readily available.

For example:

GBC revenue has changed from 2006 to 2007 by 448,000 fall divided by the starting revenue in 2006 of 5,670,400. This gives a 7.9 % fall.

	GBC			TTC		
	Actual 2006	Actual 2007	Budget	Actual 2006	Actual 2007	Budget
Revenue	5,670,400	5,222,400	5,683,200	4,308,480	5,744,640	5,385,600
Variable cost	2,521,600	2,647,680	2,550,000	1,528,380	1,604,800	1,600,000
Net profit	1,513,800	816,720	1,453,200	870,100	2,199,840	1,823,600
Asset	700,000	670,000	670,000	2,500,000	2,250,000	2,250,000
% Δ in revenue		–7.9%			33.3%	
% Δ between 07 actual revenue to budget		–8.1%			6.7%	
% Δ in profit		–46%			153%	
% Δ 07 actual profit to budget		–44%			21%	
VC / sales	44%	51%	45%	35%	28%	30%
Profit / sales %	27%	16%	26%	20%	38%	34%
Profit / assets %	216%	122%	217%	35%	98%	81%

ANSWERS TO PRACTICE QUESTIONS – SECTION A : SECTION 3

Overall GBC profit has fallen by 46%, whilst TTC has increased by 153%. This is due to a fall in revenue for GBC, partly due to lower passenger numbers and non fee paying passengers. GBC also has and a large increase in variable costs due to the environmentally friendly fuel and repairs and maintenance increasing Neither of which had been budgeted to increase at the actual rate.

> **Tutorial note**
>
> Other calculations may be used to assess performance.

The operational performance requires a lot more thought. The most important figures are the actual utilisation of the buses compared to what was budgeted. It is also important to identify the number of non fee paying passengers.

> **Tutorial note**
>
> Start with working out the levels of utilisation from the information given.

For example there are 80 seats available on each bus. How many seats are taken by fee paying passengers and then work out how many are non fee paying . Remember only GBC has non fee paying passengers.

We are given the actual utilisation for GBC and TTC for 2007, from this we can work out how many passengers were on the bus as each one holds 80 (number of seats taken up). This will include non fare paying passengers for GBC, so they need to identified. The question states that the number of non fee paying passengers have stayed the same. Therefore we are able to work out the number for 2007 and use it also for 2006.

GBC	Fee paying utilisation 2006	Actual utilisation 2006	Budget utilisation 2007	Fee paying utilisation 2007	Actual utilisation 2007
	Fare paying passengers 06 divided by 80 seats *100	Total number of passengers divided by 80 seats * 100	(given)	Fare paying passengers 07 divided by 80 seats *100	(given)
East	55%	65%	60%	50%	60%
South	80%	80%	60%	75%	75%
West	25%	32.5%	60%	23%	30%
Hopper	55%	65%	60%	50%	60%

PAPER P5 : ADVANCED PERFORMANCE MANAGEMENT

GBC	Fare paying passengers 2006	Number of seats taken up 2006	Number of seats taken up 2007	Budget passengers 2007
		Actual utilisation% * 80 seats plus non fare paying same as 2007	Actual utilisation% * 80 available seats	60% * 80 seats
East	44	52	48	48
South	64	64	60	48
West	20	26	24	48
Hopper	44	52	48	48

GBC	Fare paying passengers 06	Fare paying passengers 07	Number of non fare passengers 06	Number of non fare paying passengers 07	Total 06 Passengers
			Question states Same as for 2007	Number of seats taken 2007 less fare paying passengers 2007	Fee payers plus non fee
East	44	40	8	8	52
South	64	60	0	0	64
West	20	18	6	6	26
Hopper	44	40	8	8	52

Overall summary of levels of occupancy

	Passengers 2006	Occupancy %	Passengers 2007	Occupancy %	Change	Budget 2007
TTC						
East	48	60%	64	80%	20%	75%
South	48	60%	64	80%	20%	75%
Hopper	48	60%	64	80%	20%	75%
GBC						
East	52	65%	48	60%	-5%	60%
South	64	80%	60	75%	-5%	60%
West	26	32.5%	24	30%	-3%	60%
Hopper	52	65%	48	60%	-5%	60%

Occupancy of fee paying passengers GBC

East	44	55%	40	50%	-5%	
South	64	80%	60	75%	-5%	
West	20	25%	18	23%	-3%	
Hopper	44	55%	40	50%	-5%	

ANSWERS TO PRACTICE QUESTIONS – SECTION A : **SECTION 3**

GBC's occupancy has fallen from the levels achieved last year, whilst TTC has achieved an increase of 20% for all three areas and therefore exceeded budget of 75%. TTC may have gained some business from GBC due to the better quality buses which customers are happy to pay more for.

And finally – part (c).

The bus route in western region is providing a valuable service to the rural areas. The revenue generated is less than the cost of running the service. However, we do not know what the government funding is for.

The rural population may be dependent upon the western route as approximately 30% of the bus is in use, with about 23% in 2007 as fee paying passengers. This shows that about 7% of the occupancy is senior citizens, who may have no other form of transport.

It may be possible to assess how GBC has improved the population of the western region rather than leading to depopulation, and how it may have increased the attractiveness of living in such an area.

9 ALPHA DIVISION (DEC 07)

Key answer tips

Candidates are required to calculate residual income and comment on their findings and the relevance of three particular performance measures given in the question. Be clear and not too superficial in your answer. Finally candidates are required to calculate EVA, stating any assumptions made and three disadvantages of EVA as a measure. The final part of the question requires thought and application to the scenario and does not ask for advantages.

(a) (i)

	Year 1 $m	Year 2 $m	Year 3 $m
Net cash inflow	12.5	18.5	27.0
Less: Depreciation	15.0	15.0	15.0
Profit/(loss)	(2.5)	3.5	12.0
Less: cost of capital (at 10% of wdv)	(4.5)	(3.0)	(1.5)
RI	(7.0)	0.5	10.5

A positive NPV of $1.937m indicates that the performance is acceptable over the three-year life of the proposal.

The RI shows a negative value of $7m in year 1. This is likely to lead to its rejection by the management of Alpha Division because they participate in a bonus scheme that is based on short-term performance evaluation.

The short-term focus on performance evaluation might lead to the rejection of investment opportunities such as the one under consideration which would be detrimental to the Delta Group. Management of the Delta Group should give immediate consideration to changing the focus of the bonus scheme.

(ii) Measures of divisional profitability may be viewed as evaluating managerial performance and/or economic performance of the division. Management are likely to take the view that any contribution value used as a measure of their performance should only contain revenue or cost elements over which they have control. If each of the measures 1 to 3 shown in the question are considered the following analysis may be made:

1 **Variable short run contribution margin:**

This measure may be viewed as unacceptable to divisional management where it contains inter-divisional transfers.

In this case this should not be a problem since the use of adjusted market price is in effect equivalent to external selling price after the deduction of cost elements (e.g. special packaging) that are not appropriate to inter-divisional transfers.

2 **Controllable profit:**

This measure will be calculated by deducting controllable fixed costs from the variable short-run contribution. These costs may include labour costs and/or equipment rental costs that are fixed in the short term but are subject to some influence by divisional management. For example, divisional management action may enable efficiency gains to be achieved in order to reduce the level of fixed labour or equipment rental costs that are incurred. In addition, it will be relevant to determine whether divisional management is free to source such items as they wish or if there is some direction for them to use, for example, a Delta Group Service Division for equipment rental requirements.

The inclusion of depreciation of fixed assets as a charge in evaluating controllable contribution may be debated depending on the extent to which divisional management has control over investment decisions.

3 **Divisional profit:**

Depending on the extent to which investment decisions relating to Alpha Division are ultimately authorised at Delta Group level, depreciation may be viewed as a non-controllable cost, chargeable in arriving at the divisional profit and hence as part of divisional economic performance measurement.

Other non-controllable costs attributed to the division may be a share of Group finance and legal staff costs for services provided to the division. Such costs are non-controllable by divisional management and may be viewed as avoidable only if the division was closed.

The divisional profit figure is useful in evaluating the economic performance of the division in that it represents the contribution made by Alpha Division towards the overall profitability of the Delta Group.

ANSWERS TO PRACTICE QUESTIONS – SECTION A : SECTION 3

(b) (i) In order to compute EVA, adjustments must be made to the conventional after tax profit measures of $67m and $82m shown in the summary income statements. Since we know that financial accounting depreciation is equal to economic depreciation then no adjustment is required to take into account the fact that economic depreciation differs from financial accounting depreciation. In calculating EVA the calculation of adjusted profit represents an attempt to approximate cash flow after taking into account a charge in respect of economic depreciation. Hence non-cash expenses are added back to the profit reported in the income statement. Net interest is also added back to the reported profit because the returns required by the providers of funds are reflected in the cost of capital adjustment. It is the net interest i.e. interest after tax that is added back to reported profit because interest will already have been allowed as an expense in the computation of the taxation liability.

In computing EVA, the calculation of capital employed should be based on adjustments which seek to approximate economic value at the commencement of each period.

Due to the lack of sufficient information the book value of shareholders' funds plus long-term capital loans at the end of 2005 is used as a basis for the determination of economic capital employed at the commencement of 2006.

Goodwill is a measure of the price paid for a business in excess of the current cost of the net separable assets of the business. Payments in respect of goodwill may be viewed as adding value to the company. Therefore any amounts in respect of goodwill amortisation appearing in the income statement are added back to reported profit since they represent part of the intangible asset value of the business.

By the same token, the cumulative write off of $45 million is added back to capital employed in order to show a more realistic value of the capital base realistic value of the capital employed. This is because goodwill represents an element of the total value of a business. The value placed on goodwill should be regularly reviewed and any diminution in its value should be recognised immediately in the income statement.

The calculation of EVA in respect of the two years under consideration is as follows:

	2006 $m	2007 $m
Adjusted profit:		
Profit after tax	67	82
Amortisation of goodwill	5	5
Other non-cash expenses	12	12
Interest expense	4.2	4.2
Adjusted profit	88.2	103.2

KAPLAN PUBLISHING

	$m	$m
Adjusted capital employed:		
Year beginning	279	340
Non-capitalised leases	16	16
Goodwill	45	50
Adjusted capital employed	340	406

The weighted average cost of capital should be based on the target capital structure of 50% Debt: 50% Equity.

The calculations are as follows:

WACC 2006: (16% × 50%) + (10% × 0.7 × 50%) = 11.5%

WACC 2007: (18% × 50%) + (10% × 0.7 × 50%) = 12.5%

Therefore EVA in respect of both years can be calculated as follows:

EVA 2006 = 88.2 – (340 × 11.5%) = $49.1 million

EVA 2007 = 103.2 – (406 × 12.5%) = $52.45 million

The EVA measures indicate that the Gamma Group has added significant value during each year under consideration and thereby achieved a satisfactory level of performance.

(ii) Disadvantages of an EVA approach to the measurement of financial performance include:

- The calculation of EVA may be complicated due to the number of adjustments required.
- It is difficult to use EVA for inter-firm and inter-divisional comparisons because it is not a ratio measure.
- Economic depreciation is difficult to estimate and conflicts with generally accepted accounting principles.

Tutorial note

Other relevant discussion would be acceptable.

ANSWERS TO PRACTICE QUESTIONS – SECTION A : **SECTION 3**

Marking scheme

			Marks
(a)	(i)	Calculation of RI	3
		Comments (on merit)	3
	(ii)	For each of measures 1 to 3 including reference to managerial/economic performance and to illustrative items given in the question 3 × 3	8
			14
(b)	(i)	Adjusted profit after tax	3
		Adjusted capital employed	3
		WACC	1
		EVA	1
		Comment	1
	(ii)	Disadvantages of EVA 3 × 1	3
			11
Total			25

Examiner's comments

It was noticeable that a large number of candidates did not attempt all parts of this question. Answers to part (a) (i) were either very good or very poor. Answers to part (a) (ii) were often too superficial.

A number of candidates provided a correct solution to part (b) (i) and therefore achieved maximum marks. It was (again) very disappointing to observe the significant number of candidates who made no attempt whatsoever to provide an answer to this part of the question which potentially was worth eight marks.

Also frustrating was the significant number of candidates who provided 'advantages' of using EVA^{TM} in the measurement of financial performance when Part (b) (ii) required a brief discussion of 'disadvantages'.

10 THE HEALTH AND FITNESS GROUP (HFG) (JUN 08)

Key answer tips

In answering this questions you must be able to calculate and a comment on ROI/RI and economic value added (EVA). Candidates are required to calculate the sensitivity analysis, and give key arguments of writers such as Fitzgerald and Moon and application of these to the scenario In part (b) candidates must identify problems that the directors of HFG might experience in their wish to benchmark the performance of HFC with SFC and suggest appropriate recommendations as to how those problems might be successfully addressed.

(a) (i) **To: The Directors**

From: Management Accountant

Subject: The performance of our three health centres

Date: 6 June 2008

Further to your recent request please find below my detailed responses to the questions you have raised.

A Summary of the financial performance of the three centres is shown in the following table:

Heath centre	Return on investment (%)	Residual income ($000)	Economic value added ($000)
Ayetown	23.02	180.00	42.08
Beetown	13.96	33.00	–123.27
Ceetown	18.40	187.00	–30.09

Which of the three centres is the most successful?

This very much depends on the method used to assess the performance of the three health centres. As requested, I have undertaken calculations based on three performance measures namely, return on investment (ROI), residual income (RI) and economic value added (EVA). I have included the workings for each respective calculation in an appendix to this report.

Using ROI as a measure of financial performance indicates that Ayetown is the most successful of the three centres since its ROI was 23.02% compared with the 18.40% achieved by Ceetown and the 13.96% achieved by Beetown. However, you should bear in mind that the use of ROI can be grossly misleading since it is a relative measure and ignores absolute returns. In this respect I wish to draw your attention to the fact that Beetown earned $45,000 (11.4%) more operating profit than Ayetown and Ceetown earned $397,000 (77.5%) more profit than Ayetown.

The use of RI as a measure of financial performance indicates that Ceetown is the best performing centre, generating $187,000 of residual income. It is worth observing that Ayetown was not far behind Ceetown in terms of generating residual income of $180,000. However, Beetown only managed to generate $33,000 of residual income.

EVA™ is a specific type of residual income calculation which has attracted a considerable amount of attention during recent years. Economic Value Added equals after-tax operating profit minus the (after-tax) weighted average cost of capital multiplied by total assets minus current liabilities. EVA™ substitutes the following numbers in residual income calculations:

(a) Income is equal to after-tax profits;

(b) A required rate of return is equal to the after-tax weighted average cost of capital; and

(c) Investment is equal to total assets minus current liabilities.

Ayetown has the highest EVA. Indeed, it is the only centre which has a positive EVA. In common with RI, EVA charges managers for the cost of making investments in long-term assets and working capital. Value will only be created in circumstances where post-tax operating profit exceeds the cost of investing the required capital. In order to improve EVA, managers need to earn more operating profit using the same amount of capital, or invest capital in higher-earning projects. The use of EVA is often preferred to RI because it takes into account tax effects of investment decisions whereas pre-tax residual income measures do not.

(ii) The ROI of Beetown is currently 13.96%. In order to obtain an ROI of 20%, operating profit would need to increase to (20% × $3,160,000) = $632,000, based on the current level of net assets. Three alternative ways in which a target ROI of 20% could be achieved for the Beetown centre are as follows:

(1) Attempts could be made to increase revenue by attracting more clients while keeping invested capital and operating profit per $ of revenue constant. Revenue would have to increase to $2,361,644, assuming that the current level of profitability is maintained and fixed costs remain unchanged. The current rate of contribution to revenue is $2,100,000 − $567,000 = $1,533,000/$2,100,000 = 73%. Operating profit needs to increase by $191,000 in order to achieve an ROI of 20%. Therefore, revenue needs to increase by $191,000/0.73 = $261,644 = 12.46%.

Or alternatively 632,000 less current level of 441,000 = a 191,000 increase.

Contribution is uncertain therefore 191,000 / 1,533,000 *100 = 12.46%

(2) Attempts could be made to decrease the level of operating costs by, for example, increasing the efficiency of maintenance operations. This would have the effect of increasing operating profit per $ of revenue. This would require that revenue and invested capital were kept constant. Total operating costs would need to fall by $191,000 in order to obtain an ROI of 20%. This represents a percentage decrease of 191,000/1,659,000 = 11.5%. If fixed costs were truly fixed, then variable costs would need to fall to a level of $376,000, which represents a decrease of 33.7%.

Or alternatively variable costs are uncertain therefore 191,000 / 567,000 *100 = 33.7%

(3) Attempts could be made to decrease the net asset base of HFG by, for example, reducing debtor balances and/or increasing creditor balances, while keeping turnover and operating profit per $ of revenue constant. Net assets would need to fall to a level of ($441,000/0.2) = $2,205,000, which represents a percentage decrease amounting to $3,160,000 − $2,205,000 = 955,000/3,160,000 = 30.2%.

Or alternatively as net assets would need to fall to 2,205,000 this is a decrease of 955,000. Net assets are uncertain therefore 955,000/3,160,000* 100 = 30.2%.

(iii) The marketing director is certainly correct in recognising that success is dependent on levels of service quality provided by HFG to its clients. However, whilst the number of complaints is an important performance measure, it needs to be used with caution. The nature of a complaint is, very often, far more indicative of the absence, or a lack, of service quality. For example, the fact that 50 clients complained about having to wait for a longer time than they expected to access gymnasium equipment is insignificant when compared to an accident arising from failure to maintain properly a piece of gymnasium equipment. Moreover, the marketing director ought to be aware that the absolute number of complaints may be misleading as much depends on the number of clients serviced during any given period. Thus, in comparing the number of complaints received by the three centres then a relative measure of complaints received per 1,000 client days would be far more useful than the absolute number of complaints received.

The marketing director should also be advised that the number of complaints can give a misleading picture of the quality of service provision since individuals have different levels of willingness to complain in similar situations.

The marketing director seems to accept the current level of complaints but is unwilling to accept any increase above this level. This is not indicative of a quality-oriented organisation which would seek to reduce the number of complaints over time via a programme of 'continuous improvement'.

From the foregoing comments one can conclude that it would be myopic to focus on the number of client complaints as being the only performance measure necessary to measure the quality of service provision. Other performance measures which may indicate the level of service quality provided to clients by HFG are as follows:

- Staff responsiveness assumes critical significance in service industries. Hence the time taken to resolve client queries by health centre staff is an important indicator of the level of service quality provided to clients.
- Staff appearance may be viewed as reflecting the image of the centres.
- The comfort of bedrooms and public rooms including facilities such as air-conditioning, tea/coffee-making and cold drinks facilities, and office facilities such as e-mail, facsimile and photocopying.
- The availability of services such as the time taken to gain an appointment with a dietician or fitness consultant.
- The cleanliness of all areas within the centres will enhance the reputation of HFG. Conversely, unclean areas will potentially deter clients from making repeat visits and/or recommendations to friends, colleagues etc.
- The presence of safety measures and the frequency of inspections made regarding gymnasium equipment within the centres and compliance with legislation are of paramount importance in businesses like that of HFG.
- The achievement of target reductions in weight that have been agreed between centre consultants and clients.

APPENDIX

Calculations of ROI:

	(A) Operating profit	(B) Total assets less current liabilities	(A) ÷ (C) Return on Investment (%)
ROI:			
Ayetown	396	1,720	23.02
Beetown	441	3,160	13.96
Ceetown	703	3,820	18.40

Calculations of RI

RI:	(A) Operating profit ($000)	(B) Required rate return	(C) Total assets ($000)	(D) = (B) × (C) Required return on investment ($000)	(E) = (A) – (D) Residual income ($000)
Ayetown	396	12%	1,800	216	180
Beetown	441	12%	3,400	408	33
Ceetown	703	12%	4,300	516	187

Calculations of EVA

EVA	(A) Pre-tax operating profit ($000)	(B) = (A) × 70% Post-tax operating profit ($000)	(C) WACC	(D) Total assets less current liabilities ($000)	(E) = (C) × (D) WACC × (ta – cl) ($000)	(F) = (B) – (E) EVA ($000)
Ayetown	396	277.2	13.67%	1,720	235.12	42.08
Beetown	441	308.7	13.67%	3,160	431.97	–123.27
Ceetown	703	492.1	13.67%	3,820	522.19	–30.09

Calculation of weighted average cost of capital (WACC) for use in calculation of EVA is as follows:

	Market value ($000)			
equity	9,000	Ke	0.15	1350
debt	1,800	Kd	0.07	126
	10,800			1,476

WACC = 1,476/10,800 = 13.67%

Note that the cost of equity is 15% and the after-tax cost of debt is

$$\frac{(100-30)}{100} \times 10\% = 7\%$$

(b) There are a number of potential problems which the directors of HFG need to recognise. These are as follows:

(i) There needs to exist a sufficient incentive for SFO to share their information with HFG as the success of any benchmarking programme is dependent upon obtaining accurate information about the comparator organisation. This is not an easy task to accomplish, as many organisations are reluctant to reveal confidential information to competitors. The directors of HFG must be able to convince the directors of SFO that entering into a benchmarking arrangement is a potential 'win-win situation'.

PAPER P5 : ADVANCED PERFORMANCE MANAGEMENT

(ii) The value of the exercise must be sufficient to justify the cost involved. Also, it is inevitable that behavioural issues will need to be addressed in any benchmarking programme. Management should give priority to the need to communicate the reasons for undertaking a programme of benchmarking in order to gain the full co-operation of its personnel whilst reducing the potential level of resistance to change.

(iii) Management need to handle the ethical implications relating to the introduction of benchmarking in a sensitive manner and should endeavour, insofar as possible, to provide reassurance to employees that their status, remuneration and working conditions will not suffer as a consequence of the introduction of any benchmarking initiatives.

Marking scheme

				Marks	Marks
(a)	(i)	Calculations:			
		ROI		1.5	
		RI		1.5	
		EVA		4	
		Comments (on merit) re ROCE/RI/EVA		9	Max 14
	(ii)	Comments (on merit):			
		% changes in Turnover, Total costs, Net assets	3 × 2	6	6
	(iii)	Comments (on merit):			
		Success/quality relationship		1	
		Number of complaints as performance measure		2	
		Reduce existing level of complaints		1	
		Other measures		2	Max 5
		Professional marks (format, style, structure of report)			Max 4
(b)		Comments (on merit):			
		Problems	Up to 4	4	
		Recommendations	Up to 4	4	Max 7
Total					**36**

Examiner's comments

There were very few good answers to question 1. The vast majority of candidates were unable to provide answers to all of the question's subsections. 4 professional marks were allocated to this question in respect of the appropriateness of format, style and structure of their report but a large number of candidates were unable to gain these marks.

The requirement of part (a)(i) revealed a very large number of candidates who could not provide a commentary on, and/or a detailed calculation of economic value added (EVA), which together were potentially worth 7 marks. Moreover, few candidates were able to calculate correctly the sensitivity analysis calculations required by part (a)(ii) of the question. In dealing with requirement (a)(iii) many candidates simply summarised the key arguments of writers such as Fitzgerald and Moon but failed to apply these to the scenario thereby producing answers that would be of little value to readers of this part of the report.

In part (b) most candidates were able to identify problems that the directors of HFG might experience in their wish to benchmark the performance of HFC with SFC. However, in general, candidates had problems in suggesting appropriate recommendations as to how those problems might be successfully addressed.

ANSWERS TO PRACTICE QUESTIONS – SECTION A : **SECTION 3**

11 THE SENTINEL COMPANY (TSC) (DEC 08)

> **Key answer tips**
>
> (a)(i) Read the requirements of this question carefully. You are comparing each depot against the benchmark not each other. You need to work out how much each depot exceeds the target profit %; and to calculate the figures for the debtors in excess of 60 days and credit notes as a % of revenue. Remember when a target is for delays a business would like to achieve less than the target!.
>
> In (a)(iii) the question is clearly referring to the building blocks model so you need to know what the measures refer to within the model. Use as many examples from the scenario as possible.
>
> (a)(iv) asks you to produce a balanced argument of this performance measurement system.
>
> Part (b) League tables are topical so should have some ideas yourself. Think about how they are used in football.

(a) **Report:**

   To: The Directors of TSC

   From: Management Accountant

   Subject: The performance of our depots

   Date: 5 December 2008

   (i) **Summary analysis of points gained (1) or forfeited (0) for quarter ended 31 October 2008**

Revenue and Profit Statistics:	Donatello-town	Leonardo-town	Michaelangelo-town	Raphael-town
Revenue	0	1	1	1
Profit (see note below)	1	0	1	0
Customer Care & Service Delivery Statistics:				
Late collection of consignments	1	0	1	0
Misdirected consignments	0	1	1	0
Delayed response to complaints	1	1	1	0
Vehicle breakdown delays	0	0	1	0
Lost items	1	1	1	0
Damaged items	1	0	1	1

KAPLAN PUBLISHING

Credit Control & Administrative Efficiency Statistics:

Average Debtor weeks	0	1	1	0
Debtors in excess of 60 days	1	1	1	1
Invoice queries (% of total)	1	1	1	1
Credit notes (% of revenue)	1	1	1	0
Total points gained	8	8	12	4

Workings:

(i) Profit point calculation:

Actual results:

e.g. Donatellotown = 2.3/15 = 15.3% (1 point)

Leonardotown = 2.4/18 = 13.3% (0 point)

(ii) Debtors in excess of 60 days (% of total)

	Donatello-town	Leonardo-town	Michaelangelo-town	Raphael-town
Revenue ($000)	15,000	18,000	14,000	22,000
Debtor weeks	5.8	4.9	5.1	6.2
∴ Debtors	1,673	1,696	1,373	2,623
31–60 Days	(321)	(133)	(153)	(552)
More than 60 days	52	63	40	71
Debtors in excess of 60 days (% of total)	3.1	3.7	2.9	2.7

(iii) Value of credit notes raised as a % of revenue

e.g. Donatellotown = $45,000/$15,000,000 = 0.3%

(ii) The summary analysis in (a)(i) shows that using overall points gained, Michaelangelotown has achieved the best performance with 12 points. Donatellotown and Leonardotown have achieved a reasonable level of performance with eight points each. Raphaeltown has underperformed, however, gaining only four out of the available 12 points.

Michaelangelotown is the only depot to have achieved both an increase in revenue over budget and an increased profit:revenue percentage.

In the customer care and service delivery statistics, Michaelangelotown has achieved all six of the target standards, Donatellotown four; Leonardotown three. The Raphaeltown statistic of achieving only one out of six targets indicates the need for investigation.

With regard to the credit control and administrative efficiency statistics, Leonardotown and Michaelangelotown achieved all four standards and Donatellotown achieved three of the four standards. Once again, Raphaeltown is the 'poor performer' achieving only two of the four standards.

(iii) The terms listed may be seen as representative of the dimensions of performance. The dimensions may be analysed into results and determinants.

The results may be measured by focusing on financial performance and competitiveness. **Financial performance** may be measured in terms of revenue and profit as shown in the data in the appendix of the question in respect of TSC. The points system in part (a) of the answer shows which depots have achieved or exceeded the target set. In addition, liquidity is another aspect of the measurement of financial performance. The points total in part (a) showed that Leonardotown and Michaelangelotown depots appear to have the best current record in aspects of credit control.

Competitiveness may be measured in terms of sales growth but also in terms of market share, number of new customers, etc. In the TSC statistics available in (a) we only have data for the current quarter. This shows that three of the four depots listed have achieved increased revenue compared to target.

The **determinants** are the factors which may be seen to contribute to the achievement of the results. Quality, resource utilisation, flexibility and innovation are cited by Fitzgerald and Moon as examples of factors that should contribute to the achievement of the results in terms of financial performance and competitiveness. In TSC a main **quality** issue appears to be customer care and service delivery. The statistics in the points table in part (a) of the answer show that the Raphaeltown depot appears to have a major problem in this area. It has only achieved one point out of the six available in this particular segment of the statistics.

Resource utilisation for TSC may be measured by the level of effective use of drivers and vehicles. To some extent, this is highlighted by the statistics relating to customer care and service delivery. For example, late collection of consignments from customers may be caused by a shortage of vehicles and/or drivers. Such shortages could be due to staff turnover, sickness, etc or problems with vehicle maintenance.

Flexibility may be an issue. There may, for example, be a problem with vehicle availability. Possibly an increased focus on sources for short-term sub-contracting of vehicles/collections/deliveries might help overcome delay problems.

The 'target v actual points system' may be seen as an example of **innovation** by the company. This gives a detailed set of measures that should provide an incentive for improvement at all depots. The points system may illustrate the extent of achievement/non-achievement of company strategies for success. For example TSC may have a customer care commitment policy which identifies factors that should be achieved on a continuing basis. For example, timely collection of consignments, misdirected consignments re-delivered at no extra charge, prompt responses to customer claims and compensation for customers.

(iv) The performance measurement system used by TSC appears simplistic. However, it may be considered to be measuring the right things since the specific measures used cover a range of dimensions designed to focus the organisation on factors thought to be central to corporate success, and not confined to traditional financial measures.

Internal benchmarking is used at TSC in order to provide sets of absolute standards that all depots are expected to attain. This should help to ensure that there is a continual focus upon the adoption of 'best practice' at all depots. Benchmarks on delivery performance place an emphasis upon quality of service whereas benchmarks on profitability are focused solely upon profitability!

Incentive schemes are used throughout the business, linking the achievement of company targets with financial rewards. It might well be the case that the profit incentive would act as a powerful motivator to each depot management team. However, what is required for the prosperity of TSC is a focus of management on the determinants of success as opposed to the results of success.

(b) A central feature of many performance measurement systems is the widespread use of league tables that display each business unit's performance relative to one another. In the case of service organisations such as TSC the use of league tables emphasises the company's critical success factors of profitability and quality of service by reporting results on a weekly basis at the depot level. The fact that such league tables are used by management will actively encourage competition, in terms of performance, among depots. The individual position of a business unit in the league table is keenly observed both by the manager of that unit and his/her peers.

In theory, performance is transparent. In practice although each depot performs essentially the same function and is subject to the same modes of measurement, circumstances pertaining to different business units may vary significantly. Some depots may be situated near to the hub (main distribution centre), some may be located far away and some may be in urban zones with well developed road networks whilst others may be in remote rural areas. Measuring performance via a league table makes no allowance whatsoever for these relative differences, hence, inequality is built into the performance measurement system.

Moreover, depot managers might be held responsible for areas over which they have no formal control. The network nature of the business suggests that there will be a high degree of interdependence of depots; the depot responsible for collection will very often not be the depot responsible for delivery. Therefore, it is frequently the case that business may be gained for which the collecting depot receives the revenue, but for which the delivering depot bears the cost. Obviously this impacts upon the profit statements of both depots. The formal system might not recognise such difficulties, the corporate view being that 'the business needs to be managed'; the depots should therefore see any such anomalies as mild constraints to work around rather than barriers to break down. In such circumstances delivering depots and collecting depots should discuss such problems on an informal basis. Such informal discussions are aided by close communications between depots recognising the interdependencies of the business.

ANSWERS TO PRACTICE QUESTIONS – SECTION A : SECTION 3

		Marking scheme		Marks	Marks
(a)	(i)	Revenue		½	
		Profit		½	
		Customer care and service delivery		3	
		Credit control and administration efficiency		5	Max 9
	(ii)	Overall comment on ranking		1	
		Analysis of each of the three sections in table		5	Max 5
	(iii)	Inter-relationship of dimensions/results/determinants		2	
		Definition/examples of financial performance and competitiveness as aspects of results	$2 \times 1½$	3	
		Definition/examples of determinants of quality, resource utilisation, flexibility and innovation	$4 \times 1½$	6	Max 10
	(iv)	Comments (on merit)		5	Max 5
		Note: Requirement (a) includes 4 professional marks			Max 29
(b)		Benefits		4	
		Problems		4	Max 6
Total					**35**

Examiners comments

In part (a)(i). A minority of candidates reversed the 1/0 notation but nevertheless demonstrated an understanding of the need to rank the depots of TSC according to the 12 measures provided in the Appendix to the question and were rewarded favourably. It was also pleasing to observe that the majority of answers to part (a)(ii) were satisfactory as most candidates provided acceptable comments on the relative performance of each depot. That said, many candidates limited their evaluation of the performance of the four depots to ranking them 'first', 'second', 'third' and 'fourth' (or last)' and thereby ignoring which depots had in fact achieved (or had not achieved) the 'target values' which were at the heart of the performance measurement system of TSC. In general, answers to part (a)(iii) were satisfactory, and indeed, some were excellent. Poorer answers were offered by candidates who did not relate answers sufficiently to the examples contained in the scenario and/or chose to state that there was insufficient information contained within the question to enable them to provide a relevant assessment of TSC using the required criteria. The quality of answers to part (a)(iv) varied significantly. Many candidates achieved maximum marks whilst poorer answers referred solely to the need for more financial performance measures within TSC. In general, candidates provided satisfactory comments relating to the simplistic nature of the performance measurement system within TSC but few answers indicated the need to focus on the determinants of success rather than the results. Again, Part (b) produced a significant variation in the quality of answers provided by candidates. Many candidates achieved maximum marks whilst others evaluated potential 'benefits' without referring to any 'problems' whatsoever! Sadly, a significant number of candidates chose not to provide an answer to part (b) and in not doing so 'threw away' a potential six marks!

PAPER P5 : ADVANCED PERFORMANCE MANAGEMENT

12 ROYAL LAUREL HOSPITAL (RLH) (JUN 09)

> **Key answer tips**
>
> This question tests your knowledge on how to apply the balance scorecard model and the how to develop it for the Royal laurel Hospital. The scenario has a lot of very important information which can be applied to your answer. Ensure in part (a) you focus your answer on the performance of the hospitals with regards to the four dimensions and your answer to part (b) relates to its usefulness and how it could be improved upon.

To: The Directors of the Glasburgh Trust

From: Management Accountant

Subject: Performance of Royal Laurel and King Hardy Hospitals Date: June 2009

As requested I have prepared the attached report having adopted a balanced scorecard approach using the following dimensions:

(i) Access to services

(ii) Clinical

(iii) Efficiency

(iv) Financial management.

I should be only too pleased to provide any explanations relating to the contents of the report should you have any queries.

Signed: Management Accountant Date: June 2009

Report

(a) Re: Performance of Royal Laurel and King Hardy Hospitals for the year ended 31 May 2009.

Access to services:

Waiting times for admission to each hospital are a measure of the quality of service provided by our hospitals. Relevant data in respect of the year under review is as follows:

Inpatient statistics:

	RLH Actual	RLH Budget	KHH Actual
Total inpatients	37,000	36,500	40,000
Number of inpatients who waited more than five weeks after consultation for admission to hospital	3,330	365	320
% of inpatients who waited more than five weeks after consultation for admission to hospital	9%	1%	0.8%
Number of inpatients who waited more than 11 weeks after consultation for admission to hospital	740	0	0
% of inpatients who waited more than 11 weeks after consultation for admission to hospital	2%	–	–

The statistics in respect of inpatients to each hospital reveal that KHH provided superior access to service than RLH. RLH targeted to admit 99% of all inpatients to hospital within five weeks of their consultation. However, RLH only admitted 91% of all inpatients within five weeks from the time of their consultation. In comparison KHH admitted 90.2% of all inpatients within five weeks. Furthermore, 2% of all inpatients treated by RLH waited more than 11 weeks for admission to hospital whereas RLH had not anticipated any inpatient waiting for this length of time for admission to hospital. Again, KHH provided superior access to services with none of its inpatients having to wait more than eleven weeks prior to admission to hospital.

Outpatient statistics

	RLH Actual	RLH Budget	KHH Actual
Total outpatients	44,000	43,800	44,000
Number of outpatients who waited more than five weeks for treatment	4,400	2,190	352
% of outpatients who waited more than five weeks for treatment	10%	5%	0.8%
Number of outpatients who waited more than 11 weeks for treatment	1,320	438	220
% of outpatients who waited more than 11 weeks for treatment	3%	1%	0.5%
Number of outpatients who waited more than 13 weeks for treatment	220	0	0
% of outpatients who waited more than 13 weeks for treatment	0.5%	–	–

With regard to the access to service provided to outpatients of each hospital, then a similar picture appears.

10% of all outpatients waited more than five weeks for an appointment at RLH which was exactly twice the target of 5%. In a similar vein, 3% of all outpatients at RLH waited more than 11 weeks for an appointment against a target of 1%. Moreover, 220 outpatients at RLH had to wait more than 13 weeks for an appointment. In comparison KHH provided a far superior access to service with only 0.8% and 0.5% of outpatients waiting more than five and 11 weeks respectively for an appointment. Indeed, no outpatient at KHH had to wait for more than 13 weeks for an appointment.

Other statistics

	RLH Actual	RLH Budget	KHH Actual
Number of cancelled or delayed operations (Working 1)	592	0	160
Achievement (%) of target waiting time of two weeks for admission to the Rapid Access Chest Pains Clinic	70	98	100
Number of emergency admissions	300	400	300
Number of 12 hour 'trolley' waits for emergency admissions to a hospital bed	4	0	0
Achievement (%) of target of four hours or less time spent in Accident and Emergency ward	96	98	100

With regard to other statistics relating to 'access to service', RLH scheduled to perform 29,600 operations (Working 1) which was 400 operations more than the budgeted number of 29,200. This was due to the fact the actual number of inpatients admitted at 37,000 was greater than the budgeted number of 36,500. However, the number of operations performed was 29,008 from which indicates that 592 operations did not take place as scheduled (Working 2). Hence we can deduce that 2% of scheduled operations were either cancelled or postponed. The statistics in respect of KHH reveal that only 0.5% of scheduled operations were postponed.

It is clear that RLH did not achieve its target maximum waiting time of two weeks for admission of 98% of patients to the Rapid Access Chest Pains Clinic. In fact, it fell well short at 70% of patients requiring to be admitted to the clinic. In stark contrast KHH admitted 100% of patients to its clinic within two weeks.

Whilst the number of emergency admissions is difficult (if not impossible) to forecast with accuracy, four patients who were admitted to RLH on an emergency basis spent at least 12 hours on a 'trolley' before being allocated a hospital bed. RLH had targeted that no patient admitted to hospital on an emergency basis would have to spend 12 hours before being admitted to hospital and given the fact that such admissions can have life-threatening implications this can be regarded as poor performance. Again, in stark contrast no patient admitted to KHH on an emergency basis had to wait for 12 hours before being allocated a hospital bed.

RLH was unable to meet its target that 98% of patients admitted to the accident and emergency ward would spend less than four hours in the ward. RLH achieved a percentage of 96% whereas 100% of patients admitted to KLH's accident and emergency ward spent less than four hours in the ward.

It is quite apparent from the available statistics in respect of 'access to service' that RLH has not been able to meet its targets and that KHH has performed much better. In the absence of information regarding targets of KHH then we cannot conclude whether or not KHH has actually met its targets but we certainly can conclude that the performance of KHH is very good.

Clinical:

	RLH Actual	RLH Target	KHH Actual
% of Complaints responded to within 25 days	95	100	99
Number of deaths (inpatients)	600	730	800
Infection control – number of instances of infections reported	2	6	0
Number of drug administration errors	80	100	20
Number of staff shortages	80	60	20

In terms of a clinical focus it is apparent that KHH with 420 complaints, 1% of which are not responded to within 25 days, is better at responding to complaints than RLH which was unable to respond to 5% of the total complaints received within its target timeframe of 25 days. However one needs to be mindful that we do not know the nature of the complaints made by the patients of each hospital since a comparison of the nature of complaints can be far more revealing than the number of complaints. However, in the absence of such information it would seem reasonable to conclude that KHH is extremely capable in responding to complaints from patients.

It is observable that the number of deaths among inpatients is lower at RLH than in KHH in both absolute and relative terms. However, such a statistic should be viewed with the utmost caution since much will depend upon the seriousness of the illnesses of patients at each hospital and therefore one cannot deduce that the hospital with the lower death rate is more efficient in terms of its clinical focus.

Infection control measured in terms of the number of infections reported was excellent at KHH with no instances of infections being experienced during the year. On the other hand RLH bettered its target of six such instances but nevertheless there remains the fact that there were two reported instances of infections throughout the year.

With regard to the number of drug administration errors then staff at RLH made 80 such errors which was 20% better than the targeted number of 100. However, this was four times the level of such errors made by staff at KHH.

Again, the number of staff shortages of 80 at RLH was four times higher than that of KHH. It is reasonable to conclude that such staff shortages will inevitably precipitate problems especially within organisations such as hospitals which are so dependent upon staff being available according to hospital schedules.

Efficiency:

	RLH Actual	RLH Target	KHH Actual
Bed occupancy (number of inpatient bed nights)	138,750	146,000	134,320
Theatre utilisation (%)	88.3	88.9	96.9
Number of patient days per member of medical staff (Working 4)	8.4	7.4	9.2
Number of times of government or agency staff usage	80	60	20

Actual bed occupancy at RLH was 90.5% compared with a target of 95.3% of total bed nights available during the year. There were 500 more in patients treated than the target number of 36,500.

The average patient stay at RLH was 3.75 bed nights (Working 3) which compares favourably with a target of 4 bed nights. KHH had an actual bed occupancy rate of 87.6% and an average patient stay of 3.36 nights.

Theatre utilisation at RLH amounted to 88.3% (Working 4) of available capacity which was below the targeted level of 88.9% (36,500 × 80% = 29,200/32,850). In comparison KHH used 96.9% of available capacity which is significantly higher than RLH.

Staff productivity may be measured in terms of patient days per member of medical staff. Comparative actual and target statistics for RLH are 8.4 and 7.4 days respectively. KHH has a higher figure at 9.2 patient days per member of medical staff. More patient days per member of medical staff implies greater levels of efficiency. However, this might mean that there are issues relating to the quality of patient care. There is no information to suggest that this might be the case with regard to either hospital.

The use of government/agency staff reflects the number of staff shortages reported under the above 'Clinical focus' of this report. A hospital cannot cope with staff shortages due to the very nature of its work; i.e. patient care.

Financial:

	RLH Actual	RLH Target	KHH Actual
Revenue from clinical and non-clinical activities ($m)	54.2	55.2	60.2
Medical staff costs ($m)	22.3	22.2	19.6
Other staff costs ($m)	5.5	5.5	4.0
Income and expenditure surplus/(deficit)	(1.0)	0.0	4.0
Other operating costs (net of any other revenues received)(Working 5)	27.4	27.5	32.6
Number of days cash in hand	31	30	35

The financial information contained within the scenario is extremely limited, however, it can be deduced that RLH had a deficit of $1 million. It was targeted to operate at a zero surplus/deficit. Other than with regard to medical staff costs which were $0·1m above budget, RLH appears to have excellent cost control given that it treated more inpatients and outpatients than the budgeted numbers in respect of each category of patient.

In comparison KHH had an operating surplus of $4 million. It is noticeable that its level of operating costs ($32·6 million) is appreciably higher than the $27·4 million incurred by RLH.

RLH days cash in hand at 31 days was a day above target. By way of comparison KHH had 35 days cash in hand.

(b) The balanced scorecard approach used by the Glasburgh Trust uses four 'perspectives' or 'focuses' which are critical in the assessment of the performance of hospitals. The provision of good 'Access to services' is fundamental to the performance of each hospital because even if a hospital has excellent clinical and operating efficiency, unless patients can access the services then no benefits can be gained.

A primary consideration in the requirement for the inclusion of a clinical focus within the scorecard is the fact that 80% of inpatients are expected to undergo an operation. Hence the importance of the adoption of relevant performance measures relating to issues such as infection control and drug administration.

Resource allocation assumes critical significance in government funded institutions such as the Glasburgh Trust, hence the need for relevant performance indicators in order to assess levels of efficiency attained by each hospital. Government funded hospitals have finite resources which are funded by the taxpayer and thus in terms of public accountability it is important that appropriate performance indicators such as bed occupancy and theatre utilisation are monitored.

A focus on financial management is fundamental to any business whether they are profit seeking or not for profit organisations. By definition there is competition between publicly owned organisations for funds and hence it is critical that organisations such as the two hospitals under review are able to demonstrate that the funds made available to them are deployed in the most economic, efficient and effective manner.

The patient is in reality the 'customer' and hence a large number of the performance measures used within the scorecard are customer focused.

The scorecard utilised by the Glasburgh Trust could be improved by the inclusion of a staff perspective or focus. People are an organisation's largest asset and therefore performance measures focused upon hospital staff would add significant value to the scorecard. For example, performance indicators related to staff sickness, absence and turnover are relatively easy to measure and would assist in the management of operations within each hospital.

The usefulness of the scorecard would also be enhanced by the inclusion of a 'service quality' perspective or focus. In this regard the use of non-financial performance measures would add significant value to the scorecard. Examples of information that would enhance the usefulness of the scorecard used by the Glasburgh Trust are as follows:

- Full details of the schedule of operations in order to review the % of operations performed in accordance with scheduled activities
- The number of complaints received as a percentage of patients
- The % of patients who need a second operation because their initial operation was unsuccessful
- The number of complaints from concerned relatives of patients regarding the lack of/timeliness of information made available to them.

The scorecard could also be improved by the use of more detailed financial information in the measurement of the performance of each hospital. Examples of information that would enhance the usefulness of the scorecard used by the Glasburgh Trust are as follows:

- Details of the number of staff employed at each hospital by category of employee i.e. the number of consultants, doctors, nurses and other medical staff with a detailed breakdown of total staff costs
- A detailed breakdown of the clinical and non-clinical income received by each hospital
- A detailed breakdown of the operating costs of each hospital
- Details of the funds employed by each hospital.

Please contact me should you require any further information regarding, or clarification of, any of the matters contained in this report.

Signed:

Date:

Workings:

(1) Number of planned operations

	RLH Actual	RLH Budget	KHH Actual
Total inpatients	37,000	36,500	40,000
% of inpatients requiring a single operation	80%	80%	80%
Number planned operations	29,600	29,200	32,000

(2) Number of cancelled or delayed operations

	RLH Actual	KHH Actual
Number of planned operations (Working 1)	29,600	32,000
Number of operations performed	29,008	31,840
Number of cancelled or delayed operations	592	160
Planned operations cancelled or delayed	2.0%	0.5%

(3)	Bed occupancy (%) and average patient stay	RLH Actual	RLH Budget	KHH Actual
	Bed occupancy (number of days)	138,750	146,000	134,320
	Bed days available (42 × 10 × 365)	153,300	153,300	153,300
	Bed occupancy (%)	90.51	95.24	87.62
	Number of patients	37,000	36,500	40,000
	Average patient stay (days)	3.75	4	3.36

(4)	Theatre utilisation (%)	RLH Actual	RLH Budget	KHH Actual
	Theatre capacity – number of operations (10 × 9 × 365)	32,850	32,850	32,850
	Number of operations performed (Working 2)	29,008	29,200	31,840
	Utilisation (%) =	88.3%	88.9%	96.9%

(5)	Operating costs	RLH Actual $m	RLH Budget $m	KHH Actual $m
	Revenue	54.2	55.2	60.2
	Medical staff costs	22.3	22.2	19.6
	Other staff costs	5.5	5.5	4.0
	Operating costs (Balancing figure)	27.4	27.5	32.6
	Income and expenditure surplus/(deficit)	(1.0)	0	4.0

Marking scheme		Marks
(a)	Access to services focus	8
	Clinical focus	6
	Efficiency focus	6
	Financial management focus	3
	Maximum	20
(b)	Evaluation	6
	Recommendations	7
	Maximum	11
	Professional marks	4
Total		**35**

ANSWERS TO PRACTICE QUESTIONS – SECTION A : SECTION 3

> **Examiner's comments**
>
> In general, the answers to this question were poor. In part (a) a large number of candidates confined their comments to 'higher than' or 'lower than' or 'better than or worse than budget' using only absolute figures for the purposes of comparison. Many candidates made insufficient use of the numerical data contained in the question. Whilst many used percentage calculations, few calculated meaningful ratios. Indeed, there were some candidates who arrived at a bed occupancy rate in excess of 100%!
>
> Furthermore, many candidates prepared their report to the management of the Glasburgh Trust using no statistics whatsoever. All too often calculations were undertaken and then not explained or explained in such terms that they did not address the requirements of the question. In their answers to part (b) a large number of candidates did not evaluate the balanced scorecard used by the Glasburgh Trust or provide recommendations which would improve its usefulness as a performance management tool. A significant minority of candidates wrote all they knew about the balanced scorecard including inappropriate profitability measures, and mentioned products, delivery times and other measures not relevant to the scenario. Some candidates chose to discuss the 'performance pyramid' of Lynch and Cross or the work of Fitzgerald and Moon either in addition to or in place of the balanced scorecard of the Glasburgh Trust.

13 THE BENJAMIN EDUCATION COLLEGE (BEC) (DEC 09)

> **Key answer tips**
>
> This question is a good example of the need to remember F5 techniques – in this case, that of flexing budgets in (i). The rest of the question has the usual pitfalls such as the need for detailed discussion when assessing performance – how have figures changed, is this significant, why have they changed, what are the implications, etc?

To: The Management

From: Management Accountant

Subject: BEC and JBC Date: 11 December 2009

Please find herewith my report concerning the matters on which you recently requested information

(i) **Income statements for the year ended 30 November 2009**

	BEC Budget $	BEC Actual $	JBC Actual $
Revenue:			
Private:			
Accounting	3,456,000	3,192,000	4,000,000
Law	1,200,000	980,000	1,872,000
Marketing	1,152,000	1,120,000	2,400,000
	5,808,000	5,292,000	8,272,000

	BEC Budget $	BEC Actual $	JBC Actual $
Government funded students:			
Accounting	648,000	1,026,000	–
Law	225,000	315,000	–
Marketing	216,000	360,000	–
	1,089,000	1,701,000	–
Total revenue	6,897,000	6,993,000	8,272,000
Costs:			
Salaries:			
Lecturers	3,000,000	3,120,000	3,000,000
Administrative staff	200,000	208,000	176,000
Tuition materials	648,000	741,600	730,000
Catering	92,000	95,680	110,000
Cleaning	39,000	40,950	40,000
Other operating costs	588,000	643,800	645,000
Depreciation	40,000	40,000	60,000
Total costs	4,607,000	4,893,030	5,061,000
Net profit	2,290,000	2,099,970	3,211,000

(ii) An assessment of the performance of BEC and JBC using both financial and non-financial measure's is as follows:

Financial performance:

The key measurement will be the cost per student which for the year under review was as per the following table:

	BEC Budget	JBC Actual	BEC Actual
Total costs ($)	4,607,000	4,893,030	5,061,000
Number of students	7,200	7,200	7,560
Cost per student ($)	639.86	679.59	669.44

BEC incurred an actual cost per student which was above budget. Whilst JBC's cost per student was above the budgeted level of BEC it was below the actual cost per student incurred by BEC. The cost per student should be monitored over time in order to ascertain whether real cost savings are being achieved and should also be measured against comparable and competing organisations.

Competitive performance:

This will be measured in terms of the student population attracted to each institution. The growth rate may be measured in aggregate terms and by course. In addition the 'take-up rate' i.e. the ratio of uptake to enquiries received may be monitored by course type. The following table shows the take up rate during the year under review:

		BEC Budget	BEC Actual	JBC Actual
Accounting	Number of students	3,600	3,800	4,000
	Number of enquiries	4,800	4,750	5,000
	Take up rate	75%	80%	80%
Law	Number of students	1,500	1,400	1,560
	Number of enquiries	2,000	2,800	2,000
	Take up rate	75%	50%	78%
Marketing	Number of students	1,800	2,000	2,000
	Number of enquiries	2,400	2,500	2,400
	Take up rate	75%	80%	83.33%

BEC budgeted to have a take-up rate of 75% of all enquiries in respect of each course type. It is noticeable that they bettered this target with regard to accounting and marketing courses. However, they only achieved a take-up rate of 50% with regard to law courses. In comparison JBC had a take-up rate of 78% in respect of law courses and 80% in respect of both accounting and marketing courses.

Service quality

This is a potential issue which will certainly include the quality of teaching provided by BEC. Service quality may be measured in terms of pass rates. In the same vein it may also be measured via students' responses to questionnaires on such as guidance from staff, tutoring and the quality of lecture handouts.

The use of staff review programmes and internal reviews of the effectiveness of management committees in BEC will also be indicative of the level of service quality provided to students.

Flexibility

This may be measured in terms of the number of different modes of delivery offered to students of BEC e.g. full-time, weekday, weekend, block delivery, distance learning and linked courses which include a mix of attendance and distance learning. A further measure of flexibility lies in the availability of intermediate entry points to courses in order to enable students to gain advantage from qualifications obtained prior to joining BEC. By the same token it is also an indication of flexibility when an intermediate qualification is available for students who are unsuccessful in examinations or leave BEC for personal reasons.

The fact that JBC utilises the services of freelance staff indicates an added element of flexibility which BEC did not possess during the year under review.

Resource utilisation

The main resource of BEC is its staff. As in all such institutions, a key performance measure is the staff: student ratio.

This may be measured in respect of each course and monitored against budgeted targets over successive periods. What is rather worrying is the fact that recruitment in BEC was three times higher than budgeted in respect of accountancy, law and marketing lecturing staff and indicative of a staff turnover ratio of 20% per annum! In contrast, JBC only recruited one additional member to its entire team of lecturing staff during the year under review which might indicate that there might well be staff issues in BEC that do not exist within JBC.

Innovation

All successful businesses need new products. In this regard it is noticeable that JBC is currently developing four new courses. In comparison, BEC hasn't any new courses under development and in this regard the management of BEC should realise that innovation is key to future business success.

(iii) The performance management system (PMS) must be accepted and supported by all staff throughout the organisation. In order to achieve these aims it is essential that management address the following issues:

- the need for to buy-into the system which can only occur if chosen performance measures are regarded as fair and equitable and seen as fair by all managers and employees
- the need for managers and employees to take ownership of the results produced by the PMS and accept any changes made as a consequence of those results
- the need for leadership and education and training must be accepted throughout the organisation.
- the need for performance measures used as a basis for rewards to be linked to the degree of controllability exercised by each manager and employee.
- the need for the PMS to be clear and understandable to all managers and employees. In particular, it should place a major focus on what is critical for the business in strategic terms and also facilitate the reporting of results in a variety of relevant modes.

Please let me know if you require any further information regarding the matters discussed above.

Signed: Management Accountant

Marking scheme			
		Marks	Marks
(i)	Revenue:		
	Private students/Government funded students	3.0	
	Salaries:		
	Lecturers and administrative staff	2.0	
	Tuition materials	1.0	
	Catering	1.0	
	Cleaning	1.0	
	Other operating costs	1.0	
	Depreciation	0.5	
	Profit	0.5	10
(ii)	Financial & non-financial measures – Up to 2 each × 5	10	10
(iii)	Comments (on merit) 1 each		6
	Professional marks		4
Total			**30**

ANSWERS TO PRACTICE QUESTIONS – SECTION A : **SECTION 3**

> **Examiner's comments**
>
> In general, answers to requirement (i) were satisfactory with a number of candidates gaining maximum marks. However, it was noticeable that a large number of candidates were unable to flex the budget of BEC correctly.
>
> There was a significant variation in the quality of candidates' answers to requirement (ii) in which poorer answers offered little in terms of 'assessment' and tended to limit their analysis to 'this has gone up', 'this has gone down' etc.
>
> Again, there was a significant variation in the quality of candidates' answers to requirement (iii). Poorer answers tended to discuss performance measurement systems in a very general manner with very little, if any, 'discussion of the issues that might restrict the extent to which a performance measurement system is accepted and supported by management and employees.

14 THE RRR GROUP (RRR) (DEC 09)

> **Key answer tips**
>
> This question is a good example of the need to learn the whole syllabus. If you knew the detail concerning beyond budgeting, then this question was very straightforward.

(a) Significant items in the budget prepared for the year ending 30 November 2010 are as follows:

Sales revenue is budgeted to increase by 10% from the 2009 actual level. It is questionable whether this is likely to be achievable given cost changes that are planned as discussed below.

Cost of sales has the same percentage relationship to sales (66.7%) as in 2009. Note that the corresponding figure for 2008 was 62.5%. The percentage differences may be influenced by the change in mix of work – repairs, refurbishment, renewals that are planned for 2010.

Marketing expenditure has been reduced by $1.3m. which is a 15% reduction from the 2009 actual figure. It must be asked whether demand is sufficiently buoyant to achieve the planned 10% sales increase with this marketing reduction.

Staff training has been reduced to $1.0m which is a 25% reduction from 2009. Will the quality of work be reduced through this reduction and lead to increased costs, remedial work and customer complaints in 2010 and future years?

Uptake of orders from customer enquiries is planned at 71% compared with 66.7% in 2009 and 55% in 2008. Is this forecast improvement realistic or achievable? This requires very careful consideration especially given the planned decrease in marketing expenditure in the 2010 budget.

Problems relating to the likely achievement of the 2010 budget and its inconsistency with the 'beyond budgeting' points 1 to 3 raised in the question may be viewed as follows:

KAPLAN PUBLISHING 185

PAPER P5 : ADVANCED PERFORMANCE MANAGEMENT

'Stretch goals' are intended as moving away from fixed targets (as in the budget) that may lead to 'gaming' and irrational behaviour. Relative improvements should be the outcome of strategic changes agreed, whereas the budget focus seems to be a continuation of the 'status quo' linked to arbitrary value changes. The budgeting system is also seen to be meeting the planned target through arbitrary costs, particularly in discretionary areas such as training and marketing (see Table A in the question).

Evaluation and rewards should be based on relative improvement contracts (with hindsight). Until 2009, no such evaluation and reward processes seem to have been in place. The question indicates that a bonus system will be implemented in 2010 using a set of Key Performance Indicators as an incentive to the overall achievement of goals and the creation of value.

The existing budget process does not focus on a strategy to achieve continuous value creation for RRR. The budget planned for 2010 has a target profit of $20m which is a 33% increase on the actual profit achieved in 2009, linked to a 10% increase in sales volume. It would appear that (as discussed in answer (a) (ii) above) this expresses an arbitrary set of data that is NOT the outcome of a new charge strategy.

(b) (i) Staff bonus calculation: Year ended 30 November 2009 using Key Performance Indicators (KPIs) based on relative improvement contract factors

KPI	Weighting Factor (A)	Total Score % (B)* (see below for basis)	Weighted Score % (A) ×(B)
Revenue 2009 versus previous year (90/80)	0.15	12.50	1.875
Revenue 2009 versus competitor (90/85)	0.20	5.88	1.176
Profit 2009 versus previous year.	0.15	–6.25	–0.938
Profit 2009 versus competitor (15/15.5)	0.20	–3.23	–0.646
Quality items 2009 versus previous year:			
No. of orders requiring remedial work (W1)	0.075	31.80	2.385
No. of complaints investigated (W2)	0.075	24.20	1.815
% of enquiries converted into orders (W3)	0.15	21.30	3.195
(improvements = positive (+)			
Total	1.000	Bonus (%) =	8.863

(B)* – each KPI score value is positive (+) where 2009 value is greater than the previous year or negative (–) where 2009 value is less than previous year. Each KPI score value is the % increase (+) or decrease (–) in 2009 as appropriate

W1 $(1 - (300/440)) \times 100 = 31.8$

W2 $(1 - (100/132)) \times 100 = 24.2$

W3 2009 = $(10{,}000/15{,}000) = 66.7\%$; 2008 = $(8{,}800/16{,}000) = 55\%$

improvement in 2009 = $(66.7 - 55)/55 = 21.3\%$

(ii) The KPI appraisal and bonus process provides a broad range of indicators that may be monitored, both individually and collectively over time in respect of the relative improvement in Alpha Division. The analysis may also be used in order to give a spectrum of measures against which to compare the Alpha division relative improvement against that of other divisions in RRR plc.

In addition, the factors which improve or detract from the size of the bonus earned are clearly shown. This should act as an additional incentive for staff, particularly where an improvement in the weighted score for any particular element is required. For example, in profit versus that of competitor, which shows a negative score in the 2009 comparison in (b) (i) above.

Marking scheme

				Marks	Marks
(a)		Comments re achievability of budget and 14 its consistency with the 'beyond budgeting' philosophy (on merit)	Up to 2 each		14
(b)	(i)	Revenue 2009 versus previous year		1.0	
		Revenue 2009 versus competitor		1.0	
		Profit 2009 versus previous year		1.0	
		Profit 2009 versus competitor		1.0	
		Quality items 2009 versus previous year:			
		No. of orders requiring remedial work (W1)		2.0	
		Number of complaints investigated (W2)		2.0	
		% of enquiries converted into orders (W3)		3.0	
		Total		1.0	
					12
	(ii)	Comments (on merit)	Up to 2 each		4
Total					30

Examiner's comments

There were significant variations in the quality of candidates' answers to this question. A significant number of candidates provided good answers to part (a) and in doing so achieved very high marks.

However, it was apparent that many candidates knew little of 'Beyond Budgeting' providing answers that were not only lacking in 'depth' but also far too brief given the fact that there were fourteen marks available. It was pleasing to see a large number of candidates providing very good answers to part(b)(i) and consequently achieving very high marks. In general, answers to part (b)(ii) were satisfactory with most candidates being able to provide some relevant discussion of the potential benefits from the KPI and bonus approach both for Alpha division and throughout the RRR group.

15 THE SUPERIOR BUSINESS CONSULTANCY (SBC) (JUN 10)

> **Key answer tips**
>
> To score well in this question you have to make your answer relate to the specific circumstances in the question. So in part (i) have you written generic KPIS or are they relevant to SBC. Similarly in part (iii) have you explained the trends using typical issues or ones specific to SBC's circumstances?

(i) To: The Directors

From: Management Accountant

Subject: The Balanced Scorecard

Date: 11 June 2010

The use of non-financial performance indicators (NFPIs) has become more widespread during recent years to assess performance in organisations.

This is largely attributable to the fact that many important aspects of organisational performance cannot be measured in purely financial terms. It follows that if performance measures are restricted to financial measures alone then many important non-financial aspects of organisational performance may be ignored.

Furthermore there is a widely held view that 'what gets measured gets done' and if performance measures are restricted to financial measures alone then the focus of managers will be myopic and consequently they may be motivated by the wrong stimuli. In the past the important measure of performance have been financial in nature, with little or in extreme cases no focus whatsoever, being given to other important aspects of performance. Many commentators have argued that financial measures encourage short-termism to the detriment of the longer-term prospects of organisations.

Many NFPIs are 'lead indicators' insofar as they give an indication of likely future financial performance and therefore their measurement might reveal problems which might be addressed by management in time to take remedial action.

Skill and care must be exercised by management in the selection of NFPIs given the vast number of potential NFPIs in order to avoid an 'information overload' which could be damaging to an organisation.

The increasing attention given to NFPIs was a key factor in the development of Kaplan and Norton's 'balanced scorecard' which proposed that business performance is reviewed from four perspectives, these are:

The financial perspective – How does an organisation appear to the shareholders?

The customer perspective – How does an organisation appear to the customers?

The internal business perspective – What must an organisation excel at?

The innovation and learning perspective – Can an organisation continue to improve and create value?

For each of the four perspectives goals and measures will need to be defined – typically five measures for each perspective. The goals and measures are designed to focus attention on important factors and precipitate improved organisational performance.

The internal logic of the balanced scorecard is that goal-setting originates with customers. Then an organisation must determine what it must excel at in order to satisfy customer expectations. The innovation and learning perspective contains goals which relate to how an organisation will maintain progress and develop its processes, products and services. The results from these three perspectives will be mirrored in the financial perspective.

The directors will need to agree the 'vision' of the organisational strategy with middle management and to ensure that the vision is also shared by all employees within the organisation thereby creating an 'understood environment'. The creation of such an environment should ensure that sufficient attention is focused on all important factors within the organisation's environment which will lead to higher levels of profitability.

The following are possible measures that might feature within a balanced scorecard for SBC:

Customer perspective:

- % of sales from new clients
- % of clients from whom repeat business is gained
- Ratings from client satisfaction surveys

Internal business perspective:

- % of client projects completed on time and within budget
- % of bids for new clients which are successful
- % of employee time billed to clients

Innovation and learning perspective:

- % of time used for staff development
- % of revenues earned from new products or services

Financial perspective:

- Growth in operating cash flow
- Gross margin earned from clients
- Percentage increase in operating costs
- Expected value added (EVA ^{TM}) generated in relation to the budget.

(ii) Calculation of the cost per consultation is as follows:

		Advertising	Recruitment	IT Support
Number of consultants		20	30	50
Salary ($)		40,000	35,000	30,000
Total salaries		800,000	1,050,000	1,500,000
Number of consultations per annum	(200 per consultant)	4,000	6,000	10,000
Business Development Activity		(280)	(1,320)	(1,200)
Chargeable days		3,720	4,680	8,800
Demand for chargeable consultations		4,200	6,250	10,250
Subcontractor days		480	1,570	1,450
Cost per subcontractor day ($)		300	220	200
Cost of subcontractors ($)		144,000	345,400	290,000
Cost per chargeable consultation ($)				
Full-time consultants	Total salaries plus operating costs/chargeable days	277·55	286·86	232·95
Subcontractors	= Cost of subcontractors/ number of subcontractors	335·71	255·71	235·71

> *Tutorial note*
>
> *Any reasonable method for allocating operating costs was given credit. Here, chargeable days have been used but allocating by the number of consultants in each area or the number of consultations (inc BDA) were also accepted.*

(iii) The figures contained in the appendix reveal a forecast reduction in level of total demand of 8% over the next two years. Specifically hard hit is the recruitment business with a fall of 20% over this period with the number of recruitment consultants dropping by 33%. The figures also show that salary levels will remain constant from 2011 to 2012. This may be due to reasons such as increased competition or an economic downturn.

The forecast increase 'across all activities' in days spent on Business Development Activity, notwithstanding the projected fall in activity levels in 2011 and 2012, represent an attempt by SBC to broaden and/or retain its existing customer base.

(Additional points such as the increased use of subcontractors (based on answer to part (ii)) were also given credit.)

(iv) Potential benefits which arise from the use of subcontractors by SBC include the following:

- Increased flexibility – the use of subcontract staff where own staff are unavailable helps to avoid situations where SBC might otherwise have to cancel and/or reschedule client activities which might lead to a loss of client goodwill or even worse, the loss of clients

- The use of subcontractors might be necessitated by the lack of a particular expertise among the full-time staff employed by SBC. Thus SBC can avoid being perceived to be 'turning away' business or providing services to clients which are not of the required quality level, both of which might be harmful to its reputation

- The use of subcontractors might reduce the overall costs of SBC as it might well be the case that the number of full-time staff employed within SBC would need to be increased if subcontract staff were not available. Thus the fixed costs associated with a fixed workforce would be higher and it is quite conceivable that some of the full-time staff might have low utilisation ratios, particularly in times of low demand by clients for the services offered by SBC.

Potential problems which arise from the use of subcontractors by SBC include the following:

- The use of subcontract staff might cause resentment by full-time staff within SBC who might view the use of subcontractors as a lost opportunity to develop their own skill bases

- Subcontractors might not identify with the corporate culture of SBC and hence might operate in a way which is inconsistent with ways 'things are done' within SBC. This might create an inconsistent view of the SBC by clients who have received services from both full-time consultants and subcontractors

- The fact that there are two completely different pay schemes operating might prove problematic and cause dissatisfaction among full-time consultants and/or subcontractors.

- For example full-time staff might consider that the rate paid per day to subcontractors is too high thus giving rise to perceptions of inequity which might damage the morale within SBC.

Tutorial note

Professional marks were given under the following headings: Format, introduction, conclusion, use of subheadings, professional language, clarity. A conclusion was not required as it is difficult to formulate for this diverse report but credit was given where it was reasonably attempted.

Marking scheme

			Marks
(i)	Importance of NFPIs	Up to	4
	Balanced scorecard – discussion	Up to	2
	Balanced scorecard – SBC	Up to	7
		Maximum	13
(ii)	Chargeable days		3
	Subcontractor days		2
	Costs per consultation		2
		Maximum	7
(iii)	Comments (on merit)	Up to 2 each	6
		Maximum	5
(iv)	Potential benefits		3
	Potential problems		3
		Maximum	6
	Professional marks		4
Total			**35**

Examiner's comments

In general, answers to requirement (i) were good with a number of candidates gaining maximum marks by ensuring that their example metrics were relevant to SBC. Weaker responses often lacked focus on the importance of non-financial performance indicators and a surprisingly large minority of candidates lacked basic knowledge of the balanced scorecard, which should be considered a core topic in P5.

Requirement (ii) received answers of variable quality with many candidates not appreciating the importance of calculating the chargeable days which would exclude the business development work. A surprising number of candidates did not appreciate that the main purpose of business development was as a marketing activity.

Requirement (iii) was reasonably answered but the answers could have been improved by candidates offering more in terms of commercial reasoning, for example, the key trend in the appendix was the drop in forecast activity and this was the likely driver of the changes in the company – it was less commercially realistic to be suggesting that the drop in numbers of consultants in a previously growing business was driving the drop in demand.

Requirement (iv) was generally well answered although some candidates could have improved their answers by avoiding bullet points and demonstrating their understanding by giving fuller answers.

ANSWERS TO PRACTICE QUESTIONS – SECTION A : **SECTION 3**

16 THE EQUINE MANAGEMENT ACADEMY (EMA) (JUN 10)

> **Key answer tips**
>
> The reference to expected values and probabilities in the question requirements should have told you that risk is a key focus within this question and should thus be incorporated in your discussion as well as the calculations. Risk is likely to be a key theme in new syllabus papers, so ensure you are confident incorporating it.

(a) **Budgeted Income Statement for the year ended 31 May 2011**

			$	$
Equine College:				
Fee income – Working (1)	Student category:			
	Surgery		4,536,000	
	Dentistry		3,150,000	
	Business Management		3,402,000	11,088,000
Operating costs				(6,760,000)
Budgeted profit of Equine College				4,328,000
Riding School:				
Fee income	Rider category:			
	Beginner		1,843,200	
	Competent		2,027,520	
	Advanced		3,379,200	7,249,920
Operating costs				(6,095,000)
Budgeted profit of Riding School				1,154,920
Budgeted profit of EMA				5,482,920

Workings:

(1) Equine College fee income:
   e.g. Surgery
   Number of students (30% × 1,200) =   360
   Fee per student 12,000 × 1.05 ($)   12,600
   Budgeted Fee income ($)   4,536,000

KAPLAN PUBLISHING

(2) Riding School fee income

	Number of lessons	Charge per lesson $	Fee income $
240 horses × 4 per day × 320 days × 80% =	245,760		
Beginner (50%)	122,880	15	1,843,200
Competent (25%)	61,440	(30 × 1.1) = 33	2,027,520
Advanced (25%)	61,440	(50 × 1.1) = 55	3,379,200
			7,249,920

(b) (i)

% change in fee income	Probability	Lesson capacity	Probability	Combined probability	Equine College revenue $	Riding School revenue $	Total costs $	Net profit $	Expected value of net profit $
		90%	0.10	0.02	11,088,000	8,156,160	12,855,000	6,389,160	127,783
No change	0.20	80%	0.60	0.12	11,088,000	7,249,920	12,855,000	5,482,920	657,950
		70%	0.30	0.06	11,088,000	6,343,680	12,855,000	4,576,680	274,601
Decrease		90%	0.10	0.06	9,979,200	8,156,160	12,855,000	5,280,360	316,822
by 10%	0.60	80%	0.60	0.36	9,979,200	7,249,920	12,855,000	4,374,120	1,574,683
		70%	0.30	0.18	9,979,200	6,343,680	12,855,000	3,467,880	624,218
Decrease		90%	0.10	0.02	8,870,400	8,156,160	12,855,000	4,171,560	83,431
by 20%	0.20	80%	0.60	0.12	8,870,400	7,249,920	12,855,000	3,265,320	391,838
		70%	0.30	0.06	8,870,400	6,343,680	12,855,000	2,359,080	141,545
				1.00				Expected value of profit =	4,192,872

(ii) The use of expected values takes into account the relative likelihood of each of the possible outcomes occurring. The expected value of $4,192,872 is not one of the potential outcomes in the table, but is the weighted average of those outcomes. The use of expected values by the management of EMA implies that they have a risk-neutral attitude. A risk neutral decision-maker will ignore the variability in the range of potential outcomes and will be concerned only with the expected value of outcomes.

(iii) Possible reasons why the government of Hartland has decided to open an academy comprising an equine college and a riding school are as follows:

EMA operated the only Equine College in Hartland and operated at full capacity during the year ended 31 May 2010. This could well be an indication that the demand for equine specialists in Hartland exceeds the available supply.

Much transportation in Hartland is provided by horses and this might therefore account for the fact that the Equine College operated by EMA is currently operating at full capacity. It is reasonable to assume that the more that horses are used for transportation then the greater will be the need for specialists such as equine veterinary surgeons.

The government of Hartland 'actively promotes environmental initiatives' and therefore it might well be the case that it discourages the use of petrol and diesel propelled vehicles for both social and business purposes.

ANSWERS TO PRACTICE QUESTIONS – SECTION A : SECTION 3

Hartland is a developing country which has a large agricultural sector and therefore it is probable that horses are used in day-to-day operations e.g. farming.

Marking scheme				
				Marks
(a)	Equine College:			
	number of students			1.0
	fee income		3 × 0.5	1.5
	operating costs			0.5
	Riding School:			
	number of lessons			1.5
	fee income		3 × 0.5	1.5
	operating costs			0.5
	EMA profit			0.5
			Maximum	7
(b)	(i)	Combined probability schedule		3
		Profit and loss schedule		3
		Expected value schedule		3
			Maximum	9
	(ii)	Likelihood of occurrence		1
		Risk neutrality		1
		Other relevant comments		1
			Maximum	3
	(iii)	Reasons	3 × 2	6
Total				**25**

> **Examiner's comments**
>
> There were significant variations in the overall quality of candidates' answers to this question.
>
> Most candidates offered excellent answers to part (a) on preparing a budgeted profit figure for the academy and many scored full marks.
>
> However, when this basic understanding was tested in part (b) (i) (finding an expected value) candidates struggled. Stronger candidates scored full marks on this part but many others would have benefited from a structured approach. The issue of risk and its treatment are an important feature of business decision-making and are in the syllabus and have been mentioned in technical articles.
>
> Additionally, much of (b) (i) is assumed knowledge from F5. This lack of knowledge was then reflected in answers to (b) (ii) where few candidates discussed the implication of the use of expected value in the risk appetite at EMA.
>
> Requirement (b)(iii) for three reasons for the national government opening a competitor academy was generally well answered although some candidates did not read the question and offered six reasons briefly discussed rather than three reasons each more comprehensively discussed.

KAPLAN PUBLISHING

17 FILM PRODUCTIONS CO (FP) (DEC 10)

(a) Building and Monitoring critical success factors

Critical success factors (CSFs) are those areas of business performance where the company must succeed in order to achieve its overall strategic objectives. Monitoring CSFs are those that are used to keep abreast of ongoing operations, for example, comparison of actual results to budgets or industry averages. Building CSFs are those which look to the future of the organisation and its development, for example, the launch of niche products such as music concert films or the use of new distribution methods such as downloadable films.

(b) Information for establishing CSFs

The company can use information about the internal and external environment to set its CSFs. Relevant external information would include the structure of the industry and the strategy of FP's competitors. The geographical location of production and the main sales markets may also be relevant. Film is a hit driven industry where word of mouth can lead to success, therefore, recognition of the product and the brand ('Film Productions') by the public would lead to success. For example, the Walt Disney Company has achieved a high level of brand recognition that has enabled it to expand into other entertainment areas using characters from its films.

Relevant internal information would include measures of seasonality on sales which will dictate the timing of film releases and effectiveness of marketing campaigns. By forecasting the size of the market along with likely levels of competition, profit can be optimised. However, these forecasts will be subject to uncertainty and so the information systems will need to be flexible and allow probabilistic analysis. A CSF based on the quality of these forecasts would therefore be appropriate. Other internal sources could include measures of the cost per film and the time taken to produce a film.

Other possible information could include contingent factors (those that depend on specific threats or opportunities facing FP).

(c) Performance indicators linked to the CSFs

Audience satisfaction – performance indicators are:

- Sales per film – currently the company releases an average of 6.4 films per year and makes about $31.25 million on each one. These figures should be compared to industry averages. Trends on sales per film should be monitored for indications of changes in consumer taste.

- Brand recognition – consumers should be surveyed to identify if the FP name is known and used as an indicator of quality when selecting films. If FP regularly uses certain artists (directors or film stars) then positive consumer recognition of these names will indicate satisfaction.

- Repeat viewings – with TV showings, it will be possible to measure viewers for each showing of the film and monitor the decline in viewing over repetitions. The level of DVD purchases following a cinema release will also indicate customer satisfaction with customers actively wanting to own their own copy of a favourite film.

- Awards won – number of awards won will indicate success. However, the level of recognition of any award must be brought into account as major ones such as those voted on by the public or those whose ceremonies are widely reported have the greatest impact.

- Response of the media – scores by film critics often appear in the media and these give a measure of satisfaction although this category must be treated carefully as critics often look for artistic merit while FP is seeking commercial success and broad audience acceptance.

Profitability in operations – performance indicators are:

- Industry average margin – collect data on competitor companies to set an appropriate benchmark. This will require care to ensure that appropriate comparator companies are chosen, for example, those with a production budget similar to FP's of $18 million per film.

- Time in production – the cost of a film will depend on the length of time it takes to produce. If the film is intended to meet a current customer demand it may require to be produced quickly, in order to meet revenue targets. Therefore, the time in production will affect both sales and cost levels so altering the gross margin. Again, it would be helpful to identify if films meet their production schedule and if these schedules compare favourably to those of other film companies.

- Costs – the costs should be broken down into categories such as those for artists, production technicians and marketing. The cost structure for each film should be compared internally, to others that FP produces and also externally, to available figures for the industry.

(d) **Impact on FP's information systems**

The company website can collect audience survey results and comments posted on the site. Consumers can be drawn to the site with clips and trailers from current films and those in production. The site can log the frequency with which films are viewed and if audience members create accounts then further detail on the age, gender and location of the audience can be collected. This will allow a more detailed profile of the customer base for FP to be created and will be used to help in decisions about what films to commission in the future. The account members can be given the opportunity to score each film providing further information about satisfaction.

The company could also consider scanning the websites of its competitors to identify their performance – especially their published results which will provide benchmark information on gross margin levels.

A management information system (MIS) will collate the information from individual transactions recorded in the accounting system to allow middle level management to control the business. This system will allow customer purchases to be summarised into reports to identify both products that sell well and the customers (such as cinema chains and TV networks) who provide the main sources of revenue (indicators of satisfaction). The level of repeat business on a customer account will give an indication of the satisfaction with FP's output. The system will also produce management accounts from which gross margins will be drawn and it should be capable of breaking this down by film and by customer to aid decision-making by targeting FP's output to the most profitable areas. This will aid decision-making about the performance of the production team on a film and can be used to set rewards for each team.

An executive information system (EIS) is one that will supply information to the senior management of the organisation allowing them to drill down into the more detailed transaction reports where necessary. The EIS will provide summarised information, focused on the key performance indicators in order to allow the directors to quickly judge whether the company is meeting its CSFs. It will draw on internal sources such as the MIS and also external sources such as market data on revenues that different films are earning at the box office.

	Marking scheme	
		Marks
(a)	1 mark for general definition of a CSF. 2 marks each for a description of monitoring and building CSFs with examples appropriate to the scenario. Maximum	4
(b)	2 marks for the sources of information. 2 marks for each example including demonstration of why it is appropriate for FP. Maximum	6
(c)	2.5 marks for each suggested performance indicator with 0.5 for identification and 2 for discussion of use and relevance to FP. Maximum of 10. (Students may also discuss different margin measures such as operating and gross profit but these must be related to actual operations in order to gain much credit.) Maximum	10
(d)	3 marks for each relevant information system indicating how it links to the PIs. Maximum	9
	Professional marks for the style and structure of the discussion in the answer 2 marks.	2
Total		31

Examiner's comments

In general, answers to requirement (a) were weak with few of candidates gaining maximum marks by ensuring that their example metrics were relevant to FP. The problems were due to a lack of knowledge of the definition of monitoring and building CSFs and a lack of familiarity in using CSFs.

This became more apparent in responses to requirement (b) which was poorly attempted. This part asked for the information used in setting CSFs and then, using their reading of the scenario and general business knowledge, suggestions of suitable CSFs. Many candidates were unable to address this part of the question due to lack of knowledge of the definition of a CSF and devoted their answer purely to KPIs, as a result scoring no marks. Those candidates that read the question requirement and responded to it were quickly rewarded.

Requirement (c) was generally well answered with many candidates getting 7 or 8 out of 10. The best answers were those that used the question requirement to give a methodical structure to their answer. Those candidates who did not score well tended to provide bullet point lists of many KPIs when the question asked for four.

Candidates should look at the total marks available for the question part and realise that they are expected to develop points about each KPI suggested, not simply identify them.

Requirement (d) was generally adequately attempted. The better answers clearly linked the KPIs to changes that would be required in the design and use of the information systems mentioned. Thus, they could demonstrate knowledge of how such systems operate and the use to which the information produced is subsequently put.

> There were 2 professional marks available for this question and these were given under the headings: use of subheadings, professional language and clarity. Candidates should note that they were asked for sections and not the full report. Therefore, the standard report header, introductions and conclusions were not required except as appropriate to each section itself. (No harm was done if these were produced but mostly they wasted time.)

18 ROBUST LAPTOPS CO (RL) (DEC 10)

To: CEO

From: A Accountant

Date: 9 December 2010

Subject: Costing systems and budgetary controls at RL

Introduction

Firstly, the costing and pricing methods are reviewed and results compared between the current absorption costing method and one using Activity Based Costing (ABC). Then, the impact of the choice of cost system is evaluated. Finally, the report provides an explanation of how a company could eliminate its use of budgets but still remain in control of the business and an evaluation of whether this would be a suitable choice for RL.

(a) **Costing systems**

The costing system is important in RL not just as a method of reporting activities in the business but also because it sets the price that the customer pays and so affects competitiveness. Absorption costing is a traditional system of allocating overhead costs to products based on production activity (labour hours in RL's case). ABC is an alternative for the allocation of overheads intended to capture the different activities that lead to costs being incurred. The principle benefit of ABC is that identification and monitoring of these activities leads to more accurate cost control.

ABC is most appropriate where overheads form a large proportion of the costs (at RL they are 23% of the total which is significant but not dominant). ABC is most often used in manufacturing where there are small batch sizes and significant tailoring of the product to customer specifications as is the case with RL.

Using Order 11784 as an example, RL would normally have calculated the cost per unit of this order at $2,556 and priced it at $3,706. Using ABC, RL would have costed the units at $3,194 each and priced them at $4,631, which represents an increase of 25%. The overhead allocated to the order by the traditional method is $596 while ABC allocates $1,234 per unit sold on the order. (The detailed workings are in the attached appendix.)

ABC has captured a significant underpricing of this order. The major components of the overhead can now be identified as the time spent discussing the order and the number of purchase orders that subsequently had to be raised. Management should now investigate whether such orders should be repriced at a different margin or whether action needs to be taken to make the call handling and purchasing associated with the order more efficient. The impact on the customer and competitive position of RL should be considered especially regarding any increase in selling price.

(b) **Beyond budgeting**

The monitoring of variances between actual and budgeted variance is often the primary control mechanism available to the management of a company. Therefore, the suggestion of dropping the process which forms a major part of the finance department's efforts in a year is likely to be greeted with surprise.

The process known as going beyond budgeting involves replacing the annual system of a centrally created budget with a more flexible system of targets. Performance measurement changes from monitoring variances from the budget towards measuring achievement of strategic goals, adding value and performance against suitable benchmarks.

The new system will use forecasts produced and revised regularly by the line managers, thus devolving decision-making. The forecasts will often be more important for cashflow monitoring rather than cost control. The targets are intended to guide rather than constrain the line managers thus improving their motivation.

The approach of going beyond budgeting is considered appropriate in industries where there are rapid changes in the business environment and where intangibles such as know-how are key to competitive advantage. This appears to be the case for RL as it operates in a sector dominated by technological change. The traditional budgetary approach has drawn criticism as it sets fixed targets which are not responsive to change during the budget period. The method also sits uncomfortably with management methods such as total quality approaches since they tend to preach a continuous improvement to processes. Budgets can also struggle in organisations using other radical change approaches to management such as business process re-engineering. As RL has been going through a period of poor performance, change is likely to be a feature of its operation in the near future.

Budgets are also criticised as stifling creativity in organisations. This creativity may help RL in finding solutions to its current financial difficulties. Budgets can be perceived as an imposition of top-down control and so conflict with giving all employees power to make decisions. A culture of innovation and employee empowerment would help to combat the problems faced by RL of losses of competitive position and key staff.

Finally, budgets can encourage gaming behaviour where staff act in the interests of expanding or padding their own budgets without considering the overall impact on the company. The focus on value-added targets of going beyond budgeting can help to avoid such dysfunctional behaviour.

Conclusion

A costing system change may be warranted as ABC appears to provide valuable additional information that will assist RL in addressing its financial problems. A detailed cost benefit analysis will have to be undertaken to identify if the extra work in collecting data on activities is warranted by this improvement in information for decision-making.

Additionally, RL appears to derive its advantage from the quality of its products and so innovation and flexibility in manufacturing and handling customers' needs will be paramount. Therefore, a non-budgetary system of control could be used at RL provided sources for appropriate alternative targets can be found.

APPENDIX:

Price per unit using Absorption costing and ABC for each unit of Order 11784

Standard cost	Direct		1,959.96
	O/hd allocation		596.22
	[Standard absorption rate = 14,190,000/(23,800*3)]		2,556.18
	Profit element		1,150.28
	Price		3,706.46
Order 11784	Units ordered		16

	Total of cost of activity $000s	No of driver units	Cost per driver unit
No of minutes on calls to customer	7,735	899,600	8.60
No of purchase orders raised	2,451	21,400	114.53
No of components used in production	1,467	618,800	2.37
Administration of production (absorbed as general overhead)	2,537	71,400	35.53

	Driver units on order	Cost allocated to order $	Cost per unit on order $
No of minutes on calls to customer	1,104	9,492	593.28
No of purchase orders raised	64	7,330	458.13
No of components used in production	512	1,214	75.86
Administration of production (absorbed as general overhead)	48	1,706	106.60

ABC cost

	$
Direct	1,960.00
O/hd allocation using ABC:	
Customer service	593.28
Purchasing and receiving	458.13
Stock management	75.86
Administration of production	106.60
	3,193.87
Profit element	1,437.24
Price	4,631.11
Difference between methods	24.9%

Marking scheme

		Marks
(a)	General discussion of the two methods – 1 mark per point up to 4 marks. Discussion of illustrative calculations – 1 mark per point up to 3 marks. Further action to undertake – up to 2 marks Conclusion on system of costing – 1 mark	
	Maximum	8
	Workings:	
	Absorption cost	
	• Cost per unit – 1 mark	
	• Price per unit – 1 mark	
	ABC cost	
	• Driver rates – 2 marks	
	• Cost per unit – 1 mark	
	• Price per unit – 1 mark	
	Difference between prices – 1 mark	
	(Ignore minor rounding differences provided the candidate has used a reasonable level of detail.)	
	Maximum	7
(b)	Status of budgets – 1 mark	
	Operation of beyond budgeting – up to 4 marks	
	Appropriateness of beyond budgeting for RL – 1 mark per point up to 6 marks	
	Maximum	10
	Professional marks (format, style and structure of report) are available up to a maximum of 4.	4
Total		**29**

Examiner's comments

In part (a), candidates were asked to evaluate a traditional costing method with an activity-based one (ABC).

Calculations of the result of using both these methods were possible and expected. There were significant variations in the overall quality of candidates' answers to this question. Those candidates who could correctly calculate the relevant costs scored well as they could then provide specific evidence for their recommendations about the two methods. Indeed, a good number scored 12 or more out of 15. Those that then continued the calculations to consider the main commercial implications of the two methods on the pricing at RL often scored full marks. Sadly, a number of candidates did not appear to know how to use the ABC method which should be considered a basic technique for a management accountant.

In part (b), candidates were asked to explain a 'beyond budgeting' approach and evaluate its use at RL. This part was generally well attempted although candidates often were sketchy on the details of implementation of this approach. It was pleasing to see many candidates analysing the environment for RL as competitive and innovative and applying these as criteria for judgement about whether the beyond budgeting approach suited the company. This is a good example of making the answer specific to the scenario.

Section 4

ANSWERS TO PRACTICE QUESTIONS – SECTION B

KEY AREAS FOR MOST QUESTIONS ARE HIGHLIGHTED

STRATEGIC PLANNING AND CONTROL

19   VIRTUAL ORGANISATIONS

> **Key answer tips**
>
> The question tests your understanding of a virtual organisation and asks for issues which would lead to strengths and weaknesses. Think about the importance of relationships within a virtual organisation.
>
> The second part of the question requires knowledge about environmental analysis and its importance to a networked organisation.

(a) **Virtual networked organisations: key strategic issues as potential strategic strengths or weaknesses**

There have been many critics of virtual companies because of their perceived inherent strategic weaknesses. Charles Handy, for example, once described them as a 'bag of contracts'. Others have claimed that virtual organisations do not possess any core competences.

The best examples of virtual organisations are dot.com companies. Many Internet companies have gone bust, fuelling the criticisms described above. Even companies held out as success stories have had a very mixed performance. Amazon, for example, describes itself as: 'the premier international retailer of books, music, and movies' and claims to deliver an 'online store, reliable shipping and delivery, and renowned customer service'. However, even Amazon failed to make a net profit until recently.

Advocates of virtual companies highlight their strengths as including the following:
- flexibility
- focus
- high growth potential, and
- asset efficiency.

Virtual organisations are highly dependent on the relationships that have been developed within and outside the organisation so the ability and skills needed to foster and develop these relationships are key to whether the firm has corresponding strengths or weaknesses.

Suppliers

When looking at relationships with suppliers, the following are often key issues that may result in strengths or weaknesses:

- What happens when 'things go wrong'? How reliable are suppliers? What back-up procedures exist?
- Is the organisation over-reliant on a few suppliers or have they multi-sourced?
- What systems are in place to manage suppliers?
- What expertise exists in managing suppliers?

Customers

Having a good relationship with customers and satisfying customer needs must be viewed as threshold competences – failure to deliver will spell disaster for the firm. When looking at relationships with customers, the following are often key issues that may result in strengths or weaknesses:

- Does the organisation feel 'real' to customers to give them confidence to buy?
- How secure are its buying processes – for example, are customers' personal information and credit card details kept private?
- What record does the firm have over delivery – what percentage of orders are delivered within the advertised timescales? This obviously ties into the relationship with the delivery firm used.
- Does the quality of packaging materials used reinforce the 'reality' of the organisation?
- How does the firm deal with complaints, errors and customer queries? Many firms have been criticised by watchdog groups for outsourcing customer care to call centres, others for not having enough staff to respond to problems.

Other

Other key issues can include the following:

- Learning and innovation often arise from the experience of doing things in-house.
- Virtual organisations can have isolated areas of expertise and knowledge without being able to integrate them, resulting in a lack of capacity for innovation.
- An organisation that fails to resolve these issues of internal relationships will show a strategic weakness.

(b) **Environmental analysis in an organisation that is highly networked**

Environmental analysis has been described as 'external auditing' or 'scanning', and relates to the collection of information on the environment within which an organisation operates.

ANSWERS TO PRACTICE QUESTIONS – SECTION B : SECTION 4

Benefits

The benefits of environmental analysis for highly networked organisations are predominantly the same as for any organisation:

- Generates information to help formulate strategy and to drive change.
- Identifies opportunities to exploit and threats to defend against.
- Helps the firm choose and develop its competitive advantage.
- Allows the firm to be responsive to market developments – for example, the actions of competitors.
- Identifies changing customer's demands and helps the firm to respond appropriately.

Areas of specific concern for networked firms include:

- Understanding the environments of suppliers to be able to anticipate potential problems and how best to manage them.

Difficulties

The main areas of difficulty are as follows:

- Increased difficulty obtaining information about (often chaotic) business environments in virtual organisations than in traditionally structured organisations.
- Information gathering is usually more effective when the whole organisation is coordinated to do it. In virtual organisations it can often fall to just a few departments or individuals.
- The organisation may become cut off from useful information that will now be obtained by sub-contractors and suppliers rather than internal departments. (*Note:* Organising suppliers' forums may help here).
- There will be less scope for employees from different areas to communicate ideas through general discussion and 'chats'.

Together these can result in a failure to obtain up-to-date relevant information for decision-making.

20 UNIVERSAL UNIVERSITY (UU) (JUN 09)

Key answer tips

The first part of this question tests your understanding of both Agency theory and Expectancy theory. First of all decide how you would describe the theories and then how they would apply to the University scenario.

Agency = relationship prinicpal (university) and agent (lecturer). Does the lecturer have his/her own interests at heart or that of the university?

Expectancy theory = on the view that the individual (or group) chooses to act on the basis of a level of preference and expectation

The final part of the question looks at the hard accountability of lecturing staff. Recording/accounting for numbers, accounting for numbers and accepting responsibility.

KAPLAN PUBLISHING

(a) (i) Agency theory considers the relationship between a principal and an agent. The problem is how the agent can be motivated and monitored. The key requirements are that the agent must have to account for his/her performance to the principal and that the principal must be able to hold the agent to account. The agent performs a task through the application of judgement and skill. The outcome depends on the efforts and methods adopted by the agent.

In the context of Universal University, the lecturer is the agent in using his/her skill and judgement in the creation, delivery and assessment aspects of the department/school on behalf of the university (the principal). The lecturer may be seen as adopting a risk seeking stance in using new/innovative approaches to the teaching/learning process or a risk averse stance where he/she continues with currently used approaches to teaching and learning.

The observability of the role of the lecturer as agent may be measured, by observing outcomes achieved. Examples of such measures may include the pass rates in assessments or levels of future choice of a module by students. The effort of the lecturer may be observed insofar as all lectures took place. However, the level of effort applied by the lecturer may be more difficult to measure in the short term. It could be observed retrospectively through patterns of attendance, feedback from students or pass rates achieved.

(ii) Expectancy theory focuses on the view that the individual (or group) chooses to act on the basis of a level of preference and expectation. Expectancy theory may be illustrated by the formula:

Force or strength of motivation to do × = (Valence or strength of preference for outcome Y) × (Expectation that doing × will result in Y)

In the University example: × may be, for example, the publication of articles by the lecturer. Y may be the wish by the lecturer to achieve promotion (extrinsic preference) or a feeling of 'achievement' (intrinsic preference) from the publication recognition.

In considering the suitability of the process, it may be asked to what extent the lecturer will be motivated in publishing regularly (X), through the expectation of promotion (Y). The level of motivation will be affected by the strength of preference of the lecturer for promotion.

If promotion is a relatively insignificant aspect in relation to the overall objectives of the lecturer, there may be little strength of preference. If promotion is a significant incentive, there may be a high strength of preference.

(b) Hard accountability may be viewed in the context of three specific areas. It will require (i) the accounting for the numbers, (ii) ensuring the numbers are accounted for and (iii) the group being held accountable for the events and circumstances leading to the numbers.

In the context of the application of **hard accountability** to the lecturing staff, it may be pursued through:

(i) **'accounting for the numbers'** may be implemented by monitoring the number of articles published, role in new courses developed or innovations in methods applied. Feedback from students and the number and type of comments received about the lecturing quality and lecturer support to students. The combination of these in the context will determine its value.

(ii) **'ensuring the numbers are accounted for'** may be addressed by reporting on the reasons 'how' and 'why' the figures have occurred. For example will the publication of a specific quality of articles (X) lead to the achievement of a high choice of a module by students (i.e. HOW?). Will a high level of student complaints occur through an inability to achieve the desired quality of lecturing when it is implemented and lead to a lower level of attendance or uptake of a module (i.e. WHY?).

(iii) **'being held accountable for events and circumstances leading to the numbers'.** For example, where the lecturer is deemed responsible after attendance at lectures is poor or student pass rates achieved are unduly low. It may be deemed that the quality of the lecturing is inadequate. Senior staff may be held accountable where there is a failure to ensure that all lecturers are adequately trained, briefed, motivated.

The motivation and application of lecturing staff may be monitored on an ongoing basis in order to determine whether the work structure/environment is ensuring that the accountability of the team is being equitably reflected in areas such as rates and levels of publication OR student numbers enrolling for, and achieving success, in a module.

Tutorial note

Alternative discussion points and illustrations would be accepted.

		Marking scheme		
				Marks
(a)	(i)	Agency theory		2
		Observability of outcomes		2
		Observability of effort		2
			Maximum	6
	(ii)	Strength of motivation to do (X)		2
		Strength of preference for outcome (Y)		2
		Expectation that doing (X) will result in (Y).		2
			Maximum	6
(b)	(i)	Comments (on merit)		3
	(ii)	Comments (on merit)		3
	(iii)	Comments (on merit).		3
			Maximum	8
Total				20

PAPER P5 : ADVANCED PERFORMANCE MANAGEMENT

> **Examiner's comments**
>
> This question was the least popular of the optional questions which, in general, candidates found rather challenging. There were some very good answers to parts (a)(i) and (a)(ii) which achieved very high marks. However, there were a large number of answers which demonstrated a misunderstanding of the nature of the relationships which were the focus of the requirements of these parts of the question. In particular, there were many confused efforts to explain expectancy theory. There were also a significant number of candidates who completely ignored the scenario contained in the question. In part (b) candidates were unable to explain 'hard accountability' in the context of the three specific areas within the Universal University.

21 DIVISIONAL ACTIONS

> **Key answer tips**
>
> This question deals with the possibility of management manipulating financial performance measures. To ensure a focused answer (and economic use of time) consider the three suggestions under the four headings in the question. Group management action is required to ensure such proposals being implemented prior to forthcoming bonus calculations.

Division A

In financial accounting terms, the reduction in discretionary expenditure will lead to higher reported divisional profits than would have been the case if the original planned expenditure had taken place. Discretionary expenditure should be charged against profits as it is incurred. No provisions or accruals need to be set up at the year end because the division is not compelled to make the expenditure.

There is some question as to whether the cut in training costs and repainting costs should be separately disclosed in the financial accounts to meet the overriding objective of giving a true and fair view. This depends on the materiality of the amounts involved, but is unlikely in the context of the group as a whole.

The ethical implications are more serious. The managers of Division A have deliberately manipulated the results in order to achieve the budget and be paid their bonuses. Their duty as managers is to serve the organisation, but they have served their own interests. Perhaps the two decisions can be distinguished from each other. The repainting of the premises is not important to the group; the timing of repainting is just the sort of matter than the group management should be happy to devolve to divisional management.

The lack of training is more serious. It will probably lead to higher costs next year which the group managers would not be happy about.

Division B

In financial accounting terms, the decision to defer payment to the consultants should make no difference to the division's reported profits. If work has been carried out but not yet paid for at the balance sheet date, the division must set up an accrual for the amounts due. This will be charged against profits. So this idea should have no effect on the divisional managers' bonus payable.

The only way that the idea would increase reported profits would be if the division abandoned the accruals concept and tried to defer the charging of the expense until the consultants were paid. This would be contrary to established accounting practices, and would attract criticism from the auditors if the amounts were sufficiently material.

If the divisional managers were familiar with accounting practices, but decided not to accrue for the payments in order to be paid their bonuses, an ethical question arises. These managers have shown themselves to act unethically, and the group managers should warn the divisional managers about their conduct.

If no accruals were made this year, then next year's profits would be lower when the total cost of the contract has to be charged against profits. To avoid this kind of shock, and in the interests of giving a true and fair view, an accrual for the work carried out at the balance sheet date should be set up.

Division C

In financial accounting terms, the point of sale is the point when the purchaser starts to take responsibility for the risks and rewards of the goods. This is usually when the purchaser accepts delivery of the goods. So, by delivering goods which are accepted before the balance sheet date, the division has successfully moved the date of sale into the current financial year. The profit on such sales can therefore be included in this year's reported profits, which will help to trigger the bonus payments.

There would only be financial accounting implications to the scheme where it was decided that showing the higher profit this year, with next year's profit being lower than it would otherwise have been, destroys the true and fair view of the accounts. This is unlikely to be the case, particularly in the context of the group as a whole.

The nil inventory at the yearend could cause problems at the start of the next financial year. Any large order received early next year could not be satisfied out of inventory; the purchaser might have to wait some time for the goods to be physically produced before they can be delivered. At best this is only an inconvenience to the purchaser. At the worst the sale may be lost altogether as the purchaser takes his custom elsewhere to a supplier who can deliver from inventory. Thus a scheme that was designed to trigger bonus payments to the divisional managers in the current year could end up costing the group sales and consequent profits next year.

As in the other divisions, the divisional management have acted unethically. The possible loss of sales next year, and the pressuring of customers to accept early sales this year, simply so that managers can be paid bonuses this year, is not acceptable.

Group management action

The whole logic of establishing a divisionalised structure within a group is to allow local managements to manage their divisions as they think best, subject to meeting broad group criteria.

Normally group management will adopt a hands-off attitude of observing procedures but not interfering. Interference would be resented by the divisional managers with adverse motivational consequences.

None of the proposals in the question is actually illegal, though division B's idea would be contrary to standard accounting practice, if an insufficient accrual were established. So, the group managers may feel unwilling to get involved and criticise the proposals.

However, there is a line to be drawn between legitimate 'income smoothing' (a good thing, since stock markets value highly companies with a smooth profit record) and manipulation of results to earn bonuses this year but which will depress profits next year. The idea of the bonus scheme is to reward good operational performance, not skills at profit manipulation. So, however unwilling they may be to interfere unnecessarily, the group managers' responsibility to the stakeholders at large means that they must take up each of these issues with the divisional management, if only to prevent these proposals from being put in place every year as the bonus calculations are drawing near.

22 DIVERSE HOLDINGS PLC (DEC 05)

> **Key answer tips**
>
> This question is tightly focused on the business strategy element of the syllabus. Candidates are invited to explain the advantages of a formal strategic planning system and this discussion should involve some reference to alternative approaches. Discussion is also invited of specific strategic planning technique such as SWOT and competitive analysis.

(a) The following are some of the advantages that may be gained as a consequence of the adoption of a formal system of strategic planning:

(1) Managers are forced to consider the future. Strategic planning can assist management to form a 'vision' of the future and, in so doing, encourages creativity and the use of initiative on the part of those involved in the strategic planning process.

(2) The identification of risks which may have gone unnoticed in the absence of formal planning systems.

(3) A strategic plan focuses management attention on the need to give due consideration to an ever-changing environment in which organisations can get left behind. A strategic plan highlights the need to anticipate change and assists in helping an organisation to become more 'adaptive' thereby increasing its chances of longer term prosperity.

(4) Greater consistency will be achieved between long term, medium term and short term objectives, plans and controls. The plans should identify whether the business objectives are leading an organisation in the right direction or whether organisational objectives require re-assessment. It is vital that strategic and operational considerations are reflected in systems of performance measurement and budgetary control.

(5) Strategic planning should help to identify the opportunities for investment and the need for long term finance well in advance of requirements.

(6) All markets have a cycle. Strategic planning should help to identify the need for and timing of the launching of new products.

(7) Strategic planning will entail the review of management resources. Management does not remain unaltered for decades.

The strategic plan may identify the need for new or additional management expertise.

Note: Only four reasons were required.

(b) The use of SWOT analysis will focus management attention on current strengths and weaknesses of each subsidiary company which will be of assistance in the formulating of the business strategy of Diverse Holdings Plc. It will also enable management to monitor trends and developments in the constantly changing environments of their subsidiaries. Each trend or development may be classified as an opportunity or a threat that will provide a stimulus for an appropriate management response.

Management can make an assessment of the feasibility of required actions in order that the company may capitalise upon opportunities whilst considering how best to negate or minimise the effect of any threats.

A SWOT analysis should assist the management of Diverse Holdings Plc as they must identify their strengths, weaknesses, opportunities and threats. These may be classified as follows:

- Strengths which appear to include both OFL and HTL.
- Weaknesses which must include PSL and its limited outlets, which generate little growth and could collapse over-night. KAL is also a weakness due to its declining profitability.
- Opportunities where OFT, HTL and OPL are operating in growth markets.
- Threats from which KAL is suffering.

If these four categories are identified and analysed then the group should be strengthened.

(c) (i) Organic Foods Ltd (OFL) with a market share of 6.66% is the market leader at 30 November 2005 and is forecast to have a market share of 8% by 30 November 2007. Operating profits appear to be healthy and therefore it seems reasonable to regard OFL as a current 'strength' of Diverse Holdings Plc. This is supported by the fact that OFL has built up a very good reputation as a supplier of quality produce.

Haul Trans Ltd (HTL) was acquired on 1 December 2005 and has a demonstrable record of recent profitability. It is noticeable that the profitability of HTL is forecast to increase by 40% (excluding inflation) during its first two years of ownership. No one organisation appears to dominate the market. Forecast profits are expected to grow significantly from an almost static turnover and thus more information is required regarding how this increase in profitability is to be achieved. Management may have identified the opportunity for achieving significant cost savings and/or forming business relationships with new and more profitable customers while ceasing to service those customers who are less profitable.

Kitchen Appliances Ltd (KAL) has been identified as both a weakness and threat. KAL's market is slowly contracting, but its share is falling more quickly. It was almost the market leader at 30 November 2005. Judging by its fall in the level of operating profit KAL is carrying heavy fixed costs which must make it more difficult to compete. Indeed, it is forecast to make a loss during the year ending 30 November 2007.

KAL has suffered from squeezed margins as a consequence of competition from low cost imports. The situation may be further exacerbated as competition from abroad intensifies.

Paper Supplies Ltd (PSL) has stood still in a growing market, one which is dominated by a single supplier. PSL appears to be struggling to achieve any growth in turnover, profits and therefore cash flow. PSL cannot really compete with a narrow range of products and only two customers.

Office Products Ltd (OPL) is growing but appears unable to increase its operating profit in % terms. It appears to be operating in a high-growth market but unable to achieve a reasonable market share in spite of the fact that its products are highly regarded by health and safety experts.

(ii) The forecast situation of Diverse Holdings Plc is not without its problems. KAL and OPL require the immediate attention of management. The position of KAL is precarious to say the least. There is a choice of strategies for it:

- Outsource the manufacture of appliances
- Set up a manufacturing operation overseas
- Withdraw from the market.

Each alternative must be assessed. Whatever decision is taken it is unlikely to affect the other four subsidiaries.

PSL is also independent of the other subsidiaries. A strategic decision to widen its range of products and outlets must surely help. Hence management should endeavour to find new markets for its products, which are separate and distinct from those markets served by its appointed distributors.

In order to improve the prospects of OPL management need to adopt appropriate strategies since at the present time the company appears to be in a high growth market but is unable to capture a reasonable market share. Perhaps the answer lies in increased or more effective advertising of the endorsement of the product range by health and safety experts.

Management should endeavour to develop a strategy to integrate further its subsidiaries so that they can benefit from each other and to derive as much synergy as possible from the acquisition of HTL.

It is of paramount importance that management ensure that sufficient funds are channelled into growing OFL and HTL, which are both showing a rising trend in profitability. The group has depleted cash reserves which must to some extent be attributable to the purchase of HTL. It is possible that the divestment of KAL would provide some much needed funding.

23 ALTERNATIVE BUDGETING (JUN 06)

Key answer tips

This question invites a general discussion of the traditional budgeting model and its relevance in 'the New Economy'. In answering this question, it is important to state that the limitations of the budgeting model have long been apparent and practitioners have tried to modify that model in order to adapt it to modern circumstances. The switch from incremental to zero-based and activity based budgeting are examples of this line of thinking.

However, some contemporary management experts favour dispensing with the model altogether in favour of new alternatives. The use of performance metrics based on external benchmarks or performance indicators linked to key success factor ('KSFs') is a central element in this line of thought.

(a) The weaknesses of traditional budgeting processes include the following:

- Many commentators, including Hope and Fraser, contend that budgets prepared under traditional processes add little value and requires far too much valuable management time which would be better spent elsewhere.

- Too heavy a reliance on the 'agreed' budget has an adverse impact on management behaviour which can become dysfunctional having regard to the objectives of the organisation as a whole.

- The use of budgeting as base for communicating corporate goals, setting objectives, continuous improvement, etc is seen as contrary to the original purpose of budgeting as a financial control mechanism.

- Most budgets are not based on a rational causal model of resource consumption but are often the result of protracted internal bargaining processes.

- Conformance to budget is not seen as compatible with a drive towards continuous improvement.

- Budgeting has an insufficient external focus.

(b) (i) **Benchmarking**

Benchmarks enable goals to be set that may be based on either external measures of 'best practice' organisations or internal cross-functional comparisons which exhibit 'best practice'. A primary aim of the traditional budgeting process is the setting of realistic targets that can be achieved within the budget period. The setting of realistic targets means that the extent of underperformance against 'best practice' standards loses visibility, and thus short-term financial targets remain the predominant focus of the traditional budgeting process. It is arguable that because the budgetary reporting system purports to give managers 'control', there is very little real incentive to seek out benchmarks which may be used to raise budgeted performance targets.

Much depends upon the prevailing organisational culture since benchmarking may be viewed as an attempt by top management to impose impossible targets upon operational managers. The situation is further exacerbated where organisations do not measure their success relative to their competition.

(ii) **Balanced scorecard**

The balanced scorecard is often misunderstood because of the failure by top management to ensure that it is implemented effectively within the organisation. Thus it may be simply viewed as the addition of a few non-financial measures to the conventional budget. In an attempt to overcome this misperception many management teams now establish a performance-rewards linkage based upon the achievement of scorecard targets for the forthcoming budget period. Unfortunately this can precipitate dysfunctional behaviour at every level within the organisation.

Even in situations where the scorecard has been well-designed and well-implemented it is difficult for it to gain widespread acceptance. This is because all too often there exists a culture which places a very high value upon the achievement of the fixed annual targets in order to avoid the loss of status, recognition and rewards.

A well-constructed scorecard contains a mix of long-term and short-term measures over the four elements of the scorecard (financial perspective, internal business perspective, customer perspective, and innovation and learning perspective). These drive the company in the direction of medium-term strategic goals which are supported by cross-functional initiatives. On the other hand, the budgeting process focuses the organisation on the achievement of short-term financial goals supported by the initiatives of individual departments. Budgets can also act as an impediment to the acceptance of responsibility by local managers for the achievement of the scorecard targets. This is often the case in situations where a continued emphasis exists on meeting short-term e.g. quarterly targets.

(iii) **Activity-based models**

Traditional budgets show the costs of functions and departments (e.g. staff costs and establishment costs) instead of the costs of those activities that are performed by people (e.g. receipt of goods inwards, processing and dispatch of orders etc). Thus managers have no visibility of the real 'cost drivers' of their business. In addition, it is probable that a traditional budget contains a significant amount of non-value-added costs that are not visible to the managers. The annual budget also tends to fix capacity for the forthcoming budget period thereby undermining the potential of Activity-based management (ABM) analysis to determine required capacity from a customer demand perspective. Those experienced in the use of ABM techniques are used to dealing with such problems, however their tasks would be much easier to perform and their results made more reliable if these problems were removed.

24 PERFORMANCE MANAGEMENT (JUN 06)

> **Key answer tips**
>
> A very straight forward question asking for a discussion on key terms. It is important that you do not spend too much time on definitions but ensure that your answer includes examples relating to a NFP and profit-seeking organisation as requested. The second part asks for candidates to use an organisation of their choice and apply the structured application.

(a) **Objectives** may be viewed as profit and market share in a profit-oriented organisation or the achievement of 'value for money' in a not-for-profit organisation (NFP). The overall objective of an organisation may be expressed in the wording of its mission statement.

In order to achieve the objectives, long-term **strategies** will be required. In a profit-oriented organisation, this may incorporate the evaluation of strategies that might include price reductions, product design changes, advertising campaign, product mix change and methods changes, embracing change techniques such as BPR, JIT, TQM and ABM. In NFP situations, strategies might address the need to achieve 'economy' through reduction in average cost per unit; 'efficiency' through maximisation of the input:output ratio, whilst checking on 'effectiveness' through monitoring whether the objectives are achieved.

The annual budget will quantify the short-term **results** anticipated of the strategies. These results may be seen as the level of financial performance and competitiveness achieved. This quantification may be compared with previous years and with actual performance on an ongoing basis. Financial performance may be measured in terms of profit, liquidity, capital structure and a range of ratios. Competitiveness may be measured by sales growth, market share and the number of new customers. In a not-for-profit organisation the results may be monitored by checking on the effectiveness of actions aimed at the achievement of the objectives. For instance, the effectiveness of a University may be measured by the number of degrees awarded and the grades achieved. The level of student 'drop-outs' each year may also be seen as a measure of ineffectiveness.

The **determinants** of results may consist of a number of measures. These may include the level of quality, customer satisfaction, resource utilisation, innovation and flexibility that are achieved. Such determinants may focus on a range of non-financial measures that may be monitored on an ongoing basis, as part of the feedback information in conjunction with financial data.

A range of **business change techniques** may be used to enhance performance management.

Techniques may include:

Business process re-engineering (BPR), which involves the examination of business processes with a view to improving the way in which each is implemented. A major focus may be on the production cycle, but it will also be applicable in areas such as the accounting department.

Just-in-time (JIT), which requires commitment to the pursuit of 'excellence' in all aspects of an organisation.

Total quality management (TQM), which aims for continuous quality improvement in all aspects of the operation of an organisation.

Activity based management systems (ABM), which focus on activities that are required in an organisation and the cost drivers for such activities, with a view to identifying and improving activities that add value and eliminating those activities that do not add value.

Long-term performance management is likely to embrace elements of BPR, JIT, TQM and ABM. All of these will be reflected in the annual budget on an ongoing basis.

(b)

Tutorial note

Consider an organisation you work for or have dealt with.

An illustration of the features detailed above, framed in the context of a University as an organisation in the not-for-profit sector might be as follows:

The **overall objective** might well be stated in the mission statement of a University. An example of such a mission statement might be as follows:

'To provide a quality educational environment in a range of undergraduate and post-graduate disciplines and a quality educational focus for students and the business community.'

More specifically, objectives may be seen as the achievement of 'value for money' thereby ensuring effectiveness in areas such as:

- The provision of high added value to students.
- The establishment of a reputation for recognised expertise in specific areas of research work within the wider community..
- The provision of a high quality service to industry and commerce.

Strategies may focus on aspects such as:

- The recruitment and retention of high quality academic staff.
- The development of IT equipment and skills within the institution.
- The mentoring of students in order to ensure high added value and low drop-out rates in intermediate years of study.
- The close liaison with employers as to qualities in graduate/post-graduate employees that they will value highly.

The **determinants** used to measure the **results** of strategies might include:

- Competitiveness – cost per graduate compared to other institutions; growth in student numbers; number of staff holding a PhD qualification.
- Financial performance – average cost per graduate; income generation from consultancy work.
- Quality – range of awards (percentages of 1st class degrees); employer responses; measures of quality of delivery of education, advice to students, etc.
- Flexibility – variable entry and exit points to courses; modular structure; the variety of full-time, part-time and distance learning modes.
- Resource utilisation – staff:student ratios; quotas met by each course; accommodation filled.
- Innovation – latest IT provision in linking lecture theatres to information databases; increased provision of flexi-learning/mixed mode course provision.

The application of **business change techniques** might include the following:

- BPR with a focus on IT developments, flexible-learning or mixed mode course provision.
- JIT with a focus on moves towards student-centred uptake of educational opportunities e.g. via intranet availability of lecture and tutorial material linked to more flexible access to staff rather than a 'push' system of pre-structured times of lectures/tutorials.
- TQM with a focus on moves to improve quality in all aspects of the learning environment including delivery of lectures, access to staff and pastoral care issues.
- ABM with a focus on activities on a per student basis (both planned and actual) with a view to eliminating activities that do not add value e.g. cost per lecture per student.

ANSWERS TO PRACTICE QUESTIONS – SECTION B : **SECTION 4**

25 BUSINESS PROCESS RE-ENGINEERING

> **Key answer tips**
>
> This question tests your knowledge of Business Process Re-Engineering (BPR) and how the management accountant contributes to its planning and implementation.
>
> You need to clearly identify the different parts of the question and ensure that an appropriate amount of time is spent on each part.

(a) Business process re-engineering (BPR) is one of a number of techniques that have been advocated to overhaul existing business processes and practices with a view to radically improving organisational performance. It goes further than routine automation and rationalisation.

BPR is not confined to manufacturing processes and has been applied to a wide range of administrative and operational activities. In each case the idea is to ask radical questions about why things are done in a particular way, and whether alternative methods could achieve better results. Often the focus has been on staffing levels, the implication being that more staff are employed than are strictly needed to achieve the desired outcomes. However, this is a by-product of the technique and is not a main purpose of BPR.

(b) The management accountant contributes to planning a BPR exercise above all by providing the information required to evaluate alternatives. As mentioned above, the primary purpose of BPR is to investigate different ways in which defined outcomes can be achieved. The effects of each method on costs and profitability will be a key criterion in determining the best option, and the management accountant is well placed to provide such information.

The management accountant will work closely with operational managers to achieve this. By looking at their existing processes, and helping to formulate alternatives, the management accountant will inform himself or herself in detail about what is involved. The task then is to translate this information into financial form. The methods of reporting on processes may themselves need to be revised as a result: often adoption of BPR has gone hand in hand with a move to activity based costing.

As the term suggests, BPR is concerned with how processes are to work in practice. In implementing a BPR programme, managers will be concerned to have the appropriate information to enable them to manage new processes. Management accountants can help by reconsidering the form in which reports are presented. In many cases, the required change will be from an emphasis on transactions processing to an emphasis on decision making and control. Underlying all of this should be a focus on customer needs.

Once the appropriate information has been determined, it is equally important to ensure that it is presented appropriately. If the new emphasis is on support for decision making it is essential that managers can appreciate the information and digest it rapidly. User friendliness is an important criterion, and too much detail is as unhelpful as too little.

PAPER P5 : ADVANCED PERFORMANCE MANAGEMENT

(c) **Advantages of BPR**

(i) BPR revolves around customer needs and helps to give an appropriate focus to the business and its purpose.

(ii) BPR provides cost advantages that assist the organisation's competitive position.

(iii) BPR encourages a long-term strategic view of operational processes by asking radical questions about how things are done and how processes could be improved.

(iv) BPR helps overcome the short-sighted approaches that sometimes emerge from excessive concentration on functional boundaries. By focusing on entire processes the exercise can streamline activities throughout the organisation.

(v) BPR can help to reduce organisational complexity by eliminating unnecessary activities.

Criticisms of BPR

(i) BPR is sometimes seen (incorrectly) as a means of making small improvements in existing practices. In reality, it is a more radical approach that questions whether existing practices make any sense in their present form.

(ii) BPR is sometimes seen (incorrectly) as a single, once-for-all cost-cutting exercise. In reality, it is not primarily concerned with cost-cutting (though cost reductions often result), and should be regarded as ongoing rather than once-for-all. This misconception often creates hostility in the minds of staff who see the exercise as a threat to their security.

(iii) BPR requires a far-reaching and long-term commitment by management and staff. Securing this is not an easy task, and many organisations have rejected the whole idea as not worth the effort.

26 BUDGETING (PILOT 07)

> Key answer tips
>
> This question tests your knowledge of budgeting theory, both in general terms in part (a) and the specifics of "beyond budgeting" in part (c). Expect questions in the real exam under the new examiner to contain more application.

(a) Budgeting may be viewed as of use in planning, co-ordination, control, motivation and performance evaluation.

As a **planning aid,** the budgeting process allows for the quantification of the business plan. Alternative planning scenarios may be examined and a 'what-if' analysis applied. This feed-forward view will enable a proposed plan to be compared with the level of achievement that is required in order to provide the level of return required by the organisation. If necessary amendments can be made in order that the agreed plan will achieve the required level of return.

It may be argued that the identification and quantification of factors such as customer satisfaction may limit the level of accuracy achieved.

The **co-ordination** of business activities will be aided through the budgeting process. Areas of imbalance, for example between production capacity available and that required to satisfy demand, may be identified and investigated. The co-ordination process should also avoid individual members of management making planning that are sub-optimal for the business as a whole.

The achievement of co-ordination benefits may be diminished because of factors such as lack of adequate communication, both internally between management members and externally through inadequate links with suppliers.

The **control** of business activities may be aided through the comparison of actual results against the budget plan. Any differences may be investigated and corrective action taken.

This process may not be effective because of factors such as the type of budgeting system in use or the lack of management expertise in the interpretation of the information. For example, is actual data compared against a suitably flexed budget?

The budget should act as a **motivating** device. This should be enhanced through the feeling of involvement which participation in the budgeting process will promote. Management is more likely to identify and work toward achieving, targets that has agreed in advance. It is possible however, that management may view the budget as a pressure device in trying to get them to achieve a level of performance that they do not see as achievable.

Budgets may be used a base against which to measure actual **performance.** The measures may be quantitative in both monetary and non-monetary terms. Examples might be the monitoring of cash flow or the percentage of material losses incurred. The trend of variances between budget and actual may be monitored in order to help identify whether an 'in control' or 'out of control' situation exists.

The usefulness of the measures may be limited through factors such as lack of relevant information and/or management style and attitudes. *(Alternative relevant uses and comments would be accepted.)*

(b) Advantages claimed for the use of activity based budgeting include the following:

- Resource allocation is linked to a strategic plan for the future, prepared after considering alternative strategies. Traditional budgets tend to focus on resources and inputs rather than on objectives and alternatives.

- New high priority activities are encouraged, rather than focusing on the existing planning model. Activity based budgeting focuses on activities. This allows the identification of the cost of each activity. It also allows the ranking of activities where financial constraints limit the range of activities that may be achieved.

- There is more focus on efficiency and effectiveness and the alternative methods by which they may be achieved. Activity based budgeting assists in the operation of a total quality philosophy.

- It avoids arbitrary cuts in specific budget areas in order to meet the overall financial targets. Non-value added activities may be identified as those which should be eliminated.

- It tends to increase management commitment to the budget process. This should be achieved since the activity analysis enables management to focus on the objectives of each activity. Identification of primary and secondary activities and non-value added activities should also help in motivating management in activity planning and control.

PAPER P5 : ADVANCED PERFORMANCE MANAGEMENT

The effectiveness of activity based budgeting may be limited because of its complexity and its acceptance by management. For example accurate identification of activities and the cost drivers which determine the level of resources required for each activity may be difficult to achieve.

(c) Current research on budgeting indicates that some organisations claim that they have abandoned the major annual budget preparation exercise ('Beyond Budgeting' – Hope & Fraser (2003). It has been argued that a number of adverse impacts result from the budget. Examples of such impact are:

- Annual budgeting adds little value and takes up too much valuable management time.
- Too heavy reliance on budgetary control in managing performance has an adverse impact on management behaviour.
- The use of budgeting as a base for communicating corporate goals, setting objectives, assisting continuous improvement, etc. is seen as contrary to its original purpose as a financial control mechanism.
- Most budgets are not based on a rational causal model of resource consumption and are, therefore, of little use in determining strategy.
- The process has insufficient external focus from which to derive targets or benchmarks.
- The argument may be put that increased focus on knowledge or intellectual capital through competent managers, skilled workforce, effective systems, loyal customers and strong brands is more likely to yield improved business effectiveness. (Alternative relevant uses and comments would be accepted in all parts of the answer).

27 THE 'CARE FOR DOGS COMPANY' (CFD) (DEC 09)

> **Key answer tips**
>
> An excellent question examining the link between mission, CSFs and KPIs. In many respects this is foundational material so should have presented few problems to students.

(a) (i) A 'mission' is the purpose of an entity and its reason for existence, i.e. what is it attempting to accomplish? Henry Mintzberg has stated that 'a mission describes the organisation's basic function in society, in terms of the products and services it produces for its customers'. A large number of organisations provide a formal statement of their mission in a mission statement. Even though an entity might not have a clearly defined mission it may nevertheless have a mission statement!

A mission statement should be both memorable and succinct. It should also be 'enduring', i.e. the statement should not change unless an entity's mission changes otherwise the mission statement would serve to confuse the business community.

The mission statement should guide all employees throughout an organisation to work collectively towards the accomplishment of the corporate mission and may contain references to many stakeholder groups such as, for example, shareholders, customers, employees and the general public.

ANSWERS TO PRACTICE QUESTIONS – SECTION B : **SECTION 4**

Potential benefits of mission statements include:

- providing strategic direction to the organisation thereby assisting in the formulation of acceptable strategies
- assisting in the resolution of potential conflict among different stakeholder groups
- providing a framework within which managerial decisions can be made
- assisting in the communication of key cultural values to employees
- assisting in the presentation of a clear image of the organisation for the benefit of customers and other interested parties
- helping to prevent potential misinterpretations of the organisation's 'reason for being'.

Potential problems of mission statements include the following:

- They may be unclear
- They may be vague and therefore valueless
- They may contain 'motherhood statements'
- They may be unrealistic and not reflect reality
- There may be inconsistency between different elements
- They may be inconsistent with management action
- They may lack sufficient external focus.

(ii) Up until now it would appear that the mission statement of CFD was relevant to its central mission '….thereby providing very high value for money to all our clients'.

However, the proposed opening of the Dog Sanctuary might be considered to have changed the mission of CDC. The Dog Sanctuary is a good example of the concern of the directors of CFD for Corporate Social Responsibility. The concern is obviously not one solely based on profitability or continued 'value for money' for its customers.

Therefore one might conclude that the mission statement no longer communicates to the business world what CFD is all about and that a change in mission can necessitate a revised mission statement.

(b) Critical success factors (CSF's) are performance requirements that must be achieved if an organisation is to be successful and outperform its competition. In the context of CFD, CSFs should be regarded as those service features that are particularly valued by dog owners.

Three critical success factors are as follows:

Health – All dog owners wish their pets to be healthy and therefore it is essential that staff at CFD take all necessary steps to ensure that the premises are free of disease. A key performance indicator in this regard would be the number of dogs that become ill during a stay at CFD's premises.

Safety – Dog owners are entrusting their pets to CFD who are responsible for the safety of all dogs taken into care. A key performance indicator in this regard would be the number of accidents reported during a given period.

Cleanliness – It is vital that CFD achieve the highest possible level of cleanliness throughout its entire premises. An example of a key performance indicator with regard to cleanliness would be the length of time taken to clean the dog kennels.

(c) In order to assess the quality of service provided by the CFD the following performance measures might be used:

- The percentage of repeat bookings by dog owners which is evidence of customer satisfaction and perhaps ultimately customer loyalty.
- The percentage of dog owners who were able to book a dog stay at their preferred date and time is an indication of the availability or non-availability of the service provided by CFD.
- The percentage of dogs that were collected and delivered on time from and to the homes of dog owners.

	Marking scheme			Marks
(a)	Purpose		2.0	
	Potential benefits		3.0	
	Potential problems		3.0	8.0
	Changed circumstances	Up to 2		
	Conclusion	Up to 2		3.0
(b)	Critical success factor	3 × 2	6.0	6.0
(c)	Performance measures	3 × 1	3.0	3.0
Total				**20.0**

Examiner's comments

In general, this question was well answered. A large number of candidates provided very good answers to part (a)(i) and achieved maximum or very high marks. In contrast, there was a significant variation in the quality of candidates' answers to part (a)(ii). Poorer answers tended to completely ignore the scenario contained in the question in which candidates were required to 'advise the directors of CFD of the appropriateness of its mission statement'. That said a large number of candidates who used the scenario gained the three available marks. There were a large number of very good answers to part (b) and, in general, the quality of candidates' answers to part (b) was satisfactory. The majority of answers to part (c) were satisfactory with a large number of candidates gaining the three available marks. That said a significant number of candidates ignored the scenario choosing instead to simply list a number of irrelevant performance measures to the scenario of CFD.

28 THE RUBBER GROUP (TRG) (JUN 08)

Key answer tips

Candidates must answer each part of the question and relate to the scenario contained within the question. It is very easy with this type of question to write everything you know rather than answering the question. Remember it is the 'quality' of an answer and not the 'quantity' of an answer which is awarded credit.

Suggested answer content for each of the eight problems contained within the scenario is as follows:

(a) The nature of each of the problems relating to the use of budgeting is as follows:

Meeting only the lowest targets

- infers that once a budget has been negotiated, unless there is good reason to achieve a higher standard. the budget holder will be satisfied with this level of performance

Using more resources than necessary

- Once the budget has been agreed the focus will be to ensure that the budgeted utilisation of resources has been adhered to. Indeed the current system does not provide a specific incentive not to exceed the budget level. It may be, however, that failure to achieve budget targets would reflect badly on factors such as future promotion prospects or job security.

Making the bonus – whatever it takes

- A bonus system is linked to the budget setting and achievement process might lead to actions by employees and management which they regard as 'fair game'. This is because they view the maximisation of bonuses as the main priority in any aspect of budget setting or work output.

Competing against other divisions, business units and departments

- Competition may manifest itself through the attitudes adopted in relation to transfer pricing of goods/services between divisions, lack of willingness to co-operate on sharing information relating to methods, sources of supply, expertise, etc.

Ensuring that what is in the budget is spent

- Management may see the budget setting process as a competition for resources. Irrespective of the budgeting method used, there will be a tendency to feel that unless the budget allowance for one year is spent, there will be imposed reductions in the following year. This will be particularly relevant in the case of fixed cost areas where expenditure is viewed as discretionary to some extent.

Providing inaccurate forecasts

- This infers that some aspects of budgeting problems such as 'Gaming' and 'misrepresentation' may be employed by the budget holder in order to gain some advantage.

    Gaming may be seen as a deliberate distortion of the measure in order to secure some strategic advantage. Misrepresentation refers to creative planning in order to suggest that the measure is acceptable.

Meeting the target but not beating it

- There may be a view held by those involved in the achievement of the budget target that there is **no incentive for them to exceed that level of effectiveness.**

Avoiding risks

- There may be a prevailing view by those involved in the achievement of the budget target that wherever possible strategies incorporated into the achievement of the budget objective should be left unchanged if they have been shown to be acceptable in the past. Change may be viewed as increasing the level of uncertainty that the proposed budget target will be achievable.

(b) An illustration of each of the **problems using the data from the Battamould division/TRG scenario** is as follows:

Meeting only the lowest targets

- In the scenario, the budgeted variable cost of $200 per tonne has been agreed. There is no specific incentive for the Bettamould division to try to achieve a better level of performance.

Using more resources than necessary

- In the scenario, the current budget allows for 5% machine idle time. There is evidence that a move to outsourcing machine maintenance from a specialist company could help reduce idle time levels and permit annual output in excess of 100,000 tonnes.

Making the bonus – whatever it takes

- At present, the only sanction/incentive is to achieve 100,000 tonnes of output. There is no mention of any sanction for example, if processing losses (and hence costs) rise to 20% of material inputs.

Competing against other divisions, business units and departments

- At present, the Bettamould division sources its materials from chosen suppliers who have been used for some years. There is evidence that materials of equal specification could be sourced for 40% of the annual requirement from another TRG division which has spare capacity. Why has this not been investigated?

Ensuring that what is in the budget is spent

- In the Bettamould scenario, there is a fixed cost budget allowance of $50,000,000. We are told in the question that salaries of all employees and management are paid on a fixed salary basis. Bettamould's management will not want a reduction in the fixed budget allowance, since this could lead to the need to reduce the number of employees, which they may see as having a detrimental effect on the ability of the division to meet its annual budget output target of 100,000 tonnes.

Providing inaccurate forecasts

- In the scenario there may have been deliberate efforts to increase the agreed budget level of aspects of measures and costs. For example, by putting forward the argument that the budget requirement of 15% processing losses is acceptable because of the likelihood that ageing machinery will be less effective in the coming budget period.

Meeting the target but not beating it

- In the scenario the bonus of 5% of salary is payable as long as the 100,000 tonnes of output is achieved. This does not require that actual results will show any other aspects of the budget being improved upon. For example there is no need to consider a reduction in the current level of quality checks (25% of daily throughput) to the 10% level that current evidence suggests is achieved by competitor companies. The current budget agreement allows the Bettamould division to transfer its output to market based profit centres at $200 + $500 = $700 per tonne. There is no specified penalty if costs exceed this target level.

Avoiding risks

- Bettamould has not yet incorporated the changes listed in note 4 in the question. For example why has the sourcing of 40% of required materials from another TRC division not been quantified and evaluated. It is possible that the division with spare capacity could supply the material at cost (possibly based on marginal cost) which would be less than currently paid to a supplier external to TRC. It may be that Bettamould have not pursued this possibility because of risk factors relating to the quality of the material transferred or its continued availability where the supplying division had an upturn in the level of more profitable external business.

(c) Ways in which each of the problems might be overcome are as follows:

Meeting only the lowest targets

- To overcome the problem there must be some additional incentive. This could be through a change in the basis of bonus payment which currently only provides an incentive to achieve the 100,000 tonnes of output.

Using more resources than necessary

- Overcoming the problem may require a change in the bonus system which currently does not provide benefit from any output in excess of 100,000 tonnes. This may not be perceived as sufficiently focused in order to achieve action. It may be that engendering a culture of continuous improvement would help ensure that employees actively sought ways of reducing idle time levels.

Making the bonus – whatever it takes

- It is likely that efforts to change the 'work ethos' at all levels is required, while not necessarily removing the concept of a bonus payable to all employees for achievement of targets. This may require the fostering of a culture for success within the company. Dissemination of information to all staff relating to trends in performance, meeting targets, etc may help to improve focus on continuous improvement.

Competing against other divisions, business units and departments

- The problem may need some input from the directors of TRG. For example, could a 'be explained to management at both the Bettamould division and also dual-cost' transfer pricing system the Division with spare capacity in order to overcome resistance to problems on transfer pricing and its impact on divisional budgets and reported results? In this way it may be possible for the Bettamould division to source some of its input materials at a lower cost (particularly from TRG's viewpoint) and yet be acceptable to the management at the supplying division.

Ensuring that what is in the budget is spent

- In order to overcome the problem it may be necessary to educate management into acceptance of aspects of budgeting such as the need to consider the committed, engineered and discretionary aspects of costs. For example, it may be possible to reduce the number of salaried staff involved in the current quality checking of 25% of throughput on a daily basis.

Providing inaccurate forecasts

- In order to overcome this problem there must be an integrated approach to the budget setting process. This may be achieved to some extent through all aspects of the budget having to be agreed by all functions involved. For example, engineers as well as production line management in reaching the agreed link between percentage process losses and the falling efficiency of machinery due to age. In addition, TRC may insist an independent audit of aspects of budget revisions by group staff.

Meeting the target but not beating it

- To overcome the problem may require that the bonus system should be altered to reflect any failure to control costs per tonne at the budget level.

Avoiding risks

- In order to overcome such problems, TRC would have to provide some guarantees to Bettamould management that the supply would be available during the budget period at the initially agreed price and that the quality would be maintained at the required level. This would remove the risk element that the management of the Bettamould division may consider currently exists.

Marking scheme			
		Marks	Marks
Comments (on merit):			
(a) Nature	6 × 2	12	
(b) Illustration	6 × 1	6	
(c) Remedy	6 × 1	6	Maximum 24
Professional mark			1
Total			**25**

> **Examiner's comments**
>
> Weaker answers tended to ignore the scenario contained within the question or simply did not address the requirements of each part of the question.
>
> Some answers were very long though most were satisfactory. However candidates should be mindful that it is the 'quality' of an answer and not the 'quantity' of an answer which is awarded credit.

ANSWERS TO PRACTICE QUESTIONS – SECTION B : SECTION 4

EXTERNAL INFLUENCES ON ORGANISATIONAL PERFORMANCE

29 BOARDMAN FOODS (BF)

> **Key answer tips**
>
> While this question may appear over-mathematical, it is based on the article, "The risks of uncertainty" in October 09 by Michael Pogue.

(a) The probability that the production line has been properly maintained given that the first meal was correctly packaged, can probably be most easily found by constructing a probability table

Machine maintenance	Good		Poor	
Probability	0.97		0.03	
Food Packaging	1st item correct	1st item faulty	1st item correct	1st item faulty
Probability	0.95	0.05	0.3	0.7
Probability of each outcome	0.97 × 0.95 = 0.9215	0.97 × 0.05 = 0.0485	0.03 × 0.3 = 0.009	0.03 × 0.7 = 0.021

The probability of the first meal being correctly packaged is 0.9215 + 0.009 = 0.9305

The probability that the first meal is correctly packaged when the machine is well maintained is 0.9215

Therefore the probability that the line has been properly maintained given that the first meal was correctly packaged is 0.9215 / 0.9305 = 0.99 or 99%.

(b) **Expected value of the different levels of marketing spend**

Speed of recovery	Slow	Moderate	Rapid	
Probability	0.58	0.26	0.16	
				Total EV ($)
Marketing spend				
High	15,000 × 0.58 = 8,700	48,000 × 0.26 = 12,480	92,000 × 0.16 = 14,720	35,900
Medium	30,000 × 0.58 = 17,400	43,000 × 0.26 = 11,180	77,000 × 0.16 = 12,320	40,900
Low	22,000 × 0.58 = 12,760	44,000 × 0.26 = 11,440	51,000 × 0.16 = 8,160	32,360

The decision, based on Expected Values would be to invest in a medium level of marketing spend, which would yield the highest net expected return of $40,900.

The weakness in this approach stems from the fact that expected value calculations produce the long run average outcome which would occur if a decision was taken many times. So if BF were to undertake multiple identical campaigns each with the same associated probabilities, the average outcome would be a net return of $40,900. However, BF will only carry out this project once and, assuming they chose to spend a medium amount on marketing, they will in fact earn either $30,000 or $43,000 or $77,000 depending on market conditions. A return of $30,000 may be deemed unacceptably low.

(c) **Value of the treasury economic forecast**

The value of perfect information is the difference between the expected value in the absence of any information (calculated in part (b) above) and the expected value that would be earned with the information.

If the Treasury predicts slow recovery, then Greenlight will (correctly) choose to adopt a medium advertising spend and will earn $30,000.

If the Treasury predicts moderate recovery, then Greenlight will (correctly) choose to adopt a high advertising spend and will earn $48,000.

If the Treasury predicts rapid recovery, then Greenlight will (correctly) choose to adopt a high advertising spend and will earn $92,000.

The probabilities of such forecasts will be the same as the probabilities of the different recovery rates themselves.

The revised expected value is thus $0.58 \times 30 + 0.26 \times 48 + 0.16 \times 92 = \$44,600$

The gain, $44,600 − $40,900 = $3,700 is the value if the perfect information provided.

(d) The probabilities given for the European launch can be used to construct a joint probability table. Given these are independent events we can simply multiply the probabilities together:

Euro dollar exchange rate / Parliamentary decision	Euro strong 0.4	Euro average 0.5	Euro weak 0.1
Favourable 0.15	0.06	0.075	0.015
Inconclusive 0.3	0.12	0.15	0.03
Unfavourable 0.55	0.22	0.275	0.055

The probability of the campaign making a loss is therefore

(0.12 + 0.22 + 0.275) = 0.615

The probability of earning results of $15,000 or more is

(0.06 + 0.075 + 0.015 + 0.03) = 0.18

(e) BF has estimated that the expected value of the financial portfolio to be liquidated in one months' time will be $480,000, with a standard deviation of $47,000.

If BF uses a 95% confidence level, it will identify the reduced value of the portfolio that that has a 5% chance of occurring.

From the normal distribution tables, 1.65 is the normal distribution value for a one-tailed 5% probability level. Since we are looking for a fall in value the key value is the mean less 1.65 standard deviations.

$x = 480,000 − (1.65 \times 47,000) = \$402,450$

There is therefore a 5% probability that the portfolio value will fall to $402,450 or below.

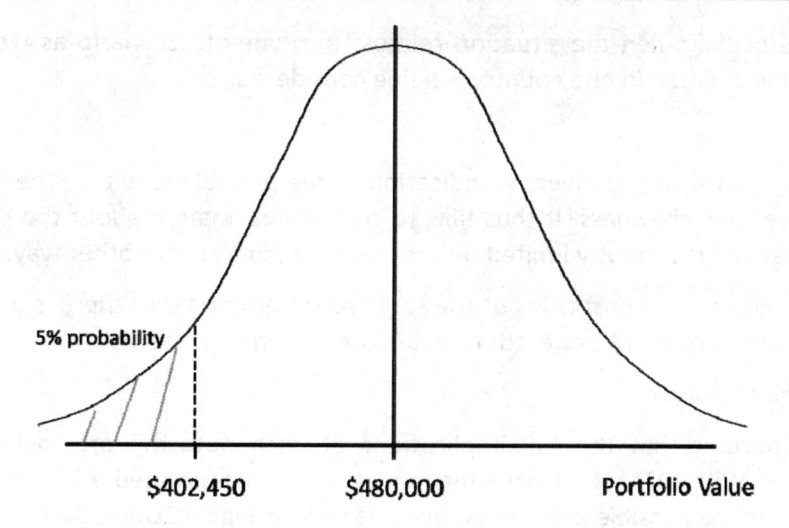

ANSWERS TO PRACTICE QUESTIONS – SECTION B : SECTION 4

[Bell curve diagram showing normal distribution with 5% probability shaded in left tail at $402,450, mean at $480,000, x-axis labelled "Portfolio Value"]

BF can use this information to decide whether the identified portfolio is likely to provide sufficient funds to finance the expansion. Depending on their attitude to risk, BF may decide to investigate the availability of other funds if $402,450 would not be enough for their requirements.

30 MTM GROUP (NOV 05)

> **Key answer tips**
>
> This question asks about expected values which it is assumed you are familiar with from earlier studies. Candidates must use the information given in the short scenario to achieve a pass.

(a) **Expected values**

The limitations of the use of expected values are discussed below:

Probabilities

The probabilities of the different outcomes are very hard to predict with much certainty. In some cases there may be objective probabilities based on past experience of similar scenarios. In others, the probabilities are much more subjective.

With MTM it is likely that the reduction in profit of 20% is based on past experience of similar legislation in other countries but the 40% chance of such a ban is speculation at best.

Possible outcomes

The expected value may not correspond to any possible outcome.

If the Government implements a ban, then profits will fall in SAC by 20%. If they don't, then profits will not change. The 8% drop is not a possible outcome and so, it can be argued, should not be used as a basis for decision making.

One-off event

Expected values can be useful when the same decision has to be made many times or when the firm has a number of independent projects with a portfolio effect. In such circumstances the expected value can be equated with the long run or overall average outcome and is thus more useful.

It is less useful when the situation relates to a 'one-off' scenario as we have with MTM. One decision in one country is being considered.

Risk

The average calculated gives no indication of the possible results, either in terms of their spread or skewness. It thus fails to convey information about the risk of those outcomes and is seriously limited unless risk is incorporated another way.

Using an 8% drop in profits is not the same as recognising that there is a 40% chance of the viability of MTM's operations in SAC being compromised!

Using the technique

It is important that the full implications of each outcome are included in any estimates. With MTM the marketing manager has incorporated a 20% drop in profit rather than the possible knock-on implication of closing SAC operations.

(b) To take into account the possible new legislation, MTM should consider the use of scenario planning where a few possible outcomes are explored rather than focusing on just one average outcome.

This could involve the following stages:

1 Develop scenarios to study the possibilities for the external environment and identify key trends and uncertainties.

MTM planners have identified two scenarios – either there will be a ban or there won't. They should also consider different times for a ban to be introduced and could also consider the possibility of a partial ban.

2 Build an analysis and strategic option against each scenario.

Rather than working with an 8% drop in profit, MTM needs to clarify its strategies assuming the ban does not occur and then consider the impact of the ban as a separate analysis. Will it compromise the viability of the operation in SAC? Why? Does MTM have production facilities in SAC or just distribution? Could MTM relocate production? Could MTM put pressure on the government for a partial ban to 'limit the damage'? MTM should construct forecasts and budgets for each scenario to consider the impact.

3 Look for the main strengths of the business and link to the scenarios

Some strategies make sense whatever the outcome, usually because they capitalise on or develop key strengths of the firm. For example, MTM has a global brand name and could seek to strengthen it in SAC by increasing its advertising spend in the short term. If the ban is agreed, then MTM has still increased awareness among its target group. If t-he ban does not materialise, then MTM should still benefit from a boost in sales.

4 Consider probability of occurrence.

5 Identify new resources and competencies that may be required.

The seriousness of a ban could prompt MTM to recruit experts in political lobbying.

6 Modify the strategic options.

The new plan may be to increase pressure on the government.

7 Constant monitoring of reality to see which scenario is unfolding.

8 Redeploy scenarios and unveil strategic options as appropriate.

31 SOCIAL RESPONSIBILITY

> **Key answer tips**
>
> This question invites a discussion of whether social responsibility conflicts with other stakeholder objectives and the feasibility of achieving these aspirations. Give examples of possible conflicts.
>
> Many students were unclear what is meant by social responsibility!

(a) (i) About 20 or so years ago, the idea that profitability was overwhelmingly the principal objective of a business would have been uncontroversial. Today's climate is different: increased public awareness of the social impact of large organisations has broadened the range of objectives which businesses must aim to achieve. New factors to be considered include pollution control, conservation of natural resources and avoidance of environmental damage.

In the short term, the measures described in the question would reduce profits; all of them involve profits or revenue forgone. And reduced profits imply reduced shareholders' wealth in the form of dividends and capital growth.

However, this analysis, though relatively straightforward in the short term, may not be so clear-cut in the long term. Many commentators argue that the reputation and image of corporations will suffer if they do not respond to heightened awareness of social responsibility amongst consumers. Given that many companies are already taking steps along this path, and making good public relations out of their efforts, there is pressure on other companies to follow suit. Failure to do so may lead to long-term decline.

(ii) A conflict between company objectives implies a picture of managers pulling in opposite directions, some trying to meet criteria of social responsibility, others hell-bent on maximising profit. Given that all of the managers in a company are drawing on the same pool of resources this is a recipe for disaster.

However, this does not mean that companies are doomed to fail if they pursue more than one objective. The ideal is to agree on a balance between conflicting objectives, and to settle on a strategy which satisfies both sets of objectives, to the extent that they can be reconciled.

(b) Part of the difficulty in pursing aspirations towards social responsibility lies in the relative novelty of the concept. Managers brought up in a culture of profit maximisation may find it hard to appreciate the importance of other objectives, and to adapt their behaviour accordingly. To 'operationalise' social responsibility involves, as a first step, making managers aware of the need for it.

This may be achieved by:

- Appropriate training
- Dissemination of targets and measures related to social objectives
- Formal incorporation of social objectives into the decision-making process
- Collaboration with other organisations to launch a common approach

- Appointment of external consultants to assess existing performance in this area and to recommend improvements
- Monitoring achievement by logging and publishing of performance indicators
- Appointment of committee to review and implement social and ethical policies.

(c) An organisation's stakeholders include:
- Owners/shareholders
- Employees
- Business contacts, such as customers and suppliers
- The general public
- The government.

Owners/shareholders will be interested primarily in profitability, but the analysis in Part(a) above suggests that long-term profitability may depend at least in part on the adoption of social objectives.

Employees obviously have a very direct interest in at least some social objectives: for example, the question mentions a policy of paying wages above national minimum levels.

Business contacts have a less direct interest in this issue. However, as a minimum, suppliers will be impressed with an ethical policy of paying debts on time, and customers who themselves have social and ethical interests may exert pressure on their suppliers to conform as well.

The general public, as already mentioned, have shown themselves increasingly aware of these issues, and prepared to back their principles with direct action (such as refusing to invest in companies whose objectives they disapprove of).

The government must meet international obligations as well as satisfying the demands of their own electorate. Both factors mean that they will take an interest in the social and ethical policies of organisations.

32 DIGWELL EXPLORATIONS

Key answer tips

In Part (a) you are required to discuss the ethical issues posed by the new mining operations within Eastborough. A brief discussion of what ethics are is a useful precursor to the specific issues: defining key terms from the requirement is often a good way to start an answer and is one of the easiest ways to get marks in the exam. A discussion of stakeholder conflicts is also required. There are many possible combinations of conflict so it is useful to pick the main conflicts and discuss these. In Part (b) you are required to outline a framework for analysing stakeholders. Mendelow's matrix is the model most people will use. This needs to be explained in relation to the scenario and the likely response Digwell will take to different groups based on their position in the matrix. In Part (a) you are not required to discuss in detail any broad ethical issues which are not related to the mining issue from the scenario. In Part (b) you do not need to discuss the business objectives or mission in detail – two topics often linked to stakeholder analysis.

(a) **Ethics**

> **Tutorial note**
>
> Start with defining ethics and then apply ethical responsibility to stakeholders.

Ethics are a code of moral principles that people follow with respect to what is right or wrong. General examples might include staying within the law, not engaging in bribery or theft, or endangering other people.

Also, a part of ethics is social responsibility: the duty towards the wider community or society in general which includes environmental issues, public safety, employment and exploitation of third world workers.

In this case ethical issues which the government should have considered when granting permission for mining include:

1   *Employment in the local area*

    The government has a duty toward people to provide them with jobs.

    In Eastborough there is significant unemployment so it is particularly important for the government to generate jobs in the area. The effect of the mining on employment levels should therefore be considered.

2   *The local economy*

    The government has an obligation to the people of Eastborough to improve the wealth of the people there. This largely depends on a successful economy. The local economy of Eastborough has been performing badly despite various initiatives based around tourism. The effect of mining on the local economy generally must be considered (i.e. jobs create income which is then spent in local shops, demand for property increases and prices rise for all in the area).

3   *Environmental concerns*

    Eastborough has a beautiful coastline with rare birds nesting there. The government has a responsibility towards society generally to preserve areas of natural beauty for all to appreciate and enjoy, and a moral obligation towards other species on the planet to protect them from extinction.

    The effects of the mining operations on the rare birds, the beauty of the coastline and any pollution caused in the locality should therefore have been considered by the government.

4   *Rights of local individuals*

    Individuals have the right for their quality of life to remain high. While employment and an improved economy may improve the quality of life of many, there may also be negative effects for some local people such as increased noise and traffic congestion.

5   *Right to free operation of business*

    Many capitalist countries believe in free trade and removing barriers to trade. This may be seen as a right of the business, and it may be considered as part of the decision to allow Digwell to open the mining operation.

Conflicts between stakeholder groups

Stakeholders are people who are affected or interested in some way by the mining operations.

In this case stakeholders include:

- national government
- local government
- local people
- wildlife protection groups
- environmental groups
- directors of Digwell
- employees of Digwell
- shareholders of Digwell.

The conflicts which may exist include the following:

1   *National vs local government*

    Local government will be interested in Eastborough and its interests. National government have to balance those needs with the needs of all people of the country. There may be a conflict over the amount of funding available to support local initiatives such as to help start up the mining operations.

2   *Unemployed vs people based near mining operations/working people*

    Unemployed people of the area will notice a direct benefit from the mining operations through increased jobs and are likely to support it. Other local residents may simply view the operations as disrupting their existing life (noise/congestion) and oppose the idea.

3   *Shareholders/directors of Digwell vs environmental/wildlife protection groups*

    Both shareholders and Directors of Digwell wish to make profits from Digwell's operations. The mining operations will enable them to make full use of an asset they own (tin reserves) and hence increase profit. They will wish it to go ahead, and may have very little interest in the broader impact.

    Environmental groups aim to protect the environment and are likely to oppose any part of the mining operation which will affect the environment irrespective of profitability.

(b) **Stakeholder mapping**

A useful model that can be used to examine stakeholders and how an organisation should deal with them is Mendelow's Matrix.

Mendelow said that there are two key aspects of understanding stakeholders:

1   *Power*

    This is the degree to which the stakeholder group can exert influence over Digwell, its operations and likely profitability. The local government, for instance, have the power to grant or refuse planning applications and hence have a lot of power in the tin mining issue.

    A local individual who feels strongly against the mining operations may have little power because whatever they do they are unlikely to be able to influence the decision. A large local group of people, on the other hand, have more power since they may be able to influence the local authority who must ensure the best interests of local people are met.

The greater the power a group has the more their views will be considered when decisions are being made. Digwell, for instance, will have ensured that all local government concerns are met in order to get permission to undertake mining.

2   *Interest*

The level of interest which the stakeholder has in the company (or in this case the mining operations) is also important to the company. If a party is not interested then the company will not need to concern itself with communicating with them or adapting to meet their needs.

In this case for instance Central Government is likely to have little interest in the local issue even though they have significant power. As long as the issue is not seen to affect national issues they are likely to remain unconcerned.

The matrix

Stakeholders can be placed into Mendelow's matrix according to their interest and power. Depending on where they fall, a different response will be necessary from Digwell.

INTEREST

POWER	Low	High
Low	**Minimal effort** General public outside Eastborough	**Keep informed** Local people Environmental groups Wildlife protection groups Digwell employees
High	**Keep happy** Central Government Digwell shareholders Large customers of Digwell	**Key player – keep close** Local Government Digwell directors

The responses required are as follows:

Key player – keep close

Key players must be kept close to the company in all major issues relating to the mining operations. For example, close relationships should be built with the local government so that they are continually kept informed of new plans. This ensures the plans are acceptable and within regulation. Any new requirements are also quickly understood and can be dealt with promptly.

Keep happy

For example, the Central Government should be kept happy by ensuring that the issue does not affect their main concern, national issues as a whole. So long as this is the case they are unlikely to get involved in this local issue and exert their considerable power. If not 'kept happy' this group can move to the 'Key player' quadrant.

PAPER P5 : ADVANCED PERFORMANCE MANAGEMENT

Keep informed

For example, Digwell employees will be very interested in the effect of the new operations on jobs. It may, for instance, create job security for them, or mean they have to relocate. It is therefore very important to ensure they understand the impact on them and expectations of them. Without formal notification, information will spread via rumour which may be inaccurate and cause undue concern. Although they have little power, the high interest displayed by members of this group can mean that they can have a strong influence on the key players.

Minimal effort

It is important to clarify which groups have little power or interest to avoid unnecessary effort being made. An example here is the general public outside Eastborough. They are likely to have little interest or power and so no effort needs to be made to keep them happy and there is little benefit from keeping them informed.

33 THE GLOBAL HOTEL GROUP (JUN 08)

Key answer tips

This is a very interesting question and must be related to the scenario. Avoid using bullet points with little or no development. The first part of the question requires candidates to think about strategic and economics factors of setting up in a different country, whilst the second part considers the cultural issues.

(a)

Tutorial note

Think about the implications of setting up business in another country.

Of vital importance is the need for reliable information on which to base the decision regarding the potential investment within Tomorrowland, since the lack of such information will only serve to increase the risk profile of GHG.

The **strategic** factors that ought to be considered prior to a decision being made to build and operate a hotel in Tomorrowland are as follows:

The competition

The key notion here is that of the position of GHG relative to its competitors who may have a presence or intend to have a presence in Tomorrowland. The strategic management accounting system should be capable of coping with changes that can and will inevitably occur in a dynamic business environment. Hence it is crucial that changes such as, the emergence of a new competitor, are detected and reflected within strategic plans at the earliest opportunity.

The government

The attitude of the government of Tomorrowland towards foreign organisations requires careful consideration as inevitably the government will be the country's largest supplier, employer, customer and investor. The directors need to recognise that the political environment of Tomorrowland could change dramatically with a change in the national government.

Planning and control of operations within Tomorrowland

Planning and control of operations within Tomorrowland will inevitably be more difficult as GHG might not possess sufficient knowledge of the business environment within Tomorrowland. Indeed their nearest hotel is at least 3,000 kilometres away. It is vital the GHG gain such knowledge prior to commencing operations within Tomorrowland in order to avoid undue risks.

The sociological–cultural constraints

While it is generally recognised that there is a growing acceptability of international brands this might not be the case with regard to Tomorrowland.. In this respect it is vital that consideration is given to recognition of the relationships in economic life including demand, price, wages, training, and rates of labour turnover and absenteeism.

Resource utilisation The attitude towards work, managers (especially foreign nationals) and capitalist organisations could severely impact on the degree of success achieved within Tomorrowland

A primary consideration relates to whether or not to use local labour in the construction of the hotel. The perceived 'remoteness' of Tomorrowland might make it an unattractive proposition for current employees of GHG, thereby presenting the directors of GHG with a significant problem.

Communication

Consideration needs to be given to the communication problems that arise between different countries and in this respect Tomorrowland is probably no exception. Language barriers will inevitably exist and this needs to be addressed at the earliest opportunity to minimise any risks to GHG.

The **economic** factors that ought to be considered prior to a decision being made to build and operate a hotel in Tomorrowland are as follows:

Resource availability

The hotel should be designed having given due consideration to the prevailing climatic conditions within Tomorrowland which might necessitate the use of specific types of building materials. It might well be the case that such building materials are not available locally, or are in such scarce supply in which case local supply would prove to be uneconomic.

Another consideration relates to local labour being available and reliable in terms of its quality.

Currency stability/restrictions

The stability of the currency within Tomorrowland assumes critical significance because profit repatriation is problematic in situations where those profits are made in an unstable currency or one that is likely to depreciate against the home currency, thereby precipitating sizeable losses on exchange. Any currency restrictions need to be given careful consideration. For example, it might be the case that hotel guests would be prohibited from paying accommodation bills in a foreign currency which would be problematic if the local currency was weak.

Legislation

All local and International legislation should be given careful consideration. It might be the case that local legislation via various licences or legal requirements favour local hotels.

Demand

The potential demand within Tomorrowland will be linked to the local economy. It is a developing economy and this may bode well for GHG. However, again the need for reliable information about the size of the market, the extent of competition, likely future trends etc is of fundamental importance.

Financing

An important decision lies in the availability and associated costs of financing in Tomorrowland which might not have mature enough capital markets due to its developmental state. Hence GHG might need to finance using alternative currencies.

Note: Other relevant comments would be acceptable.

(b) The directors of GHG should be mindful that the effectiveness of a locally employed workforce within Tomorrowland will be influenced by a number of factors including the following:

The availability of local skills

If Tomorrowland is a lower wage economy it is quite conceivable that a sufficient number of employees possessing the requisite skills to undertake the construction of a large hotel cannot be found. If there are insufficient local resources then this would necessitate the training of employees in all aspects of building construction. This will incur significant costs and time and needs to be reflected in any proposed timetable for construction of the hotel. As far as the operation of the hotel is concerned then staff will have to be recruited and trained which will again give rise to significant start-up costs. However, this should not present the directors of GHG with such a major problem as that of training construction staff. Indeed, it is highly probable that GHG would use its own staff in order to train new recruits.

Attitudes to work

The prevailing culture within Tomorrowland will have a profound impact on attitudes to work of its population. Attitudes to hours of work, timekeeping and absenteeism vary from culture to culture. For example, as regards hours of work in the construction industry in countries which experience very hot climates, work is often suspended during the hottest part of each day and recommenced several hours later when temperatures are much cooler. The directors of GHG need to recognise that climatic conditions not only affect the design of a building but also its construction.

A potentially sensitive issue within regarding the use of local labour in the construction of the hotel lies in the fact that national holidays and especially religious holidays need to be observed and taken into consideration in any proposed timetable for construction of the hotel. As regards the operation of a hotel then consideration needs to be given to the different cultures from which the guests come. For example, this will require a detailed consideration of menus to be offered.

ANSWERS TO PRACTICE QUESTIONS – SECTION B : **SECTION 4**

However, it might well be the case that the local population might be unwilling to prepare dishes comprising ingredients which are unacceptable to their culture due to, for example, religious beliefs.

Marking scheme			
			Marks
(a)	Comments (on merit):		
	Strategic/economic factors	10 × 1.5	Maximum 14
(b)	Impact on effectiveness	2 × 3	6
Total			**20**

Examiner's comments

This was the most popular of the option questions with many candidates producing good answers to both parts of the question. Part (a) was generally well answered. Poorer answers to part (a) were often reduced to bullet points with little or no development. Whilst Part (a) was generally well answered, there was a significant variation in the quality of answers to part (b). Poorer answers invariably ignored the scenario contained in the question.

34 FRANCHISING FOR YOU LTD (F4U) (JUN 09)

Key answer tips

A fairly straight forward NPV question. Candidates firstly need to calculate contribution as sales revenue less variable cost. Then calculate NPV, be careful about the timing of the cashflows especially the development costs. Remember the rule about inflation either inflate the cashflows and discount at the money rate or to make it easier and quicker remove the inflation from the money cost and ignore inflating the cashflows. In part (b) you are required to understand "intellectual capital", just think logically what the two words mean. Intellectual means analytical thinking in a professional capacity. In part (c) imagine why focusing on financial measures is not enough when analysing performance. Then the final part (d) is based on the information given in the question and is very straight forward on maximax and maximin.

(a) Contribution per franchise = sales revenue – variable cost
= $20,000 – $6,000 = $14,000

Net operating cash flow each year before taxation = ($14,000 × 300) – $600,000 = $3,600,000 Net operating cash flow each year after taxation = $3,600,000 × 70% = $2,520,000

Net present value (NPV) at a discount rate of 11%

Net operating cash flow – initial investment – development costs

= (2,520,000 × 4.231) – (6,000,000) – (1,000,000 × 0.812) – (1,000,000 × 0.731) = $3,119,120

The positive NPV indicates that the proposal should be undertaken.

> **Tutorial note**
>
> A real discount rate of 11% has been used. It has been calculated as follows:
> (1 + money cost of capital)/(1 + rate of inflation) – 1
>
> = (1 + 0.1544)/ (1 + 0.04) – 1
>
> = 0.11 or 11%

(b) There are barriers to the creation and revision of a performance measurement system. Key drivers are not easily measured. This applies specifically to the issue of intellectual capital.

Intellectual capital will include assets such as employee know-how, skills and creativity. Such assets cannot be measured using traditional financial measures. It is necessary to identify and value a number of alternative measures such as years of experience or service of key employees, or the proportion of employees generating new ideas for the development of the business.

The rise of intellectual capital statements has been driven by the decreasing information relevance of aspects of traditional financial statements. There is a role for accountants (in particular management accountants) in classifying the intellectual (and intangible) assets in the organisation.

In F4U the development of new franchises will rely heavily on the intellectual capital input. This will require the ongoing development of existing employee knowledge and expertise and the recruitment of new expertise/knowledge as required by the trend in the franchise range.

There will be specific costs incurred in the retention and development of existing staff expertise and in the acquisition of new staff/expertise and its development within the ethos of F4U.

(c) A Performance Measurement system (PMS) must be comprehensive for the following reasons:

- Financial is only one dimension of value – as such it is inadequate in evaluating strategic performance of an organisation in its entirety.
- Financial measures are traditionally backward looking – in today's volatile markets, a poor predictor of future performance.
- Financial measures take no account of the intangible value drivers – especially important in knowledge intensive companies.
- Fixation with bottom line profit pushes for short-term decisions to boost earnings streams in short term.
- Alternative perspectives are needed to satisfy demands of providing a sustainable competitive environment.

The effectiveness of a PMS based solely on financial performance may be reduced due to key drivers not being easily measured such as, for example, the degree of innovation required for new franchises.

Also, there may be conflict between the PMS with the culture of an organisation. The culture will probably focus on innovation in franchise development. This will not be enhanced by a solely financial based PMS. It is important that a culture is developed which recognises and rewards the contribution of employees to achieving corporate goals and strategy fulfilment.

It is important to focus on sustaining competitive advantage through superior strategic management in all aspects of franchise development and implementation. There is a need for better business intelligence capability from both within the organisation and from external sources, in the assessment of likely demand for new franchise areas and how best to satisfy such demand. In this regard there is need for non-financial performance measures in order to enhance the effectiveness of the PMS.

(d) The maximax rule looks for the largest possible outcome. In this case F4U will choose a fee per franchise of $18,000 where there is a possibility of an NPV of $4,348,226. This may be seen as risk seeking since F4U has not been put off by the possibility of a lower NPV than if a $22,000 fee is charged and variable costs are $6,000 or $7,000.

The maximin rule looks for the fee per franchise which will maximise the minimum possible NPV. Hence maximin is a risk averse strategy. In this case F4U will choose a fee per franchise of $22,000 where the lowest NPV is $2,674,865. This is better than the lowest figures applying where franchise fees of $18,000 or $20,000 apply.

The minimax regret rule requires the choice of the fee per franchise which will minimise the regret from making the wrong decision. Regret in this context is the opportunity lost through making the wrong decision. Using the calculation from the payoff matrix given in the question, a regret matrix may be created as follows:

Regret matrix

Fee per franchise ($000)

		$18	$20	$22
Variable cost	5	0	340,596	74,043
per franchise	6	177,702	355,404	0
($000)	7	429,446	444,255	0
Maximum regret		429,446	444,255	74,043

This shows that the minimax regret rule leads to the choice of a fee per franchise of $22,000. This minimises the regret to an amount of $74,043.

Marking scheme			
			Marks
(a)	Margin after tax		2
	Discount rate		2
	NPV		1
	Decision		1
		Maximum	6
(b)	Elements		4
	Issues		4
		Maximum	6
(c)	Comments (on merit)		6
(d)	Maximax		2
	Maximin		2
	Minimax regret criterion		3
		Maximum	7
Total			25

PAPER P5 : ADVANCED PERFORMANCE MANAGEMENT

> **Examiner's comments**
>
> There were significant variations in the quality of candidates' answers to this question.
>
> Answers to part (a) revealed that the majority of candidates were unable to calculate correctly the discount rate. A large number of candidates also included the development costs in the tax calculations of F4U.
>
> In general, answers to part (b) were poor. A significant number of candidates appeared to attempt to 'guess' the answer and a sizeable number made no attempt to answer part (b) which was potentially worth six marks.
>
> There were a large number of very good answers to part (c) which achieved high marks. However, in answering part (c) many candidates offered a discussion of a variety of non-financial performance measures instead of discussing ways in which reliance solely on financial performance measures can detract from the effectiveness of the performance management system within an organisation, as required by the question.
>
> There were many correct answers to part (d) with candidates achieving maximum marks. However, a significant number of candidates demonstrated a lack of knowledge of maximax, maximin and minimax regret decision rules. What is more, a significant number of candidates made no attempt to answer this subsection of the question which was potentially worth seven marks.

35 FGH TELECOM (FGH) (DEC 10)

> **Tutorial note**
>
> *Requirement (a) could be answered using any sensible set of headings for example, PEST and PESTEL.*
>
> *The working given in this solution is more detailed than would be required to produce a good answer to this question. It is here to give detailed explanation of the calculations.*

(a) Government regulations relevant to FGH's environmental strategy include requirements to recycle materials, limits on pollution and waste levels along with new taxes such as carbon levies to add additional costs. Performance indicators would be additional costs resulting from failure to recycle waste, fines paid for breaches and the level of environmental tax burdens.

The general economic climate is relevant to the strategy including factors such as interest, inflation and exchange rates. For FGH, the general economic environment is not good and cost savings from reductions in energy use would help to offset falling profits. Also, the difficulties indicated in raising capital could be monitored through the firm's cost of capital. This would be especially relevant if the environmental initiatives lead to significant capital expenditure for FGH.

Trends and fashions among the general public appear to be relevant for FGH as the public will be end-users of its services and environmental action could improve the brand image of FGH. Suitable performance indicator would be based around a score in a customer attitude survey.

Technological changes in the capabilities available to FGH and its competitors will affect its environmental strategy. New environmentally efficient technologies such as hybrid cars and solar recharging cells would be relevant to the cost and product sides of FGH. Performance indicators would involve measuring the impact of the use of new technology on existing emission data.

(b) The company has a target of cutting emissions by 60% of their 2001 values by the year 2017. Overall, it has cut emissions by 38% in the first nine years of the 16-year programme. There was a reduction of 16% in the last year of measurement. If this rate of improvement is maintained then the company will reduce its emissions by 82% (62% × (84% ^ 7)) by 2017. However, it should be noted that it is unlikely that there will be a constant rate of reduction as it normally becomes more difficult to improve as the easy actions are taken in the early years of the programme.

The initial data are rather complex and so to summarise, three categories for the three types of transport were considered (Road, Rail and Air). The largest cut has been in rail related emissions (63%) while the contribution from road transport has only fallen by 38%. The road emissions are the dominant category overall and they are still falling within the programmed timetable to reach the target. However, it is clear that air travel is not falling at the same pace but this may be driven by factors such as increasing globalisation of the telecommunication industry which necessitates travel by managers abroad to visit multinational clients and suppliers.

One unusual feature noted is that the mix of transport methods appears to be changing. Rail travel appears to be declining. This is surprising as rail is widely believed to be the lowest emitting method from these forms of travel. However, caution must be exercised on this conclusion which may be due to a change in the emissions technology relating to each category of travel rather than the distance travelled using each method.

The major change that is apparent from the basic data is the move from petrol to diesel-powered motor vehicles which in the commercial fleet appears nearly complete. It will be more difficult to move company and private cars to diesel-power as there will be an element of choice on the part of the car user in the type of car driven.

Working:

Measured in millions of kgs	2001 Base year	2009	2010	Change on base year
Commercial Fleet Diesel	105.4	77.7	70.1	−33%
Commercial Fleet Petrol	11.6	0.4	0.0	−100%
Company Car Diesel	15.1	14.5	12.0	−21%
Company Car Petrol	10.3	3.8	2.2	−79%
Other road travel (Diesel)	0.5	1.6	1.1	120%
Other road travel (Petrol)	3.1	0.5	0.3	−90%
Rail travel	9.2	9.6	3.4	−63%
Air Travel (short haul)	5.0	4.4	3.1	−38%
Air Travel (long haul)	5.1	7.1	5.4	6%
Hire Cars (Diesel)	0.6	1.8	2.9	383%
Hire Cars (Petrol)	6.7	6.1	6.1	−9%
Total	172.6	127.5	106.6	

	2001	2009	2010	Change on base year
Index	100%	74%	62%	
YoY change			−16%	

Simplifying categories

	Base year			
Road travel	153.3	106.4	94.7	−38%
Air travel	10.1	11.5	8.5	−16%
Rail travel	9.2	9.6	3.4	−63%
Total	172.6	127.5	106.6	−38%

Mix of travel method in each year

	Base year		
Road travel	89%	83%	89%
Air travel	6%	9%	8%
Rail travel	5%	8%	3%

(c) The analysis could be improved by collecting data on the total distances travelled so that employee behaviour can be tracked. This would allow measurement of the effect of switching away from physical meetings and using teleconferencing facilities. This may be particularly effective in cutting air travel which has been noted as a problem area.

It would also allow assessment of the homeworking scheme which should reduce total distance travelled. Although, the full environmental benefit will not be apparent as much of the travel would have been a regular commute to work which an employee will not be able to claim and so is unlikely to record.

Finally, the collection of distance travelled data will allow a measure of the effect of changing modes of transport by calculating an average emission per km travelled.

Marking scheme		
		Marks
(a)	1 mark per factor identified as relevant for each section of the broad sections of the analysis (PEST or PESTEL sections are appropriate and competition could be an additional area considered). Up to 1 mark for each performance indicator relevant to the factors identified. Maximum of 8.	
	Maximum	8
(b)	Up to 4 marks for analysis of basic data, commenting on overall picture and achievement of target	
	Up to 2 marks for simplifying data into broad categories and commenting	
	Up to 4 marks for analysis of mix of methods of travel and commenting	
	(Another acceptable categorisation could be related to fuel type: petrol, diesel and aviation – rail is problematic as it is a mix of diesel and electricity but reasonable assumptions will be acceptable)	
	Maximum	9
(c)	1 mark per point reasonably made up to	3
Total		**20**

ANSWERS TO PRACTICE QUESTIONS – SECTION B : **SECTION 4**

> **Examiner's comments**
>
> Part (a) was generally well done although a number of good candidates ignored the request for illustrative performance indicators.
>
> Part (b) was an analysis of a table of raw data which showed up basic weaknesses in some candidates' skill set. It was well-answered by only a minority of candidates.
>
> Many candidates wasted their time by limiting their comments to only writing out lists of statements such as
>
> 'Commercial Fleet Diesel use has fallen from 105.4 to 70.1' or even 'Commercial Fleet Diesel use has gone down'. First, this is stating the obvious to anyone who read the table but also, this is far too detailed for most reporting purposes.
>
> An appropriate plan of attack for this part might have been:
>
> 1   consider the 'big picture' – whether the overall target for emission reduction be met;
>
> 2   break down the data into smaller but meaningful (and manageable) chunks – Road, Rail and Air transport; and
>
> 3   discuss the individual lines of the data table focussing on the data that explains the overall picture of emission changes, for example, the switch from petrol to diesel powered motor vehicles is complete in commercial vehicles and has lead to large reductions in emissions but such a change may be more difficult in company cars as employees may resist such a change.
>
> Good candidates analysed the numerical data given in the scenario. They created information from the data given and provided the reader of their answer with new insight into the key factors driving the reduction in emissions.
>
> Part (c) was often poorly done as a result of the failure to address the requirement which asked for the data to be related to the reduction initiatives mentioned in the scenario. Many candidates got a mark for general suggestions of further useful data but few related this to the reduction initiatives.

PERFORMANCE MEASUREMENT SYSTEMS AND DESIGN

36 MOTOR COMPONENT MANUFACTURER (DEC 02)

> **Key answer tips**
>
> The main theme of the question is 'external sources of information' for the purposes of planning and controlling business operations. Requirement (a) invites discussion of information needs, (b) invites discussion of information sources and (c) invites discussion of information systems.

(a)   **Information areas**

Customers – What are their needs and expectations? Are the needs changing? What is the potential for products and markets?

Competitors – Who are they? What are they doing? Can their ideas/products be copied? Size? Pricing policy? Profitability? Market share?

Suppliers – Information is required concerning:
- quality of supplier
- prices
- potential of new suppliers
- financial viability of suppliers

New entrants – what is the risk of a new entrant to the market?

Substitute products – difficult to anticipate and usually arising from advances in technology.

Legal Framework

Compliance requirements to meet statutory standards e.g. safety, labelling and working conditions.

Political and ecological framework

The motor vehicle industry business will be influenced by government transport policy, vehicle emission standards and the health and safety laws concerned with production methods.

Financial and economic environment

Business activity is influenced by general level of economic activity. Inflation rates, interest rates, foreign exchange rates and the levels of imports and exports all impact upon business. All of the above issues are likely to have consequences for the company in terms of future:
- business activity levels
- financial performance
- production method
- costs
- business viability
- market trends

and therefore need to be considered in the preparation of budgets – they will influence the future revenues, costs and growth of the company.

Social changes

For example, increased use of motor vehicles (or, indeed, decreased use of motor vehicles because of ecological concerns).

Technological changes

For example, new, more reliable components could reduce the need to supply replacement products. An example would be the use of long-life LEDs in rear and brake lights instead of traditional bulbs.

(b) **Sources**

Market research – commissioned or generally available from secondary sources.

Trade reports – magazines and conferences.

Suppliers – price lists and brochures.

Government reports – general reports and the occasional specific report on industrial sectors.

ANSWERS TO PRACTICE QUESTIONS – SECTION B : SECTION 4

Government statistics – economic indicators, industrial output, consumer spending, inflation rates.

Newspaper and other media reports – a great deal of this information is now available on the Internet – more accessible.

(c) **Implementation**

- Data capture systems need to be developed with assigned responsibility for obtaining the information.
- Monitoring systems are required to ensure that new information and new information sources are identified and utilised.
- Ensure that the appropriate people receive the information that they require – avoid sending everyone all the data – may result in it being dismissed.
- Dissemination of the information via:
    - company magazine
    - e-mail/Internet
    - occasional meetings to discuss the impact of significant issues
- May need to categorise the information as being relevant for strategic or operational decisions – that this categorisation may influence the frequency and detail required.
- Do the people preparing the budgets have the competence to interpret and incorporate the information provided into their estimates?
- Is the information distributed in its raw form or is it modified to meet the internal users specific needs?

37 PRECISION PARTS

> **Key answer tips**
>
> This question which focuses upon position appraisal, requires you to assess the validity of management accounting data for strategic planning purposes. You must also suggest how benchmarking could be applied to information for strategic planning purposes. As a general point, it is worth noting that the examiner regularly shows an interest in the role of the management accountant in strategy. Ensure you relate your answer to the scenario.

(a) The management accounting reports which are currently provided to the management of W Ltd comprise monthly cost variance reports covering direct materials, direct labour, variable and fixed production overheads, and regular sales price and volume variance reports. These will help management in its control of the company's operations, by focusing on areas where results actually achieved are materially different from those expected.

But **controlling activities is only one aspect of management accounting**. Other important responsibilities are the formulation of strategy and optimising the use of resources. The inward-looking reports currently produced focus only on what is happening within the company by reporting internally generated numbers to internal managers who are expected to adjust their internal actions.

A successful business must react to changes in its external environment and be outward looking. The current reports are inward-looking and appear to have no strategic content. However punctually and comprehensively they are produced, they are still inadequate as information to assist the board's strategic decision making.

(b) Effective strategic planning starts with the **setting of objectives** and a **position audit** of the company. W Ltd appears to want to increase its profits, but it is unclear whether objectives exist in terms of earnings per share, products/markets, productivity, etc.

A position audit examines the current situation of the company in terms of resources, products, markets, operating systems, internal organisation, current results and returns to stockholders. The audit should be carried out now as a matter of urgency and repeated regularly to keep the information up to date. Planning is not an activity that can be carried out once a year and then forgotten about during the rest of the year; to be valuable it must be a regular ongoing process.

Environmental analysis considers the environmental conditions within which the company will be operating, looking at product demand, production technology, competition, etc. This analysis is particularly lacking from the management information that the management accounting department has previously provided.

Specific reports are recommended to be prepared as follows:

(i) Statement of objectives

(ii) Position audit

- Resources (people, fixed assets, finance)
- Products and markets
- Operating systems (including use of technology)
- Organisation
- Results (segmental analysis of profits, returns to shareholders)

(iii) Environmental analysis

- Product demand: what market share is currently achieved and forecast for the future?
- Customers: why do the existing customers buy from W Ltd? Perhaps the company possesses specific skills or technology, or prices its products keenly. Whatever it is, the source of competitive advantage must be identified and built upon.
- Workforce: numbers and skill levels of existing employees. Why is so much work being turned away? If there is a shortage of skilled employees, new people must be trained or recruited.
- Technology: if it is a shortage of machines that is leading to so much work being turned away, then the cost of new machines should be compared with the forgone profits.

The **segmental analysis of results** recommended in the position audit should show the profits currently achieved on each of the company's existing products. Often profits can quite easily be improved by stripping out loss-making lines and shifting resources to the highest-profit products. Similar segmentation can be carried out by customer and by market. Without this information managers cannot make correct decisions about the products that the company should choose to make.

The **current budgetary control system could be improved** by calculating planning and operational variances rather than the traditional variances now reported. Line managers could then concentrate on improving operational matters for which they are genuinely responsible. The disadvantage of planning and operational variances is that too often all adverse variances are explained away as being planning errors.

The **standard costing system could be improved** by setting standards on the basis of activity-based costing (ABC) rather than any other method. This will identify the cost drivers for each process and is particularly important if the standard cost plus pricing basis is to be persevered with. A market-based pricing method would be preferable since it offers the prospect of maximising profits.

Finally, **information on current and future cash flows** must be reported regularly to managers. Companies fail because they run out of cash, not because they are unprofitable, and cash control will become important if any expansion plan is implemented. A monthly statement of current and forecast cash flows would be a valuable source of information to managers.

(c) **Benchmarking** is a continuous, systematic process for evaluating the products, services and work processes of organisations that are recognised as representing best practices for the purpose of organisational improvement.

Essentially you compare your organisation with another in the hope of identifying ways of improving your output, organisational structure, etc.

The exercise will be most useful if the companies benchmarking each other are in the same industry and have similar technology. Thus W Ltd should look for another small-scale engineering company with a similar cost structure to its own. It is likely that this will be a competitor to W Ltd who might be unwilling to co-operate with the exercise so, if both parties are to benefit without endangering their commercial secrets, it is usual that benchmarking is limited to specified non-sensitive areas and that the exercise is mutual. Thus each company agrees to co-operate with the representatives of the other company in showing their operations.

Since W Ltd knows that its management information system is currently less than excellent, it could seek to benchmark MISs between companies to learn what system a successful company is operating. This may however prove difficult to agree, since the information in any MIS will be highly commercially sensitive. Perhaps proformas and document flow charts can form the basis of the benchmarking exercise rather than the actual MIS schedules and numbers.

It may be more realistic to try and benchmark the MIS of a company which is not in direct competition with W Ltd but which does have a reputation for excellence concerning its strategic planning. The disadvantage is the possible lack of relevance to W Ltd of the information generated in the other company; for example, a much larger company might have more tiers of management which have no counterpart in W Ltd's structure.

In conclusion, if W Ltd has appreciated that its current system for developing information for strategic planning needs improving, benchmarking the MIS of a similar company with a proven excellent MIS could bring benefits to W Ltd. However, a relationship of trust must be established between two companies before benchmarking can be implemented, and such mutual trust may not be possible between two rival companies in direct competition.

38 ACCOUNTING SYSTEMS (JUN 03)

> **Key answer tips**
>
> The theme of this question is the behavioural issues associated with the design and operation of management accounting systems. The requirements of the question are capable of interpretation and answers might have been pitched at either a practical or conceptual level. Candidates should be given credit for illustrating these issues with specific references to a work environment.

(a) The role of a management accountant is to provide information which can be used to assist and guide management in the pursuit and achievement of organisational objectives. The management information provided is read, interpreted and responded to by people within the organisation, and their responses will determine the quality of the decisions made and the extent to which corporate objectives are achieved. Management accountants should be aware of this relationship and endeavour to ensure that the information that they supply is used in a way that benefits their organisation. The design and operation of a management accounting system should anticipate the behavioural consequences that are likely to arise as a result of its activities. A management accountant who fails to consider these repercussions or denies responsibility for them is likely to operate a dysfunctional system. This is most likely to manifest itself in a failure to secure goal congruence between the interested parties. The management accounting system will need to consider the particular culture of the organisation, adjust to whether it has a hierarchical or democratic structure, its attitude towards employee empowerment and the extent of delegated team decision making.

(b) *Performance Monitoring:*

There is a general acceptance of the idea that an organisation that monitors performance and rewards individuals for 'good performance' is more likely to encourage behaviour that is consistent with the objectives of the organisation. This involves the organisation 'transmitting signals' to its people as to what it deems desirable activities and outcomes in the workplace. This approach has resulted in such terms and activities as, performance monitoring, performance related pay, payment by results, bonus systems – the reward for the achievement of desired outcomes could be money, promotion, job security, preferred work activities, alternative work environments. Unfortunately this is a very complex task and problems are likely to arise in a number of areas:

- It is very difficult in many work environments to measure individual performance – and if you resort to team performance, it is difficult to gauge the contribution from individual members.

- It is difficult to ensure that individual targets are not inconsistent with other individuals or corporate objectives.

- Current measured performance may discourage consideration of longer term issues that may have adverse repercussions.

- Can a performance monitoring system comprehensively measure the key variables e.g. the desire to achieve greater volume/activity may be at the cost of quality that is more difficult to identify and appraise.

- Measure fixation – concentrating on the measurement process and not on what needs to be achieved.
- Misrepresentation – 'creative' responses that give a favourable view of activities.
- Myopia – short sighted viewpoint with limited consideration to long term issues.

The problems highlighted above can be managed if the following points are considered:

- Do not underestimate the scale of the task in designing a performance monitoring system.
- Consider the expectations and likely responses of all the parties concerned – take a broad view.
- Ensure that the people designing and operating the system have a comprehensive understanding of the organisation's activities and the interrelationship between all of the stakeholders.
- Ensure that all parties involved believe that they will be beneficiaries of the system.
- Be prepared to reappraise and modify – it is unrealistic to believe that it can be perfected at the first attempt.

Budgeting

Adverse behavioural consequences of budgeting can arise from insufficient consideration being given to the task during the planning stage. The targets set may be perceived as:

- Imposed
- Complicated
- Unfair
- Irrelevant
- Easy
- Unachievable

This is likely to foster the 'them and us' syndrome and the consequential failure to achieve goal congruence. These undesirable consequences may be avoided by consulting with all interested parties, setting challenging but achievable targets, considering other people's perception of the targets and anticipating their likely responses. On the other hand, if budget holders are given complete autonomy or are permitted to have a significant influence on budgetary targets, they may be tempted to build in 'slack' to give themselves an easy life which is not in the interests of their organisation.

Having implemented the planning stage, we need to turn our attention towards control. Behavioural problems can arise from:

- A failure to distinguish between controllable and non-controllable factors for each particular budget holder – people will feel aggrieved for being accountable for what they do not control.
- A failure to account for the changing circumstances that have arisen since the budget was determined – may require budget adjustments and/or a flexible budget approach.

- Failure to reward favourable variances – budget under spending that automatically results in cuts in future budget provision merely encourages spending of the entire budget, not something that should be encouraged.
- Budget constrained approach – a requirement to conform to budget may stifle attempts at improvement.
- Insufficient participation in budgetary control and poor communication of the reasons for change decisions may alienate staff.

Transfer Pricing

Transfer pricing is primarily concerned with ensuring that semi-autonomous business units behave in a way that contributes towards the achievement of corporate and not merely divisional objectives. An effective transfer pricing system encourages divisional managers with autonomous decision making authority to automatically pursue the interest of the corporation whilst endeavouring to maximise the performance of their own business unit. Their decisions are made with self (divisional) interest as the driving factor, but coincidentally benefit the entire company. Effective transfer pricing systems consciously endeavour to harness selfish divisional behaviour to induce decisions that foster goal congruence.

Problems can arise when inappropriate prices are set that result in 'wrong signals' being sent and non-optimal decisions being made:

- Too high a price may result in unused capacity, lost contribution, reduced incentive to find external markets and unnecessary external sourcing from the buying division.
- Too low a price may result in 'excessive' internal trading and a loss of valuable external business.

To avoid these pitfalls the transfer pricing determination should consider:

- The cost behaviour (fixed and variable) of the different divisions.
- The adequacy of the information available to the divisions concerning both internal and external prices.
- Both the short and long run consequences of the prices set – internal and external markets and capacity levels.
- The degree of autonomy given to the divisions.

39 GMB CO (DEC 07)

Key answer tips

The whole question relates to activity based techniques. Firstly prepare an analysis of expense items, be careful not to ignore the information on batches and therefore arrive at an incorrect solution. Part (b) asks candidates to identify cost drivers and consider their appropriateness and part (c) asks for practical problems of implementing an activity-based system, not to describe what it is.

ANSWERS TO PRACTICE QUESTIONS – SECTION B : **SECTION 4**

(a) **Order Number 377: Summary total cost statement**

	$000	$000
Unit-based costs:		
Direct material cost ($180 × 5,000)	900	
Direct labour cost ($150 × 5,000)	750	
Power cost ($120 × 5,000)	600	
		2,250
Batch-related costs:		
Design work ($30,000 × 5)	150	
Machine set up ($34,000 × 5)	170	
Production scheduling ($60,000 × 5)	300	
Selling – batch expediting – ($60,000 × 5)	300	
Admin. – invoicing & accounting ($24,000 × 5))	120	
Distribution ($12,000 × 5)	60	
		1,100
Product sustaining costs:		
Engineering design & support (per order)	350	
Production line maintenance (per order)	1,100	
Marketing (per order)	200	1,650
Total cost excluding business/facility sustaining costs		5,000
Total cost excluding business/facility sustaining costs		5,000
Business/Facility sustaining costs:		
Relating to production, administration, selling and distribution based on overall business/facility time used. 30% × $5,000,000		1,500
Total cost of order		6,500

Note: Number of batches = 5,000 units/1,000 = 5 batches

(b) A cost driver is the factor that determines the level of resource required for an activity. This may be illustrated by considering costs for each of the four levels in Order Number 377.

Unit based costs:

Direct material costs are driven by the quantity, range, quality and price of materials required per product unit according to the specification for the order.

Direct labour costs are driven by the number of hours required per product unit and the rate per hour that has been agreed for each labour grade.

Batch related costs:

The number of machine set-ups per batch is the cost driver for machines used.

The number of design hours per batch is the cost driver for design work.

Product sustaining costs:

The number of marketing visits to a client per order is the cost driver for marketing cost chargeable to the order.

The number of hours of production line maintenance per order is the cost driver for production line cost.

Business sustaining costs:

These costs are absorbed at a rate of 30% of total cost excluding business sustaining costs. This is an arbitrary rate which indicates the difficulty in identifying a suitable cost driver/drivers for the range of residual costs in this category. Wherever possible efforts should be made to identify aspects of this residual cost that can be added to the unit, batch or product related analysis.

The cost drivers are useful in that they provide a basis for an accurate allocation of the cost of resources consumed by an order. In addition, investigation of the cause(s) of a cost driver occurring at its present level allows action to be considered that will lead to a reduction in the cost per unit of cost driver.

Examples of causes that might be identified are:

Material price may be higher than necessary due to inefficient sourcing of materials. This may be overcome through efforts to review sourcing policy and possibly provide additional training to staff responsible for the sourcing of materials.

The number of machine set-ups per batch may be due to lack of planning of batch sizes. It may be possible for batch sizes in this order to be increased to 1,250 units which would reduce the number of batches required to fulfil the order from five to four. This should reduce overall costs.

The amount of production line maintenance (and hence cost) required per order may be reduced by examining causes such as level of skill of maintenance carried out – by GMB's own staff or out-sourced provision. Action would involve re-training of own staff or recruitment of new staff or changing of out-source providers.

(Alternative relevant examples and discussion would be acceptable for all aspects of part (b).)

(c) The benefits of an activity-based system as the basis for product cost/profit estimation may not be straightforward. A number of problems may be identified.

The selection of relevant activities and cost drivers may be complicated where there are many activities and cost drivers in complex business situations.

There may be difficulty in the collection of data to enable accurate cost driver rates to be calculated. This is also likely to require an extensive data collection and analysis system.

The problem of 'cost driver denominator level' may also prove difficult. This is similar to the problem in a traditional volume related system. This is linked to the problem of fixed/variable cost analysis. For example the cost per batch may be fixed. Its impact may be reduced, however, where the batch size can be increased without a proportionate increase in cost.

The achievement of the required level of management skill and commitment to change may also detract from the implementation of the new system. Management may feel that the activity based approach contains too many assumptions and estimates about activities and cost drivers. There may be doubt as to the degree of increased accuracy which it provides.

(Alternative relevant examples and discussion would be acceptable.)

Marking scheme			
			Marks
(a)		Unit level costs	1
		Batch related costs	2
		Product sustaining costs	1
		Business sustaining costs	1
			5
(b)		Identification and appropriateness of cost driver of levels 1 to 4 expenses	6
		Causes of the cost drivers 1–3	3
		Possible benefits	3
			10
(c)		Comments (on merit)	5
			5
Total			20

Examiner's comments

This proved to be the least popular choice among the optional questions contained in Section B of this examination paper. In general, those candidates who chose to answer this question provided satisfactory answers. Many candidates provided a correct solution to part (a) and achieved maximum marks. Regrettably, many candidates ignored the information on batches and therefore arrived at incorrect solutions. Answers to part (b) were invariably of a satisfactory nature and many candidates provided very good answers to part (c).

40 THE ORNAMENTAL COMPANY (TOC) (DEC 08)

Key answer tips

This question is far easier than it first looks. Part (a) asks for variable cost per unit under an activity based approach, which is simple to calculate from the information.

Part (c) of this question could be completed first as it is easy to answer. Relate your points to companies like the ornamental group.

(a) The management accountant of TOC would have calculated the variable costs per unit as follows:

Workings:

(i) Direct material cost per unit:

	Fountain	Goblin
Total costs ($)	450,000	150,000
Production units	2,000	4,000
Cost per unit ($)	225.00	37.50

(ii) Direct labour cost per unit:

	Fountain	Goblin
Total costs ($)	300,000	100,000
Production units	2,000	4,000
Cost per unit ($)	150.00	25.00

(iii) Variable overheads:

Material related overhead cost = 30% × $2,400,000 = 720,000

Labour related overhead cost = 70% × $2,400,000 = $1,680,000

Material related overhead has material volume that is required as the cost driver.

Total volume factor =

	Units	Required per unit	
Fountain	2,000	4	8,000
Goblin	4,000	7	28,000
Other	16,000	4	64,000
Total volume factor =			100,000

Material related overhead per unit of volume = $720,000/100,000 = $7.20. Therefore, overhead cost per product unit will be as follows:

Product:

Fountain $7.20 × 4 = $28.80

Goblin $7.20 × 7 = $50.40

Labour related overhead has the number of operations that are performed as the cost driver.

Total operations factor =

	Units	Required per unit	
Fountain	2,000	6	12,000
Goblin	4,000	5	20,000
Other	16,000	4	64,000
Total volume factor =			96,000

Labour related overhead per operation = $1,680,000/96,000 = $17.50.

Therefore, overhead cost per product unit will be as follows:

Product:

Fountain $17.50 × 6 = $105.00

Goblin $17.50 × 5 = $87.50

Product unit costs using an ABC approach to product costing would be:

	Fountain	*Goblin*
	$	$
Direct material costs	225.00	37.50
Direct labour costs	150.00	25.00
	375.00	62.50
Variable overhead		
Material related	28.80	50.40
Labour related	105.00	87.50
Total variable cost	508.80	200.40

(b)   SGG is willing to purchase the Fountain at $750 per unit and the Goblin at $150 per unit. At these prices TOC will achieve sales of 2,000 units of the Fountain and 4,000 units of the Goblin. The product costs per unit together with the respective contribution per unit may be calculated using either the existing basis for the absorption of variable overhead cost by product units or alternatively by employing an ABC approach which attempts to give recognition to the cost drivers which causes costs to occur.

Product information (by unit) is as follows:

	Fountain		*Goblin*	
	Current basis	ABC basis	Current basis	ABC basis
	$	$	$	$
Direct material cost	225.00	225.00	37.50	37.50
Direct labour cost	150.00	150.00	25.00	25.00
Variable overhead cost:				
Material related	90.00	28.80	15.00	50.40
Labour related	157.50	105.00	26.25	87.50
Total variable cost	622.50	508.80	103.75	200.40
Selling price	750.00	750.00	150.00	150.00
Contribution	127.50	241.20	46.25	(50.40)
Contribution:sales (%)	17.00	32.16	30.83	(33.60)

At present TOC will not undertake any work which does not yield an estimated contribution to sales ratio of 28%. The current basis of product costing would suggest that The Goblin should be produced as per the request of SGG as a contribution:sales ratio of 30.83% would be obtained. However, the current basis of product costing would suggest that TOC should not undertake production of The Fountain because at a selling price of $750 per unit, the estimated contribution:sales ratio of 17% would be lower than the desired contribution:sales (%) of 28%.

Using an activity based costing approach which gives management greater visibility of the true costs of each product would lead TOC to a different production strategy. TOC would opt to produce The Fountain for SGG since a contribution:sales ratio of 32.16 would be obtained. However TOC would decline to undertake the production of the Goblin since it would result in a negative contribution:sales ratio of (33.60%).

(c) **Activity-based management (ABM)** is a method of identifying and evaluating activities that a business performs using activity-based costing to carry out a value chain analysis or a re-engineering initiative to improve strategic and operational decisions in an organisation. Activity-based costing establishes relationships between overhead costs and activities so that overhead costs can be more precisely allocated to products, services, or customer segments. Activity-based management focuses on managing activities to reduce costs and improve customer value.

Kaplan and Cooper (1998) divide ABM into operational ABM and strategic ABM:

Operational ABM is about 'doing things right', using ABC information to improve efficiency. Those activities which add value to the product can be identified and improved. Activities that don't add value are the ones that need to be reduced to cut costs without reducing product value.

Strategic ABM is about 'doing the right things', using ABC information to decide which products to develop and which activities to use. This can also be used for customer profitability analysis, identifying which customers are the most profitable and focusing on them more.

A risk with ABM is that some activities have an implicit value, not necessarily reflected in a financial value added to any product.

For instance a particularly pleasant workplace can help attract and retain the best staff, but may not be identified as adding value in operational ABM. A customer that represents a loss based on committed activities, but that opens up leads in a new market, may be identified as a low value customer by a strategic ABM process.

ABM can give middle managers an understanding of costs to other teams to help them make decisions that benefit the whole organisation, not just their activities' bottom line.

Marking scheme		
		Marks
(a)	Production costs (2*4)	8
		8
(b)	Contribution:sales ratios	2
	Comments re the acceptability of products (4*1)	4
		6
(c)	Comments (on merit) (6*1)	6
		6
Total		**20**

Examiner's comments

In general, the answers to this question were very poor.

In their answers to part (a) a minority of candidates were able to calculate correctly the ABC costs for direct materials and direct labour for each product. A much smaller number of candidates were able to calculate correctly the material and labour related overheads in respect of the products.

Rather alarmingly a significant number of candidates did not understand how to calculate the contribution to sales ratio for the two products as required by part (b).

In their answers to part (c) the vast majority of candidates discussed the adoption of activity-based costing (ABC) as opposed to Activity-based management (ABM) and in doing so not only failed to achieve some relatively easy marks but also sacrificed precious examination time. Many candidates did not provide any answer whatsoever and in not doing so 'threw away' a potential six marks.

41 REPORT (PILOT 07)

Key answer tips

Basic bookwork required for this question. Only attempt this type of question if you are sure of the subject. Note the structured approach in the answer. Marks will be awarded for using the report format and presentation.

To: Manager:

From: An accountant

Date: x/x/xxxx

Draft report on 'How to design an effective management information system'

1 **Introduction**

   This brief report summarises how an effective management information system can be designed.

2 **The objectives of management accounting information systems**

   Management accounting information has three principal objectives:

   (i) aid to short-term planning and strategic planning

   (ii) to facilitate control and decision making

   (iii) to provide the base for the effective use of management accounting techniques.

   These planning, controlling and decision-making activities are essential if the organisation is to achieve its objectives. These objectives may encompass a wide range of issues from high-level strategic plans to the control of detailed operating activities, such as the labour hours worked during the month. There is therefore a need to identify the information needs for a broad range of business activities.

3 The range of information

Given a spectrum from long-term strategic to short-term operational information needs, the data sources will probably exhibit the following characteristics:

- Strategic information needs will tend towards long-term, external and global data, which is obtainable from customers, suppliers, trade associations and government.
- Detailed operational information needs are likely to come from within the business.

4 Recording and reporting issues

The recording and processing methods adopted need to consider:

- Collecting and recording monetary and non-monetary information
- The influence and needs of management accounting techniques
- The influence of IT systems
- the type of business entity.

In deciding on the format of the reports generated, consideration should be given to:

- Analysis and dissemination to relevant individuals and groups
- Management culture, structure and style
- The appropriate accuracy, detail and speed, and any trade-off between them
- Security, access and controllability issues
- The need for systems compatibility and other organisations
- The needs, skills and systems knowledge of the potential users.

5 Other issues

Other general issues that need to be considered are:

- Expected planned life of the system
- Developments in MIS
- Available resources and time constraints in terms of commissioning dates.

Tutorial note

The above discussion should include reference to a specific organisation of which the candidate has experience/knowledge.

The design of the system should consider the management accounting tools that are likely to be utilised e.g. budgeting, costing, TQM, benchmarking. Can the system deliver the information needs of these techniques?

42 ENVIRONMENTAL INFORMATION

> **Key answer tips**
>
> This question tests your knowledge and awareness of external environmental information, and its use to complement internal information.
>
> In answering this question you need to ensure that you link your answer to the realisation of corporate objectives to earn a good mark.

The traditional focus of management accounting has been on factors internal to the organisation. Much attention has been given to the processes and outputs undertaken by the firm. Management accountants have provided significant benefits by analysing processes and outputs in financial terms (e.g. by variance analysis) and identifying areas where efficiency and effectiveness could be improved.

This philosophy grew up particularly in manufacturing businesses. As production became concentrated in ever larger firms there was a real need to exercise control. This was the great strength of traditional management accounting.

However, this picture has been changing dramatically over recent decades. For one thing, the relative importance of manufacturing industry has been changing compared to that of service industry. And in both sectors the level of competition between firms has increased. In this new arena, the traditional ambit of management accounting is not wide enough. It ignores competitive pressures, environmental factors, and the pace of change.

Faced with this situation, management accountants have responded by drastically changing their focus. The new outlook is sometimes referred to as strategic management accounting or SMA. Its approach is characterised by equal attention to internal and external factors affecting the organisation. Often this is evidenced by formal SWOT analysis: strengths, weaknesses, opportunities and strengths.

Management accountants are well placed to contribute to SWOT analysis. Apart from providing analysis in financial terms, they can equally deal in non-financial measures such as market share and quality.

Once possible strategies have been identified management accountants attempt to evaluate them. Cost structures will often be important: not just the organisation's own cost structure, but also those of competitors. Detailed analysis in this area can provide important insights into potential competitive advantages.

After implementation the role of the management accountant is in evaluating progress towards objectives. To an extent, this is a continuation of the traditional role already described above. However, there are also important differences. Management accountants are concerned with continual modification of the chosen strategy in the light of actual and predicted outcomes. As a result of this SMA is concerned with a much longer timescale than traditional management accounting.

Strategic management is the art of managing employees in a way that maximises the potential of achieving the business objectives. Management accountants collate and analyse information to help set and evaluate objectives.

STRATEGIC PERFORMANCE MEASUREMENT

43 HEG (DEC 07) *Walk in the footsteps of a top tutor*

> **Key answer tips**
>
> This question requires candidates to calculate the sales margin of a new operation, with a little bit of sensitivity on the price of ingredients and for you to explain five critical success factors; these should be related to the information given in the question. Finally how an ERPS would aid the role of a management accountant and not to describe what it is.

(a) Volume equals 4% of 625m = 25m

Selling price per unit includes SFG mark up of 33.3%, therefore 2.40/1.3333 = 1.80 as actual selling price for HEG.

Revenue = 25m * 1.80 = 45m

Now draw up the income statement entering the revenue, followed by costs calculated as shown over the page:

Forecast Income Statement of HSC for the year ending 31 December 2008:

	$000
Revenue (as above)	45,000
Materials (25m * 0.70)	(17,500)
Packaging (5m * 015)	(3,750)
Distribution (8% * 45m)	(3,600)
Fixed costs (given)	(5,401)
Total costs	(30,251)
Profit	14,749
Profit/sales as a % ((14,749/45,000)*100)	32.78%
Target rate of return (%)	32.00%
Target return ($000)	14,400
(This is calculated as 32% * 45,000)	
	$000
Materials can increase by the excess profit over budget (14,749 − 14,400)	349
Material costs could increase to	17,849
Therefore increase = ((349/17,849)*100)	1.994%

Based on the information provided an expected return on sales amounting to 32.78% of revenue would be made in which case the statement made by the finance director was correct.

The finance director was correct to be concerned with an increase in the cost of all ingredients as the return % is very sensitive to an increase in the price of ingredients purchased by HEG, as material costs cannot rise in price by more than $349,000 which represents an average increase amounting to 1.994%.

This shows that the target margin is very sensitive to an increase in the price of ingredients purchased by HEG. However, these ingredients come from suppliers chosen by SFG and therefore outside HEG's control.

(b)

> *Remember a critical success factor is a performance requirement that is fundamental to competitive success. Managers typically monitor a number of these in order to keep up to date.*

The main critical success factors are as follows:

Product quality

The fact that the production staff have no previous experience in a food production environment is likely to prove problematic. It is vital that a comprehensive training programme is put in place at the earliest opportunity. HSC need to reach and maintain the highest level of product quality as soon as possible.

Supply quality

The quality of delivery into SFG supermarkets assumes critical significance. Time literally will be of the essence since 90% of all sandwiches are sold in SFG's supermarkets before 2 pm each day. Hence supply chain management must be extremely robust as there is very little scope for error.

Technical quality

Compliance with existing regulations regarding food production including all relevant factory health and safety requirements is vital in order to establish and maintain the reputation of HSC as a supplier of quality products. The ability to store products at the correct temperature is critical because sandwiches are produced for human consumption and in extreme circumstance could cause fatalities.

External credibility

Accreditation by relevant trade associations/regulators will be essential if nationwide acceptance of HSC as a major producer of sandwiches is to be established.

New product development

Whilst HSC have developed a range of healthy eating sandwiches it must be recognised that consumer tastes change and that in the face of competition there will always be a need for a continuous focus on new product development.

PAPER P5 : ADVANCED PERFORMANCE MANAGEMENT

Margin

Whilst HSC need to recognise all other critical success factors they should always be mindful that the need to obtain the desired levels of gross and net margin remain of the utmost importance.

> *(i) Only five critical success factors were required.*
>
> *(ii) Alternative relevant discussion and examples would be acceptable.*

(c)

> *Enterprise Resource Planning (ERP) is a term usually used in conjunction with ERP software or an ERP system which is intended to manage all the information and functions of a business or company from shared data stores.*

The introduction of ERPS has the potential to have a significant impact on the work of management accountants. The use of ERPS causes a substantial reduction in the gathering and processing of routine information by management accountants. Instead of relying on management accountants to provide them with information, managers are able to access the system to obtain the information they require directly via a suitable electronic access medium.

ERPS integrate separate business functions in one system for the entire organisation and therefore co-ordination is usually undertaken centrally by information management specialists who have a dual responsibility for the implementation and operation of the system.

ERPS perform routine tasks that not so long ago were seen as an essential part of the daily routines of management accountants, for example perpetual inventory valuation. Therefore if the value of the role of management accountants is not to be diminished then it is of necessity that management accountants should seek to expand their roles within their organisations.

The management accountant will also control and audit the ERPS data input and analysis. Hence the implementation of ERPS provides the management accountant with an opportunity to change the emphasis of their role from information gathering and processing to that of the role of advisers and internal consultants to their organisations. This new role will require management accountants to be involved in interpreting the information generated from the ERPS and to provide business support for all levels of management within an organisation.

ANSWERS TO PRACTICE QUESTIONS – SECTION B : **SECTION 4**

Marking scheme		
		Marks
(a)	Profit 6 × 0.5	3
	Profit/Sales %	1
	Materials – price sensitivity	2
		5
(b)	Critical success factors 5 × 2	10
		10
(c)	Comments (on merit)	
	Nature of work	3
	Changing role	3
		5
Total		**20**

Examiner's comments

There were a large number of correct solutions to part (a) of the question. However, it was disappointing to observe an equally large number of incorrect solutions.

In their answers to part (b) most candidates were able to explain three critical success factors and a significant number of candidates discussed five (CSFs) as required.

Answers to part (c) varied significantly. The better answers produced by candidates were not only high in quality but were also concise. Poorer answers, which were often quite lengthy, resulted from the 'scattergun' approach adopted by candidates.

44 THE MOTHERHELP COMPANY (TMC) (DEC 08)

Key answer tips

In part (a) planning gap should make you think of strategy and corporate appraisal. Do not try to calculate the planning gap as this cannot be calculated and is also not asked for. Explain the planning gap and the three strategies other than the existing one within the Motherhelp Company. Part (b) is asking for you to give reasons for the potential problems that may occur in acquisition. Part (c) requires you to think yourself what might be the governments concerns and the reasons for these concerns. Try to think about the environment and general issues such as emissions and legislation. The final part (d) is asking you to determine the value of government assistance to business and the pros and cons of this aid.

(a) A 'planning gap' is the gap between the forecast position based upon an extrapolation of projected current activities and the forecast of the desired position. The planning gap is most often measured in terms of demand but may also be reported in terms of net profit, return on capital employed etc.

TMC has a projected market share of 22% at the end of 2010. It is clear from the information given that the directors of TMC have a target market share which is higher than this, hence the planning gap.

Gap analysis diagram:

[Gap analysis diagram showing $ Revenue on y-axis and Years on x-axis, with lines representing Ultimate objective, Future projects, and Current operations, and a GAP indicated between the ultimate objective and future projects/current operations.]

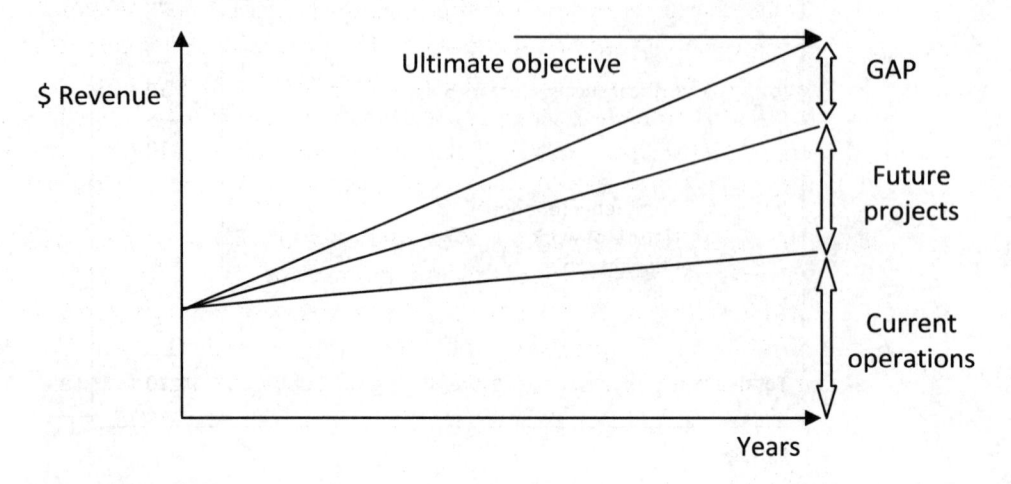

An organisation will forecast the likely performance of its existing projects and also the expected contribution of future projects. This is far more difficult since future projects are subject to much greater uncertainty than current operations and therefore forecasts of future projects have a much wider margin of error.

Where a gap exists, additional strategies are required. In this respect the directors of TMC might make use of Ansoff's growth vector matrix which identifies various options that might be considered in order to close the planning gap.

- A market penetration strategy aims to increase sales within existing markets.
- A market development strategy aims to find additional markets for existing products.
- A product development strategy aims to find additional products for an organisation's existing customers.
- A diversification strategy aims to reduce the risks of a business or to increase its growth prospects by entering new industries.

The above strategies are not mutually exclusive. An organisation might well pursue a penetration strategy whilst seeking to enter new markets. However, such a strategy would not be pursued by TMC since there is a projected fall in the birth-rate in Happyland after 2010.

Other strategies that can be used include efficiency strategies which are designed to increase profits (or throughput) by making better use of resources in order to reduce costs. Also it is possible to reduce the planning gap by divesting of loss-making business units.

(b) Three potential problems that TMC might encounter in the proposed acquisition of CBC are as follows:

(i) TMC is forecast to have a 22% share of the market for disposable nappies at the end of 2008. If TMC was to acquire CBC at that time it would then have a market share of ($681m + $155m)/$3,095m = 27%. Much will depend on prevailing legislation. It might be the case that the Director General of Fair Trading may ask the Competition Commission (CC) to investigate if any organisation controls 25% or more of the market. The Secretary of State may do likewise in circumstances where the proposed takeover would lead to the creation of a firm that would control 25% or more of the market.

(ii) The directors of TMC need to be aware of the precise nature of the cultural problems that CBC has experienced during recent years as this could be very damaging to its business if the acquisition of CBC goes ahead. In an extreme case the organisational cultures of TMC and CBC might be incompatible. The directors of TMC need to make a very careful assessment as to whether it would be possible to transform a negative culture into a positive one. If they consider that this would prove to be very difficult then they might be best advised not to proceed with the acquisition.

(iii) The directors of TMC have no experience of managing such acquisitions and this might mean that the integration of CBC into TMC would prove problematic. It is obvious that the organisational cultures are markedly different. It is probable that the systems are different as well as the management styles, employee skills and business infrastructure.

> **Tutorial note**
>
> Alternative relevant discussion would be acceptable.

(c) The government of Happyland will be concerned by the negative impact on the environment. The growth in the number of children born in Happyland will have raised the demand for disposable nappies as is evidenced from the market size data contained in the question.

In some countries disposable nappies make up around 4% of all household waste and can take up to five hundred years to decompose! The government will be concerned by the fact that trees are being destroyed in order to keep babies and infant children in nappies. The disposal costs incurred by the government in terms of landfill etc will be very high, hence its green paper on the effect of non-biodegradable products in Happyland. The costs of such operations as the landfill for such products will need to be funded out of increased taxation.

It might be beneficial for the directors of TMC to develop more eco-friendly products such as washable nappies which, by definition, are recyclable many times over during the life of the 'product'. Many parents are now changing to 'real nappies' because they work out cheaper and better for the environment than disposables.

(d) Governments may act as an aid to business performance in the following ways:

- A government can increase aggregate demand for goods and services by increased government spending and/or by reducing taxation so that firms (and individuals) have more after tax income available to spend.

- Government policy may encourage firms to locate to particular areas. This is particularly the case where there is high unemployment in such areas.

- Government policy via the use of quotas and import tariffs might make it more difficult for overseas firms to compete in domestic markets.

- A government can regulate monopolies in particular with regard to the prices they charge and the quality of their goods and services.

PAPER P5 : ADVANCED PERFORMANCE MANAGEMENT

– Government policy can regulate the activities of those firms which do not act in the best interests of the environment.

> **Tutorial note**
>
> *Alternative relevant discussion would be acceptable.*

	Marking scheme	Marks
(a)	Explanation	2
	Strategies (3*1)	3
		Max 5
(b)	Problems 3 × 2	6
		Max 5
(c)	Concerns of government	3
	Alternative strategy	3
		Max 5
(d)	Comments on merit (5*1)	Max 5
Total		**20**

Examiner's comments

This was the best answered of the three optional questions. Part (a) was answered very well or very badly insofar as candidates either did or did not understand the term 'planning gap'. Those who did not understand the term not only 'threw away' a potential five marks but also wasted valuable time in 'guessing' its meaning.

Answers to part (b) were, in general, satisfactory as the majority of candidates made sound use of the information contained in the question and referred to the issues of cultural problems, lack of experience of acquisitions and the impact of government action.

Again, in general, most candidates' answers to part (c) were satisfactory. Usually issues relating to non biodegradable nappies were cited however, few candidates drew attention on 'washable nappies' as an eco friendly alternative.

A significant number of candidates provided very good answers to part (d). However, many candidates needed to suggest a greater range of government actions in order to have achieved higher marks.

Rather worrying is the fact that a number of candidates did not provide any answer whatsoever and in not doing so 'threw away' a potential five marks!

ANSWERS TO PRACTICE QUESTIONS – SECTION B : SECTION 4

45 STATUTORY TRANSPORT AUTHORITY

> **Key answer tips**
>
> Your answer should explain the criteria for evaluating options, quantifying a social service and discuss funding for a transport service. You are not required to recommend an option or give a detailed evaluation of each proposal.

(a) When evaluating different options to find the best value for money, a statutory transport authority should consider:

Financial criteria

Financial objectives should be set, against which all three options can be evaluated. M Ltd is offering to provide a limited service with no authority funding whereas O Ltd requires a subsidy from the authority of $3,000 per week but provides a more flexible service and N Ltd requires variable funding.

Standard of service

This covers criteria such as frequency of service, timing of the services, facilities offered for disabled passengers and reliability.

Each of the three options plans a different standard of service. M Ltd is offering a limited, fast service. N Ltd plans a more flexible service with O Ltd offering the most flexible service of all. The practicality of each of the options proposed should be evaluated.

The area covered

M Ltd's and N Ltd's proposals only offer services between urban areas. O Ltd is catering for people living in rural areas who would not be served by M Ltd's and N Ltd's proposals.

Acceptability to the local population

Local people need to be consulted to establish their travelling needs. Meeting the needs of people will be a value for money factor because if it doesn't meet their requirements people will not use it.

(b) A statutory transport authority can quantify the value of a social service transport undertaking in many ways, including:

Financial measures

- Cost per passenger mile.
- Revenue per vehicle mile.
- Contribution per vehicle mile.
- Profit/loss per passenger mile.

Efficiency measures

- Capacity loadings of vehicles on each route.
- Punctuality rates for each service.
- Reliability ratio e.g. services cancelled and breakdown rates.

Other measures

- Reduction in other motor vehicle traffic.
- Number of passengers carried.
- Average length of journey.
- Analysis of use e.g. percentage of journeys made for leisure, travel to work and visits to hospital.
- Customer satisfaction.
- Impact on the quality of life of local people.

(c) Sources of funding for a rural transport facility, other than passenger fare revenues and public funds, include:

- Revenue could be earned by carrying advertisements on the inside and outside of vehicles and at vehicle stops. Companies could also pay to have vehicles painted in their corporate colours.
- Through tickets could be sold for longer journeys using other services. Commission could be charged for the sale of these through tickets.
- Tickets can be sold to include travel and entry to local tourist attractions. Again commission could be charged for the tourist attraction part of the price.
- Contract hire for school transport services and staff bus services for local employers in the area covered.
- Private vehicle hire on an ad hoc basis for local organisations.
- Running excursions during the tourist seasons.
- Providing a back-up service for railway operators during engineering work and other emergencies.

46 MISSION STATEMENT (DEC 02)

Key answer tips

The question invites discussion of the role of the 'Mission Statement' in the planning and control of business operations. Taken together, the three requirements invite a wide ranging discussion of business strategy formulation and the link between strategy and performance evaluation.

(a) A Mission Statement describes the organisation's basic function in society. Typically, the elements of a Mission Statement will include:

Purpose: Why does the organisation exist? A company exists primarily to create wealth for its shareholders whereas a hospital exists to care for the sick.

Strategy: It may specify the business that the organisation is in, the product and service areas it is going to operate and the necessary competences that need to be present.

Values and culture: It may state the beliefs, ethical standpoints and principles under which activity is to be carried out.

The statement can range from short snappy sentences ('Absolutely, Positively, Overnight' for a parcel courier service) to a page long description of business intentions (for, example, for public sector organisations). Whatever the length, it should guide all employees at all levels to work collectively towards the achievement of the corporate mission – 'a guiding light'.

It may attempt to incorporate several of the stakeholders (for example, shareholders, customers, employees), and increasingly, the environment.

(b) The Mission Statement can play an important part in the planning process by providing:

- a framework within which the plans must be developed
- a focus on strategies
- a screening device for unacceptable projects, practices and activities
- a communication device to establish a common acceptable corporate culture.

This framework should impact upon both high level strategic plans e.g. what areas of business are acceptable, and on operational planning decisions such as sources of supply and the way customers are dealt with by staff.

In terms of the owners, the statement may incorporate:

(i) A broad intention to enhance shareholder wealth.

(ii) This then needs to be converted into specific goals such as to provide a return on investment and/or increase share value.

(iii) Then measurable targets will be developed, e.g. 20% return on investment annually and/or a share price increase of 5% in excess of the industry average.

(iv) To achieve the required 20% return on investment may necessitate the profit margin on sales to be 43%.

The mission statement will therefore result in the cascading down of increasingly more detailed plans and targets. These targets will be set for the corporate entity, business sub-units and individuals. They will provide the basis of the performance measurement when they are compared with the outcomes. Good performance should relate to the extent that we are achieving the mission. Performance is concerned with assessing the extent that a desire, goal, objective or target has been achieved – a comparative judgement. To what extent have we achieved what was set out to be done?

(c) Potential problem areas:

- The wording of the statement may be rather vague and abstract and therefore provide limited assistance in developing strategies
- The content of the statement may provide the management with non-congruent goals. For example, maximising shareholder wealth may conflict with any ethical statements made in the mission. Trade-offs between quantifiable financial targets and non-quantifiable goals complicate the assessment of managerial performance
- The potential for inconsistent goal setting can occur between departments, differing managerial levels and over time
- The mission statement is occasionally regarded by employees as 'political window dressing' and does not in their view reflect actual company strategy and the actions of management – this may result in adverse behavioural consequences
- The statement does not normally stipulate a time horizon for the achievement of the mission so problems can arise in assessing how well the organisation is doing.

47 PROJECT X (JUN 03)

> **Key answer tips**
>
> The question invites candidates to explore the basic issues associated with business investment appraisal. Requirement (a) involves a fairly elementary computational exercise using a number of relevant techniques. Requirements (b) and (c) invite a discussion of the strengths and limitations of the techniques used in (a).

> **Tutorial note**
>
> The best outcome will have the highest possible revenue and lowest costs.

(a) (i)

	Best outcome		
Year	1	2	3
	$m	$m	$m
NBV	54.0	36.0	18.0
Revenues	84.0	94.5	105.0
Less direct costs	45.0	54.0	63.0
= Net cash flow	39.0	40.5	42.0
Less depreciation	18.0	18.0	18.0
= Profit	21.0	22.5	24.0
Less imputed interest (8% of NBV)	4.32	2.88	1.44
= Residual income	16.68	19.62	22.56
ROI	100 × 21/54 = 39%	100 × 22.5/36 = 62.5%	100 × 24/18 = 133%

Year	Cash flow	Discount factor (8%)	DCF
0	(54.0)	1.000	(54.0)
1	39.0	0.926	36.1
2	40.5	0.857	34.7
3	42.0	0.794	33.3
		NPV =	50.1

ANSWERS TO PRACTICE QUESTIONS – SECTION B : SECTION 4

> **Tutorial note**
>
> The worst outcome will have the lowest possible revenue and highest costs.

(ii)

	Worst outcome		
Year	1	2	3
	$m	$m	$m
NBV	54.0	36.0	18.0
Revenues	76.0	85.5	95.0
Less direct costs	55.0	66.0	77.0
= Net cash flow	21.0	19.5	18.0
Less depreciation	18.0	18.0	18.0
= Profit	3.0	1.5	0.0
Less imputed interest (13% of NBV)	7.02	4.68	2.34
= Residual income	(4.02)	(3.18)	(2.34)
ROI	100 × 3/54	100 × 1.5/36	100 × 0/18
	= 5.6%	= 4.2%	= 0%

Year	Cash flow	Discount factor (8%)	DCF
0	(54.0)	1.000	(54.0)
1	21.0	0.885	18.6
2	19.5	0.783	15.3
3	18.0	0.693	12.5
		NPV =	(7.6)

(b) **Residual Income:**

This measures net income after deducting an imputed interest charge on the capital employed. It is intended to ensure that the decision making and performance assessment process incorporates the finance (interest) cost of securing funds for a project. It prompts the question – is this project a good use for scarce and costly funds?

Strengths

- Signals to project sponsors that funding of projects involves finance costs
- Can be used to discriminate between projects that generate returns above and below the cost of capital
- Is a flexible tool as projects carrying differing risks can have separate rates of interest imputed

Weaknesses

- It does not facilitate comparison between projects that vary in size because it is an absolute measure of surplus
- Many difficulties can arise in deciding an appropriate and accurate measure of the capital employed on which to base the imputed interest charge (see further comments on ROI)

Return on Investment:

It gauges the efficiency of the project to generate outputs (profits) from resources input (required investment). It can be used to assess short and long term decisions.

Strengths

- It is directly related to the standard accounting process and is widely understood
- It appeals to investors who are interested in assessing the percentage return on an investment
- It permits comparison to be drawn between projects that differ in their absolute size
- It permits the performance of semi-autonomous business units to be compared with each other and with an aggregated figure

Weaknesses

- It can be difficult to identify the appropriate value of the investment – there are problems associated with the valuation of 'assets' in relation to their earning power. What are 'assets'? Many 'costs 'are expensed, R&D for example, and do not form part of the asset base of an organisation but nevertheless make a significant contribution to the earning power of the entity. On the other hand, intangibles like brands and customer lists can be regarded as legitimate 'assets' in a balance sheet but are notoriously difficult to value.
- Both recorded profit figures and asset values are subject to unscrupulous manipulation by senior managers in an attempt to artificially enhance the ROI performance of their organisations – candidates should be given credit for referring to recent (2002) scandals within large US companies.
- It is not easy to compare the performance of investment centres if they have calculated their depreciation in different ways or have assets that vary in their age profile
- The ROI is likely to increase as assets depreciate and therefore this may deter necessary asset replacement if managers are assessed on short run ROI performance – short term ROI performance indicators may discourage long term optimal decisions being taken
- Where a conglomerate sets a common ROI target that has to be achieved for all new projects, it may present problems in assessing performance fairly where:
- the target return makes no allowance for projects with varying risk
- where the various parts of the business operate in differing business environments

Net Present Value:

Unlike the other two indicators NPV considers the time value of money – it is concerned with not only how much, but also with when. Therefore it is particularly suitable for decisions whose consequences have a long time horizon e.g. capital projects.

Strengths

- The emphasis on cash flows is particularly appealing to shareholders who are seeking short and long term cash returns
- The use of cash flows is less subject to manipulation and subjective decisions than profits bases on accrual accounting (see above comments on ROI)
- It considers the opportunity cost of not holding money
- Risk can be allowed for by adjusting the cost of capital

Weaknesses

NPV estimates require a number of assumptions concerning critical variables such as:

- the duration of the cash flows?
- the timing of the cash flows within the life of the project – it is very difficult to accurately profile cash flows over long time periods
- determining the appropriate cost of capital to apply to the project and whether this should remain constant over the life of the project. This is especially difficult when the organisation is not able or is unwilling to arrange long term fixed interest funding.
- the heavy reliance on estimates and subjective decision making permits and encourages project sponsors and other interested parties to submit optimistic projections that cannot be easily refuted.

(c) Issues to consider may include:

- The anticipated project risk – is it known and can it be measured?
- Is the project the commencement of a much larger and longer term plan? An apparently poor performing project in the short term may proceed because of the long term prospects.
- The synergy and relationship between different projects may need to be considered – the role of the project within the corporate plan.
- The potential for an individual project to alter the overall risk of a company's business activities e.g. a single project has the potential, if combined with certain other projects, to lower overall risk, and consequently the corporate cost of capital.
- When will the project commence – now or later? Is postponement feasible? Is this project an integral element of a broader plan?

48 THE CHILDRENS TOY COMPANY (CTC) (JUN 08)

> **Key answer tips**
>
> Candidates must firstly demonstrate their ability to assess product profitability and comment on their findings. Next they are required to undertake a DCF analysis regarding the introduction of 'Nellie the Elephant' and some sensitivity. The final part asks for suggestions on alternative strategies and must be related to the scenario.

(a) (i) **Statement of Product Profitability**

	2008				2009			
	Bruno	Kong	Leo	Total	Bruno	Kong	Leo	Total
	000	000	000		000	000	000	
Sales units	180	150	60		120	48	72	
Selling price per unit ($)	40	50	60		40	50	60	
Sales revenue	7,200	7,500	3,600	18,300	4,800	2,400	4,320	11,520
Variable cost	2,160	2,625	1,440	6,225	1,440	840	1,728	4,008
Contribution	5,040	4,875	2,160	12,075	3,360	1,560	2,592	7,512
Product fixed overheads	3,800	2,400	2,040	8,240	2,400	1,340	2,100	5,840
Product profit	1,240	2,475	120	3,835	960	220	492	1,672
Company fixed overheads				1,650				1,650
Profit/Loss				2,185				22

(ii) The statement of product profitability shows that CTC is forecast to achieve a profit of $2.185 million in 2008 giving a profit:sales ratio of 11.9%. However, the forecast profit in 2009 is only $22,000 which would give a profit:sales ratio of just 0.19%! Total sales volume in 2008 is 390,000 units which represent 97.5% utilisation of total annual capacity. In stark contrast, the total sales volume in 2009 is forecast to be 240,000 units which represents 60% utilisation of total annual capacity and shows the expected rapid decline in sales volumes of Bruno and Kong products. The rapid decline in the sales of these two products is only offset to a relatively small extent by increased sales volume from the Leo product. It is vital that a new product or products with healthy contribution to sales ratios are introduced. Management should also undertake cost/benefit analyses in order to assess the potential of extending the life of Bruno and Kong products.

(b) (i)

	01 Jun 2008	31 May 2009	31 May 2010	31 May 2011
Initial investment	–3,900,000			
Working capital	–500,000	–200,000		700,000
Contribution (at 50%)		2,000,000	4,500,000	2,500,000
Fixed overheads		–1,600,000	–1,440,000	–1,296,000
Net cash flow	–4,400,000	200,000	3,060,000	1,904,000
Discount factor at 12%	1.000	0.893	0.797	0.712
DCF	–4,400,000	178,600	2,438,820	1,355,648
NPV	–426,932			

ANSWERS TO PRACTICE QUESTIONS – SECTION B : SECTION 4

The negative net present value indicates that the introduction of Nellie the Elephant is not viable on financial grounds.

(ii) Let X = the change in the contribution to sales ratio (%)

For Nellie the Elephant to become financially viable, an increase in the contribution to sales ratio (%) is required. This can be calculated as follows:

$(4 \times X \times 0.893) + (9 \times X \times 0.797) + (5 \times X \times 0.712) = 0.426932$

i.e. $3.572X + 7.173X + 3.56X = 0.426932$

∴ $14.305X = 0.426932$

∴ $X = 0.02985$

This means that the required contribution to sales ratio (%) = 0.50 + 0.02985 = 0.52985 or 52.985%. This would result in a net present value = 0.

Tutorial note

An alternative method is NPV/PV 'uncertain cash flows'.

We know that sales revenue is 4000 (80 *50), 9000 and 5000.

The sales ratio is uncertain as financially viable.

PV = (4,000 *0.893) + (9,000*0.797) + (5,000*0.712) = 14,305

427 / 14,305 = 0.029 + 0.50(sales ratio currently)

= 0.529 or 52.9%

(iii) If no new products are available then CTC must look to boost revenues obtained from its existing product portfolio whilst seeking to reduce product specific fixed overheads and the company's other fixed overheads. In order to do this attention should be focused on the marketing activities currently undertaken.

CTC should consider selling all of its products in 'multi product' packages as it might well be the case that the increased contribution achieved from increased sales volumes would outweigh the diminution in contribution arising from reductions in the selling price per unit of each product.

CTC could also apply target costing principles in order to reduce costs and thereby increase the margins on each of its products. Value analysis should be undertaken in order to evaluate the value-added features of each product. For example, the use of non-combustible materials in manufacture would be a valued added feature of such products whereas the use of pins and metal fastenings which are potentially harmful to children would obviously not comprise value added features. CTC should focus on delivering 'value' to the customer and in attempting to do so should seek to identify all non-value activities in order that they may be eliminated and hence margins improved.

PAPER P5 : ADVANCED PERFORMANCE MANAGEMENT

Marking scheme				Marks	Marks
(a)	(i)	Sales revenue		1	
		Variable costs		1	
		Contribution		1	
		Product margin by product		1	
		Company fixed overheads/net profit		1	Maximum 4
	(ii)	Comments (on merit):	4 × 1	4	4
(b)	(i)	Initial investment		0.5	
		Working capital		1.5	
		Contribution		1	
		Fixed overheads		1	
		NPV/Decision		1	Maximum 4
	(ii)	Approach to problem		3	
		Correct answer		1	4
	(iii)	Comments (on merit):	Up to 4	4	4
Total					**20**

Examiner's comments:

The majority of candidates provided a satisfactory answer to parts (a) (i) and (ii) of this question. Whilst many candidates also provided a good answer to part (b) (i), a large number of candidates made no attempt whatsoever to provide an answer to part (b) (ii) which was potentially worth 4 marks. Many candidates who did attempt part (b) (ii) did not undertake a DCF analysis regarding the introduction of 'Nellie the Elephant' even though the need for one was clearly signalled by the inclusion of multiple years, end of year cash flows and the provision of the cost of capital. There was a significant variation in the quality of answers to part (b) (iii). Again, poorer answers tended to ignore the scenario contained in the question.

49 VISION PLC (DEC 06)

Key answer tips

A good question asking candidates to demonstrate their ability to assess the profit gap. Then to explain Ansoff's product matrix and how the product range would feature within the matrix. Be careful not to spend too much time explaining the matrix. It is more important to apply it to the product range.

ANSWERS TO PRACTICE QUESTIONS – SECTION B : SECTION 4

(a)

Year ending 30 November	2007 $000	2008 $000	2009 $000
Existing portfolio	40,000	42,000	44,000
Oceanic division	2,000	5,400	12,790
Shops	25,000	26,600	28,312
Racquets	16,000	17,000	18,000
Birdcam-V	25,000	25,000	25,000
Forecast profit	108,000	116,000	128,102
Target profit			150,000
Shortfall i.e. profit-gap			21,898

Working 1:

Birdcam-V

Demand function is P = 1,450 – 0.01q, giving MR = 1,450 – 0.02q

Profit is maximised when: marginal revenue = marginal cost i.e. when:

1,450 – 0.02q = 180

∴ 0.02q = 1,270 and q = 63,500

Using the demand function P = 1,450 – 0.01q then

P = 1,450 – 0.01(63,500)

P = 1,450 – 635 = $815

Therefore profit per annum can be calculated as follows:

			$
Revenue	63,500	× $815	51,752,500
Variable costs	63,500	× $180	11,430,000
Contribution			40,322,500
Fixed overheads	$45,967,500/3		15,322,500
Profit per annum			25,000,000

(b) (i) Ansoff's product-market matrix is as follows:

	Existing	**Products**	New
Markets Existing	Market Penetration Strategy		Product Development Strategy
New	Market Development Strategy		Diversification Strategy

The design of the matrix will focus the attention of the management of Vision plc on strategic responses in order to promote growth in profits. Use of the matrix will enable management to evaluate and select alternative strategic options in order to reduce or eliminate the 'profit-gap'. Management will be able to use information relating to the past in assessing the potential future benefits that may derive from the adoption of alternative strategies. The model, like many other models, has little predictive capability. However, in using the model, management will be able to take into account the level of risk attaching to each of their strategic options. For example, the adoption of a strategy of market penetration entails the lowest risk whereas a diversification strategy has the highest risk especially when the entry strategy is not based upon the core competencies of Vision plc.

(ii) **Market penetration**

With regard to existing products it would appear that a strategy of market penetration is being followed, whereby attempts are made to sell existing products into existing markets. This is a low risk strategy which is most unlikely to lead to high rates of growth, reflected in the forecast increase of 2% per annum in the years ending 30 November 2008 and 2009. Management seeks here to increase its market share with the current product range. In pursuing a penetration strategy the management of Vision plc may to some extent be able to exploit opportunities including the following:

- Encouraging existing customers to buy more of their brand
- Encouraging customers who are buying a competitor's brand to switch to their brand
- Encouraging non-users within the segment to buy their brand

'Strengths' within the current portfolio will need to be consolidated and any areas of weakness addressed with remedial action.

Market development

The purchase of the retail outlets will enable management to sell existing products via new channels of distribution. The products of both the Astronomy and Outdoor Pursuits divisions could be sold via the retail outlets. Very often new markets can be established in geographical terms. Management could, for example, look to promote the sale of microscopes and associated equipment to overseas hospitals.

Product development

The launch of the Birdcam-V is an example of a product development strategy whereby new products are targeted at existing markets. Very often, existing products can be improved, or if an organisation possesses adequate resources, completely new products can be developed to meet existing market needs. Some of the main risks here lie in the 'time to market' and product development costs which frequently go well beyond initial estimates.

Diversification

The purchase of Racquets Ltd is an example of diversification on the part of Vision plc since the products and markets of Racquets Ltd bear no relationship to the existing products and markets of the company. In this regard the diversification is said to be unrelated.

The establishment of the Oceanic division could be regarded as a related diversification since existing technology will be used to develop new products for new markets. The success of this strategy will very much depend on the strength of the Vision brand.

50 BETTER AGRICULTURE GROUP (BAG) (DEC 08)

Key answer tips

This is a transfer pricing question with a twist! Be careful not to become confused between litres and Kg and try to apply the basic principles of transfer pricing.

Part (b) of this question refers to quality costs and the four subcategories and was very straightforward.

(a) (i) In order to facilitate BAG profit maximising decisions the following strategy should apply:

Division C should offer to transfer chemical CC to Division B at marginal cost plus opportunity cost. This would apply as follows:

– 40,000 kilograms of CC at $105 per kilogram since this is the price that could be achieved from sales to external customers of BAG.

– 60,000 kilograms of CC at marginal cost of $50 per kilogram since no alternative opportunity exists.

Division B has a sales forecast of 360,000 litres of product BF. This will require 360,000/4 = 90,000 kilograms of chemical CC input.

Based on the pricing by Division C indicated above, Division B would choose to purchase 60,000 kilograms of CC from Division C at $50 per kilogram, since this is less than the $55 per kilogram quoted by the independent supplier.

Division B would purchase its remaining requirement for 30,000 kilograms of CC from the independent supplier at $55 per kilogram since this is less than the $105 per kilogram at which Division C would offer to transfer its remaining output – given that it can sell the residual output to external customers of BAG.

(ii) **Division B:**

	External selling price of $105 per kilogram		External selling price of $95 per kilogram	
		$m		$m
Sales	360,000 × $120	43.20	360,000 × $120	43.20
Costs:				
Variable conversion costs	360,000 litres × $15	5.40	360,000 litres × $15	5.40
Material costs:				
CC – internal transfers	60,000 kg × $50	3.00	30,000 kg × $50	1.50
– external purchases	30,000 kg × $55	1.65	60,000 kg × $55	3.30
Fixed costs		18.00		18.00
Total costs		28.05		28.20
Net profit		15.15		15.00

Division C:

Sales:				
External sales	40,000 kg × $105	4.20	70,000 kg × $95	6.65
Transfers to B	60,000 kg × $50	3.00	30,000 kg × $50	1.50
		7.20		8.15
Costs:				
Variable	100,000 × $50	5.00		5.00
Fixed		2.00		2.00
Total costs		7.00		7.00
Net profit		0.20		1.15
BAG net profit		15.35		16.15

An alternative working – with data showing the consolidated BAG profit is as follows:

		$m		$m
Sales:				
Division B	360,000 × $120	43.20	360,000 × $120	43.20
Division C	40,000 × $105	4.20		
External			70,000 × $95	6.65
		47.40		49.85

		$m		$m
Costs:				
Variable conversion costs	360,000 litres × $15	5.40	360,000 litres × $15	5.40
Material costs:				
Internal transfers	100,000 at $50	5.00	100,000 kg at $50	5.00
External purchases	30,000 kg × $55	1.65	60,000 kg × $55	3.30
Fixed costs – Division B		18.00		18.00
Fixed costs – Division C		2.00		2.00
		32.05		33.70
Net Profit		15.35		16.15

The financial viability of the change will be affected by the accuracy of the increased external sales level to 70,000 kilograms at $95 per kilogram. A sensitivity analysis study could be used to monitor the impact on overall profit from a range of possible price:demand relationships.

(b) Quality costs may be monitored by measuring costs of non-conformance and costs of conformance.

Costs of non-conformance occur when the product fails to reach the design quality standards. Such costs may be subdivided into internal failure costs and external failure costs.

Internal failure costs occur when the failure is detected before the transfer of the product to the customer.

External failure costs occur when the failure to reach the required standards is not detected until after the product has been transferred to the customer.

Costs of conformance are those incurred in reducing or eliminating the costs of non-conformance. Such costs may be subdivided into appraisal costs and prevention costs.

Appraisal costs are those associated with the evaluation of items such as purchased material and services in order to ensure that they conform to the agreed specification.

Prevention costs are those associated with the implementation of a quality improvement programme. Such costs are planned in advance and their implementation should lead to continuous improvement.

Examples of quality costs relevant to Division C may include:

Internal failure costs: cost of materials scrapped due to poor receipt and storage procedures or losses of CC output due to poor processing routines.

External failure costs: cost of quality problems with batch of CC not detected until it has reached Division B. This may require free replacement of the batch and compensation for loss of output by Division B.

Appraisal costs: evaluation of purchased material and services in relation to the manufacture of CC to ensure that it conforms to the agreed specification; e.g. inspection and testing before use.

PAPER P5 : ADVANCED PERFORMANCE MANAGEMENT

Prevention costs: the cost of implementation of staff training and the costs of equipment testing to ensure that it conforms to the specification standards required for the production of CC.

(Alternative relevant examples would be accepted.)

Marking scheme				Marks
(a)	(i)	40,000 kgs of CC @ $105		1
		60,000 kgs of CC @ MC $50		2
		B purchase 90,000 kgs		1
		B purchase 60,000 kgs of CC from C		1
		B purchase 30,000 kgs of CC from IS		1
				Max 6
	(ii)	Revenue		2
		Costs		3
		Profit		1
				Max 6
(b)		Category of quality cost (4*2)		8
Total				20

Examiner's comments

In general, the answers to this question were very poor.

In their answers to part (a) a minority of candidates were able to calculate correctly the ABC costs for direct materials and direct labour for each product. A much smaller number of candidates were able to calculate correctly the material and labour related overheads in respect of the products.

Rather alarmingly a significant number of candidates did not understand how to calculate the contribution to sales ratio for the two products as required by part (b).

In their answers to part (c) the vast majority of candidates discussed the adoption of activity-based costing (ABC) as opposed to Activity-based management (ABM) and in doing so not only failed to achieve some relatively easy marks but also sacrificed precious examination time. Many candidates did not provide any answer whatsoever and in not doing so 'threw away' a potential six marks.

51 UNIQUE COMPONENTS LTD (PILOT 07)

Key answer tips

Make sure in part (a) that it is clear who's perspective you are taking. Part (b) looks intimidating but is actually quite straightforward if you read the requirements carefully.

(a) (i) The existing external selling price will be $41.21 + 35% mark-up = $55.63. We may assume that at this price Creative Division is able to obtain a market for all of its production capacity. If some units are transferred to other divisions within the same group, the opportunity cost to Creative Division is the external sales value foregone. However, it is possible that Creative Division has costs that will not apply to inter-divisional transfers such as packaging and negotiating costs. For example, if such costs were $6 per unit, then a transfer price of $49.63 would leave Creative Division with the same reported profit. This adjusted selling price would enable the management at the receiving division(s) to make a decision about transfers from Creative Division rather than from external suppliers, on a basis that would lead to group profit maximising decisions (other factors being equal).

(ii) If Creative Division has some spare capacity for which no external business is available, it may be asked to offer component A at marginal cost. Assume that this is $35 per unit. Once again, management at the receiving division(s) could make a decision about transfers from Creative Division rather than from external suppliers, on a basis that would lead to group profit maximising decisions (other factors being equal). It may be decided as part of Group policy to allow transfers to be made on the basis of marginal cost + a lump sum to allow for a share of the fixed costs of Creative Division. The size of this fixed sum would have to be agreed between management at Creative Division and each receiving division.

(iii) A dual pricing system may be used as part of Group accounting policy. In this case, Creative Division may be allowed to use the external price ($55.63) for its profit reporting. It would, however, offer to transfer at marginal cost ($35.00) if spare capacity existed. Unless an external source was available at less than marginal cost, the receiving division would buy from Creative Division. A group profit adjustment would be made on consolidation of profits at the year-end.

(b) A number of points may be raised, by examining the data-table analysis, and the combined probability matrix provided. The data-table shows the range of values of product unit cost for product A for a range of values of number of cut in Shaping AND quantity of timber (square metres) required. We can check the current value of product unit cost of $41.21 which is the value in the data-table where the number of cuts per unit in Shaping is 40 and the timber required is 0.60 square metres.

An analysis of the management team attitudes may be viewed as follows:

(i) A fall of 12% from the current level would result in a unit cost of $41.21 × 88% = $36.26. However, the combined probability of this cost level being achieved is only 18% (this can be abstracted from the probability matrix). This might, therefore, be seen as a 'risk seeking' stance if management decide to proceed with the re-design.

(ii) Other members of the management team are not willing to proceed with the re-design if it might lead to a cost increase from the current level. There is a 32% combined probability that the changes could result in a unit cost greater than the current level of $41.21. But there is also a 66% likelihood that the unit cost of product A could be less than the current level. This is a 'risk averse' stance since management are not swayed by the 66% likelihood that unit costs may fall.

PAPER P5 : ADVANCED PERFORMANCE MANAGEMENT

(iii) The expected value solution ($39.84) is the weighted average view i.e. the sum of each possible value of unit cost × the combined probability of each occurring. This may be viewed as a 'risk neutral' view of the likely unit cost. In this case since it is less than the current value of $41.21 management would proceed with the redesign of product A.

52 SSA GROUP (DEC 09)

Key answer tips

This is a tough question on transfer pricing, so it is vital that you focus on the key aspects – in particular how transfer prices affect managers' decisions from a divisional perspective and whether those decisions are best for the company as a whole.

(a) (i) As regards Quotation 1 in respect of the year ending 31 December 2010, the management of Division B would purchase ankle supports from a local supplier in order to increase the profitability of Division B. An internal transfer price from Division A of $10.50 ($15 less 30%) would appear unattractive in comparison with a locally available price of $9. The management of Division B is encouraged to seek the maximisation of reported profit as its key objective.

Division A has spare production capacity of 10,000 units (Maximum available = 160,000 units and the 2010 budget total demand is 150,000 units). Division A could, therefore, supply 10,000 units of ankle supports at its marginal cost of $7 per unit ($350,000/50,000) i.e. at a total cost of $70,000. However the external supplier would charge $9 per unit, giving a total price of $90,000 for the 10,000 units.

In order to have decisions leading to the maximisation of SSA group profit, Division A should, therefore, quote its marginal cost of $7 per unit for each of the 10,000 units required by Division B.

SSA Group profit will then increase by ($9 – $7) × 10,000 = $20,000.

As regards Quotation 2 in respect of the year ending 31 December 2010, the management of Division B would again purchase from a local supplier in order to increase the reported profitability of the division if Division A quotes a transfer price of $10.50 ($15 less 30%).

Division A could potentially have supplied 18,000 ankle supports by using (i) spare capacity for 10,000 units and (ii) switching 8,000 units of production from sales of the type of support that earns the lowest contribution per unit.

The 10,000 units of spare capacity can be supplied at marginal cost of $7 per unit as in Quotation 1.

The additional 8,000 units would have to be diverted from the type of existing support that earns the lowest contribution per unit. The situation is as follows:

Product	Knee Support	Ankle Support	Elbow Support	Wrist Support
Selling price per unit ($)	24	15	18	9
Variable cost per unit ($)	10	7	8	4
Contribution per unit ($)	14	8	10	5

Division A should offer to transfer the additional 8,000 ankle supports by diverting production from the least profitable type of support. The wrist support earns the lowest contribution per unit ($5). Hence Division A should offer to transfer the additional 8,000 ankle supports at marginal cost + contribution foregone = $7 + $5 = $12.

In this case, Division B would reject the offer and would buy externally at $9 per unit. This would ensure that SSA Group profit is not adversely affected by any transfer decision.

(ii) The management of the SSA Group needs to ensure that the management of all divisions takes into consideration all internal and external information relevant to divisional and, much more importantly, group circumstances.

As a starting point, the basic principle which underpins transfer pricing is that transfer prices should be set at a level which covers the marginal costs plus any opportunity cost to the SSA Group. If the basic principle is applied correctly then any subsequent decision made regarding whether to make internal transfers or external sales of products or internal purchases as opposed to external sourcing of products should lead to the most profitable outcome from the standpoint of the group as a whole.

What is best for the SSA Group as a whole is dependent upon the capacity utilisation of its divisions. In this example everything depends on the capacity utilisation of Division A.

What is of vital importance is that the marginal revenues and marginal costs of the SSA Group are known, understood and applied by management.

(b) If Division B buys from a local supplier the financial implications for the SSA group are as follows:

	$
Division A sales:	
60,000 wrist supports at a contribution of $5 per unit	300,000
Taxation at 40%	120,000
After tax benefit of sales	180,000
Division B purchases:	
18,000 ankle supports at a cost of $9 per unit	162,000
Taxation benefit at 20%	32,400
After tax cost of purchases	129,600
Net benefit to SSA Group = $180,000 – $129,600	$50,400

If Division B buys internally from Division A the financial implications for SSA group are as follows:

Division A sales: $ External:

52,000 wrist supports at a contribution of $5 per unit	260,000
18,000 ankle supports to Division B at a contribution of ($15 × 70%) − $7 = $3.5 per unit	63,000
	323,000
Taxation at 40%	129,200
After tax benefit of sales	193,800
Division B purchases:	
18,000 ankle supports at cost of $10.50 per unit	189,000
Taxation benefit at 20%	37,800
After tax cost of purchases	151,200
Net benefit to SSA Group	$42,600

The SSA group will be $50,400 − $42,600 = $7,800 worse off if Division B purchases the ankle supports from Division A, as opposed to purchasing an equivalent product from a local supplier.

Marking scheme

				Marks
(a)	Quotation 1	Up to 4		4.0
	Quotation 2	Up to 4		
(b)	Comments (on merit)	Up to 2 each	4.0	8.0
	Calculations (on merit)			
	Purchase from local supplier		3.0	
	Purchase from Division A		4.0	
	Conclusion		1.0	8.0
Total				**20.0**

Examiner's comments

There were some very good answers to parts (a)(i) and (a)(ii) which achieved very high marks. In their answers to part (a)(i) a significant number of candidates did not recognise that Division A had spare production and consequently were unable to provide a correct solution. It was disappointing to observe a number of candidates being unable to correctly identify which of the products yielded the lowest contribution. In general, answers to part a (ii) were satisfactory with a significant number of candidates achieving all four available marks. There were a significant number of poor answers to part (b). Some candidates confused themselves by applying the 30% discount to the market price of the buying division (B), not that of the selling division (A).

ANSWERS TO PRACTICE QUESTIONS – SECTION B : SECTION 4

53 LOCAL GOVERNMENT HOUSING DEPARTMENT (JUN 10)

> **Key answer tips**
>
> This question requested analysis of concepts surrounding the upgrading of housing stock by a local authority. To improve your answer ensure you use the scenario of a local authority working for the benefit of the community as a base for your explanations.

(i) Value for money audits may be seen as being of particular relevance in not-for-profit organisations where they are an important performance assessment tool. The VFM audit focuses on the achievement of objectives of the organisation in a way that ensures the most economic, efficient and effective manner. This may be complicated by the inter-relationship of objectives.

In the scenario the principal objective is the provision of the upgrade of the air-conditioning systems, ensuring that the quality of the system is satisfactory to LGHD. A subsidiary objective is to ensure satisfaction of the occupants of the premises with the quality and ease of use of the upgraded system.

An extension of the objectives is to ensure that the upgrade is seen to satisfy cost-benefit criteria, both in terms of the upgrade and the subsequent maintenance and operational advice to be provided by the contractors.

The principals are LCGD as the provider of funds and the house occupiers as recipients of the improved service.

The agents are the contractors who are tasked with the installation and maintenance of the upgrade plus the advice to users (occupants) during the initial two year period.

(ii) The focus on the achievement of the objectives of the proposed improvements will benefit from consideration of the relevance of each of Economy, Efficiency and Effectiveness. The three Es are likely to be seen as possibly being in conflict with each other in terms of the achievement of objectives.

Economy will be seen as being achieved by aiming at minimising the average cost per house for the upgrade and subsequent maintenance and advice. This may be aimed at choosing the lowest quote per house for the proposed upgrades. A possible problem with this approach is that the quality of the work done may be compromised resulting in dissatisfaction of occupants.

Efficiency may be seen as the maximisation of the input:output ratio. In this exercise, this may be measured through maximising the number of houses that can have the air-conditioning upgrade with the funds available.

Effectiveness requires the achievement of the objectives (both principal and subsidiary) of the proposal. This may be measured by focusing on factors such as:

- The quality of upgrade obtained
- The level of improvement in air-conditioning achieved
- The extent to which external noise is eliminated
- Residents' feedback indicates that the benefits will outweigh any inconvenience caused by the upgrading work
- LCGD considers that 'value for money' has been achieved.

(iii) Intangibility in the context of the LGHD proposal relates to the likelihood that it is less likely that there will be a single measurable output. The upgrading of the air-conditioning systems is likely to require different amounts of input effort from one property to another. In addition, the provision of maintenance and advice to occupiers over the first two years after the upgrade is unlikely to be able to be valued with certainty. Intangible factors such as the professionalism of the contractors may be difficult to value. Also the level of advice likely to be sought by occupiers may vary considerably.

Heterogeneity refers to a possible variability in the standard of performance in the provision of the service. The quality of advice given to house occupiers may vary according to the expertise and/or level of commitment of the engineer giving the advice. Alternatively, the engineer may be underperforming because of some work stress factor.

Simultaneity refers to the provision and consumption of the service coinciding and hence making it difficult to apply all relevant checks and tests before its use. In the LGHD exercise, it should be possible to test the quality of an upgrade before it is accepted by LGHD. However, the provision of maintenance and operational advice will take place throughout the two-year period after installation. This means that there should be some safeguard provisions in the contract to ensure that deficiencies from the agreed maintenance and advice aspects can be addressed as required.

Perishability refers to the inability to 'store' the service in advance. A particular problem may be where extreme weather conditions (hot or cold) lead to an overload of the air-conditioning units. Will there be any provision in the contract to ensure that the contractors will provide additional help – especially during the initial two year period?

Marking scheme

			Marks
(i)	Value for money		3
	Principal and agent		3
		Maximum	6
(ii)	Economy, efficiency, effectiveness	Up to 2 each	6
(iii)	Explanation of terms, the extent of their influence and problems arising for each heading	Up to 2 each	8
Total			20

Examiner's comments

Requirement (i) regarding a value for money audit was reasonably answered although many candidates did not appreciate there are multiple principal/agent relationships in the scenario (home occupants/ LGHD; LGHD/contractors). A number of candidates did not read the requirement and offered general comment about VFM in the scenario when the relevance of a VFM audit was requested.

Requirement (ii) was typically well done with most candidates displaying knowledge of the meaning of the 3E's and their application to the scenario.

ANSWERS TO PRACTICE QUESTIONS – SECTION B : **SECTION 4**

> Requirement (iii) was generally poorly done with few candidates indicating clearly that the four terms relate more to services than tangible products. Some candidates understood the meaning of the four terms but did not clearly relate them to the situation at LGHD. Candidates would score high marks by giving examples of how each term affects LGHD's situation and then providing any problems to which this would give rise.

54 PIPE DREAM

> **Key answer tips**
>
> In part (a) you should make the most of the comments given and aim to relate each comment to the reward scheme. In part (b) it will be important that you relate your answers to the scenario rather than simply regurgitate the pocket notes.

(a) The main features of TQM are as follows:

  (i) The primary aim within a system of TQM is to meet the needs and requirements of customers and achieve full customer satisfaction. Juran argued that having identified its customers' needs, an entity should develop products that meet those needs and it should seek to optimise the product features so that they meet the needs of the entity as well as those of its customers. The entity should then develop a process for making the product, and should optimise the process.

  (ii) TQM should be applied to all aspects of an entity's activities, not just to production operations, and to all employees, whatever their job.

  (iii) TQM must involve everyone within the organisation, and there must be a commitment to quality from everyone. To achieve this commitment, there must be committed leadership and a change of organisational culture. The concept of empowerment of employees is very closely associated with TQM: management must give more power to employees to make their own decisions, and should learn to trust them to do what is best.

  (iv) All quality-related costs should be measured and managed. These costs can be classified as prevention costs, inspection costs, internal failure costs and external failure costs. An aim should be to minimise the total of these costs. In TQM, the view is that by investing in prevention, total quality costs will be minimised. In the long-run, it is cheaper to prevent poor quality than to look out for it or rectify the problem when something goes wrong. Crosby developed the concept of 'getting things right first time', so that failures do not happen.

  (v) An entity must develop systems for monitoring quality performance and to support quality improvements. Deming is associated with developing systems of statistical quality measurement and statistical quality control. Establishing quality standards and monitoring actual performance against those standards has also led to the development of international standards for quality systems (for example, the ISO 9000 series).

(b) The main problems with introducing TQM into operations are likely to be getting the total commitment of senior management and the willing support of employees. A radical change is needed in culture and in attitudes towards the customer and quality. For management, the changes must involve greater empowerment to employees and greater trust.

Since the cultural changes required are so large, it might take time to introduce a system of TQM successfully.

A starting point should probably be to win the enthusiastic support of management. Managers should be given training in TQM concepts and practices, so that they understand what TQM is about and what they, as managers, should be expected to do. Without the full support of management, employees are unlikely to be persuaded that TQM is worthwhile.

Employees need to understand the importance of meeting quality standards, and the entity should establish quality standards for its operations. Employees should be encouraged to achieve the quality standards, and actual performance should be reviewed against the targets. The principles of Six Sigma might be introduced, so that statistical quality control is applied throughout the production process, and the levels of waste and defective output are reduced to minimal levels.

Quality should perhaps be written into all of the entity's procedures and systems. A criticism of TQM is that it might become too bureaucratic and procedure-led. Nevertheless, the entity might benefit from reviewing its management of quality systems, in accordance with the ISO 9001: 2000 guidelines.

(c) The emphasis in TQM is on the prevention of mistakes. Arguably, it could be almost as wasteful to incur additional costs on manufacturing goods to an unnecessarily small tolerance as it would to waste money on correcting defects or scrapping waste products. For example, if Pipe Dream's customers require pipes of a particular length, plus or minus two millimetres, there is no need to aim to manufacture pipes that are within a tenth of a millimetre of the specification. Making pipes that were that close to the target might offer advantages if there were no cost associated with doing so, but otherwise the company should develop processes that are intended to get all output to within the intended standards of output.

TQM is essentially about understanding the needs of customers (both internal and external) and working towards meeting those needs. For example, a motorist who wishes to purchase an inexpensive car might be prepared to tolerate the use of cheaper materials in trimming and decorating the interior of the car, but might still prize durability and reliability in the car itself. There is no need for a car manufacturer who is aiming at the cheaper end of the market to produce cars that are built to the same standard as those produced by the manufacturers of premium markets.

ANSWERS TO PRACTICE QUESTIONS – SECTION B : SECTION 4

55 UNIVERSAL POTTERY COMPANY (UPC)

> **Key answer tips**
>
> With any question it is vital that you relate your comments to the scenario given. This is particularly relevant to the parts of the syllabus dealing with quality as many students are tempted to write down everything they know instead of applying the points to the company given, in this case, UPS.

(a) **Quality**

Quality has become an increasingly important issue in organisations. For some companies it is an important differentiator, allowing the organisation to pursue a high price/high quality strategy. For other organisations, such as UPC, the quality threshold requirements for their products have increased significantly over the last few years. Customers have increased expectations of product construction, longevity and reliability. Quality is rarely absolute; and it is usually constrained by such factors as selling price. This particularly applies in UPC's market where it is likely that the quality of the product is limited by the relatively low price consumers are willing to pay for it. Quality concerns how a product meets its designed purpose and satisfies its original requirements. The target selling price is likely to be one of those requirements.

At UPC quality appears to be defined in terms of the physical condition of the products (no breakages, cracks or chips) and in the accurate positioning of the printed image on the product. These are the reasons given by the UPC management for setting up the inspection team. However, this perception of quality would have to be confirmed by the customer. It may be that other issues, such as the density of the printed image, are also important to the customer but have not yet been fed back to UPC.

Many definitions of quality include references to the customer. They stress meeting the requirements of the customer or user of the product. UPC might benefit from re-considering who it perceives to be the customer. Their current perception appears to be that the customer is the gift shop that sells the product. It is not the ultimate person or consumer who buys the product from the shop and uses it. For this consumer, other issues may be significant such as:

- The ability to wash the item in a dishwasher.
- The long-term safety of the product, for example: the handle does not break off a cup and spill its content on the drinker.
- The long-term clarity of the image on the item after many washes.

Investigating the issue of quality from the perspective of the consumer may identify other problems that need addressing.

Finally, quality has to be considered in the context of responsibility. UPC currently uses a courier company to deliver its products to the gift shops. This means that freedom from breakage is only partly under UPC's control. The delivery condition of products is partly determined by the care with which the courier company handles the package. Hence delivery quality depends on courier performance as well as on packaging care. In contrast, the quality of the printed image on the item is completely within the control of UPC.

Quality control

Quality Control (QC) is primarily concerned with checking and reviewing work that has been done. It is an inspection system for ensuring that pre-determined quality standards are being met. In theory, the responsibility for the control of quality lies with the person undertaking the process, whether it is the production of goods, delivery of a service or the passing of information. QC is the part of quality management focused on fulfilling quality requirements.

In many quality control systems, sample products are removed and inspected. Defects in these sampled products may lead to the whole batch being inspected and defective items destroyed. This is essentially the role of the inspection team at UPC, where 1 in 20 packed packages are inspected for accuracy of printing and correctness of packing. Incorrect packing in a sampled package will lead to the inspection (and potential re-packing) of all packages packed by that employee. Failure in the accuracy of the printed image is likely to lead to the destruction of the whole batch, and the re-setting of the production imaging machine to address the positional inaccuracy of the image.

It has to be stressed that, in this instance, quality control is a sampling activity and so it is very likely that defective batches will get through to the customer. To criticise the inspection unit for failing to find defective batches ('the quality inspection team is just not working') fails to recognise the sampling nature of the role.

In the context of UPC there are at least three further factors that inhibit effective quality control.

- The quality control of the positioning of the image takes place too late in the process. It should take place before packing, not after it. Valuable packing time and materials can be wasted by packing items with defective images which are found when the package is inspected.
- The reward system for packers is based on the throughput of packages rather than the quality of packing. In the past many manufacturing organisations have valued productivity more than quality and reflected this in their reward system. This is the case at UPC where faults in packing are not reflected in the reward system of the packers. In fact, the very opposite appears to be true. Packers are incentivised to pack quickly, not effectively. Beckford suggests that 'a major barrier to quality may be built into the reward system of the organisation'.
- There is evidence that the inspection team has participated in the achievement of the required throughput targets by passing packages that did not meet the required quality. This is clearly giving the wrong message, but the inspection team is only reflecting the need for the company to meet certain deadlines.

Quality Assurance

Quality Assurance (QA) is the part of quality management focused on providing confidence that quality requirements will be fulfilled. It may be defined as a set of procedures designed to ensure that quality standards and processes are adhered to and that the final product meets or exceeds the required technical and performance requirements. Quality assurance covers activities such as product design, development, production, installation and servicing. It also sets the pre-determined standards required for effective quality control. If quality control is primarily concerned with detecting defective products, then quality assurance is primarily about the prevention of quality problems through planned and systematic activities.

There is little evidence of quality assurance at UPC. However, the company may wish to consider:

- Setting quality targets and delegating responsibility for achieving those targets to the people who are meant to achieve them. In UPC it would be preferable to give responsibility for product quality to the employees who actually make the products and to reflect this in their reward structure. One of the roles of QA is to enable quality improvement initiatives. A possible initiative is to investigate the purchasing of imaging machines (or adopting the current ones) with a facility to automatically assess the accuracy of the image before printing. If the image falls outside certain tolerances then it may be feasible for the machine to automatically adjust it before printing. If these machines were installed, it would be the responsibility of QA to ensure that they were calibrated correctly and to verify that every product had undergone the necessary check.

- QA also offers quality advice and expertise and trains employees in quality matters. They would set standards for materials used in packing and establish systems for monitoring raw materials sent by suppliers to ensure that these standards were met. It may also be possible to improve how items are physically laid out in the package to reduce the chance of damage. The internal layout of the packages may be constructed in such a way that they only allow products to be packed in a prescribed pattern. QA would be involved in defining that prescribed pattern and training packers to use it – as well as subsequently monitoring that the prescribed pattern had been followed.

- The increased importance of quality means that many customers now demand some proof that the supplier is capable of consistently producing quality products. This proof is part of the 'confidence' factor of QA and may be demonstrated by a third party certification, such as ISO 9000. Certification helps show the customer that the supplier has a commitment to consistently supplying a quality product. QA will be concerned with gaining and maintaining such certification and this should assist the company in securing and retaining contracts.

At UPC the current inspection team is focused on QC. The responsibility for this should be moved to the production process itself or to the people who actually undertake that process. The inspection team could then focus on QA, setting standards for quality, establishing how those standards should be monitored, and then ensuring that such monitoring is being performed. In making this transition, the company will move to a culture of attempting to prevent faults rather than relying solely on detecting them.

(b) In many ways Six Sigma started out as a quality control methodology. It focused on measurement and the minimisation of faults through pursuing Six Sigma as a statistical measure of some aspects of organisational performance. However, Six Sigma has developed into something much more than a process control technique. It includes a problem-solving process called DMAIC and a comprehensive toolkit ranging from brainstorming to balanced scorecards and process dashboards. It also has defined team roles for managers and employees, often with martial arts names such as Black Belt, Green Belt and Master Black Belt.

Six Sigma was first used in organisations in the early 1990s. However, it was its adoption and promotion by Jack Welch, the CEO of GE that brought Six Sigma wider publicity. He announced that 'Six Sigma is the most important initiative GE has ever undertaken'. As Paul Harmon comments, 'Welch's popularity with the business press, and his dynamic style, guaranteed that Six Sigma would become one of the hot management techniques of the late 1990s'.

Six Sigma uses an approach called DMAIC in its problem solving process. This stands for Define, Measure, Analyse, Improve and Control. Three aspects of this are considered below in the context of how they would address the problems at UPC.

Defining the problem

Part of defining the problem is the identification of the customer. It is important to understand what customers really want and value and one of the main themes of Six Sigma is its focus on the customer. Six Sigma explicitly recognises the 'voice of the customer' (VOC) in its approach. In the UPC situation quality requirements are currently defined by the physical condition of the goods and by the alignment of the image. However, this may be a limiting view of quality because there is no evidence of any systematic investigation of the requirements of the customer. Solving these problems may not lead to any significant long-term gain; they may be quickly replaced by other 'quality issues'. Furthermore, the customer is also perceived in a limited way. These quality requirements are in the eye of the gift shop owner who is interested in saleable products.

The end customer – the consumer – who buys and uses the product may have other requirements which can also be addressed at this time. By considering the VOC the problem and scope of the project becomes re-defined and the solution of the problems potentially more valuable.

Measurement

Measurement is fundamental to Six Sigma. This includes the gathering of data to validate and quantify the problem. The creation of the inspection team was based on initial evidence about an increase in breakages. This needs to be quantified. The inaccurate printing of the image had been quantified as 500 units per month, out of the 250,000 shipped out of the company. This equates to a failure rate of 0.2%, so that 99.8% of items are shipped with a correctly aligned image. This sounds quite reasonable but it still raises issues and complaints that have to be dealt with, as well as creating wastage costs of $10,000 per month. The problem is that even a relatively low percentage of defects can lead to a lot of unhappy customers. Aiming for Six Sigma would reduce defects down to about one faulty item per month, reducing the wastage cost to $20.

Analysis

Analysis is concerned with understanding the process to find the root cause. Six Sigma focuses on processes and their analysis. Analysis concerns methods, machines, materials, measures, Mother Nature and people. The alignment problem needs investigation to find out what causes the imaging machine to irregularly produce misaligned images. Management currently appear to blame the machine but it may be due to the way that certain people load the machine. The analysis of the breakages is particularly important. It is unclear at present where these breakages occur (for example, are some of the items broken before they leave UPC's despatch facility) or are they all broken in transit? Neither is it understood why the breakages occur. Management appear to blame the packers for packing incorrectly and not following the correct method. However, it may be that the material is just not strong enough to withstand heavy handling by couriers who are outside the control of UPC. Additionally, the breakages may be due to some manufacturing problem or raw material imperfection in the items that break. Six Sigma stresses understanding the problem before solving it.

ANSWERS TO PRACTICE QUESTIONS – SECTION B : **SECTION 4**

Although DMAIC has been selected as the framework for the sample answer, focusing on other aspects of Six Sigma would be acceptable – as long as they are presented in the context of the UPC scenario.

Marking scheme		
		Marks
(a)	Up to 2 marks for the definition of quality	
	Up to 3 marks for issues of quality at UPC	
	Up to 2 marks for the definition of quality control	
	Up to 3 marks for issues at quality control at UPC	
	Up to 2 marks for the definition of quality assurance	
	Up to 3 marks for issues at quality assurance at UPC	
		15
(b)	Up to 3 marks for description of Six Sigma	
	Application of Six Sigma to UPC up to a maximum of 7 marks.	
		10
Total		**25**

Examiner's comments

The first part of question four focused on the current and potential role of quality, quality control and quality assurance at UPC, the supplier of pottery souvenir items. Many candidates were unclear about the distinction between the three concepts and (like question two) too many answers did not use the comprehensive information provided in the scenario. Many answers were too theoretical and, in fact, a significant number of answers failed to explicitly reference UPC at all.

The second part of the question asked candidates to examine how adopting a Six Sigma approach would help address the quality problems at UPC. Clearly some candidates had not prepared themselves for this area of the syllabus at all as no answer was provided. Other candidates knew some of the key concepts, such as DMAIC, but failed to apply them to the scenario. One marker commented that 'often candidates looked no further than the packaging process as being the problem, but quite a few did recognise that other factors such as raw materials and handling by the courier company might contribute to the problem. Students need to appreciate that putting a sticking plaster on the obvious problem does not necessarily constitute total quality management'. However, it must also be recognised that some candidates were very well prepared for this question, applied the concepts specifically to UPC, and as a result scored full marks on this part of the question

56 TELECOMS AT WORK (TAW) (JUN 08)

Key answer tips

This may appear a very complicated question in actual fact it is very straight forward. The key is to be able to analyse the costs into the different categories of quality costs. Then calculate the total for each type of quality cost and the overall total. The second part requires an assessment of which option gives the better savings. Presentation is very important in this question

(a)

> **Tutorial note**
> Ensure you have the following headings and that you have split costs correctly into each heading.

	Quantity	Rate $	Total costs $000	% of sales
Prevention costs:				
Design engineering	48,000	96	4,608	1.28
Process engineering	54,000	70	3,780	1.05
Training			180	0.05
Total prevention costs			8,568	2.38
Appraisal costs:				
Inspection (manufacturing)	288,000	50	14,400	4.00
Product testing			72	0.02
Total appraisal costs			14,472	4.02
Internal failure costs:				
Rework (Manufacturing)	2,100	4,800	10,080	2.80
Total internal failure costs			10,080	2.80
External failure costs:				
Customer support (Marketing)	2,700	240	648	0.18
Transportation costs (Distribution)	2,700	280	756	0.21
Warranty repair (Customer service)	2,700	4,600	12,420	3.45
Total external failure costs			13,824	3.84
Total costs (P, A, IF and EF)			46,944	13.04
Opportunity costs	1,800	7,200	12,960	3.60
Total quality costs			59,904	16.64

% of Total Quality:			
Prevention	2.38%	16.64%	14.30%
Appraisal	4.02%	16.64%	24.16%
Internal failure	2.80%	16.64%	16.83%
External failure	3.84%	16.64%	23.08%
Lost sales	3.60%	16.64%	21.63%
			100.00%

The total of prevention, appraisal, internal failure, and external failure costs should not be assumed to represent the total costs of quality for TAW or any other organisation. Quality cost statements frequently exclude opportunity costs such as foregone contribution margins and profit from lost sales, lost production or lower prices that are consequences of poor quality. This is because opportunity costs are difficult to estimate and are often not recorded by accounting systems. It should be recognised that opportunity costs can be substantial and provide much impetus to quality-improvement programmes.

(b) Option:

Cost of quality items:	Rate		Option 1 $	Option 2 $
		$		
Additional design engineering costs	2,000	96		192,000
Additional process engineering costs	5,000	70		350,000
Additional inspection / testing costs	10,000	50	500,000	
Savings in rework costs:				
Option 1	720	1,920	–1,382,400	
Option 2	960	1,920		–1,843,200
Savings in customer support costs:				
Option 1	600	96	–57,600	
Option 2	840	96		–80,640
Saving in transportation costs:				
Option 1	600	210	–126,000	
Option 2	840	210		–176,400
Savings in warranty repair costs:				
Option 1	600	1,700	–1,020,000	
Option 2	840	1,700		–1,428,000
Opportunity savings:				
Option 1	300	7,200	–2,160,000	
Option 2	360	7,200		–2,592,000
Incremental savings/(costs)			–4,246,000	–5,578,240

Option 2, i.e. redesigning and strengthening the casings is preferable since it is projected to result in incremental savings amounting to $5,578,240 – $4,246,000 = $1,332,240.

Marking scheme

			Marks	Marks
(a)	Prevention costs		2	
	Appraisal costs		1	
	Internal failure costs		1	
	External failure costs		2	
	Opportunity costs		1	
	Correct percentages		1	
	Opportunity costs – comment		2	
	Presentation		1	
				11
(b)	Additional design engineering costs		0.5	
	Additional process engineering costs		0.5	
	Additional inspection and testing costs		0.5	
	Savings in rework costs:	2 × 0.5	1	
	Savings in customer support costs:	2 × 0.5	1	
	Saving in transportation costs:	2 × 0.5	1	
	Savings in warranty repair costs:	2 × 0.5	1	
	Opportunity savings:	2 × 1	2	
	Advice/reason		1.5	
				9
Total				20

Examiners comments

This was the least popular choice from among the option questions. However, when attempted, the question produced some excellent answers which earned very high marks. In general answers to part (a) were satisfactory. Poorer answers demonstrated confusion regarding the different categories of quality costs. There was a significant variation in the quality of answers to part (b) with a number of candidates achieving maximum marks for a correct solution. However, there was also a number of unsatisfactory answers which invariably comprised poorly laid out, incorrect calculations.

57 GIBSON & CHEW

Key answer tips

It is important that you separate out each part of the requirement. Part (a) wants a generic answer on staff appraisal schemes. Part (b) then wants you to apply this answer to the particular scenario in the question.

(a) Informal appraisal is very much a part of the day to day activity of the manager. Consciously or sub-consciously managers continually make judgements on what they see, hear and read with regard to work colleagues, customers, products, technology and systems. Staff appraisal systems are an attempt to formalise the process by which managers judge the performance of their subordinates.

In practice, formal staff appraisal schemes are used for a variety of purposes including:
- problem identification and problem solving
- fixing remuneration and rewards
- staff development, career planning, training needs
- performance assessment, performance improvement, providing feedback
- communicating goals, targets and expectations.

Formal appraisal at predetermined intervals is not a substitute for the continuous and informal appraisal which takes place between effective managers and their staff, but provides a framework of good practice which benefits the appraiser, appraisee and the organisation. Formal appraisal systems are often structured around documentary procedures in which:
- forms are initially issued to appraiser and appraisee for self-assessment and management assessment,
- an appraisal interview takes place based on comments made on the forms,
- an agreed consolidated form is produced which summarises the outcomes expected as a result of the interview,
- which then forms the basis of monitoring and becomes part of the input for the next appraisal round.

Appraisal systems do not have to make use of the appraisal interview but the inclusion of the interview is considered good practice in aiding problem solving, giving feedback, generating motivation and assisting in the ongoing learning process.

The appraisal process can attempt to measure employee personality, behaviour or performance. Measurement can be either qualitative which usually involves the use of a narrative report or quantitative using rating scales. For example a series of behavioural attributes such as 'keeps accurate work records' or 'communicates well with clients' are assessed on a four, five or sometimes six point performance scale.

Some organisations seek to integrate their appraisal schemes into a full scheme of performance assessment, which encompasses job descriptions, objective setting, individual target setting, individual development goals to meet targets and the appraisal system itself. Individual goals can, in turn be linked into the objectives of the organisation through group goals using management by objectives, key result areas and critical success factors.

The operation of the appraisal system should be aligned to the desired culture of the organisation. Staff appraisal is one means by which the organisation permeates its culture through to its employees. It follows that there is no one best way to operate a staff appraisal scheme – the scheme should fit the management style of the organisation – but there are guidelines and experience from practice which suggest rules for effective operation. These are considered in part (b) to the question.

(b) A badly operated staff appraisal scheme can do more harm than good. For this reason G&C is correct in considering abandoning the scheme unless the operation of the scheme can be improved. It appears from the information provided that the scheme was introduced by the two senior partners which suggests a possible reason for some of the problems experienced. Appraisal systems need specific expertise in scheme design and implementation which is unlikely to be found in the partnership. External help and assistance may be necessary.

It is important that there is a clear understanding of the objectives of the scheme. For example, there appears to be confusion at G&C as to when the scheme is being used for staff development, performance assessment and determining the annual bonus. These three different scheme roles have been described as potential reviews, performance reviews and reward reviews (Randell, 1984). Randell suggests that, to avoid the inherent conflict between these three roles and the subsequent confusion in both the appraiser and appraisee, the appraisal process should concentrate on only one of the three. For example, it can be seen that if an appraisal interview is dealing with potential and performance then the appraiser is being required to operate in the conflicting roles of both judge and helper (Fletcher and Williams, 1985). As a guideline to G&C, it is considered that performance review based appraisal systems produce the most satisfactory results.

There are limits in terms of both time and suitability to the number of employees that an appraiser can satisfactorily appraise. Gibson and Chew have appraised about 25 staff each. At up to one half of a day required to prepare for, conduct, document, and monitor for each employee it is not surprising that it has taken two busy partners two years to deal with all their staff. Limits need to be placed on the numbers each manager can appraise which suggests that G&C will need to involve other partners and managers in the role of appraiser (a maximum of six appraisees is a useful rule). Decisions need to be made as to whether the appraiser is to be an immediate supervisor (parent approach) or the supervisor's supervisor (grandparent approach).

The appraisal process should operate on a cascading mode from senior staff down to the most junior staff and not in a random uncoordinated manner. In other words a manager will only appraise his/her appraisees after he/she has been appraised. At the same time the whole appraisal process should be completed within a reasonable time period (six months maximum).

Some writers suggest a number of factors which govern successful appraisal schemes. These include:

- Clear cut management understanding of the purpose and objectives of the appraisal scheme. It is important that G&C communicated this purpose to all employees who are to take part in the appraisal process.

- Management ownership of the scheme, that is, the scheme is operated for the benefit of the appraiser, appraisee and the partnership and not simply for the benefit of the two senior partners. The benefits of the scheme will need to be 'sold' to all staff.

- The scheme is 'open', that is the appraisee is given full feedback of the results of the appraisal system and has every opportunity to contribute to the appraisal process. Style here is important: if G&C are operating on the basis of 'tell' rather than 'tell and listen' then the appraisee will adopt a passive role in the process.

- The appraisal criteria must relate to the job performance and in so far as possible be objective rather than subjective. Designing criteria scales is a particularly skilled activity where G&C may need specialist help.

- Appraisal skills are new to most managers and require appraisers to be trained in appraisal interviewing. Successful appraisal interviews require careful preparation prior to the interview, a structured plan for the interview, documentation of action plans and a willingness to follow up and monitor progress. It is often helpful to provide awareness training for the appraisees as part of the process of gaining commitment to the scheme. Scheme training should include Gibson and Chew as well as their staff.

- The scheme should be simple to operate and require the minimum of form filling and administration.
- Follow up action must be taken up to underpin scheme credibility. For example, if training needs are identified then action should be taken to put together a development plan for the appraised. It appears from the comments that G&C are failing to monitor performance issues raised in the appraisal interview.

It will be impossible for G&C to evaluate accurately the benefits, if any, of the present scheme. However, much experience suggests that organisations which promote good practice and procedures in dealing with their employees end up with a more motivated and competent workforce which in turn feeds through to improved business performance. Finally, it should be noted that formal appraisal is not a substitute for the continuous feedback which employees need from their supervisors. Systems cannot substitute for the short and frequent comments praising, encouraging, coaching and sometimes reprimanding which all good managers carry out continually.

58 EQUIGUARD

Key answer tips

Part (a)

Key to success:

Try to come up with a wide range of issues with the current system (the examiner complained that some students didn't create enough points to score 15 marks).

Explain why the system used is a problem and what issues it is causing for the business.

Extra marks may be given for coming up with suggested improvements.

Dangers:

Not enough breadth or depth to the issues. A bullet pointed list of issues will not get enough marks to pass. The examiner wants the issues to be assessed – so each can be split into three elements (what is the issue, why does it cause problems for the business, how could/should it be changed). Then each identified deficiency can gain you three marks each.

Part (b)

Key to success:

There were two new proposals so it was important to spread tie equally between them.

There were three sentences given on each measure, so discuss the elements of each sentence.

Dangers:

Ignoring the measures that were suggested by the HR director and suggesting your own instead. Students were not asked for alternative measures – instead they had to analyse the measures that were suggested in the question.

(a) High labour turnover is not always a problem for an organisation. Some companies, particularly those pursuing a strategy of cost leadership, can tolerate low commitment and high turnover, employing unskilled workers who are easy to recruit and train. However, this is not the case at Equiguard where the engineers play a key role. The high turnover of engineers is of particular concern for two reasons.

- The scenario suggests that the company have two primary sets of customer-facing employees. The customer support clerks, who record and schedule repairs, and the engineers who actually fix the faults. Of these, only the engineers meet the customers face-to-face. Hence the motivation of the engineers, their commitment to the company and their proficiency in undertaking the repair is vital to Equiguard. Their behaviour will affect how the customer perceives the company and also the probability of them renewing their warranty agreement. High labour turnover in such a key customer-facing job is a major issue.

- The cost of training engineers is significant. The case study suggests that it costs the company approximately $6,000 to train an engineer when they join the company. Table 1 shows that Equiguard spends an average of $1,000 per year in keeping each engineer up-to-date with new products and product changes.

- Although this figure is lower than its competitors, it is still a significant investment compared with other industries. The training costs are additional to other recruitment costs incurred by the company. These costs would include advertising the posts and the cost of organising and conducting job interviews.

Hence the high turnover of engineers is a significant problem to Equiguard.

Table 1 is primarily concerned with the *reward options* offered by Equiguard and two of its competitors. Reward options usually contain three elements – base pay, performance pay and indirect pay. Organisations have to decide how each of these three components should be balanced in the reward mix. Equiguard have taken an approach which stresses base pay and pays little attention to performance and indirect pay. Although their annual average pay is greater than their competitors, engineers cannot gain extra pay to reflect work-related performance. Equiguard's approach fails to recognise that many organisations (including two of its competitors) now reward their employees with a level of pay dependent upon an individual's performance. Performance related pay ties additional payments directly to the performance of the task. This may be at an individual or team level or both. Both of Equiguard's competitors offer this. Its absence was recognised by two engineers in the exit survey;

- 'There is no point in doing a good job, because you get paid no more than doing an ordinary one. Average work is tolerated here.'

- 'The real problem is that the pay structure does not differentiate between good, average and poor performers. This is really de-motivating.'

This absence of performance related pay has also been recognised by the HR director who has proposed two performance related pay measures (one individual and one team-based). Performance related pay may also be distributed organisation-wide. Additional income can be given to employees to reflect the size, growth or profitability of the firm. Table 1 again suggests that Equiguard is not competitive in this area, with both Safequipe and Guarantor offering profit-sharing schemes.

Indirect pay (or employee benefits) is the part of the reward management package provided to employees in addition to base and performance pay. Health and life insurance, pension plans, company cars and social club membership are all examples of indirect pay. Table 1 includes two measures that might be relevant here; days holiday and expenditure on training. Again Equiguard performs less well than its competitors. A failure to invest in employees is likely to contribute to poor performance and high labour turnover. It appears that the company sees training as a cost rather than as an investment and employees' knowledge as a threat rather than an opportunity. Human Resource Development perceives that an organisation's investment in the learning of its people 'acts as a powerful signal of its intentions' (Bratton and Gold). That the company is sending out the wrong signal is suggested by a further quote from the exit survey.

- 'This is the first place I have worked where learning new skills in not encouraged. There is no incentive to improve yourself. The company seems to believe that employees who gain new skills will inevitably leave, so they discourage learning.'

Equiguard needs to revisit its reward mix. High labour turnover and the comments of the exit survey suggest that annual salary is not the prime determinant of satisfaction.

(b) In performance related pay, income is tied to the level of ability and output. Advocates of this approach suggest that a job's performance measures demonstrate to the employee what the employer considers to be the key tasks they want employees to perform. Measures also suggest what level of performance is expected in those key tasks. However, for these measures to be successful, the employee has to perceive that the measures are both relevant and achievable. There are at least two significant issues here (both of which appear in the performance measures suggested by the HR director).

- Firstly, that the parameters that underpin the measure are under the control of the employee who is attempting to achieve a defined performance. There is little point in setting targets that are outside the scope of the employee's influence.

- Secondly, that the measures that relate to the employee are not at odds with the measures applicable to the whole organisation. So employees are not encouraged to work in a way that maximises their income but which reduces the performance or profitability of the organisation as a whole.

The HR director at Equiguard has proposed two performance measures. The first is a team-based bonus based on an average time it takes for the company to respond to a repair request. He proposes that this should be based on the time taken between the customer request for a repair being logged and the date of the engineer attending to fix the problem. He argues that customers value quick response times and so the shorter this time the greater the bonus should be. Although quick response to a customer request for a repair is important, the potential problem with this measure is that it is influenced by parameters largely outside the influence of the team. Firstly, it depends upon the availability of an engineer and this availability is largely determined by how many engineers the company decides to employ. Secondly, the scenario makes it clear that the visit is scheduled 'at the earliest possible time convenient to the customer'. This may be some considerable time in the future, particularly for householders who have to make arrangements to stay at home to allow the engineer access to the equipment they are repairing. To make this a legitimate performance measure the lead time to repair has to be in the hands of the team, which it clearly is not.

In addition, the HR director proposes an individual bonus. This will be based on the average time taken for an engineer to fix a reported fault once they have arrived. This is the average time taken for the engineer to repair the fault from the start time of the job to its completion. He argues that the company values quick response time as this increases efficiency and so the quicker the fix the greater the bonus.

At least this measure is partly in the hands of the repairer. However, there are at least three problems with this measure:

- The length of the repair is likely to depend upon the complexity of the problem and the design of the equipment being repaired. The measure would penalise engineers working on complicated problems on complex equipment.

- The length of the repair may influence the quality of the repair. There might be a temptation to perform a relatively quick fix, with a high probability of a future failure. Indeed the measure might encourage engineers to maximise their income by performing a number of quick repairs that do not address the underlying problem. The effect of this on Equiguard could be potentially disastrous. Their current business model depends upon the company minimising calls and repairs during the warranty period. In contrast, the performance measure might lead to more calls, increasing the pay of the engineer but undermining the profitability of the company.

- There could be problems with engineers reliably reporting the correct start and end time of a job. The engineer may be tempted to falsify these times, reducing job time but perhaps increasing the time apparently spent in travelling and performing administration.

	Marking scheme	
		Marks
(a)	Up to 3 marks for each deficiency identified by the candidate	12
(b)	Evaluation of HR director's suggested measures: measure 1 – companywide measure: up to 5 marks	
	Evaluation of HR director's measures: measure 2 – individual measure: up to 5 marks	8
Total		**20**

Examiner's comments

The first part of the question asked candidates to assess the deficiencies of the company's current rewards management system. This was answered fairly well by candidates, although in some cases not enough points were made to get the marks on offer. The second part of the question asked candidates to analyse the limitations of new performance measures proposed by the HR Director. It is relatively difficult to spot these deficiencies in the time-constrained pressurised environment of an examination. However, many candidates did, providing answers that scored eight or more of the ten marks on offer for this part question. This was very heartening.

59 BUSINESS SOLUTIONS (JUN 02)

> **Key answer tips**
>
> The issues raised by a company divisionalising are always going to be an important feature of this paper. This is a standard transfer pricing question involving the usual array of situations, and should represent some very easy marks. There are a number of other indicators which could be suggested for part (c), but it is important to justify yours in the context of the case study.

(a) **Scenario (i)**

If North uses the external consultant, the daily contribution to the company is $1,200 − $500 = $700. If North uses a consultant from South the daily contribution to the company is $1,200 − $100 = $1,100. Therefore the cross charge rate should be set on a level where both North and South will perceive that they will benefit – above $100 and below $500 – say $300.

Scenario (ii)

If North uses the external consultant, the total contribution for one day's consultancy in both North and South divisions would be:

	Income	VC		
North	1,200	500		
South	400	100		
	1,600	− 600	=	$1,000

If the South consultant goes to North, then the total contribution would be:

$1200 − $100 = $1,100

Therefore it is best if North employs the South consultant – by setting the cross charge above $400 and below $500, say $450, both parties will benefit and agree to the transaction.

Scenario (iii)

If the North uses the South Consultant, the total contribution will be:

$1200 − $100 = $1,100

If North employs the external consultant, the total contribution will be:

	Income	VC		
North	1,200	500		
South	700	100		
	1,900	− 600	=	$1,300

The lost contribution of the work in South ($600) exceeds the incremental cost ($400) of the external consultant undertaking the work.

The company therefore needs to set a cross charge that discourages a consultant going North i.e. above $500 but below $700.

Assumptions:

- The objective of the company is to maximise contribution in the short run (not long run considerations).
- The long term business consequences of rejecting work in the south (scenario ii) can be ignored.
- The divisional managers' behaviour and responses determined only by short term sectional (divisional) financial performance measurement.
- Access to all the decision making data that the separate divisions use.

(b) **Reasons for re-organisation**

- The need to have local knowledge applied specifically to local decisions.
- A divisional company offers the opportunity to make decentralised speedy decisions – especially with a rapidly changing environment.
- It permits senior managers to concentrate on global strategic issues – detailed operational activities are dealt with separately by those most suitable.
- It permits junior managers to experience broader decision making and can be used as part of their development programme.
- Local semi-autonomous decision making is likely to be a motivating factor for managers (less central control).
- A divisional structure may reduce the complexity and cost of the communication systems within an unitary hierarchical structure.

Suggested problems

- Senior management may have difficulty in 'letting go' – permitting decision to be made locally.
- Senior management may become involved in resolving disputes between the divisions.
- The divisions might eventually compete against each other to the detriment of the entire company.
- Some divisional decisions may not be in the best interests of the entire company (problems of local optimality v global optimality) – ensuring goal congruence.
- The potential waste from the duplication of functions.

(c) **Possible indicators**

A number of indicators could be used. These should be measured for the business as a whole and where appropriate for each division separately to enable comparison between them. Examples include:

- Growth in the business – which could be measured both in absolute terms and in terms of market share. The management need to monitor whether the growth experienced in the last decade is continuing.
- Levels of repeat business (as a measure of customer satisfaction). For North division it would be particularly beneficial to analyse this according to the consultant used (North, South or sub-contract) to indicate whether the assumption that the quality of the work is the same whoever carries it out.
- Business turned away by division – to give an indication of whether there is additional scope for expansion and unmet demand.
- Average fee per day, which may reflect the market demand or the type of jobs being undertaken. In addition it is important to monitor this to ensure that the cross-charging system is based on assumptions which are still valid.

ANSWERS TO PRACTICE QUESTIONS – SECTION B : SECTION 4

60 BETTASERVE (PILOT 07)

> **Key answer tips**
>
> With the new syllabus it is questionable the extent to which you will be asked to evaluate a proposal in this way. However, it is still a good question to consider the implications of decisions.

(a) (i) Corporate vision may be seen as looking forward through the defining of markets and the basis on which the company will compete. Bettaserve plc has defined the 'gold standard' proposal for one of its product ranges as a specific market opportunity. It envisages competing through the identification of key competitors and by close co-operation with its customers in providing services to meet their specific design and quality standards.

The corporate vision is seen as being achieved through a focus on internal efficiency and external effectiveness. The 'gold standard' proposal may be seen as illustrating a specific sub-set of the corporate mission since it:

- has its own distinct business concept and mission – the 'gold standard' focus;
- has identified the key competitors; and
- is a suitable area for the management of its own strategies – close co-operation with customers and the provision of services to meet their design requirements.

(ii) The 'gold standard' proposal may be measured in both marketing and financial terms. Will it achieve market growth and an improved market position? The projected sales ($m) in schedule 1 shows growth of 20% in 2008 ($36m/$30m) and a further 11.1 % in 2009 ($40m/$36m). In addition, market position is anticipated to improve, with a market share of 12.5%, 14.4% and 15.4% in years 2007, 2008 and 2009 respectively (e.g. 2007 = $30m/$240m).

The net profit/ sales percentage is also expected to increase each year. The figures are 6%, 29.3% and 37.25% for 2007, 2008 and 2009 respectively (e.g. 2007 = $1.8m/$30m). The profit increase is partly linked to the projected fall in quality costs, both costs of conformance (appraisal and prevention) and costs of non-conformance (internal and external failure) as shown in Schedule 1. It is also linked to the increase in volume of business as fixed costs have a reduced effect.

(iii) The marketing success of the proposal is linked to the achievement of customer satisfaction. The success will require an efficient business operating system for all aspects of the cycle from service design to after sales service to customers. Improved quality and delivery should lead to improved customer satisfaction. Schedule 1 shows a number of quantitative measures of the expected measurement of these factors:

- Quality is expected to improve. The percentage of services achieving design quality standards is expected to rise from 95% to 98% between 2007 and 2009. In the same period, rectification claims from customers for faulty work should fall from $0.9m to $0.2m and the cost of after sales rectification service should fall from $3m to $2m.

- Delivery efficiency improvement may be measured in terms of the increase in the percentage of sales expected to meet planned delivery dates. This percentage rises from 90% in 2007 to 99% in 2009.

(iv) The financial success of the proposal is linked to the achievement of high productivity. This should be helped through reduced cycle time and decreased levels of waste. Once again Schedule 1 shows a number of quantitative measures of these factors:

- The average total cycle time from customer enquiry to delivery should fall from 6 weeks in 2007 to 5 weeks in 2009. This indicates both internal efficiency and external effectiveness.
- Waste in the form of idle capacity of service personnel is expected to fall from 10% to 2% between 2007 and 2009. Also, service enquiries not taken up by customers, is expected to fall from 7.5% of enquiries in 2007 to 2.5% of enquiries in 2009. These are both examples of ways in which improved productivity may be measured. Both will be linked to the prevention and appraisal costs, which are intended to reduce the level of internal and external failure costs.

(b) The analysis of the 'gold standard' proposal shows a hierarchy of performance measures. The performance pyramid shown below indicates how strategies to assist in the achievement of corporate vision may be cascaded down through a number of levels. The analysis discussed and evaluated in section (a) consists of a number of interrelated areas of focus. The marketing and financial success of the proposal is the initial focus for the achievement of corporate vision. Marketing and financial strategies must be formulated and inter-related. They must be linked to the achievement of customer satisfaction and high productivity at the next level in the hierarchy. Increased flexibility of methods should also be aimed for. This should help (internally) in achieving improved productivity and also (externally) in an improved level of customer satisfaction. High quality standards will improve customer satisfaction and in turn will assist in market retention and growth.

As discussed in part (a), customer satisfaction may be achieved through a more detailed focus on improved quality and delivery. Productivity may be improved through reductions in service cycle times and waste elements.

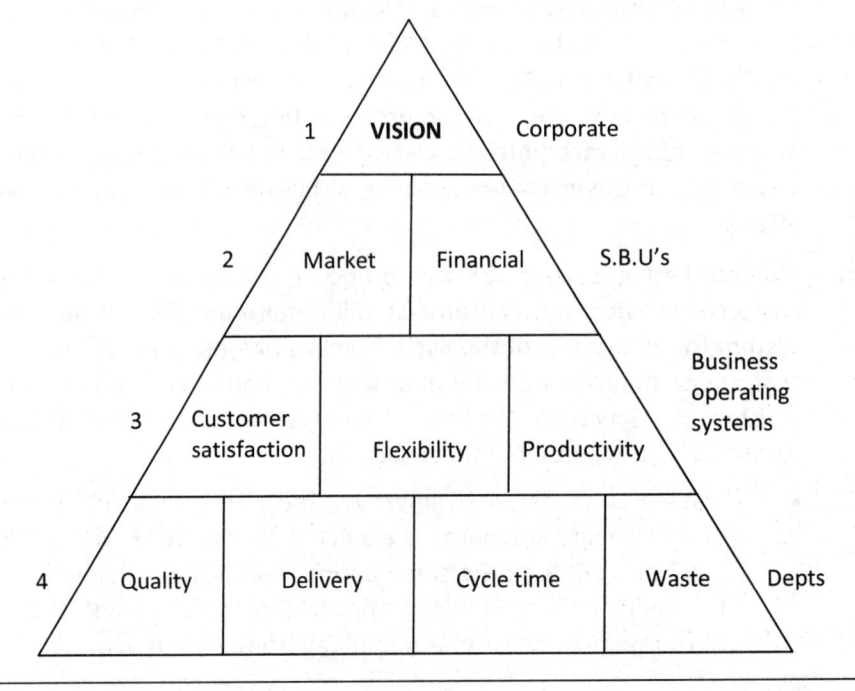

```
                    1  /  VISION  \        Corporate

                 2 /  Market  | Financial  \   S.B.U's

                                                    Business
              3 / Customer    |           |        \  operating
                 satisfaction | Flexibility | Productivity  systems

           4 / Quality | Delivery | Cycle time | Waste \   Depts
```

ANSWERS TO PRACTICE QUESTIONS – SECTION B : SECTION 4

61 SUPERIOR SOFTWARE HOUSE (SSH) (DEC 08)

> **Key answer tips**
>
> Set out your answer using the headings in the question. Consider what measures are appropriate per division and which ones for the group. E.g. ROCE, EBITDA, Gearing for the group! You need to comment on your calculations. You need to aim for at least seven calculations plus commentary for fourteen marks.
>
> In part (b) Think why is the operations manager pushing for delivery at all costs, are his statements ethical?
>
> In part (c) What makes software fit for use? Are there any standards?
>
> In part (d) You are asked about non financial performance measures to ensure that you have a more balanced view of performance.

(a) To: Directors

From: Management Accountant

Date: 5 December 2008

Subject: Financial performance of operations in Bonlandia and Karendia

Further to your recent request please find detailed below my analysis of the financial performance of our operations for the two-year period ended 30 November 2008. I have included operating statistics in the appendix which is attached to my report.

Sales revenue

The turnover in Bonlandia increased by 4.3% whereas the turnover in Karendia increased by 40% which is excellent bearing in mind that operations only commenced in 2006. The overall growth in turnover achieved during 2008 amounted to an acceptable level of 8.75%.

Profits

The operation in Bonlandia did not perform as well in 2008 with net profit falling by $152,000 (5.6%). The operation in Karendia made a loss of $348,000 in 2008 compared with a loss of $750,000 in 2007. It appears that although turnover in Karendia increased by 40% during 2008 further growth in revenues (or cost reductions) will be essential in order for the Karendia operation to become profitable. The change in the structure of industry in Karendia may enable this growth to be achieved.

The overall profit of SSH has increased from $1,050,000 to $1,350,000, an increase of 28.6%. Non-operating costs have increased from $3,400,000 (2007) to $3,842,000 (2008), an increase of 13%. It is worth noting that interest payable has fallen by $50,000 which is a direct result of the repayment of $500,000 of debt finance. The increased amount of marketing expenditure has enabled both operations to achieve growth in turnover. However, the additional revenue of $600,000 in Bonlandia in 2008 appears modest. In this regard one might question the effectiveness of the marketing strategy of SSH. EBITDA (earnings before interest, taxation, depreciation and amortisation) rose from $2,450,000 to $2,760,000. The return on capital employed increased from 15.9% in 2007 to 16.7% in 2008.

Costs

Salaries have increased by 8.5% in Bonlandia and 4% in Karendia. These increases may reflect local conditions in the labour market for software specialists. Software and consumables costs have only increased by 2% and 8% respectively in Bonlandia and Karendia. Bearing in mind that turnover of each operation has increased then it is quite conceivable that SSH are benefiting from economies of scale that exist with regard to the provision of software and consumables. However, the increase of 8% in Karendia may be indicative of poor cost control. Other operating costs have increased by 2.9% in Bonlandia but increased by 9% in Karendia, which might be indicative of poor cost control.

Utilisation of non-current assets

The 2008 non-current assets utilisation ratios of Bonlandia and the overall business show a decrease over those of 2007.

The ratio in respect of the Karendia operation indicates a decrease from 2 times to 1.75 times. However, this is acceptable given that operations in Karendia have been recently established.

It might well be the case that, for example, recently acquired non-current assets may not yet have been brought fully into use or perhaps were acquired towards the end of 2008. The Karendia operation is clearly in a rapid-growth phase hence the need for such investments in non-current assets.

Other information

It would be useful to have data relating to previous years in order to observe longer term trends of revenues and costs for each operation. Certainly, data for 2006 in respect of the Karendia operation would enable a 'complete' picture to be taken. This would enable a much better assessment of current recent years.

It would be extremely useful to have competitor information in order to assess relative market share and establish how they are performing in the Bonlandia and Karendia markets compared with the operations established by SSH.

It is clear that long-term borrowings have decreased during 2008 and that SSH has sufficient cash flow to be repaying debt finance. However, it would be useful to have a detailed breakdown of the working capital of each operation in order to confirm this.

It would also be useful to have future market and financial projections in respect of operations in Bonlandia and Karendia which should reflect the actual results achieved in 2007 and 2008.

Signed: Management Accountant

APPENDIX

	2008			2007		
	Bonlandia	Karendia	Group	Bonlandia	Karendia	Group
% growth in sales revenue	4.3	40	8.75			
Sales margin before interest (%)	17.45	(12.4)	12.64	19.3	(37.5)	12.2
Return on capital employed (%)			16.7			15.9
Earnings before interest, depreciation and amortisation ($000)			2,760			2,450
Non-current asset turnover ratio	1.62	1.75	1.64	1.75	2.00	1.77
Debt:Equity ratio (%)			43.7			57.7
Gearing ratio (%)			30.4			36.6

(b) In a market place such as that in which SSH competes, product and service quality assumes critical significance. Quality is a key determinant of the financial results and the level of competitiveness achieved by SSH. This will always be the case and therefore quality may be viewed as a strategic necessity if SSH is to prosper in the future. Therefore, the statements of the manager of Bonlandia operations are myopic at best and unethical at worst! Businesses use software in a variety of different ways but poor quality software can do serious harm to businesses.

Much will depend on the extent to which a business uses its information for strategic reasons as opposed to meeting operational needs.

The more a business uses its information systems for strategic reasons then the greater the potential damage suffered as a consequence of poor quality software. It is wrong for the manager of Bonlandia operations to knowingly promote the installation of poor quality business software in clients' businesses. The effects can be costly to clients in terms of poor planning, control and decision-making with potential losses of client goodwill and reputation.

(c) The following are important considerations regarding the quality of the business software:

- The software is error-free as this will improve its reliability. Whilst in practice this might not always be achievable the directors of SSH must recognise the dangers involved in supplying bespoke software which may prove damaging to their clients' businesses with the resulting loss of client goodwill.

- The software should meet quality control standards such as those specified by the ISO (International Standards Organisation).

- The software must be delivered on time. Late delivery of business software will prove problematic since clients may rely on updated software to meet new customer needs or to fulfil revised business objectives.

- The software must meet the initial specification of the customer. In meeting the specification SSH will be demonstrating that the software has been produced correctly with an appropriate focus on the requirements of end users.

- The software must be usable i.e. as well as being able to do what it is supposed to do it is important that it is easy to use.
- The software should be capable of being updated in the light of future changes that occur in the clients' requirements.

(d) The following performance measures which could be used to assess the quality of service provided to its clients:

- The reliability of staff in keeping to scheduled appointment times with clients
- The responsiveness of staff to client enquiries or requests for assistance
- The quality of communications between SSH and its clients
- The competence of its staff in providing training to its clients
- The access times to staff upon the request of clients
- The availability of staff to meet emergency needs of clients
- The security of the data of its client base.

Note that only six were required and other measure would be accepted.

Marking scheme		Marks	Marks
(a)	Comments (on merit) and calculations		11
	Items of additional information		3
			14
(b)	Comments (on merit)	4 × 1	4
(c)	Comments (on merit)	4 × 1	4
(d)	Performance measures	6 × ½	3
Total			**25**

Examiner's comments

In general part (a) was well answered, although some candidates showed lack of basic analysis. Many candidates provided either quantitative ratios or comment but not both, and a number of candidates ignored the requirement to 'highlight additional information'. Regrettably, many candidates provided an answer that was so brief that they obviously ignored the fact that was a potential fourteen marks available. In general, answers to part (b) were satisfactory. However, poorer answers were confined to comments concerning the bonus of the operational manger of Bonlandia with little or no regard for the effect of the views of the operational manager on the business of SSH. It was pleasing to observe that part (c) produced some very good answers, especially given the importance of 'quality software' in the modern business environment. In part (d) candidates' answers varied significantly. Better answers suggested performance 'measures' (as required), whereas poorer answers referred to performance 'criteria' such as 'cleanliness', 'appearance' and 'responsiveness'. The worst answers, (as always in this type of question requirement), simply provided a bullet note list of criteria extracted from the 'balanced scorecard', 'performance pyramid', or the work of Fitzgerald and Moon. That said, the poorer answers were also presented in the form of one word 'bullet points'

ANSWERS TO PRACTICE QUESTIONS – SECTION B : SECTION 4

PERFORMANCE EVALUATION AND CORPORATE FAILURE

62 ROYAL BOTANICAL GARDENS

> **Key answer tips**
>
> This question tests your knowledge of the balance scorecard, how to apply the model and the process employed to develop the scorecard for the botanical gardens.
>
> The scenario has a lot of very important information which can be applied to your answer. Ensure you go through each perspective and relate them to the botanical gardens.

(a) **Board briefing**

The concept of the Balanced Scorecard was introduced by Kaplan & Norton in the early Nineties to recognise what they considered to be two primary deficiencies in the implementation phase of many corporate plans.

First, they recognised that, although many organisations measure performance ratios these are primarily focused on historical figures and may have little to do with future success. Although such ratios are important they do not address important aspects of future strategy, particularly those concerned with the satisfaction of customers and their loyalty, organisational learning and the commitment of employees.

Additionally, they believed that, although strategic initiatives were formulated, these often had little impact on organisational behaviour or performance since they were not translated into measures which management and staff could understand and use.

Moving away from purely financial measures they claimed that what really mattered was the strategy implementation process and described **three processes**:

1   Management – how the leader runs the organisation, how decisions are made and implemented

2   Business – how products are designed, orders fulfilled, customer satisfaction achieved, for example

3   Work – how work is operationalised, purchased, stored, and manufactured.

The Balanced Scorecard was developed to address any deficiencies in these areas and encompasses **four key principles**:

1   Translating the vision through clarifying and gaining consensus

2   Communicating and linking by setting goals and establishing rewards for success

3   Business planning to align objectives, allocate resources and establish milestones

4   Feedback and learning to review the subsequent performance against the plan.

They recognised that there should be, on every scorecard, **four perspectives**:

1. Financial perspective – 'To succeed financially, how should we appear to our shareholders?'

2. Customer perspective – 'To achieve our vision, how should we appear to our customers?'

3. Internal perspective – 'To satisfy our shareholders and customers, what business processes must we excel at?'

4. Future – the innovation and learning perspective. 'To achieve our vision, how will we sustain our ability to change and improve?'

For each perspective, a number of objectives, appropriate measures and target levels of performance together with initiatives for their achievement, would be defined. Thus the measures chosen under each perspective would reflect the strategic imperatives under which the organisation operates at the time.

Although the Balanced Scorecard was originally developed for commercial organisations, over the last few years it has found increasing use in the not-for-profit sector, where the same perspectives are equally important, but measured in a different way.

The Royal Botanical Gardens would benefit from the introduction of a Balanced Scorecard by:

- Placing the whole organisation in a learning process, aligning everyone to strategy in a single framework. The Balanced Scorecard has potential to improve itself over time by testing cause – effect hypotheses, refinement of the metrics selected, the measurement processes employed, resource allocation and identification of suitable initiatives.

- Encouraging more rational budgeting in a world of rapid change where resource allocations are based on performance and systematic, fact-based management replaces intuition.

- Encouraging and facilitating the anticipation of future outcomes and their impact on the organisation.

- Raising the visibility of what is happening, prioritising what most needs to be changed and helping to identify best practices.

In addition to the internal, managerial, benefits that the balanced scorecard can bring to the organisation it has the potential to demonstrate to external stakeholders that their mandates and objectives are being met. In this particular case, where the Government will need to be convinced to maintain, or even increase, the grant in aid, the measures incorporated can demonstrate that objectives over and above value for money are being achieved. It would make it easier for the Garden's negotiators to demonstrate the achievements in terms of assistance to education, industry, tourism and national prestige.

However, it must be recognised that it requires sustained effort to implement fully and requires a high level of organisational commitment. Its introduction may create fear and uncertainty since it raises both visibility and accountability. As with all other performance measurement techniques it will not solve problems – only strategy and initiatives and their successful implementation can do that.

(b) It is important that the Balanced Scorecard is developed by a team of individuals and the commitment of the senior management is obtained. The team should be cross organisational and contain representatives of all functional groups within the Gardens.

The main tasks of the teams are as follows:

- Identify strategic themes
- Define perspectives and desired outcomes
- Create a strategy map
- Define performance measures and targets
- Develop strategic initiatives to achieve targets.

Once the team has been established the mission statement should be analysed to identify the strategic themes that are encompassed by the statement. This will provide a more specific focus for planning.

For instance the following themes, among others, might be distilled from the mission statement:

- Knowledge and understanding through research
- Knowledge and understanding through display
- Conservation by living and preserved collections
- Belonging to the Nation.

The next task will be to define the perspectives – the diverse ways of looking at the organisation from the perspective of different stakeholders. Also to define the meaning of mission success for each perspective and strategic theme.

The different stakeholders for The Royal Botanical Gardens are many and would include, for example:

1. Financial perspective – government and research foundations that fund some of the work

2. Customer perspective – universities who use the facilities

3. Internal perspective – botanists using the facilities for research

4. Future – the innovation and learning perspective – educationalists attached to the Gardens.

Within the strategic theme of knowledge and understanding through research, these perspectives might lead to the following desired outcomes:

1. Financial perspective – government funders would look for value for money in the collection of novel plants and materials and the production of research papers.

2. Customer perspective – universities who deal with the Gardens would look for seamless access to any plants and materials they required in a cost-effective way.

3. Internal perspective – the botanists who work within the Gardens would look for support in their research so that they can work productively and advance the boundaries of science.

4. Future – the innovation and learning perspective – the educationalists might wish to raise the profile of the facilities and attract people to this area of study and would look to find innovative ways to bring people in.

For each strategic theme, the team would need to develop a chain of causes and effects that would be expected to lead to the desired outcomes. Each of these chains would be mapped onto a strategy map. Systems dynamics techniques would help in this area.

For instance considering the provision of samples to Universities from a future perspective would mean enhancing information management, improving the employee climate and changing the skills gap. The botanists who work in the Gardens might see themselves in competition with the Universities. A co-operative approach would improve relationships, while seeking citation or acknowledgement in any research published. From the internal perspective looking for process efficiencies in picking and despatch would lead to more cost effective operations satisfying the financial perspective, while the enhanced service levels would, from the customer perspective, make them more likely to acknowledge assistance in research publications.

The definition of performance measures and targets would be achieved by answering the question 'how will we know if this theme/desired outcome is being achieved?' and deciding how each goal should be measured for example surveys or other means of data collection. If available, baseline data should be examined to set schedules and targets for improvement.

For instance, measures for the theme/outcome of provision of samples to Universities might include:

- Financial – cost per sample provided, revenue generated from advice and consultancy
- Customer – satisfaction surveys, amount of repeat business
- Internal – citations in published research, published research
- Future – new universities seeking samples; reduction in number of unsatisfied requests.

63 SPECIALIST CLOTHING COMPANY (JUN 06)

Key answer tips

This is a business strategy question that invites candidates to demonstrate an appreciation of the Boston Consulting Group matrix. Specifically, the question requires an explanation of the BCG model and its relevance to the determination of strategies for a manufacturing business on the basis of past and forecast financial data.

(a) The management of The Specialist Clothing Company Ltd (SCC) could use the Boston Consulting growth share matrix in order to classify its subsidiary companies in terms of their rate of market growth and relative market share. The model is based on the premise that an analysis of the market of a strategic business unit (SBU) i.e. division, can be assessed by reference to its growth rate and that its relative market share best indicates the strength of an organisation. The model uses four categories, these are:

Stars

A star product has a relatively high market share in a high growth market. The fashion division is experiencing strong growth in a rapidly growing market. It is forecast to have a market share of 10% by the end of 2007 and therefore it seems reasonable to categorise the Fashion division as a star.

Problem children (sometimes called question marks)

The distinguishing feature of a problem child is that they have a relatively low market share in a high-growth market. The Children's division would appear to fall into this category. The market leader enjoys 35% of the market whilst SCC Ltd appears to be struggling to achieve any growth in turnover and hence profits and therefore cash flow remain relatively static. Similarly, the Industrial division would appear to be a problem child since it operates in a relatively high-growth market but appears unable to achieve a reasonable market share. It would appear that the introduction of sales of industrial clothing via mail-order has not been successful.

Cash cow

A cash cow is characterised by a relatively high market share in a low growth market and should generate significant cash flows.

The Leisure division appears to be a cash cow since it has a very high market share (70%) in what can be regarded as a low-growth market.

Dog

A dog is characterised by a relatively low market share in a low growth market and might well be loss making and therefore have negative cash flow. The Footwear division would appear to fall into this category since its market share is relatively low and forecast to fall during each of the next two years in what is a low-growth market.

The forecast situation of SCC Ltd is far from ideal. It has a dog (the Footwear division) and two problem children (Industrial and Children's divisions) that require the immediate attention of management. The dog classification of the Footwear division is precarious to say the least. Competitors within low growth markets will invariably offer high levels of resistance to any attempts to reduce their share of a low-growth or declining market. As far as the problem children are concerned, management need to devise appropriate strategies to convert them into stars since at the present time they appear to be in high growth markets but are unable to capture a reasonable market share. The cash generated by the Leisure division should be applied to ensure the continued upward trend of the only current star (the Fashion division) and then applied to assist in the development of the problem children.

(b) The four quadrants of the Boston-growth share matrix summarise expected profits and resultant cash flows and recommends an outline strategy to follow which rather simplistically may be summarised as invest in stars, scrutinise the problem children, milk the cows and divest the dogs.

Value Chain Analysis

It is vital that the management of SCC Ltd undertake a value chain analysis of each of its divisions in order to identify and eliminate all non-value added activities, thereby improving profitability and cash flow without necessarily increasing turnover or market share.

Divestment of the Footwear division

Serious consideration should be given to the divestment of Footwear division. This will enable resources to be redirected to divisions categorised as problem children i.e. the Industrial and Children's divisions.

Support the Stars

As far as the Fashion division is concerned, it is obviously in a growth market and currently performing well. It is vital, given the forecast performance of the other subsidiaries that the management of SCC Ltd do not concentrate on the poor performers to the detriment of its only star.

(c) There are numerous criticisms that have been made regarding the BCG growth share matrix. Two such criticisms are as follows:

- It is a model and the weakness of any model is inherent in its assumptions. For example many strategists are of the opinion that the axes of the model are much too simplistic. The model implies that competitive strength is indicated by relative market share. However other factors such as strength of brands, perceived product/service quality and costs structures also contribute to competitive strength.

- Likewise the model implies that the attractiveness of the marketplace is indicated by the growth rate of the market. This is not necessarily the case as organisations that lack the necessary capital resources may find low-growth markets an attractive proposition especially as they tend to have a lower risk profile than hi-growth markets.

- There are problems with defining the market. The model requires management to define the marketplace within which a business is trading in order that its rate of growth and relative market share can be calculated. This can prove problematic in comparing competitors since if they supply different products and services then the absence of a consistent basis for comparison impairs the usefulness of the model.

Tutorial note

Other valid criticisms include the following:

The application of the BCG matrix may prove costly and time-consuming since it necessitates the collection of a large amount of data.

The use of the model may also lead to unfortunate consequences, such as:

- *Moving into areas where there is little experience.*
- *Over-milking of cash cows.*
- *Abandonment of potentially healthy businesses labelled as problem children.*
- *Neglect of interrelationships among businesses, and*
- *Too many problem children within the business portfolio largely as a consequence of incorrect focus of management attention.*

64 BPC (DEC 07)

> **Key answer tips**
>
> Part (a) requires candidates to not only describe Porter's five forces model but more importantly apply it to the scenario contained within the question. Part (b) the requirement is to discuss performance indicators which might indicate that JOL Co might fail as a corporate entity, not the use of performance indicators in a more general sense.

(a) In order to assess the attractiveness of the option to enter the market for spirally-wound paper tubes, the directors of BPC could make use of Michael Porter's 'five forces model'.

In applying this model to the given scenario one might conclude that the relatively low cost of the machine together with the fact that an unskilled person would only require one day's training in order to be able to operate a machine, constitute relatively low costs of entry to the market. Therefore one might reasonably conclude that the threat of new entrants might be high. This is especially the case where the market is highly fragmented.

The fact that products are usually purchased in very large quantities by customers together with the fact that there is little real difference between the products of alternative suppliers suggests that customer (buyer) power might well be very high. The fact that the paper tubes on average only comprise between 1% and 2% of the total cost of the purchaser's finished product also suggests that buyer power may well be very high.

The threat from suppliers could be high due to the fact that the specially formulated paper from which the tubes are made is sometimes in short supply. Hence suppliers might increase their prices with consequential diminution in gross margin of the firms in the marketplace.

The threat from competitive rivals will be strong as the four major players in the market are of similar size and that the market is a slow growing market. The market leader currently has 26% of the market and the three nearest competitors hold approximately 18% of the market.

The fact that Plastic Tubes Co (PTC) produces a narrow range of plastic tubes constitutes a threat from a substitute product. This threat will increase if the product range of PTC is extended and the price of plastic tubes is reduced.

The fact that a foreign-based multinational company is considering entering this market represents a significant threat from a potential new entrant as it would appear that the multinational company might well be able to derive economies of scale from large scale automated machinery and has manufacturing flexibility.

Low capital barriers to entry might appeal to BPC but they would also appeal to other potential entrants. The low growth market, the ease of entry, the existence of established competitors, a credible threat of backward vertical integration by suppliers, the imminent entry by a multi-national, a struggling established competitor and the difficulty of differentiating an industrial commodity should call into question the potential of BPC to achieve any sort of competitive advantage. If BPC can achieve the position of lowest cost producer within the industry then entry into the market might be a good move. In order to assess whether this is possible BPC must consider any potential synergies that would exist between its cardboard business and that of the tubes operation.

From the information available, the option to enter the market for cardboard tubes appears to be unattractive. The directors of BPC should seek alternative performance improvement strategies.

(b) It would appear that JOL's market share has declined from 30% to (80 – 26)/3 = 18% during the last three years. A 12% fall in market share is probably very significant with a knock-on effect on profits and resultant cash flows. Obviously such a declining trend needs to be arrested immediately and this will require a detailed investigation to be undertaken by the directors of JOL. Consequently loss of market share can be seen to be an indicator of potential corporate failure. Other indicators of corporate failure are as follows:

Six performance indicators that an organisation might fail are as follows:

Poor cash flow

Poor cash flow might render an organisation unable to pay its debts as and when they fall due for payment. This might mean, for example, that providers of finance might be able to invoke the terms of a loan covenant and commence legal action against an organisation which might eventually lead to its winding-up.

Lack of new production/service introduction

Innovation can often be seen to be the difference between 'life and death' as new products and services provide continuity of income streams in an ever-changing business environment. A lack of new product/service introduction may arise from a shortage of funds available for re-investment. This can lead to organisations attempting to compete with their competitors with an out of date range of products and services, the consequences of which will invariably turn out to be disastrous.

General economic conditions

Falling demand and increasing interest rates can precipitate the demise of organisations. Highly geared organisations will suffer as demand falls and the weight of the interest burden increases. Organisations can find themselves in a vicious circle as increasing amounts of interest payable are paid from diminishing gross margins leading to falling profits/increasing losses and negative cash flows. This leads to the need for further loan finance and even higher interest burden, further diminution in margins and so on.

Lack of financial controls

The absence of sound financial controls has proven costly to many organisations. In extreme circumstances it can lead to outright fraud (e.g. Enron and WorldCom).

Internal rivalry

The extent of internal rivalry that exists within an organisation can prove to be of critical significance to an organisation as managerial effort is effectively channelled into increasing the amount of internal conflict that exists to the detriment of the organisation as a whole. Unfortunately the adverse consequences of internal rivalry remain latent until it is too late to redress them.

Loss of key personnel

In certain types of organisation the loss of key personnel can 'spell the beginning of the end' for an organisation. This is particularly the case when individuals possess knowledge which can be exploited by direct competitors, e.g. sales contacts, product specifications, product recipes, etc.

Marking scheme		
		Marks
(a)	Comments (on merit):	
	Each of the five forces 5 × 2	10
	Conclusion	1
		——
		10
(b)	Comments (on merit)	
	Fall in market share significant	1
	(with percentage 18%)	1
	Indicators 6 × 1.5	9
		——
		10
Total		20

Examiner's comments

Part (a) was generally well answered with a significant number of candidates achieving maximum marks. However, many candidates who could describe Porter's five forces model were unable to apply it to the scenario contained within the question. Answers to part (b) were generally not as good as those to part(a).

A significant number of candidates did not observe the requirement to discuss performance indicators which might indicate that JOL Co might fail as a corporate entity, but discussed the use of performance indicators in a more general sense.

65 DENTAL HEALTH (JUN 05)

Key answer tips

The question turns around performance evaluation in the context of a service operation. The theoretical part of the question (requirements (b) and (c)) draws on the recent writings of Fitzgerald and her collaborators. In the UK performance measurement in healthcare has been the subject of recent high profile discussion in regard to NHS hospital and primary care trusts. It may be appropriate to refer to the Peters principle – what gets measured gets done. An insensitive use of performance measures can induce unintended results.

(a) **Dental Health Partnership**

Summary Profit and Loss Account for the year ended 31 May 20X5

	$	
Fees received	1,226,880	(Note 1)
Other Operating Income	20,800	
Total Income	1,247,680	
Material and consumables	446,400	
Less: fixed costs		
Salaries	538,880	
Establishment costs	85,000	
Other operating costs	75,775	
Total costs	1,146,055	
Net profit for the period	101,625	

Calculation of % of total capacity required to break-even during the year ended 31 May 20X5.

	$
Fees received	1,226,880
Less: variable costs	446,400
Contribution	780,480

Total number of consultations	28,800
Weighted average contribution per patient visit	= $780,480/28,800
	= $27.10
Total fixed costs:	
Salaries	538,880
Establishment costs	85,000
Other operating costs	75,775
	699,655
Less: fixed income	20,800
Total fixed costs less fixed income	678,855

Divide by weighted average contribution per patient visit: $678,855/$27.10 = 25,050 consultations.

Total capacity for patient visits = 28,800/0.8333 = 34,560 per annum

Therefore percentage of maximum capacity required in order to break-even is 25.050/34,560 = 72.5%

Note 1: *Fees received:*

Adult fees = Payment plus Government refund Children/Senior Citizens = Government refund

Adjusted patient mix is as follows:

Adults	50% × 2 =	100%
Children		40%
Senior Citizens		10%
Total		150%

The weighted average fee per patient is as follows:

Type of patient treatment:		$
None	0.70 × $12 =	8.40
Minor	0.20 × $50 =	10.00
Major	0.10 × $100 =	10.00
Total		28.40

Therefore fees received during the year ended 31 May 20X5 = 28,800 × 1.5 × $28.40 = $1,226,880.

Note 2: *Capacity:*

Each dentist had a maximum of 24 patients per day but on average treated 20 patients per day which equates to 83.333% of maximum capacity.

(b) The major characteristics of services which distinguish services from manufacturing are as follows:

Intangibility

When a dentist provides a service to a client there are many intangible factors involved such as for example the appearance of the surgery, the personality of the dentist, the manner and efficiency of the dental assistant. The output of the service is 'performance' by the dentist as opposed to tangible goods.

Simultaneity

The service provided by the dentist to the patient is created by the dentist at the same time as the patient consumed it thus preventing any advance verification of quality.

Heterogeneity

Many service organisations face the problem of achieving consistency in the quality of its output. Whilst each of the dentists within the Dental Health Partnership will have similar professional qualifications there will be differences in the manner they provide services to clients.

Perishability

Many services are perishable. The services of a dentist are purchased only for the duration of an appointment.

(c) In order to assess the quality of patient care provided by the Dental Health Partnership the following performance measures might be used:

- The percentage of 'on time' treatment of those patients who arrived prior to their appointment time would provide an indication regarding the effectiveness of the scheduling of appointments by the Dental Health Partnership.

- The percentage of patient appointments which were re-arranged at the request of the Dental Health Partnership. Rearranged appointments represent the provision of a lower level of service provision to clients who may, as a result, switch to an alternative dental practice.

- The percentage of patients who return for treatment after their first appointment would provide an indication that they were satisfied with the service they received.

- The percentage of patients who were able to gain an appointment at their preferred date and time is an indication of the availability of the service to clients.

66 BLA LTD (DEC 03)

Key answer tips

Part (a) requires to comment on the performance of BLA using the information supplied and five indicators from Fitzgerald & Moon.

Part (b) asks for three factors in determining standards e.g. participation and commitment to achievement.

(a) The Fitzgerald et al framework proposes six dimensions of performance which are controlled by service industries. Their propositions include that two of these, namely financial performance and competitiveness are the 'results' of actions previously taken and reflect the success of the chosen strategy.

The remaining four dimensions of quality, flexibility, resource utilisation and innovation are factors that determine competitive success now and in the future. The performance of BLA Ltd can now be analysed under this framework.

(i) **Financial performance**

Summary Income statement for the year ended 31 October 20X3

	Budget	Actual
	$000	$000
Fee income (W1)	6,075	6,300
Costs:		
Consultants' salaries (W2)	2,025	2,025
Bonus (W3)		90
		2,115
Other operating costs	2,550	2,805

	Budget $000	Actual $000
Subcontract payments (W4)	0	18
	4,575	4,938
Net profit	1,500	1,362

(W1) Fee income

    Budget   40,500 chargeable consultations × $150

    Actual   42,000 chargeable consultations × $150

(W2) Consultants' salaries

    45 consultants × $45,000

(W3) Bonus

    40% of $(6,300,000 – 6,075,000)

(W4) Subcontract payments

    120 consultations × $150

It is clear that BLA has not performed as well as expected during the year to 31 October 20X3. Whilst client income is above budget, other operating expenses reached a level which is more than 10% higher than the budget for the year, and thus it would be extremely useful to have a more detailed breakdown of other operating expenses for the year. Consultants have earned an aggregate bonus of $90,000 (42,000 – 40,500) × $150 × 40% in respect of activity above budgeted levels. Payments to subcontractors amounted to $18,000. Actual profit amounts to $1,362,000 against a budget of $1,500,000. It would be extremely useful to see the results of the previous two years in order to assess whether there are any discernible trends in revenues and costs. The budget for the following year should be reviewed in the light of the actual performance of this year with particular reference to checking the footing of the assumptions upon which it has been prepared.

(ii) **Competitiveness**

Competitiveness may be measured in terms of market share or sales growth and the relative success in obtaining business from enquiries made by customers. The turnover of BLA Ltd for the year to 31 October 20X3 is above budget. Again it is desirable to see the results of recent years since it might well be the case that BLA Ltd has achieved steady growth which is indicative of a high level of competitiveness in future years.

BLA provided 1,200 consultations on a no-fee basis with a view to gaining new business. Also, during the year BLA consultants provided 405 non-chargeable 'remedial' consultations. Both of these non-chargeable activities might be viewed as initiatives to increase future levels of competitiveness.

It is useful to look at the extent to which BLA Ltd were successful in converting the enquiries received from both existing and new client enquiries into new business.

The percentages are as follows:

		Budget		Actual
Conversion rate from enquiries				
New clients	(24,300/67,500)	36.0%	(22,400/84,000)	26.7%
Repeat clients	(16,200/32,400)	50.0%	(19,600/28,000)	70.0%

70% of enquiries from the existing client base resulted in additional consultancy work for BLA Ltd. This is indicative of strong customer loyalty, suggesting that existing clients are satisfied with the service provided. However, the company was unable to reform as well with regard to enquiries from potential 'first time' customers, only achieving a conversion ratio of 26.7%, which is approximately 74% of the intended number of 'first time' clients that were budgeted for. This indicates that there is probably room for improvement in the ways in which BLA Ltd deals with enquiries from prospective clients. The company should review its marketing strategies with a view to improving its conversion ratio.

In absolute terms new business was approximately 7.8% below budget whereas repeat business was 21.0% above budget.

As regards the nature of the chargeable activities undertaken by the consultants, it can be seen that Exterior Design is 14.6% below budget, whereas Interior Design and Garden Design are 6.4% and 35.1% above budget.

(iii) **Service quality**

Quality of service is the totality of features and characteristics of the service package that bear upon its ability to satisfy client needs. Flexibility and innovation in service provision may be key determinants of service quality. To some extent the increase in the number of complaints and non-chargeable consultations associated with the remedying of those complaints is indicative of a quality problem that must be addressed. This problem needs to be investigated. BLA Ltd only provides advice to clients and only recommends contractors when asked to do so by clients. It would be interesting to see how many of the complaints related to recommendations made by BLA Ltd. Assuming consultants could have otherwise undertaken chargeable work, the revenue forgone as a consequence of the remedial consultations was $60,750. Client complaints received during the year were nearly double the budgeted level. Also the number of remedial consultations was 405 against a budgeted level of only 45, which is exactly nine times higher than budget!

Perhaps BLA Ltd should review and, if necessary, limit the amount of remedial consultancy provided to any one particular client. The business development consultations can be viewed as an innovative measure with a view to gaining additional business.

(iv) **Flexibility**

Flexibility may relate to the company being able to cope with flexibility of volume, delivery speed or job specification.

Hence, flexibility might be substantiated by looking at the mix of work undertaken by the consultants during the year. The following table gives a comparison of actual and budgeted consultations by category of consultant.

ANSWERS TO PRACTICE QUESTIONS – SECTION B : SECTION 4

Consultations by category of consultancy service

	Budget %	Actual %	Increase/(decrease)
Exterior Design	40.0	32.9%	(7.1%)
Interior Design	40.0	41.0%	1.0%
Garden Design	40.0	26.1%	6.1%

It is a deliberate policy of BLA Ltd to retain 45 consultants thereby maintaining flexibility to meet increasing demand. The delivery speed will be increased as a consequence of the retention of consultants. It would appear that a change has occurred in the mix of consultants which may well be a response to changing market requirements. Again, it would be useful to see recent years statistics in order to consider trends but notably garden design looks to be a growth area hence the three new consultants recruited during the year. The mix of consultants should be such that BLA Ltd can cope with a range of job specifications. The fact that links have been retained with retired consultants will give an added dimension of flexibility in times of very heavy demand upon its consultants.

(v) **Resource utilisation**

Resource utilisation measures the ratio of output achieved from those resources input. In this scenario the mean number of consultations per consultant may be used as a guide.

Average consultations per consultant

	Budget	Actual	Increase/(decrease)
Exterior Design	900	922	2.4%
Interior Design	900	957	6.3%
Garden Design	900	912	1.3%

It is interesting to note that all categories of consultant are being utilised above budgeted levels. Consequently an aggregate bonus amounting to $90,000 was paid in respect of the year ended 31 October 20X3. There are potential problems if the quality of the service provision is falling. In this regard it would be useful to have more detailed analysis of the client complaints in order to ascertain whether a large proportion relate to any one category of consultancy and/or contractor. BLA Ltd has adopted an innovative approach that requires consultants to undertake non-chargeable business development consultations which have at their heart the intention of generating new business. Hence in the immediate sense there is a trade-off between resource utilisation and innovation.

(vi) **Innovation**

Innovation should be viewed in terms of its impact on financial performance, competitiveness, service-quality, flexibility and resource utilisation in the short, medium and long term. Certainly the non-chargeable activity in terms of 'business development' is an innovative feature within the business of BLA Ltd, as is the non-chargeable remedial consultancy provided to clients who experience problems at the commencement of building works. The acquisition of 'state of the art' business software is by its very nature innovative.

The result of its use is reflected in the significant increase of 35.1% above budget achieved in garden design consultations. This has probably enabled BLA Ltd to differentiate its services from those of its competitors and enhance its reputation. Certainly the management of BLA Ltd will be hoping for a similar increase in business as a consequence of the use of the software by its external and interior design consultants. The management should ensure the introduction of the software has not caused the increase in the number of complaints received.

(b) **Participation:** In establishing targets, the importance of individuals taking ownership of the standards has long been established: this is often facilitated by the adoption of a budgetary system based on employee participation. This is also considered to be beneficial to the organisation since it alleviates, or at the very least reduces, many of the dysfunctional consequences associated with particular control models. In particular, managers who participate in the standard-setting process are more likely to accept the standards set, feel less job-related tension and have better relationships with their superiors and colleagues. Participation does, however, provide opportunities for the introduction of budgetary slack in order that any subsequent monitoring of activities presents a favourable outcome.

Realistic standards: Budgets need to be realistic enough to encourage employees to perform, but not set at levels so high that they are demotivated. The challenge to management lies in finding the balance between what the company views as achievable and what the employee views as achievable as this often proves to be a source of organisational conflict.

Equity: It is important that the standards of performance measurement chosen by management facilitate a fair comparison across all similar business units and that equity is seen to prevail in measuring the performance of those units. There may be circumstances where some business units have an inherent advantage unconnected with their own deliberate initiatives. For example, some business units will be subject to higher levels of environmental uncertainty than others. In situations where higher levels of uncertainty exist, there will be a need for greater reliance to be placed on subjective judgement in appraising performance, with consequently less reliance being placed on objective, financial data. It would be inappropriate and inequitable to measure the performance of two completely different business contexts in an identical manner.

67 PERFORMANCE PYRAMID (JUN 06 – AMENDED)

> **Key answer tips**
>
> The question draws on a variety of topics relating to concepts of performance management in a service environment. The key point to appreciate is the distinction between effectiveness (the achievement of required outcomes at minimum cost) and efficiency (achieving maximum output from given inputs). A good answer to this question demonstrates an appreciation of the range of financial and non-financial performance metrics that can be used to measure both efficiency and effectiveness, and the need to take account of qualitative issues as well.

ANSWERS TO PRACTICE QUESTIONS – SECTION B : **SECTION 4**

(a) (i) **EAJ**

Financial performance and Competitiveness

Summary Income Statement for the year ended 31 May 20X6

	Budget $000s	Actual $000s
Fee income:		
New	2,940	3,150
Existing	6,930	8,085
	9,870	11,235
Costs:		
Consultants salaries	5,000	5,000
Bonus		294
Other operating costs	3,600	4,500
Total costs	8,600	9,794
Net profit	1,270	1,441

It is clear that EAJ performed well during the year ended 31 May 20X6. Fee income was 13.8% above budget, in spite of the fact that other operating costs were 25% higher than budget. The management of EAJ should investigate what caused this significant overspend and therefore it would be extremely useful to have a more detailed breakdown of other operating costs.

Consultants earned an aggregate bonus of (($11,235,000 – $9,870,000) – (450 × 2 × $700)) × 40% = $294,000 in respect of activity above budgeted levels. Actual net profit was $1,441,000 against a budgeted net profit of $1,270,000. In spite of the overspend on other operating costs, EAJ is achieving rapid growth in levels of net profit. In 20X5 (its second year of trading) net profit was 50% higher than in its first year. In 20X6 net profit has increased by 60.1% over 20X5 net profit.

EAJ could measure its competitiveness in terms of sales growth and the relative success in obtaining business from enquiries made by customers.

In assessing sales growth it needs to be borne in mind that this is the 'start-up' phase of EAJ. However, EAJ increased sales revenue from $4,000,000 in its first year to $11,235,000 in its third year of operation, which is very impressive. EAJ's success in obtaining business from enquiries made by customers for the year ended 31 May 20X6 is shown in the following table.

Conversion rate from enquiries:	Budget	Actual
New clients	35.0%	30.0%
Repeat clients	50.0%	60.0%

KAPLAN PUBLISHING

60% of enquiries from existing clients resulted in additional chargeable consultancy days for EAJ. This may well indicate that EAJ is starting to build customer loyalty despite the fact that the organisation has only been in existence for three years. With regard to enquiries from potential 'first time' clients, EAJ achieved a conversion ratio of 30.0%, against a budgeted conversion ratio of 35% that was budgeted. However, in absolute terms new business was approximately 7.1% above budget whilst existing business was 16.7% business above budget.

As regards the nature of the chargeable activities undertaken by the consultants it can be seen that Distribution software implementation was 20.6% below budget, whereas Accounting and Manufacturing implementations were 26.2% and 33.3% respectively above budget.

EAJ provided 300 consultations on a no-fee basis with a view to gaining new business. Also, during the year EAJ consultants provided non-chargeable 'remedial' consultations. Both of these non-chargeable activities might be viewed as initiatives aimed at increasing future levels of competitiveness. However, each remedial consultation could be viewed as inefficiency.

(ii) **External effectiveness**

In order to achieve 'external effectiveness' EAJ has to satisfy its customers. Customer satisfaction may be defined as meeting customer expectations. The quality of service provision and delivery are operational criteria that can be used to monitor levels of customer satisfaction. To some extent, the increase in the number of complaints and non-chargeable consultations associated with the remedying of those complaints is indicative of a quality problem that must be investigated and addressed. In particular the number of chargeable days for implementation of distribution applications is significantly below budget and it might well be the case that poor service 'delivery' is giving rise to the need for remedial consultations.

Assuming consultants could otherwise have undertaken chargeable work at a rate of $700, revenue amounting to $630,000 was lost as a consequence of having to undertake remedial consultations. It would appear that EAJ does not budget for complaints.

A summary of client complaints received by EAJ is shown in the following table:

Year ended 31 May	20X4	20X5	20X6
Number of complaints	160	225	280
Number of clients	320	500	700
Complaint: client ratio (%)	50%	45%	40%

Whilst it can be seen that the complaint: client ratio is improving, it should be recognised that this may be due to the fact that the size of the client base is increasing very rapidly. Such a trend might be expected during the first few years of operation, especially in a business such as EAJ.

The harsh fact is that the number of complaints is increasing in absolute terms. In order to be able to better assess customer satisfaction, complaints need to be analysed since the nature of complaints may well be of far more relevance than the number of complaints!

The number of customer support desk queries resolved is improving; i.e. 20X4 (85%); 20X5 (95%) and 20X6 (99%). This will further enhance the level of customer satisfaction. The fact that the number of accounts in dispute is falling whilst the number of clients is increasing significantly on a year-on-year basis may also be an indication of improved customer satisfaction. The increase in the number of new customers and the increased revenues generated per customer are probably indicators of increasing levels of customer satisfaction.

(iii) **Internal efficiency**

Internal efficiency may be assessed by reference to flexibility and productivity. Flexibility relates to the business operating system as a whole whilst productivity relates to the management of resources such as, in the case of EAJ, consultants time.

Flexibility might be substantiated by looking at the mix of work undertaken by the consultants during the year. The following table gives a comparison of actual and budgeted consultations by category of consultant.

Consultations by category of consultant:

	Budget %	Actual %	Increase/(decrease)
Accounting	40.0	44.2	4.2%
Distribution	30.0	20.8	(9.2%)
Manufacturing	30.0	35.0	16.7%

It is a deliberate policy of EAJ to retain 100 Consultants thereby maintaining flexibility to meet increasing demand. The delivery speed will be increased as a consequence of the retention of consultants. It would appear that a change has occurred in the mix of consultants which may well be a response to changing market requirements. Again, it would be useful to see recent year's statistics in order to consider trends.

Productivity can be measured by the ratio of output achieved from those resources input. In this scenario the average number of chargeable days per consultant may be used as a guide.

Average number of chargeable days per consultant

	Budget	Actual	Increase/(decrease)
Accounting	168	212	26.2%
Distribution	168	160	(4.8%)
Manufacturing	168	192	14.3%

The implementation of distribution application software was more than 20% below budget. Chargeable distribution consultancy days based on the original budget of 168 days per consultant would produce a total of 4,200 chargeable days which is 200 more than the actual levels. Again this might be indicative of a quality problem.

'Cycle time' would appear to be improving as evidenced by the increasing number of on-time implementations as well as the reduction in the implementation time of each application. In this respect EAJ needs to be certain that the reduction in implementation time has not caused a diminution in the quality of service delivery. Consequently an aggregate bonus amounting to $294,000 was paid in respect of the year ended 31 May 2006. EAJ needs to ensure that the incentive provided by the bonus is not causing a loss of 'internal efficiency'.

With regard to the bonus paid to consultants then it is questionable whether the bonus should be shared equally by consultants since chargeable activity levels clearly vary between categories of consultant.

(b) Particularly at higher levels of management, non-financial information is often not in numerical terms, but qualitative, or soft, rather than quantitative. Qualitative information often represents opinions of individuals and user groups. Decisions often appear to have been made on the basis of quantitative information; however qualitative considerations often influence the final choice, even if this is not explicit. In both decision making and control, managers should be aware that an information system may provide a limited or distorted picture of what is actually happening. In many situations, sensitivity has to be used in interpreting the output of an information system.

Conventional information systems are usually designed to carry quantitative information and are sometimes less able to convey qualitative issues. However the impact of a decreased output requirement on staff morale is something that may be critical but it is not something that an information system would automatically report.

The following difficulties in measurement and interpretation mean that qualitative factors are often ignored:

- Information in the form of opinions is difficult to measure and interpret. It also requires more analysis.
- Qualitative information may be incomplete.
- Qualitative aspects are often interdependent and it can be difficult to separate the impact of different factors.
- Evaluating qualitative information is subjective, as it is not in terms of numbers – there are no objective formulae as there are with financial measures.
- The cost of collecting and improving qualitative information may be very high.

Despite the challenges it presents, there may be ways of improving the use of qualitative information. Where it is important to make use of qualitative information, it is essential to ensure that users are aware of any assumptions made in analysis and of the difficulties involved in measuring and counting it. It is sometimes possible to quantify issues which are initially qualitative, by looking at its impact. For example when looking at service quality it is possible to consider the cost of obtaining the same quality of service elsewhere. Even if it is not possible to quantify issues precisely, attempting to do so is likely to improve decision making as the issues are likely to have been thought through more thoroughly.

68 THE SUCCESS EDUCATION CENTRE (SEC) (PILOT 07)

Key answer tips

This is a fairly straightforward question on performance assessment and one you should be able to score well on, provided you discuss the differences in figures and try to explain why they have happened and possible implications.

For example, costs have not risen as fast as revenue. This could be due to the presence of fixed costs but also to economies of scale.

ANSWERS TO PRACTICE QUESTIONS – SECTION B : SECTION 4

(a)

	2006			2007		
	Homeland	Awayland	Group	Homeland	Awayland	Group
% growth in sales revenue				11.1%	30%	14.5%
Sales margin before interest (%)	20	(17.5)	13.2	24.5	1.2	19.7
Return on capital employed (%)			18.6			26.0
EBITDA ($000)			1,125			1,690
Fixed asset turnover ratio	1.6	4.0	1.8	1.8	2.4	1.9
Debt: Equity ratio			62.5			35.6
Gearing ratio			38.4			26.2

Sales revenue

The turnover in Homeland increased by 11.1% whereas the turnover in Awayland increased by 30% which is excellent bearing in mind that operations only commenced in 2005. The overall growth in turnover achieved during 2007 amounted to a healthy 14.5%.

Profits

The operation in Homeland has achieved an increase of 36% in net profit which is an excellent result given the operation only commenced during 2003. The operation in Awayland made a very small profit of $15,000 in 2007 compared with a loss of $175,000 in 2006. The overall profit of SEC has increased from $575,000 to $1,115,000, an increase of 93.9%. Non-operating costs have increased from $475,000 (2006) to $525,000 (2007), an increase of 10.5%. It is worth noting that interest payable has fallen by $25 million which is a direct result of the repayment of $250,000 of loan stock. The increased amount of marketing expenditure has enabled both operations to achieve substantial growth in turnover. EBITDA rose from $1,125 million to $1,690 million.

Costs

Tuition materials and consumables costs have only increased by 2% and 3.3% respectively in Homeland and Awayland. Bearing in mind that turnover of each operations has increased substantially then it is highly probable that SEC are benefiting from economies of scale that exist with regard to the provision of tuition materials and consumables. Salaries have increased by 5% in both Homeland and Awayland. Other operating expenses have increased by 4% in Homeland and remained static in Awayland which shows excellent cost control.

Non-current (fixed) Asset utilisation

The 2007 utilisation ratios of Homeland and the overall business remain at a similar level to those of 2006 with the exception of that of Awayland which has fallen from 4 times to 2.4 times. However, this is acceptable given that operations in Awayland have only been recently established. It might well be the case that, for example, recently acquired buildings may not yet have been brought fully into use or perhaps were acquired towards the end of 2007. Awayland is clearly in a rapid-growth phase hence the need for such investments in fixed assets.

(b) It would be useful to have data relating to 2005 in order to observe a three year trend for Homeland and the full picture of Awayland. This would enable a much better assessment of current performance and the identification of significant factors that have arisen during the past four years.

It would be extremely useful to have competitor information in order to assess relative market share and establish how they are performing in the Homeland and Awayland markets compared with SEC.

It is clear that long-term borrowing has decreased during 2007 and that SEC has sufficient cash flow to be repaying loan stock. However, it would be useful to have a detailed breakdown of the working capital of each operation in order to confirm this.

It would also be useful to have future market and financial projections in respect of operations in Homeland and Awayland which should reflect the actual results achieved in 2006 and 2007.

(c) The following factors may need to be taken into account in an assessment of the comparative financial performance of the two divisions.

- The size of each market
- The number of competitors in each market
- The different types of service provision e.g. frequency and modes of course delivery, available from competitors
- The strength of the SEC brand
- The availability of resources within each country, in particular, suitably qualified lecturers.

(d) EBITDA

- EBITDA is easy to calculate and understand.
- The use of EBITDA (earnings before interest, taxation, depreciation and amortisation) will focus management attention on cash flow from operations and hence is a measure of underlying performance.
- Whilst taxation and interest payable remain important considerations in essence they represent distributions to the government (taxation) and a charge for financing. Neither taxation nor interest payable is relevant to the underlying success of the business of SEC.
- EBITDA is a useful measure of the managerial performance in situations like that of SEC where managers have no control over acquisition and financing policy since it excludes costs associated with assets (depreciation and goodwill) and debt finance (interest).

69 CUNDY AQUATIC PURSUITS (CAP) (DEC 09)

Key answer tips

This is a fairly straightforward question on performance assessment and one you should be able to score well on.

To do this make sure you "make the numbers talk" and explain any differences / movements by reference to the scenario given.

(a) From the information available it would appear that the business of CAP has been in decline for at least the last three years. Turnover has fallen during each of the last three years and profit levels have also fallen during the same period of time. Relevant performance measures are as follows:

	2006	2007	2008	2009
% growth/(reduction) in Turnover	1.5	(3.0)	(3.8)	(9.1)
Operating costs as a % of Turnover	81.9	82.5	83.1	85.7
Net profit margin (%)	18.2	17.5	16.9	14.3
Turnover per Aqua Park ($m)	5.893	5.517	5.133	4.516
Dividend cover				1.5

It is noticeable that the net profit percentage has fallen from 18.2% in 2006 to 14.3% in 2009 and that turnover per Aqua Park has been reducing on a year by year basis.

Operating costs have also fallen during each of the last three years. The fact that turnover has declined at a faster rate than operating costs may be indicative of the fact that a significant proportion of operating costs are in the nature of fixed costs. A detailed analysis of operating costs would be most valuable given the decline in profitability during recent years.

In addition, dividend cover at 1.5 (21m/14m) is currently very low. If profits continue to fall, then it will not be possible to maintain the current level of dividend. Indeed, the recent trend in profitability raises the question as to how the proposed expansion into Robland is going to be financed.

The liquidity position of CAP is also a cause for concern since there is only a small balance at the bank insufficient to meet the trade and other payables owing by CAP at 30 November 2009.

The relatively low P/E ratio may be attributable to a market perception of low future growth and concerns regarding the company's future well-being due to the $110m ($100m + $10m premium) repayment of redeemable preference shares in 2010.

(b) **Financial considerations:**

Before consideration is given as to how the proposed expansion into Robland would be financed, CAP will have to raise $110m in order to redeem the preference shares currently in issue. The proposed expansion into Robland will require a further $120m (40 × $3m), therefore a total of $230 million of additional finance would be required.

The raising of equity finance does not appear to be a feasible solution because of Jody Cundy's desire to control the business. Jody currently owns 55% of the ordinary share capital. Any significant public issue of shares might dilute his shareholding to below 50%, a situation which would obviously be unacceptable to him as he has stated on many occasions he always wants 'to control this business'.

Furthermore, the very poor dividend cover together with the relatively low price earnings ratio would suggest that it is not a good time for CAP to consider a public flotation.

The raising of debt finance might well prove more attractive. However, this would require the directors of CAP to convince potential lenders that the reduction in profitability during recent years will cease. The gearing level is not too high and there appears to be adequate security (non-current assets $220m, net current assets $30m) that could be offered to potential lenders as security for debt finance.

The potential exit from Robland would be easier if an autonomous operating subsidiary was to be created as this would facilitate the future sale of the business in Robland.

Economic considerations:

The potential demand within Robland will be linked to the local economy. In this regard it is of paramount importance that CAP gives most careful consideration to the reliability of the market research study commissioned by Jody Cundy. The accuracy of information about market size, the extent of competition, likely future trends etc is of crucial importance.

The potential instability of the currency within Robland assumes critical significance because profit repatriation can be difficult in situations where those profits are made in an unstable currency such as the Rob, or one that is likely to depreciate against the home currency, thereby precipitating sizeable losses on exchange. Any currency restrictions in Robland need to be given careful consideration.

The attitude of the government of Robland to incoming organisations must be assessed very carefully and all local legislation should be given careful consideration. It might be the case that legislation in Robland favours comparable local Aqua Parks already in operation.

Social considerations:

CAP operates in the leisure sector and therefore the disposable income of inhabitants of Robland assumes critical significance because people spend their income on 'essentials' as opposed to 'would like to have' goods and/or services.

Correct decisions regarding the location of the aqua-parks in Robland would be vital to the success of the proposed expansion. In making this decision CAP would be aided by the findings of the market research study which should contain information regarding the geographical and age distributions of the population within Robland.

However, there is nothing to suggest that CAP has any expertise in site appraisal and selection. Furthermore, Robland is situated a long way from Lizland and therefore CAP should engage the services of an established consultancy in Robland to provide advice regarding the location and exterior design of each of its aqua-parks.

CAP will need to consider other issues such as the availability of suitably qualified staff and wage rates payable in Robland.

CAP should also consider lifestyles, attitudes and customs within Robland which all influence the design and facilities of the aqua-parks.

	Marking scheme		Marks
(a)	Financial performance:		
	Margin	3.0	
	Dividend cover	1.0	
	Liquidity	1.0	
	Price earnings ratio	1.0	6.0
(b)	Issues:		
	Financial	5.0	
	Economic	5.0	
	Social	5.0	14.0
Total			**20.0**

ANSWERS TO PRACTICE QUESTIONS – SECTION B : **SECTION 4**

Examiner's comments

In general this question was well done with most candidates using the scenario in a satisfactory manner. A large number of candidates achieved maximum marks by providing a very good evaluation of the financial performance of CAP and the vast majority of candidates achieved high marks. However, it was noticeable that a significant number of candidates did not recognise that CAP would need to redeem preference shares in 2010 and would require additional finance of $110 million in order to do so. Poorer answers were simply confined to ratio analysis with very little, if any, evaluation of financial performance. In general, answers to part (b) were of an acceptable quality. This part of the question did reveal a significant number of candidates who assumed that retained earnings were available to finance the redemption of preference shares or the proposed expansion into Robland, which is a major conceptual misunderstanding that is particularly worrying at this stage of the qualification.

---

70 THE SPARE FOR SHIPS COMPANY (SFS) (JUN 10)

Key answer tips

This is a fairly tough question that looks at ABC and ABM. Ensure that you have learnt the key knowledge aspects of both of these.

(a) (i) The differences in the reported cost estimates calculated under each of the two costing systems are significant. This is especially the case with regard to Job order 973. The management accountant's calculations for the cost estimates produce the following increase/(decrease) in reported costs:

	Job order 973	Job order 974
	$	$
Unit cost per job under existing system	1,172.00	620.00
Unit cost per job under activity based costing	1,612.00	588.89
Increase/(decrease) in reported cost	37.54%	(5.02)%

Job order 973 shows an increase in reported cost of 37.54% [(1,612 – 1,172)/1,172] whereas Job order 974 shows a decrease in reported cost of 5.02% [(88.89 – 620)/620].

A common occurrence when activity-based costing is implemented is that low-volume products show an increase in their reported costs while high-volume products show decreases in their reported costs. This is very much the case with regard to the products which are the subjects of Job orders 973 and 974.

The reported costs also differ due to the following:

- Job orders 973 and 974 differ in the way they consume activities in each of the five activity areas within SFS's premises
- The activity areas differ in their indirect cost allocation bases. In particular no activity area uses direct labour hours as the basis of allocating indirect costs.

Two areas where the differences in reported product costs might be important to SFS are as follows:

Product design – since it is more probable that those involved in the design of products will find the results produced by the activity-based approach to be much more credible. This is especially the case in a machine oriented environment where direct labour hours are unlikely to be the major cost-driver. Activity-based costing can be of more assistance to product designers and may signal areas where cost reductions can be achieved, for example using fewer cuts on the lathe and/or reducing the number of machine hours required in the milling area.

Product pricing – The application of activity-based costing shows that the cost of Job order 973 is being understated while the cost of Job order 974 is being overstated. The management of SFS should be aware of the danger of failing to recover the costs incurred on Job order 973. Conversely, they may well be overpricing Job order 974 which might well entail losing business to its competitors.

(ii) Two problems SFS would have had to deal with in the successful implementation of an activity-based costing system are as follows:

(i) initially it would be very time consuming to collect a large amount of data concerning the activities relating to each job undertaken by SFS. Hence the cost of buying, implementing and maintaining a system of activity-based costing is likely to be significant.

(ii) it would be vital to identify the real 'cost-drivers' within the activity-based costing system of SFS otherwise results given by the ABC system would be inaccurate leading to incorrect decisions by management.

Tutorial note

Additional credit was available for staff/culture issues which would be resolved by adequate training and motivation to change.

(b) Operational ABM is about 'doing things right'. Those activities which add value to products can be identified and improved. Activities that do not add value should be reduced in order to cut costs without reducing product value. Where for example a product or service has been estimated to require a longer activity time than other products or services then every effort should be made to find ways of reducing the number of hours required.

Strategic ABM is about 'doing the right things' using the ABC information to decide which products to develop and which activities to use. It can focus on profitability analysis, identifying which products/customers are the most profitable and for which sales volume should be developed.

An activity may have implicit value not necessarily reflected in the financial value added to any service or product. SFS might decide to cut back on the level of expenditure involved in servicing customers. This may lead to a poorer perceived value by customers of the service provided by SFS with a consequent fall in demand.

There are risks attaching to the use of ABM insofar as ABM can give the wrong signals. For example a particularly pleasant work environment can help attract and retain the best staff, but may not be identified as adding value in operational ABM. By the same token, a customer that represents a loss based on committed activities, but that opens up leads in a new market, may be identified as a low value customer by a strategic ABM process.

Tutorial note

Other risks or potential problems were also accepted such as pricing errors arising or the cost/benefit of such an expensive system.

Marking scheme

				Marks
(a)	(i)	Comments (on merit):		
		Cost per unit comparisons		2
		Reasons for differences		2
		Potential consequences	Up to 2 each	4
			Maximum	8
	(ii)	Problems	Up to 2 each	4
(b)		Comments (on merit):		
		Operational ABM		2
		Strategic ABM		2
		The implicit value of an activity		2
		Risks		2
			Maximum	8
Total				20

Examiner's comments

Overall, answers to this question were mixed. The comparison of different methods of costing and performance measurement is a basic element of this paper and surprisingly, many candidates seem unprepared for part (a) (i).

Better answers to this part focussed on how the two methods can produce different answers by comparing their underlying approaches. Again, candidates scored more heavily if their answer used the information in the scenario as illustrative example of the general points made about the different costing methods. Most candidates realised that there were price implications arising from the two costs but few realised the internal process implications for example in designing products.

Requirement (a) (ii) requested two problems associated with implementation of an activity-based costing system using 'state of the art' IT systems. Candidates who focussed on the implementation stage and considered how it might be affected by such an IT system scored well. A few candidates cleverly took two subheadings and then discussed issues within these in order to ensure that they scored the two marks available for each problem.

PAPER P5 : ADVANCED PERFORMANCE MANAGEMENT

> Requirement (b) related the ABC system used earlier in the question to the broader use of activity analysis in management of the company. There were effectively four parts to this question the three topics itemised plus the risks of using ABM. There was a wide spread of marks to this part with a few knowledgeable candidates scoring close to full marks but a number of weaker answers which failed to relate the general definitions of operational and strategic ABM to SFS. Many candidates did not realise that implicit value was the value which does not immediately appear in traditional performance measurement systems but nevertheless, is important in a long-term management of a successful business.

71 LOL CO (DEC 10)

> **Key answer tips**
>
> This was a straightforward question provided you understood the main ideas surrounding VBM and EVA. Unfortunately many students were uncertain on these key concepts.

(a) The value-based approach takes the primary objective of the business to be maximising shareholder wealth and seeks to align performance with this objective. The principle measure used at the strategic level will be economic value added $^{(EVA^{TM})}$. EVA^{TM} is equivalent in the long term to discounted cash flow which is widely used as the valuation method for shares by equity analysts. (Other relevant value measures might be market value added and shareholder value added.)

By using this as the sole measure of performance, management is focused and they will be able to avoid conflicts which occur when there are multiple objectives and measures. The measure can be applied to decisions at all levels within the organisation (strategic, tactical and operational) so that the company is unified in its goal. As only a single measure is used, the variables which drive performance are clear within the calculation of EVA™. These value drivers can be used by managers to achieve their value-based targets which are set from the strategic value-based goal.

(b) The performance of LOL has declined with earnings per share falling by 23% (W2) from last year. Normally, this would imply that the company would be heavily out of favour with investors.

However, the share price seems to have held up with a decline of only 12% compared to a fall in the sector of 26% and the market as a whole of 35% (W3). The sector comparison is more relevant to the performance of LOL's management as the main market index will contain data from manufacturing, financial and other industries. Shareholders will be encouraged by the implication that the market views LOL as one of the better prospects within an outperforming sector.

This view is consistent with the calculated positive EVA^{TM} for 2010 ($22.6m, (W1)) which LOL generated. EVA^{TM} has fallen from 2009 but it has remained positive and so the company continues to create value for its shareholders even in the poor economic environment. It therefore remains a worthwhile investment even in a falling market.

Workings:

(W1)

EVA calculations for the periods given are

	2009 $m	2010 $m
Profit after interest and tax	35.0	26.8
Interest (net of tax at 25%)	3.0	5.9
Net operating profit after tax (NOPAT)	38.0	32.6
Capital employed (at year start)	99.2	104.1

Assumptions:

Economic and accounting depreciation are equivalent.

There are no non-cash expenses to adjust in the profit figure.

There are no operating leases to be capitalised.

There are no additional adjustments to make regarding goodwill.

Cost of Capital

WACC = (%e × Ke) + (%d × Kd)

2009	(50% × 12.7%) + (50% × 4.2%)	=	8.45%
2010	(50% × 15.3%) + (50% × 3.9%)	=	9.60%

EVA = NOPAT − (Capital employed × WACC)

2009	38.0 − (99.2 × 8.45%)	=	29.6
2010	32.6 − (104.1 × 9.6%)	=	22.6

(W2)

	2009	2010	Change
EPS (profit after interest and tax/av no of shares) cents	21.88	16.75	−23.4%

(W3)

Stock market information	2009	2010	Change
Main market index	2,225.4	1,448.9	−34.9%
Retailing sector index	1,225.6	907.1	−26.0%
LOL share price ($'s)	12.2	10.7	−12.3%

(c) VBM provides focus on shareholder wealth but it can be argued that a single profit measure can do the same. Value measures are considered to be superior to profit measures because they take into consideration the capital employed and cost of capital. These variables are less clear in a profit measure. Also, although value measures are calculated from profit figures they are adjusted in order to bring them closer to a cash flow measure of performance which is less affected by the various accounting adjustments such as depreciation. (Here we have assumed in calculating EVA™ that accounting and economic depreciation are the same but with greater information on the company we may be able to make a better estimate to the cash performance of the company.)

A disadvantage of value-based measures like EVA™ compared to profit is the unfamiliarity and complexity of the calculation. The calculation of the cost of capital is encumbered by the assumptions of CAPM and it is based on historic data which may not be repeated in the future (share values are based on expected dividend flows). These difficulties can be overcome by a process of education and training for the staff and shareholders. Additionally, the use of EVA™ as the sole value-measure as suggested by Stern Stewart may be too simple and overlook other value drivers.

As a tool for decision-making, EVA™ can be subject to manipulation by choosing projects with low initial costs to provide a short-term boost to the value measure in the same way as profit measures. It may not address the weaknesses in project appraisal that drive many companies to use net present value, which recognises the increase in shareholder wealth over the life of the whole project in question.

Marking scheme

		Marks
(a)	Up to 2 marks on the explanation of VBM and then up to 2 marks on how it aids focus in the management process Maximum	4
(b)	**Workings:**	
	NOPAT	1
	Capital employed	1
	Cost of capital	1
	EVA™	1
	Assumptions 0.5 each up to a maximum of	1.5
	EPS	1
	Share price 3 × 0.5	
	Comments: 1 mark per reasonable point up to 2 on EPS and share price and 2 on EVATM.	12
(c)	1 mark for each point made up to a maximum of	4
Total		20

Examiner's comments

Requirement (a) requested an explanation of value-based management (VBM) and how it aids management focus. Candidates often scored a pass but not full marks on this part. There were often lengthy and irrelevant discussions about non-financial factors which suggest incomplete knowledge of VBM.

Requirement (b) asked for an evaluation of LOL's performance using EVA, EPS growth and the share price. It was also typically passed but few candidates scored 9 or more out of 12. The assessment of the numerical work was often lacking. Candidates infrequently compared the change in share price of LOL to the market and sector performance – which demonstrated that the company was doing well in a falling market. Some candidates could not perform the EVA computation which was surprising as this is a key performance measure and the scenario offered few of the possible technical adjustments. Having performed the calculation of EVA, a significant minority then failed to note that it was positive choosing to focus on the fact that it had fallen from the previous year. This again showed weak understanding of such a key concept.

Requirement (c) was the most difficult part of the question and was generally poorly done, probably as a result of the failure to explain VBM which was illustrated in part (a).

ANSWERS TO PRACTICE QUESTIONS – SECTION B : SECTION 4

72 RM BATTERIES CO (DEC 10)

> **Key answer tips**
>
> This was a straightforward question on corporate failure provided you answered the question set. Many students failed to add value to their comments in part (b) and often misread or ignored the requirement in parts (c) and (d).

(a) Quantitative models such as the Altman Z-score use publicly available financial information about a firm in order to predict whether it is likely to fail within the two-year period. The method uses a model equation into which the financial data is input and a score obtained. The advantages of such methods are that they are simple to calculate and provide an objective measure of failure. However, they only give guidance below the danger level of 1.8 and there is potential for a large grey area in which no clear prediction can be made. Additionally, the prediction of failure of those companies below 1.8 is only a probabilistic one, not a guarantee. The model is based on a statistical analysis of historic patterns of trading by a group of companies and may not be relevant unless the company under examination falls within the same economic circumstances and industry sector as those used to set the coefficients in the model. These models are open to manipulation through creative accounting which can be a feature of companies in trouble.

Qualitative methods are based on the realisation that financial measures are limited in describing the circumstances of a company. Models such as Argenti's rely on subjective scores to certain questions given by the investigator. A score above a certain level indicates potential disaster. The advantage of the method is the ability to use non-financial as well as financial measures and the judgement of the investigator but this is also a weakness as there is a danger that the investigator will give scores to ensure the conclusion agrees with first impressions.

(b) The Z score of RMB in 2010 is 1.45 which is below the danger level of 1.8 and so indicates that RMB is in danger of becoming insolvent within the next two years. The Z score has been falling for the last two years through the grey area between the safe level of 3 and the danger level of 1.8.

During this period, the variables in the model have been roughly static or have shown significant declines. About half of the decline of the Z-score from 2.7 to 1.4 can be explained by the deterioration of variable x4 which measures the market value of the company's shares to its debt.

Debt has been building due to the investment programme and the share price (and so the market value) has fallen by 14% over the last year. It would be helpful to identify the relative performance of the share price against RMB's competitors to see if this is related to the company's specific problems or is due to general market conditions. The other significant reduction is in variable x3 which shows a failure to derive profit from the assets available. However, this could be a timing effect as the profits from the new product will occur over many subsequent accounting periods but the asset value will increase immediately in line with the investment programme.

(c) The qualitative problems can be broken down according to the Argenti model into three broad areas: defects, mistakes made and symptoms of failure. RMB exhibits the following defects – a domineering CEO, a failure to split CEO/Chairman roles and a passive senior management. These are structural problems within the company that will obstruct any effort to change direction if that direction is leading the company downwards.

It appears that RMB may also be making mistakes (in fact, the company illustrates all three of the classic errors noted by Argenti). It is overtrading as revenue rises and this is mainly funded by debt. As a result, gearing has risen from 107% to 197% and interest cover has fallen from 8.8 to 2.0. Additionally, the future of the company seems to depend on one big project. The higher gearing increases the financial risk that the company will fail to make its loan repayments. The dependence on the single new product demonstrates a lack of diversification which also signals greater risk.

Finally, symptoms of failure are not yet apparent from the information to hand. This may imply that there is still time to correct matters as these are often the final signals of failure e.g. creative accounting being employed to massage the financial statements.

(d) The outlook for RMB appears bleak when only looking for the bad points, however, the company is still making profits ($65m in 2010) and its revenues are growing (by 23% over the last year). This suggests that customers are taking up the new product. It is not surprising that in the early stages of this project that the capital expenditure is high and returns have yet to materialise.

Overall, the company is clearly showing signs of financial strain from the project but more work is required before coming to a final conclusion. Further data required would include a cash flow projection to ensure that as the product matures there will be funds to pay the new borrowings. The decline in operating margin from 21% to 10% requires explanation and action as this indicates problems in control of the business. Detailed cost information would assist in identifying the source of margin problems. The share price movement should be compared to the change in the market as a whole to identify if the fall in price is due to problems unique to RMB or if this is due to general economic conditions.

Marking scheme		
		Marks
(a)	1 mark for each point made. Up to 3 for each type of model. Maximum	6
(b)	1 mark for each point made. Maximum of 5 marks. Maximum	5
(c)	0.5 mark for identifying problem and up to 1 mark for explaining how this relates to corporate failure. Maximum of 5 marks. Maximum	5
(d)	1 mark for each point explained. To score full marks some appreciation of the information not captured by parts (b) and (c) must be demonstrated. Maximum of 4 marks. Maximum	4
Total		**20**

ANSWERS TO PRACTICE QUESTIONS – SECTION B : SECTION 4

> **Examiner's comments**
>
> Part (a) required a general discussion of the strengths and weaknesses of both qualitative and quantitative models. This was generally done well although some candidates tried to structure their answer as the strengths and weaknesses of models in general which would not be a helpful method in real life, where a comparison of the models is likely to be more useful.
>
> Part (b) asked for comments on an analyst's spreadsheet which provided the data and results of a Z-score calculation. Answers to this part were generally good although many candidates restricted their comment on the Z-score to repeating the comment given in the question (RMB is 'at risk of failure within two years') when the data given was requiring a more analytical answer about which factors within the model were driving the score down and so leading to this prediction. A minority of candidates restricted their comments to the company's statements of income and financial position when the question required comment about the spreadsheet data and consequently their answers lacked relevance.
>
> Part (c) asked for the application of qualitative-type models to failure prediction at RMB. This was generally well done with many candidates making good use of the Argenti model and the factors mentioned in the scenario. Unfortunately, some candidates ignored the word 'qualitative' in the requirement and wasted time writing about quantitative factors.
>
> Part (d) was poorly answered with many candidates ignoring the requirement to assess the results of previous answers and only picking up marks for suggesting additional data to gather

CURRENT DEVELOPMENTS AND EMERGING ISSUES IN MANAGEMENT ACCOUNTING AND PERFORMANCE MANAGEMENT

73 TOTAL TIMBER GROUP (TTG)

> **Key answer tips**
>
> Environmental management accounting is a key topic area that you should ensure you know at least the basics of.

The executive board of TTG, by focusing entirely on the sustainability and legality of their timber supplies, are interpreting environmental issues very narrowly.

The purpose of EMA is to widen this focus to take account of the environmental costs associated with all aspects of their products, processes and services. The aim is not to provide an environmental reporting framework but rather to provide financial and non-financial environmental information in such a way the management team can make better decisions about products and projects and so better manage their overall environmental performance.

The first aspect of EMA that would be of value to TTG is in helping them to define environmental costs more broadly. Factors such as toxic waste products in production processes, fuel inefficiency in delivery vehicles and poor energy usage in retail outlets would all be considered environmental costs of TTG's business, but may well not be taken into consideration at present.

EMA breaks down environmental costs into four areas.

- **Conventional costs** such as buying raw materials and labour. TTG will already be recording spending in these areas, but may not be thinking about the environmental impact of inefficiencies in their use.

    For example, even the inks used to print size, grade etc. on the timber may be damaging to the environment, need to be regularly refilled meaning more downtime or need expensive storage because of their volatility.

- **Hidden costs** – these costs will be captured within the management accounts but then tend to become lost in general overheads – this would include items such as energy and water usage and waste disposal all of which have significant environmental impacts.

- **Contingent or future costs** – these may include later management of environmental damage caused by production processes or distribution breakdown.

- **Image and relationship costs** – TTG are clearly aware of the importance to their clients and therefore to their brand of their environmental credentials. Improving the environmental impact of their entire operations will provide them with a valuable marketing tool when attempting to win corporate contracts (where the clients will themselves be under pressure to show a 'green' supply chain) as well as appealing to the individual DIY market.

The next benefit of EMA is in providing accounting techniques which will assist TTG in identifying the actual environmental costs they are incurring. Most conventional accounting systems cannot isolate environmental costs and instead allocate them to general overheads. Management are therefore not aware of their existence so cannot make any move to control or reduce them.

EMA can collect two types of information to inform management decisions; physical data on the use of materials and resources such as water and energy, and monetary information on the financial costs and revenues and potential savings of environmental matters.

Input / output analysis

This can help to identify inefficiencies in conventional costs, and some hidden costs such as energy and water. It records physical flows in and out of the process to identify what happens to the inputs – from product, to recycled waste materials to loss. For example, actual weight of wood into a timber production process would be compared with the joint weights of the final products, the sawdust sold on as a by-product, the waste collected for disposal etc. This would allow TTG to measure how efficiently they were using the wood. Efficient usage in the long run means fewer trees cut down and less environmental impact.

An extension of this technique is known as flow management, which measures the flow of not just physical quantities but also costs and values of materials through all aspects of the business, from those used in production to those used in running the business as a whole and those needed for delivery and disposal.

Activity based costing (ABC)

This involves allocating internal costs to cost centres and drivers on the basis of the activities causing the costs. Some environment-related costs such as those relating to disposal of chemicals used in wood treatment will be attributed to joint cost centres. However environment-driven costs (such as capital costs of pollution monitoring and waste disposal equipment and expenses such as increased record keeping costs) often go unrecognised within general overheads. ABC removes these costs from overheads, and instead traces them to specific products and services so that polluting, wasteful or environmentally damaging products take a higher level of cost. This helps management to focus on the processes that drive the costs and work to improve them.

Lifecycle costing

This involves considering the costs associated with a product over its entire lifecycle – from the initial production through to its final disposal as waste or as a recycled new product. From an environmental perspective this means that a product which cannot be recycled, or which requires high energy inputs to convert, will have a higher cost. This would allow TTG to rethink the way in which items are made; for example, wood itself can be recycled but the addition of chemicals in treating or painting the product, and fixings made of other materials would hinder this.

Total Quality Management (TQM)

TQM involves monitoring and measuring all aspects of quality failure – including external failure such as complaints and bad publicity as well as more obvious factors such as waste and quality testing. It has as its basis a culture of excellence, continuous improvement and total elimination of failure. This approach would help TTG to focus on the importance of improving every aspect of their business, and applied to environmental failure – as measured by the accounting techniques described above – it could produce significant gains in their environmental performance.

Once TTG had better defined their environmental costs and introduced ways of identifying and measuring them more accurately, the information generated can then be used to control and even eliminate them. Managers can be appraised on the true environmental costs of their activities, and targets set to incentivise them to reduce them. Costs can be built into the investment appraisal process for new projects, and potential savings built into the budgets for current ones. TTG can work to become truly environmentally responsible and if properly implemented should be able to cut costs (both internally and externally) and increase revenues at the same time.

74 PUBLIC SERVICES

Key answer tips

The central theme of the question is performance management and measurement in the provision of public services. The three requirements of the question invite consideration of different aspects of this theme.

The requirements are all capable of wide interpretation. Issues that might be addressed include the determination of objectives, efficiency, effectiveness, value-for- money and benchmarking. References to practical topics such as 'contracting-out', Executive Agencies and Private Finance Initiatives are relevant.

(a) *Examiner's note:* A structured approach could take many alternative forms, this suggested answer represents one approach – candidates are likely to offer many variations. The request for a 'structured' approach is to avoid candidates merely listing a series of random indicators without consideration to the relationship between them and their contribution towards overall performance assessment.

'Overall performance' refers to a comprehensive coverage of the major issues that are generally regarded as important in assessing a public service.

They could be broken down into three categories:

1   Financial indicators (assessing efficiency)

2   Non-financial quantitative indicators (assessing effectiveness)

3   Qualitative indicators that are difficult to quantify (assessing effectiveness)

Financial:

- Cost per unit of activity/unit cost measurement e.g. per hospital bed per annum, annual cost per pupil, per arrest, each call to attend a fire.
- A comparison between actual and budgeted or standard cost (variance analysis) – flexible budget approach may be adopted to relate costs to activity levels.
- Bench marking costs against other regions and/or 'best practice'.
- An indicator that measures cost recovery against service delivered – e.g. fees received from dental patients who are required to contribute towards the cost of a service – may be set at a ratio to total costs incurred.
- The ratio of one cost component to the total cost of the service e.g. what percentage are staff costs of the total costs – this could be supplemented by bench marking ratios.

Non-financial (quantified):

- Units of activity delivered within a period e.g. operations undertaken, number of children attending school, criminals arrested, fires attended.
- Flexibility and speed of response e.g. time taken for ambulances to arrive, hospital waiting lists and time elapsed between diagnosis and treatment.
- Quality of Service/output measures – pupils' test marks, crime rates, life expectancy, the number of hospital deaths arising from infections, numbers of people rescued from fires.
- Utilisation of resources e.g. – bed occupancy ratios, average class size, ratio of police vehicles currently operational.
- Number of complaints received.
- Accessibility – e.g. distance to nearest hospital or school.

Qualitative:

- Public confidence in the service – the strength of the expectation that –
- a criminal will be arrested
- a pupil will receive a 'good' education
- a patient will be 'well looked after' in hospital
- the fire service will respond rapidly when required
- The morale of the work force
- The 'attitude' of the staff – do they appear concerned, helpful and confident when dealing with the public
- How effective are they at meeting the information needs of their 'customers.'
- Cleanliness, comfort security – do people feel 'comfortable' within the premise owned by the public service (school and hospital) – it is part of 'quality', but it is difficult to quantify.

(b) Common problems are likely to include:

- The simultaneous pursuit of multiple and sometimes conflicting objectives – the private sector frequently has a single prime objective e.g. maximisation of shareholder wealth.
- Political interference – this may result in policy U-turns or long term organisational objectives being sacrificed for short term political gains.
- They are usually monopoly services therefore making it difficult to assess relative performance. Attempts to overcome this via bench marking with other regions can be problematical owing to geographical variations in operating environments.
- It is very difficult to measure outputs that public services provide. What is the 'output' of the fire service? The private sector has measurable units of output whether it is goods or services – they charge for them! They also have a measure of net output – their profits.
- Financial constraints e.g. a private company could decide to borrow money if it thought it were in its interest, but a public body may be forbidden to undertake such action – the service may not have the freedom to act in what it regards as its own interest.
- The temptation to judge outputs on the value of inputs – employing more people, spending more money on a service and building new premises is frequently taken to represent improved service provision – this is not necessarily true.

(c) Ways to overcome the problems outlined above:

- Change in the governance to restrict political interference.
- Facilitate regional benchmarking by introducing adjustment factors to compensate for known regional disparities e.g. permit higher rates of pay in high wage locations and allowing for variations in the socio-economic composition of the population.
- Undertake cost-benefit analysis of projects in an effort to place a monetary value on the service provision.
- Accept that it is difficult to monitor their performance in a quantifiable and objective way, and therefore appoint and trust independent agencies staffed by experts who will make subjective decisions based upon their experience and the information presented to them.

75 SHAREHOLDER VALUE ANALYSIS

Key answer tips

In Part (a) you need to discuss the term shareholder value and the difficulties encountered in its assessment – noting that the analysis is based on discounted cash flows. You should discuss the fact that the focus should be long-term, EPS is unreliable and that a 10-year horizon for calculation of NPV from cash flows has been advocated. In Part (b) you could use the 'Balanced Scorecard' technique as a basis for your answer.

REPORT

To: Finance director
From: Management accountant
Date: XX/XX\XX
Re: Shareholder value in our reporting system

(a) The term 'shareholder value' reflects the view that when a person invests his money in a company he does so in the expectation that his wealth will increase. To paraphrase Robert Kaplan, 'the overall goal of the corporation is to generate long-term economic value'.

There are various crude ways in which this can be measured. For example, earnings per share or the market value of the company. However, EPS is fallible and market values are transient. Finance directors want to evolve a method of measurement that is neither crude nor transient but which provides strategic direction to improving long-run gains for shareholders. Writers such as Rappaport have suggested a 10-year horizon for the calculation of NPV from cash flows as a measure of shareholder value. This also is highly subjective.

Companies such as Apple have experimented with the identification of various value drivers, many of which are non-financial but are expressed in terms of financial surrogates (i.e. financial measures which reflect the value drivers). The essence of the exercise is to identify those matters that influence competitive advantage, thus affect the chances of longevity of the business, and ultimately an increase in shareholder economic value.

(b) The traditional basis of reporting divisional performance has been angled towards financial measures that are relatively short-term, such as return on investment (ROI), or residual income (RI), or even controllable profit. The more modern orientation towards maximisation of shareholder value demands a process of re-education. The balanced scorecard approach originally written up in the Harvard Business Review has now been widely accepted in both the US and the UK.

The technique is to focus on four perspectives that influence competitive advantage. This is set out in the chart below:

Financial perspective	*Internal business perspective*
ROI	% items needing reworking
Cash flow	Cost per unit
Project NPV	Efficiency measures
Customer perspective	*Innovation and learning perspective*
Satisfaction	% revenue from new business
New business	Products launched
Repeat business	Qualifications obtained by staff

Reports structured around this concept are more forward looking and concerned with continuous improvement associated with techniques such as re-engineering. The technique focuses on a variety of indicators, both long-term and short term.

Traditional financial indicators are not overlooked. They are complemented by non-financial indicators which have considerable strategic significance. No single measure will provide a focus on the key variable that ensures long-term survival and growth, namely sustained competitive advantage. In the past, the fixation on financial data meant that the unmeasurable (in financial terms) was downgraded to a soft variable: interesting but difficult or impossible to measure. What were once regarded as 'soft' variables (unmeasurable) have now become hard variables. The identification of critical success factors and the mechanisms for measurement will focus efforts on improving those features of business activity and bring about greater economic value.

The **design of the scorecard** will vary according to the entity assessed. Some years ago (before its takeover by RBS) the National Westminster Bank discovered that it needed one scorecard for retail banking and another for group results. However, the most striking aspect of the literature has been the recognition of non-financial issues and their impact on financial plans and investment appraisal processes.

The scorecard also **changes the way in which reports go to the board** and the way in which information is communicated to stakeholders. A stakeholder in a bank does not want just a recital of dry financial statistics. The information that is needed should inform him on the crucial issues of competitive advantage, product innovation and customer satisfaction. The common thread is the customer; if we lose customers we lose our business. Hence the importance of the customer perspective.

The **development of the appropriate indicators** to satisfy the four perspectives will take time and effort. The pioneer in this field, Rockware, developed their scorecard over a year-long project which involved customers, management and their principal shareholder. They acknowledge benefits in efficiency, profitability and customer satisfaction.

The balanced scorecard approach encourages managers to think about the strategic consequences of their actions. A decision to cut advertising could boost ROI but lose long-term benefits in market share. A decision to reduce headcount could destroy morale and quality standards even if profits rise in the short run.

In conclusion, although the immediate consequence might be an administrative burden to cope with, experience reports that the trade off should be cohesive and effective for management at group and divisional level.

76 PD

> **Key answer tips**
>
> This is a straightforward question asking about two new developments in management accounting. However it is important to ensure that you answer not solely in general terms but in the context of the scenario given in the question. Relate the prism and EMA to the scenario.

(a) The Performance Prism is an approach to performance measurement which is designed to take account of the interests of all stakeholders, such as suppliers, employees, legislators, and local communities. In doing this it takes a broader approach to stakeholder interests than many other performance management models which pay limited attention to stakeholders other than customers and shareholders.

The Performance Prism is based on the principle that the performance of an organisation depends on how effectively it meets the needs and requirements of all its stakeholders. It takes stakeholder requirements as the starting point for the development of performance measures and recognises the need to work with stakeholders to ensure that their needs are met. The framework can be used to identify measures at all levels within the organisation.

The Performance Prism has five facets which are different perspectives on performance which prompt specific questions. The answers to these questions form the starting point for defining performance measures.

These facets are as follows:

- **Stakeholder satisfaction – Who are our key stakeholders and what do they want and need?** For PD, key stakeholders include environmental pressure groups and legislative bodies. For example the pressure groups want to see PD making better use of its non-renewable resources and reducing emissions of pollution. The latter will also be a concern of legislative bodies.

- **Strategies – What strategies do we need to put in place to satisfy the wants and needs of our key stakeholders, while satisfying our own requirements too?** A possible strategy for PD to pursue to respond to the wants of environmental pressure groups would be the development of new products which use less non-renewable resources and which use new manufacturing processes which result in lower emissions.

- **Processes – What processes do we need to put in place to enable us to execute our strategies?** For example PD may need to look at a different approach to product research and development to meet the demands of the strategy identified.

- **Capabilities – What capabilities do we need to put in place to allow us to operate, maintain and enhance our processes?** Examples of capabilities which PD will need to have are waste management, improved new product development and environmental management accounting.

- **Stakeholder contribution – What contributions do we want and need from our stakeholders if we are to maintain and develop these capabilities?** PD could for example consider working with environmental pressure groups to identify particular areas of concern and possible solutions.

Once the answers to the above five questions have been answered, PD can use the results to identify performance measures which enable the company to monitor the success of the processes put in place. Some of these indicators could also be used to convey to the public that PD is working to improve the environmental impact of its activities.

Example indicators are:

- Numbers of new products developed
- Levels of emissions
- usage and cost of resources such as water, electricity and fuel.

(b) Many organisations are beginning to recognise that environmental awareness and management are not optional, but are important for long-term survival and profitability. All organisations are faced with increasing legal and regulatory requirements relating to environmental management. They also need to meet customers' needs and concerns relating to the environment and to demonstrate effective environmental management to maintain a good public image. Organisations are also recognising the importance of sustainable development. In addition most organisations can make cost savings by improved use of resources such as water and fuel. This is particularly evident in the case of PD.

EMA is concerned with the accounting information needs of managers in relation to corporate activities that affect the environment as well as environment-related impacts on the corporation. It could be used by PD to enable the company to:

- Identify and estimate the costs of environment-related activities
- Identify and monitor the usage and cost of resources such as water, electricity and fuel and to enable costs to be reduced
- Ensure environmental considerations form a part of capital investment decisions and new product developments
- Assess the likelihood and impact of environmental risks
- Ensure routine performance monitoring includes environment-related indicators benchmark activities against environmental best practice.

77 SPORTS COMPLEX

Key answer tips

Part (a) is a straightforward application of relevant cashflows. However, you must explain your treatment of items to get full marks. Part (b) on breakeven follows on from part (a) so it is important that the marker can follow your figures should they be different in part (a). Part (c) requires you to have learnt some detail on environmental reporting.

(a)

Sports Complex – Heat recovery proposal
Cash flows for year to 31 May 20Y0

	Accept proposal $	Reject proposal $
At 25% level of recovery		
Variable swimming pool costs	43,312	115,500
New equipment hired	75,000	
Employee to supervise equipment	17,500	
	135,812	115,500

The proposal should be rejected on financial grounds since there is a net increase in cost of $20,312 if it is accepted.

Notes:

1 At 25% heat recovery we have 125,000 units of heat available (500,000 × 25%). This is sufficient for 62.5% of the 200,000 units of heat required by the swimming pool. This means that 37.5% of the variable costs from the existing system will remain, i.e. 37.5% × $150,000 × 70% × 1.1 = $43,312.

If the proposal is rejected, the total variable costs for 20X9 are relevant, i.e. $150,000 × 70% × 1.1 = $115,500.

PAPER P5 : ADVANCED PERFORMANCE MANAGEMENT

2   The new equipment hire charge of $75,000 is an incremental cost of the proposal.

3   The salary of $17,500 to the employee is avoidable if the proposal is rejected. Therefore it is an incremental cost of the proposal.

4   The survey fee of $30,000 is irrelevant since the money has already been spent, i.e. it is a sunk cost.

5   The ice rink heat extraction cost of $120,000 (plus 10% price increase) will remain whether or not the new heating scheme for the swimming pool is implemented. It is, therefore, irrelevant to the decision. It may be omitted entirely or shown to apply to both acceptance and rejection of the proposal.

(b) For a breakeven situation we require residual variable heating costs from the existing system to be $115,500 − ($75,000 + $17,500) = $23,000.

Hence units of heat required from the existing system

= 200,000 × 23,000/115,500 = 39,827 units.

This means that units from ice rink extraction = 200,000 − 39,827 = 160,173 units.

This gives a heat recovery percentage from the ice rink of 160,173/500,000 = 32%.

> *Tutorial note*
>
> *A number of alternative presentations could be used.*
>
> *If X = percentage heat recovery from the ice rink we have heat extraction units from the existing system*
>
> *= 200,000 − 500,000X*
>
> *Now, variable cost per unit of heat in year to 31 May 20Y0 from the existing system*
>
> *= ($150,000 × 1.1 × 70%)/200,000 = $0.5775*
>
> *For a breakeven position on financial grounds:*
>
> *(200,000 − 500,000X) × $0.5775 = $23,000*
>
> *Solving, X = 32%*

(c) Organisations are beginning to recognise that environmental awareness and management are not optional, but are important for long-term survival and profitability. All organisations:

- Are faced with increasing legal and regulatory requirements relating to environmental management
- Need to meet customers' needs and concerns relating to the environment
- Need to demonstrate effective environmental management to maintain a good public image
- Need to manage the risk and potential impact of environmental disasters
- Can make cost savings by improved use of resources such as water and fuel
- Are recognising the importance of sustainable development, which is the meeting of current needs without compromising the ability of future generations to meet their needs.

Environmental management accounting is concerned with the accounting information needs of managers in relation to corporate activities that affect the environment as well as environment-related impacts on the corporation. This includes:

- Identifying and estimating the costs of environment-related activities
- Identifying and separately monitoring the usage and cost of resources such as water, electricity and fuel and to enable costs to be reduced
- Ensuring environmental considerations form a part of capital investment decisions
- Assessing the likelihood and impact of environmental risks
- Including environment-related indicators as part of routine performance monitoring
- Benchmarking activities against environmental best practice.

78 BIOTEC

Key answer tips

It is vital to this question that you answer the requirement set and relate your comments to the scenario. In particular, the use of public sector league tables is a source of ongoing debate so make sure you are aware of, and can apply, the arguments concerned.

(a) **Financial performance management and control**

The key problems facing BIOTEC are as follows:

- Financial control – preventing BIOTEC from overspending its budget for 20X1/20X2
- Loss of key staff
- League tables – losing funding in the future if they do not perform well

Each of these will be addressed in turn.

Financial control – preventing a deficit

It is vital that BIOTEC avoids an overspend. While we are not told the consequences of failure, it is likely to include a cutback in future funding or even closure. This will be difficult in a context of a culture where overspends have become normal and hence acceptable.

The size of, and diversity within, BIOTEC implies it is the sort of complex organisation that would benefit from a common system of financial control based on financial ratio analysis.

However, financial control usually takes place within a context of budgetary reporting where actual expenditure is compared to budget expenditure. This is usually reported both on a period and year-to-date basis. It is also common for the periodic reporting, which is usually done monthly, to be accompanied with forecasts of expenditure for the remainder of the budget year. Budgets may be modified during the budget year if a fundamental change has occurred and they are often kept continually up-to-date by the use of 'rolling' budgets.

However, many of the components required for a system of budget reporting are not in place in BIOTEC. BIOTEC does not have an adequate management accounting function and the Director only knows 'approximately' the aggregated spending which has taken place. For effective control to take place there would need to be disaggregation of the total budget and this would be normally analysed within responsibility centres which reflected BIOTEC's organisational structure. For example, research projects could be grouped by areas such as weapons, medical, food and drink and so on.

Neither, does BIOTEC have a formal system for forecasting expenditure and, as it normally has a deficit at the year end, there is a weakness here which needs to be rectified.

Even if a system of actual v budget with rolling forecasts is introduced, there is still the problem of capital rationing. If an overspend is forecast on certain projects then the "obvious" action would be to limit their funding for the rest of the year.

However, this might be a mistake if it results in research being delayed that had high value, either in humanitarian terms or in terms of potential future profitability. Assessing the potential benefits of research is notoriously difficult, even part way through a project.

Staffing issues

At present staff who successfully discover new innovations are leaving for more lucrative positions elsewhere. Further research, such as exit interviews, will be required to determine whether they are leaving for the higher financial returns or to continue to have involvement with the development of their ideas (assuming they join companies who have won licences for such development).

The financial gain can be addressed through higher pay or a bonus system linked to recognition of their achievements. This is likely to be based on KPIs linked to non-financial aspects of project success, such as establishing a patent, rather than cost control or other financial targets. In this respect a greater emphasis on financial based performance management is unlikely to help the problem. However, if BIOTEC is changed into an investment centre and allowed to develop innovations further, then this conclusion will change.

League tables

The main risk for BIOTEC is losing funding in the future if they do not perform well in league tables.

It appears that ROI will feature as a primary measure in future league tables. ROI is usually analysed into its components which examine Income: Sales and Sales: Investment. These ratios are then analysed in their turn. However, little of this analysis could be performed within BIOTEC at present, as it has no sales revenue and the value of its assets is not recorded within BIOTEC.

BIOTEC does not generate any income and does not receive the benefits of the commercial exploitation of its innovations. Bringing the process for patenting innovations and exploiting them within BIOTEC would be a major contribution towards BIOTEC becoming commercial. However, this is a separate issue to the introduction of financial ratio analysis. If BIOTEC was to earn income from its innovations, it would be more appropriately constituted as a profit centre or, possibly, an investment centre.

Summary

Financial ratio analysis will be able to make a contribution towards BIOTEC becoming commercial. However, this will be limited as many of the aspects of a commercial business are currently missing within BIOTEC, notably having income.

(b) **League tables**

The government are considering setting up league tables to assess the performance of research facilities to assist funding decisions.

Advantages of league tables

- Implementation should stimulate competition between research facilities resulting in better cost control. This is important in an environment of cutbacks in funding and should result in better value for money overall.
- In time the league tables will make it easier to identify and adopt best practice. As a result, the quality of the service should improve.
- Monitors and ensures accountability of the providers.
- Performance is transparent.

Disadvantages

- Encourages providers to focus on performance measures rather than the quality of the service. In the context here the danger is that more "pure" research would be abandoned in favour of shorter term projects that have a more obvious commercial application.
- Similarly many significant breakthroughs have only come after many initial failures. A system of league tables would encourage managers to abandon projects that do not show promise early on.
- May encourage creative reporting, although public sector audits will go some way to alleviate this
- The value of any performance indicator depends on the quality of any data in the calculation. The data management systems in the public sector do not always provide quality data.
- Many of the outcomes valued by society are not measurable but many of the performance indicators have been selected on the basis of what is practical rather than what is meaningful. For example, the projects that generate the highest commercial value in terms of ROI may not be the same as those that enhance wellbeing or protect the environment.
- Differences between facilities may make comparisons meaningless, e.g. a facility focussing just on weapons may have very different results from another looking at crops.
- A poor ranking may have a negative impact on public trust and employee morale. For example, the press are likely to question breakthroughs form a facility with a low ranking, casting doubts over the truth of any announcements
- A poor ranking may lead to a worsening of future performance, e.g. more able staff may not want to join a research facility with a poor ranking, thus compounding its lack of skills.
- Supplying the necessary data and forms to comply with the league table administration would be costly and time consuming.

Conclusion

In summary the problems with evaluating research mainly on financial grounds would make the usefulness questionable at best.

79 BENNETT PLC (DEC 03)

> **Key answer tips**
>
> An interesting question that requires candidates to criticise the evaluation. Work through each line and think about whether the figures are relevant, clear and in sufficient detail. The second part of the question is asking you to explain and apply Target Costing to the scenario. Ensure that you do both.

(a) In order to evaluate the investment, numerous problems had to be addressed by the management of Bennett plc. Firstly, there was a need to incur expenditure of $200,000 on market research relating to the proposal. This expenditure constitutes a 'sunk cost' and therefore has been excluded from the evaluation by the finance director. It must be acknowledged that there is no guarantee as to the precision of the estimate of market size arrived at by the market research consultancy. It is clear that the management of Bennett plc are placing a high degree of reliance on the consultants' assessment. As the new project requires a sizeable capital investment, the estimate of sales assumes critical significance.

It is noticeable that the intended selling price of the product varies in each of years 1 – 4. This reflects the desired intention of the board of directors to maintain a 5% share of the total market in each of the four years of the estimated life of the product. The changes in selling price are intended to help procure this desired level of market share. There is a linear relationship between selling price per unit and sales units. The finance director has used a price/demand relationship of $P = 90 - 0.0002Q$ to estimate the selling price to be charged in order to achieve the required sales quantities of the product in each year.

Quotations will almost certainly have been obtained to substantiate the initial capital outlay in respect of required plant and equipment to enable manufacture to commence. It is highly probable therefore that the Year 0 outlay is accurate. Likewise, the requirement for the injection of working capital should also be free from material error. Any error regarding the timing of the release of working capital will be related to the inaccuracy in the estimated life of the product.

The marketing director's estimates in respect of the intended advertising campaign total $2.6 million in undiscounted terms. The estimates and the phasing of this amount should be subjected to a detailed examination. If it were possible to defer some of the expenditure, then the NPV and IRR arrived at in the forecast, and hence the projects desirability, would be improved.

An estimated variable cost of $35 per unit has been assumed to remain constant for the expected four-year life of the product. This may be an unrealistic assumption and ignores any efficiency gains and/or benefits from 'learning' and 'experience' that could arise.

The estimated fixed costs should be reviewed to ensure that they are truly attributable to the investment. These costs are forecast to remain 'fixed' for the four-year life of the project and this may also be too simplistic an assumption.

The finance director chose to use two performance measures, Net Present Value (NPV) and Internal Rate of Return (IRR), in appraising the investment. Each of these measures is based on the use of discounted cash flow analysis.

When evaluating investments with a simple cash flow profile i.e. those involving a one-off investment outlay followed by a stream of cash inflows, both the NPV and IRR methods produce the same 'accept' or 'reject' decisions.

The finance director might well appreciate that an advantage which accrues from the use of the NPV method is the simplicity with which results are stated. NPV is an absolute measure of performance which produces a result expressed in $s which directly reflects the changed wealth position expected as a consequence of undertaking an investment. However, because NPV is an absolute measure of performance it does not easily allow two investments of very different scales to be compared. By way of contrast, the Internal Rate of Return produces a result which is shown as a percentage, and this result has to be compared with a required rate of return before a decision regarding whether to invest or not can be made. Since IRR is a relative measure, it could be used by the finance director to compare returns on investment projects which differ significantly in scale.

However, because internal rate of return (IRR) ignores the relative size of investments, it should not be used to select between mutually exclusive projects since the project with the highest IRR might have the lowest absolute return.

In view of the number of variables contained in the forecast, the management of Bennett plc should apply sensitivity analysis to the forecasted cash flows, in order to gain a more comprehensive appreciation of the financial implications of the project.

(b) **Target costing** should be viewed as an integral part of a strategic profit management system. The initial consideration in target costing is the determination of an estimate of the selling price for a new product which will enable a firm to capture its required share of the market. Then it is necessary to reduce this figure to reflect the firm's desired level of profit, having regard to the rate of return required on new capital investment and working capital requirements. The deduction of required profit from the proposed selling price will produce a target price that must be met in order to ensure that the desired rate of return is obtained. Thus the main theme that underpins target costing can be seen to be 'what should a product cost in order to achieve the desired level of return'.

Target costing will necessitate comparison of current estimated cost levels against the target level which must be achieved if the desired levels of profitability, and hence return on investment, are to be achieved. Thus where a gap exists between the current estimated cost levels and the target cost, it is essential that this gap be closed.

In the case of Bennett plc it is apparent that if the market research findings regarding market share has been accurately forecast at appropriate selling prices for the four-year life of the project, then costs must be reduced from the currently estimated level if the proposal is to be acceptable at a 'hurdle rate' of 14%.

The management of Bennett plc should be aware that it is far easier to 'design out' cost during the pre-production phase than to 'control out' cost during the production phase. Thus cost reduction at this stage of a product's life cycle is of critical significance to business success. A number of techniques may be employed in order to help in the achievement and maintenance of the desired level of target cost. Attention should be focused upon the identification of value added and non-value added activities with the aim of the elimination of the latter. The product should be developed in an atmosphere of 'continuous improvement'. In this regard, Total Quality techniques such as the use of Quality Circles may be used in attempting to find ways of achieving reductions in product cost.

Value engineering techniques can be used to evaluate necessary product features such as the quality of materials used. It is essential that a collaborative approach is used by the management of Bennett plc and that all interested parties such as suppliers and customers are closely involved in order to engineer product enhancements at reduced cost.

The target cost-setting process

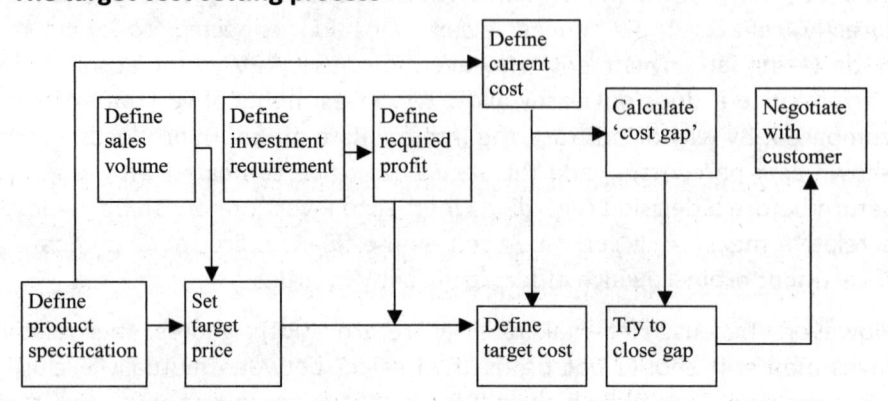

```
                                    ┌─────────┐
                                    │ Define  │
                                    │ current │
                                    │  cost   │
                                    └────┬────┘
   ┌────────┐   ┌──────────┐   ┌────────┐│   ┌──────────┐   ┌──────────┐
   │ Define │   │  Define  │   │ Define ││   │Calculate │   │ Negotiate│
   │ sales  │──▶│investment│──▶│required├┴──▶│'cost gap'│──▶│   with   │
   │ volume │   │requirement│  │ profit │    │          │   │ customer │
   └────────┘   └────┬─────┘   └────────┘    └──────────┘   └──────────┘
                     │                                             ▲
                     ▼                                             │
   ┌────────┐   ┌────────┐                  ┌────────┐   ┌──────────┐
   │ Define │   │  Set   │                  │ Define │   │  Try to  │
   │product │──▶│ target │─────────────────▶│ target ├──▶│close gap │
   │specif'n│   │ price  │                  │  cost  │   │          │
   └────────┘   └────────┘                  └────────┘   └──────────┘
```

Source: Sakurai, H, Journal of Cost Management for the Manufacturing Industries, 'Target costing and how to use it', iii No 2, (1989).

80 THE BETTER ELECTRICALS GROUP (BEG) (JUN 10)

> **Key answer tips**
>
> This is a question on target costs rather than target costing so ensure you answer the question set.

(a) At present, the variable manufacturing costs are targeted to be at a level of 35% of sales value. Fixed costs are expected to increase by $400,000 in 2012 which may be indicative of an increase in the level of activity.

The use of cost targeting would necessitate comparison of current estimated cost levels against the targets which must be achieved if the desired levels of profitability, and hence return on investment, are to be achieved. Thus where a difference exists between the current estimated cost levels and the cost target, it is essential that this gap be closed. The gap between the cost targets and current expected cost levels regarding the application for 'platinum' status may be analysed into internal and external failure costs. Internal failure costs arise when products or services fail to meet design quality standards and such failures are detected before the product or service is passed to the customer. For example, incorrect processing of customer orders prior to supplying goods or services to customers, excessive idle capacity of personnel would constitute internal failure costs. External failure costs arise after products or services have been passed to the customer and would include costs incurred in order to address rectification claims from customers. Internal failure costs are expected to fall from 21.92% of the cost target to 7.5% of the cost target in 2013. External failure costs are expected to fall from 27.2% of cost target to 6.13% of cost target in 2013.

Prevention and appraisal costs are discretionary costs incurred by management in an attempt to reduce the costs of internal and external failures. Prevention costs are incurred as a consequence of management actions with regard to achievement of the desired quality standards to enable the cost target to be achieved, such as for example the costs incurred in training sales administration staff. Prevention costs are expected to fall from $4.2m in 2011 to $1.32m in 2013.

Appraisal costs are costs incurred in order to ensure conformance with agreed quality standards. These would include costs incurred in ensuring quality negotiation procedures with customers. Appraisal costs are expected to decrease by $100,000 to $0.7m in 2012 and to remain at that level during 2013.

(b) (i) The application for 'platinum status' quality certification may be measured in both financial and marketing terms. The net profit/sales percentage is expected to increase each year. The figures are 8.33%, 31.67% and 43.89% for 2011, 2012 and 2013 respectively (e.g. 2011 = $2m/$24m). The profit increase is partly linked to the projected fall in quality costs, both costs of conformance (appraisal and prevention) and costs of non-conformance (internal and external failure) as shown in the appendix. It is also linked to the increase in volume of business as fixed costs have a reduced effect. Will BEG achieve market growth and an improved market position? The projected sales in the appendix shows growth of 25% in 2012 ($30m/$24m) and a further 20% in 2013 ($36m/$30m). In addition, market position is anticipated to improve, with a market share of 8%, 9.38% and 10.59% in years 2011, 2012 and 2013 respectively (e.g. 2011 = $24m/$300m).

(ii) In order to achieve external efficiency BEG has to satisfy its customers. Customer satisfaction may be defined as meeting customer expectations. The quality of service provision and delivery are operational criteria that can be used to monitor levels of customer satisfaction. The success will require an efficient business operating system for all aspects of the cycle from product design to after sales service to customers. Improved quality and delivery should lead to improved customer satisfaction. Schedule 1 shows a number of quantitative measures of the expected measurement of these factors:

- Quality is expected to improve. The percentage of products achieving design quality standards is expected to rise from 92% to 99% between 2011 and 2013. In the same period, rectification claims from customers for faulty work should fall from $0.96m to $0.1m and the cost of after sales rectification service should fall from $1.8m to $0.8m.
- Delivery efficiency improvement may be measured in terms of the increase in the percentage of sales expected to meet planned delivery dates. This percentage is forecast to increase from 88.5% in 2011 to 99.5% in 2013.

(iii) Internal efficiency may be assessed by reference to flexibility and productivity. Flexibility relates to the business operating system as a whole whilst productivity relates to the management of resources such as staff time. This should be helped through reduced cycle time and decreased levels of waste. Once again the appendix shows a number of quantitative measures of these factors:

- The average total cycle time from customer enquiry to delivery is forecast to reduce from 49 days in 2011 to 40 days in 2013. This indicates both internal efficiency and external effectiveness.

- Waste in the form of idle capacity of service personnel is expected to fall from 12% to 1.5% between 2011 and 2013. Also, service enquiries not taken up by customers are expected to fall from 10.5% of enquiries in 2011 to 3% of enquiries in 2013. These are both examples of ways in which improved productivity may be measured. Both will be linked to the prevention and appraisal costs, which are intended to reduce the level of internal and external failure costs.

Whilst we do not know the precise standards that are required to be achieved in order to gain 'platinum' status quality certification one can conclude that BEG has forecast vast improvements in several aspects of its performance during the three-year period under review.

Marking scheme

			Marks
(a)	Comments (on merit):		
	Cost targets		4
	Costs of quality		4
		Maximum	8
(b)	(i) Financial performance and marketing		4
	(ii) External effectiveness		4
	(iii) Internal efficiency		4
		Maximum	12
Total			20

Examiner's comments

Part (a) required an explanation of cost targets and their relevance to the application for platinum status (the quality certification) and an analysis of forecasts of those costs for the next three years. There was some evidence of misreading the question as being about target costing rather than the more basic use of target costs in achieving this quality standard. However, candidates who took this track made relevant points and were given some credit. Those candidates who scored well did so by appreciating that these were forecast numbers and so gave an indication of the company's plans not its history. Therefore, a good answer commented on how the increased quality costs of 2011 fed through to improved quality in the later years yielding lower costs. Many candidates would have benefited from considering the cost categories within each year rather than across each category. There was frequently little evidence of understanding how spending in one category affects the others – especially, the effect of conformance activity on non-conformance activity.

Part (b) required an analysis of general forecast performance under three headings. The successful candidates made clear how their points linked to the specific headings demonstrating their appreciation of the meaning of that heading. They provided quantified analysis of the data in the appendix and linked it to business objectives under the heading. Again, the weaker candidates provided trend analysis but did not demonstrate an appreciation of how this then affected the business within the headings e.g. by satisfying customers and so being externally effective.

Professional Pilot Paper – Options module

Advanced Performance Management

Paper P5

Time allowed
Reading and planning: 15 minutes
Writing: 3 hours

This paper is divided into two sections:

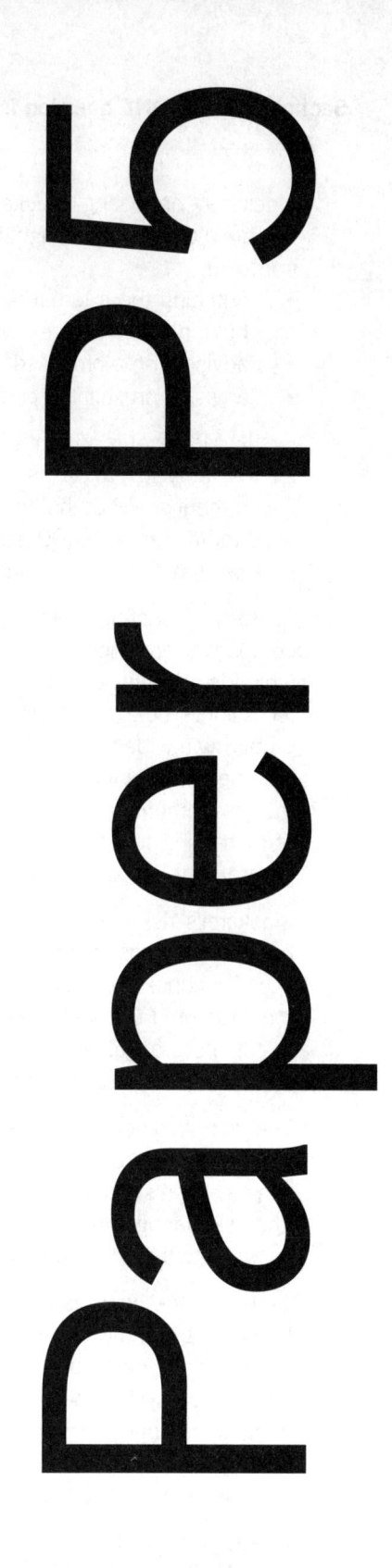

Section A – THIS ONE question is compulsory and MUST be attempted

Section B – TWO questions ONLY to be attempted

**Do NOT open this paper until instructed by the supervisor.
During reading and planning time only the question paper may be annotated. You must NOT write in your answer booklet until instructed by the supervisor.
This question paper must not be removed from the examination hall.**

The Association of Chartered Certified Accountants

Section A: THIS ONE question is compulsory and MUST be attempted

1   Mackerel Contracting (Mackerel) is a listed defence contractor working mainly for its domestic government in Zedland. You are a consultant brought in to advise Mackerel on a number of issues facing the company. The board need a report from you:
   - outlining the external factors affecting the profitability of a potential new contract and how these factors can be built in to the choice of the design budget which is ultimately set,
   - advising on a proposed change to the company's information systems and
   - advising on suitable performance measures for Mackerel.

Firstly, Mackerel is currently considering tendering for a contract to develop a new armoured personnel vehicle (APV) for the army to protect its soldiers during transport around any future battlefield. The invitation to tender from the government specifies that the APV should take two years to develop and test, and be delivered for a full cost to Mackerel of no more than $70,000 per unit at current prices. Normally, government contracts are approximately priced on a cost plus basis with Mackerel aiming to make a 19% mark-up.

At the last briefing meeting, the institutional shareholders of Mackerel expressed worry about the volatility of the company's earnings (currently a $20.4m operating profit per annum) especially during the economic downturn which is affecting Zedland at present. They are also concerned by cuts in government expenditure resulting from this recession. The Zedland minister for procurement has declared 'In the current difficult economic conditions, we are preparing a wide ranging review of all defence contracts with a view to deciding on what is desirable within the overall priorities for Zedland and what is possible within our budget.' The government procurement manager has indicated that the government would be willing to commit to purchase 500 APV's within the price limit set but with the possibility of increasing this to 750 or 1,000 depending on defence commitments. In the invitation to tender document, the government has stated it will pay $7.5m towards development and then a 19% mark-up on budgeted variable costs.

Mackerel's risk management committee (RMC) is considering how much to spend on design and development. It has three proposals from the engineering team: a basic package at $7.5m (which will satisfy the original contract specifications) and two other improved design packages. The design packages will have different total fixed costs but are structured to give the same variable cost per unit. It is believed that the improved design packages will increase the chances of gaining a larger government order but it has been very difficult to ascertain the relevant probabilities of different order volumes. The RMC need a full appraisal of the situation using all suitable methods.

The risk manager has gathered information on the APV contract which is contained in appendix A. She has identified that a major uncertainty in pricing the vehicle is the price of steel, as each APV requires 9.4 tonnes of steel. However, she has been successful in negotiating a fixed price contract for all the steel that might be required at $1,214 per tonne. The risk manager has tried to estimate the effect of choosing different design packages but is unsure of how to proceed to evaluate the different options.

Secondly, the board is also considering a change to the information systems at Mackerel. The existing systems are based in the individual functions (production, sales, service, finance and human resources). Currently, reports are submitted by each function and then integrated at head office into the board papers that form the main strategic information system of the company. The board are considering the implementation of a new system based on an integrated, single database that would be accessible at any of the company's five sites. The company network would be upgraded to allow real-time input and update of the database. The database would support a detailed management information system and a high-level executive information system.

Finally, the chief executive officer (CEO) of Mackerel believes that this new information system will provide the opportunity for a change in how performance is evaluated within the company. The company's mission is to maximise shareholder wealth and currently, the board use total shareholder return (TSR) as an overall corporate measure of performance. The CEO has asked you consider the general impact of the new information system and also, how profit based measures such as return on capital employed (ROCE) compare to newer measures such as economic value added (EVATM) with regard to meeting the overall goals of Mackerel and its external measure of performance.

Appendix A

Budgeted cost for APV
Variable cost per unit

	$	
Steel	11,412	9.4 tonnes at contracted prices
Engine/transmission	9,500	
Electronics	8,450	
Other	4,810	
Labour	13,800	

Design and development (fixed total) $

Package
Type 1	7,500,000
Type 2	8,750,000
Type 3	10,000,000

Risk manager's assessment of likely government order:

Demand	Probability		
	Type 1	Type 2	Type 3
500	85%	25%	20%
750	10%	50%	50%
1,000	5%	25%	30%

Required:

Write a report to the board of Mackerel to:

(i) Analyse the risks facing the management of Mackerel and discuss how the management team's attitude to risk might affect their response. (9 marks)

(ii) Evaluate the APV project using metrics and methods for decision-making under risk and uncertainty, and assess the suitability of the different methods used. (19 marks)

(iii) Recommend an appropriate choice of method of assessing the project and therefore, a course of action for the APV contract. (3 marks)

(iv) Evaluate the potential impact of the introduction of the new executive information system on operational information gathering and strategic decision-making at Mackerel. (8 marks)

(v) Assess how profit based measures such as return on capital employed (ROCE) compare to newer measures such as economic value added (EVA™) given Mackerel's overall goals. (7 marks)

Question 1 includes professional marks for the format, style and structure of the discussion of your answer.
(4 marks)

(50 marks)

Section B – Two questions from the three given must be attempted.

2   Albacore Chess Stores (Albacore) is a chain of twelve shops specialising in selling items associated with the game of chess: boards, pieces, clocks, software and books. Three years ago, the company was the subject of a venture capital buyout from a larger group. A new senior management team was put in place after the buyout. They have the aim of running the business in order to maximise profits.

The Chief Financial Officer (CFO) along with the other members of senior management sets the annual budget and uses a standard costing approach with variance analysis in order to control individual shop performance. The head office handles all capital purchases and brand marketing. All inventory purchasing is done centrally and the shop opening times are set as standard across the company. As an illustration of senior management attitude, the CFO had set the budget for 2011 staff costs at $7 per hour for part-time staff and this was rigorously observed in the period.

Each shop is run by a manager who reports their financial results to the operational director at head office. The shop managers recruit and manage the staffing of their shop. They have some autonomy in setting prices locally and have been given authority to vary prices by up to 10% from a master list produced by the CFO. They also have a local marketing budget agreed each year by the shop's manager and the marketing director as part of the annual appraisal process.

The shop managers have approached the Chairman of Albacore to complain about the way that they are managed and their remuneration. They feel that their efforts are unrecognised by senior management. One manager commented 'I have had a successful year in hard economic circumstances. I have run a number of promotions in the shop that have been well received by the customers. However, the budgets that are set are impossible to achieve and as a result I have not been paid any bonus although I feel that I have done everything in my power to bring in good profits.'

The shop managers at Albacore are paid a basic salary of $27,000 with bonuses of up to 30% of basic salary dependent on two factors: performance above budget and the operational director's assessment of the manager's performance. The budget for the next year is prepared by the CFO and presented by the operational director at the shop manager's annual appraisal.

The Chairman has come to you to ask if you can consider the system of performance assessment for the shop managers and give an independent perspective on the reward systems at Albacore. She has heard of variance analysis but is unsure as what would be relevant in this situation. She has provided the following illustrative branch report from the previous year for one shop:

Albacore Chess Stores
Tunny Branch Year to Sept 2011

		Budget $	Actual $	Variance $
Sales		266,000	237,100	-28,900
Cost of sales		106,400	94,840	11,560
Gross profit		159,600	142,260	-17,340
Marketing		12,000	11,500	500
Staff costs	Manager	27,000	27,000	0
	Part-time staff	38,000	34,000	4,000
Property costs		26,600	26,600	0
Shop profit		56,000	43,160	-12,840

Notes:
Property costs includes heating, lighting and rental.
Positive variances are favourable.

End of report

The manager of this shop commented at the appraisal meeting that she felt that the assessment was unfair since her failure to make budget was due to general economic conditions. The industry as a whole saw a 12% fall in revenues during the period and the budget for the period was set to be the same as the previous period. She was not paid a bonus for the period.

Required:

(a) Evaluate the suitability of the existing branch report as a means of assessing the shop manager's performance and draft an improved branch report with justifications for changes. *(13 marks)*

(b) Analyse the performance management style and evaluate the performance appraisal system at Albacore. Suggest suitable improvements to its reward system for the shop managers. *(12 marks)*

(25 marks)

3   Pharmaceutical Technologies Co (PT) is a developer and manufacturer of pharmaceuticals medical drugs in Beeland. It is one of the 100 largest listed companies on the national stock exchange. The company focuses on buying prospective products drugs from small bio-engineering companies that have shown initial promise in testing from small bio-engineering companies. PT then leads these through three regulatory stages to launch in the general medical market. The three stages are:

1   to confirm that the safety of the drug product (does it harm humans?), with small scale trials;,
2   to test the efficacy of the product (does it help cure?), again in small scale trials; and
3   finally, large scale trials to definitively decide on the safety and efficacy of the product.

The drugs are then marketed through the company's large sales force to health care providers and end users (patients). The health care providers are paid by either health insurance companies or the national government dependent on the financial status of the patient.

The Beeland Drug Regulator (BDR) oversees this testing process and makes the final judgement about whether a product can be sold in the country.

Its objectives are to protect, promote and improve public health by ensuring that:
- medicines have an acceptable balance of benefit and risk;,
- the users of these medicines understand this risk-benefit profile; and
- new beneficial product development is encouraged.

The regulator is governed by a board of trustees appointed by the government. It is funded directly by the government and also, through fees charged to drug companies when granting licences to sell their products in Beeland.

PT has used share price and earnings per share as its principal measures of performance to date. However, the share price has underperformed the market and the health sector in the last 2 two years. The chief executive officer (CEO) has identified that these measures are too narrow and is considering implementing a balanced scorecard approach to address this problem.

A working group has drawn up a suggested balanced scorecard. It began by identifying the objectives from the board's medium term strategy:
- Create shareholder value by bringing commercially viable drugs to market
- Improve the efficiency of drug development
- Increase shareholder value by innovation in the drug approval process

The working group then considered the stakeholder perspectives:
- Shareholders want an competitive return on their investment
- Payers Purchasers (governments, insurers and patients) want to pay a reasonable price for the drugs
- Regulators want an efficient process for the validation of drugs
- Doctors want safe and effective drug products
- Patients want to be cured

Finally, this leads to the proposed scorecard of performance measures:
- Financial – share price and earnings per share
- Customer – number of patients using TTPT products
- Internal business process – above exceed industry-standard quality of on design and testing; time to regulatory approval of a product
- Learning and growth – training days undertaken by staff; time to market of new product; percentage of drugs bought by TTPT that gain final approval.

This balanced scorecard now needs to be reviewed to ensure that it will address the company's objectives and the issues that it faces in its business environment.

Required:

(a) **Evaluate the performance measures proposed for PT's balanced scorecard.** (10 marks)

(b) **Briefly describe a method of analysing stakeholder influence and analyse the influence of four different external stakeholders on the regulator (BDR).** (8 marks)

(c) **Using your answer from part (b), describe how the application of the balanced scorecard approach at BDR would differ from the approach within PT.** (7 marks)

(25 marks)

4   PLX Refinery Co is a large oil refinery business in Kayland. Kayland is a developing country with a large and growing oil exploration and production business which supplies PLX with crude oil. Currently, the refinery has the capacity to process 200,000 barrels of crude oil per day and makes profits of $146m per year. It employs about 2,000 staff and contractors. The staff are paid $60,000 each per year on average (about twice the national average in Kayland).

The government of Kayland has been focussed on delivering rapid economic growth over the last 15 years. However, there are increasing signs that the environment is paying a large price for this growth with public health suffering. There is now a growing environmental pressure group, Green Kayland (GK), which is organising protests against the companies that they see as being the major polluters.

Kayland's government wishes to react to the concerns of the public and the pressure groups. It has requested that companies involved in heavy industry contribute to a general improvement in the treatment of the environment in Kayland.

As a major participant in the oil industry with ties to the nationalised oil exploration company (Kayex), PLX believes it will be strategically important to be at the forefront of the environmental developments. It is working with other companies in the oil industry to improve environmental reporting since there is a belief that this will lead to improved public perception and economic efficiency of the industry. PLX has had a fairly good compliance record in Kayland with only two major fines being levied in the last eight years for safety breaches and river pollution ($1m each).

The existing information systems within PLX focus on financial performance. They support financial reporting obligations and allow monitoring of key performance metrics such as earnings per share and operating margins. Recent publications on environmental accounting have suggested there are a number of techniques (such as input/output analysis, activity-based costing (ABC) and a lifecycle view) that may be relevant in implementing improvements to these systems.

Currently, the refinery has the capacity to process 200,000 barrels of crude oil per day and makes profits of $146m per year. It employs about 2,000 staff and contractors. The staff are paid $60,000 each per year on average (about twice the national average in Kayland). PLX has had a fairly good compliance record in Kayland with only two major fines being levied in the last eight years for safety breaches and river pollution ($1m each).

PLX is considering a major capital expenditure programme to enhance capacity, safety and efficiency at the refinery. This will involve demolishing certain older sections of the refinery and building on newly acquired land adjacent to the site. Overall, the refinery will increase its land area by 20%.

Part of the refinery extension will also manufacture a new plastic, Kayplas. Kayplas is expected to have a limited market life of five years when it will be replaced by Kayplas2. The refinery accounting team have forecast the following data associated with this product and calculated PLX's traditional performance measure of product profit for the new product:

All figures are $m's

	2012	2013	2014	2015	2016
Revenue generated	25.0	27.5	30.1	33.2	33.6
Costs					
Production costs	13.8	15.1	16.6	18.3	18.5
Marketing costs	5.0	4.0	3.0	3.0	2.0
Development costs	5.6	3.0	0.0	0.0	0.0
Product profit	0.6	5.4	10.5	11.9	13.1

Subsequently, the following environmental costs have been identified from PLX's general overheads as associated with Kayplas production.

	2012	2013	2014	2015	2016
Waste filtration	1.2	1.4	1.5	1.9	2.1
Carbon dioxide exhaust extraction	0.8	0.9	0.9	1.2	1.5

Additionally, other costs associated with closing down and recycling the equipment in Kayplas production are estimated at $18m in 2016.

The board wishes to consider how it can contribute to the oil industry's performance in environmental accounting, how it can implement the changes that this might require and how these changes can benefit the company.

Required:

Write to the board of PLX to:

(a) Discuss and illustrate four different cost categories that would aid transparency in environmental reporting both internally and externally at PLX.
(6 marks)

(b) Explain and evaluate how the three management accounting techniques mentioned can assist in managing the environmental and strategic performance of PLX.
(9 marks)

(c) Assess the impact of implementing an input/output analysis on the information systems used in PLX.
(3 marks)

(d) Evaluate the costing approach used for Kayplas's performance compared to a lifecycle costing approach, performing appropriate calculations.
(7 marks)

(25 marks)

End of Question Paper

Answers

Pilot Paper P5
Advanced Performance Management

Answers

1 To: Board of Mackerel Contracting
From: A Accountant
Date: XX XXX 20XX
Subject: APV contract, new information system and performance measurement

Introduction

Mackerel has to make a decision on which level of design expenditure and so on which type of APV to tender. This choice will be dictated by the objectives of the business and its appetite for risk.

(i) **Risks and risk appetite for APV contract**

It is natural to assume that the main objective of a business is the maximisation of shareholder wealth and in the context of the APV project the main measure of performance will be the profit made on the contract as this will drive the earnings over which the institutions are concerned.

However, in a decision where there is risk and uncertainty, the company also has to decide on its appetite for risk. Risk appetite is usually divided into three categories:
- risk averse individuals tend to assume the worst outcome and seek to minimise its effect
- risk seekers are interested in the best outcomes and seek to maximise their returns under these circumstances
- risk neutral individuals are interested in the most probable outcome

The risks for Mackerel arise from uncertainties in its external environment. The key stakeholders in this situation are the government (the customer) and Mackerel's shareholders. The other factor giving rise to uncertainty is the forecast price of steel, the main raw material in the APV's construction.

The shareholders have indicated a concern over earnings volatility and so seem to be risk averse. This is commercially sensible in a recessionary situation where the company's survival could be placed at risk if a large project (such as the APV) were to fail. The project can be seen to be large for Mackerel as the expected profit is $5m if package 1 is chosen and this is material when compared to the current operating profit of $20.4m.

A risk averse approach might also be called for where winning the bid could lead to additional future work so that securing a deal is more important than optimising profit. This appears to be the case here as the government is the major customer of Mackerel.

The demand level for the APV is also uncertain as the recession could lead to cuts in government expenditure. Defence spending is often considered more discretionary than spending on public services (such as pensions) especially if there is not an immediate threat of conflict. Thus, it has been difficult to predict the probabilities of the different demand levels. Given that there are significant fixed costs of design and development, these different levels have a material impact on the return from the project.

These problems in quantifying the level of risk will affect the choice of method of analysing the return from the contract. Mackerel should evaluate the contract using different methods and come to a conclusion based on the most appropriate one for its objectives and risk appetite.

A further source of risk is the danger of cost over runs. If successful in its tender, Mackerel will be working towards a fixed price for the contract ($7.5 m + budgeted variable cost per unit plus 19%). Any over runs of actual cost as compared to budget will reduce the profit margin earned.

A major cost risk is the cost of the primary raw material of production (steel). However, this has been fixed by the forward purchase of the steel for the contract. This has eliminated the risk of price fluctuations during the contract.

(ii) **Risk evaluation methods and results**

As was stated earlier, it is natural to assume that the main objective of the business is the maximisation of shareholder wealth and in the context of the APV project the main measure of performance will be the profit made on the contract. Although discounted cashflow would be a superior approach, there is insufficient data available here to calculate it.

The first priority is too ensure that the contract complies with the government requirement of a maximum per unit cost of $70,000 to Mackerel. The results per the Appendix 2 are:

Cost per unit	Demand		
	500	750	1,000
Package			
1	62,972	57,972	55,472
2	65,472	59,638	56,722
3	67,972	61,305	57,972

This complies with the contract specifications.

The total profit for each design package under the different demand levels is calculated at the Appendix 2 as:

Profit ($)	Demand		
	500	750	1,000
Package			
1	4,557,302	6,835,953	9,114,604
2	3,307,302	5,585,953	7,864,604
3	2,057,302	4,335,953	6,614,604

There are four possible approaches to selecting a package. The methods depend on the information available and the risk appetite of the decision-maker.

If we assume that there is insufficient information to make an estimate of the probabilities of the different demand levels then we are making a decision under uncertainty and there are three common methods of approach which depend on the risk appetite of the decision-maker (maximax, maximin and minimax regret). I have calculated payoff and regret tables in Appendix 1. The results can be summarised as follows:

Risk seekers and the risk averse will use profit under the different demand scenarios to make the appropriate choice.

Risk seekers will aim to maximise the possible returns from the different demand scenarios. The maximax method would be appropriate in this situation and here the company would be advised to choose design package 1 which will have a maximax profit of $9.1m.

Risk averse decision-makers will aim to maximise the minimum possible returns from the different demand scenarios. The maximin method would be appropriate in this situation and here the company would be advised to choose design package 1 which will have a maximin profit of $4.6m.

Pessimistic decision-makers will choose to focus on the lost profit (regret) compared to the best choice under that demand scenario. They aim to minimise the maximum level of regret that they can suffer under any demand scenario. This minimax regret method shows the company would be advised to choose design package 1 which will lead to no regret.

These conclusions should not be surprising as design package 1 has considerably lower fixed costs and yet is scalable to cope with all levels of demand.

A risk neutral manager does not take an optimistic or pessimistic stance. They will choose the option that yields the maximum expected value. This method depends on the use of probabilities for each of the outcomes. The risk manager has attempted to quantify the probabilities of the different levels of demand given the different design packages employed. It would be wise to involve both the design and sales teams in these estimates as such estimates are usually highly subjective and a broad canvassing of opinion may help to gain more accurate values.

The estimated probabilities allow the calculation of an expected profit for each choice of design package. Appendix 2 shows that the maximum expected profit of $5.6m arises if design 2 is chosen. This is due to the much greater likelihood of higher demand in that case. Design 3 does not seem to increase the chances of higher demand sufficiently to outweigh the extra fixed cost of $1.25m compared to design 2.

(iii) **Recommendation**

In this situation, the choice of method will depend on the risk appetite of Mackerel, whether this type of decision is likely to be repeated many times and the accuracy of the probability estimates. As Mackerel shareholders seem risk averse, the profit under the contract is significant compared to the operating profit of the whole company and the economic environment is difficult so the low risk method of maximin seems appropriate. The use of expected values appears questionable as the probability estimates have not been widely debated and in the current economic circumstances, the company's survival may be at risk and so the repeated trials necessary to make this method valid may not arise.

Design package 1 should be chosen as with unknown probabilities, it carries the least risk. The company could seek to sharpen the probability estimates and review the implications for company survival before considering the use of expected values although there is the potential to make an additional expected profit of $573k if we could justify choosing design 2 over design 1.

The risk over steel prices has been removed by using forward (advance) contracts to cover the purchase of the material required. As steel is used in many of the company's products, this should be investigated as a general risk management technique for the company.

(iv) New information system

The executive information system (EIS) will bring a number of benefits in decision-making at the strategic level at Mackerel but at certain costs and with certain problems at the operational and strategic levels. The key danger is that the tangible increase in costs is not balanced by the intangible (and difficult to quantify) benefits of the new system.

At the operational level, the data gathering will generate new costs as the expectations of users for immediate update of the system drive demand for less batch input of data. This problem represents an opportunity to automate the input of data in order to fully benefit from real-time data availability.

At the strategic level, the benefits relate to improved decision-making as the EIS should allow drill-down access to the more detailed operational records but the initial presentation of data should be based on the key performance indicators for the company. This system should also be linked to external data sources so that senior management do not fall into the trap of only looking inwards in the organisation at the risk of ignoring wider issues in the business environment (for example, the risks associated with the APV contract such as the effect of the recession and the attitude of government). These will represent new data sources and so again increase the cost of the system.

The new system will increase the amount of information and analysis that it will be possible for senior managers to perform. It will present opportunities for better decision-making using the more up-to-date information. However, it may present the problem of information overload for senior managers. Therefore, the system will need to be designed to give access to only those areas that it is appropriate for any given manager to see.

The data used in decision-making will be more robust as a single database will reduce the problem of redundancy where multiple copies of the same data are held on different systems. This will remove the danger of inconsistencies and reduce the storage required by the company. This benefit will be felt at the tactical level of the company were such data consistency will aid inter-functional communication.

The EIS would allow access to decision support systems such as large spreadsheet models built in order to pull data out of the database for use in forecasting and appraising projects (for example, demand forecasting and risk modelling of the APV contract).

The EIS will also give access to tactical information such as budgets in order to help the executive control the business.

In order to gain the maximum benefit from the new system, executive managers will need to be trained and this training should occur just before the new system is available so that they are in a position to use it immediately.

(v) Performance measures at Mackerel

The proposed new performance measures should be judged against the overall mission which is to maximise shareholder wealth and so optimise total shareholder return (TSR). It should be noted that TSR reflects both dividend returns and capital gains and so deals with both the current performance of the business (current dividend payments) and its expected future performance (as this dictates the share price).

The return on capital employed (ROCE) is calculated on profit before interest and tax divided by capital employed in a project or at the company as a whole. ROCE is a simple, commonly used measure of performance. However, it can encourage delays to investment in new assets since this measure improves as assets are depreciated with age. ROCE has the disadvantage of being based on profit measures of performance rather than cash. Measures such as NPV use cash flows which are less subject to the interpretation of accounting rules and are more directly aligned with shareholder interests. It is unclear that ROCE will align with the overall performance measure of TSR since TSR depends on share price and dividends paid. In particular, the fact that share price is based on a long-term view of dividend prospects makes the use of short period-based measures (such as profit) less valuable.

EVATM is an absolute performance measure. It involves a more complex calculation than ROCE with many adjustments to the accounting figures of profit and net assets, such as the use of replacement costs for asset values and economic depreciation rather than accounting depreciation.

Many of the EVATM adjustments are intended to avoid distortion of results by accounting policies that are present in ROCE. EVATM has the advantage that by treating certain costs as investments it encourages appropriate capital expenditure.

However, EVATM depends on historical data while shareholders will be focused on future performance. Thus, while EVATM is more directly aligned with the objective of increasing shareholder wealth, it too falls short of measuring shareholders' expectations which are present in the share price.

Conclusions

Given the current risk appetites of key stakeholders and economic environment, it is recommended that the design package 1 for the APV be chosen, as it carries least risk.

The new EIS represents an opportunity to gain considerable strategic advantage provided the costs of the new system are properly understood and controlled.

Neither ROCE nor EVATM represent a perfect match to the company's main external measure of performance (TSR) due to their backward looking nature. However, EVATM may be closer to the spirit of TSR in measuring increased shareholder wealth.

Appendix 1

Variable cost

Steel	11,412	9.4	Tonnes at $1,214
Engine/transmission	9,500		
Electronics	8,450		
Other	4,810		
Labour	13,800		
	47,972		

Payoff table

Demand	500	750	1,000	Max payoff	Min payoff
Design package					
1	4,557,302	6,835,953	9,114,604	9,114,604	4,557,302
2	3,307,302	5,585,953	7,864,604	7,864,604	3,307,302
3	2,057,302	4,335,953	6,614,604	6,614,604	2,057,302

Maximum of the maximum payoffs — package 1 — 9,114,604
Maximum of the minimum payoffs — package 1 — 4,557,302

Regret table

Demand	500	750	1,000	max regret
Design package				
1	0	0	0	0
2	1,250,000	1,250,000	1,250,000	1,250,000
3	2,500,000	2,500,000	2,500,000	2,500,000

Minimum of max regret package 1   0

Appendix 2

Demand	500	750	1,000
Variable cost	23,985,800	35,978,700	47,971,600
Fixed cost			
Package 1	7,500,000	7,500,000	7,500,000
Package 2	8,750,000	8,750,000	8,750,000
Package 3	10,000,000	10,000,000	10,000,000
Total cost			
Package 1	31,485,800	43,478,700	55,471,600
Package 2	32,735,800	44,728,700	56,721,600
Package 3	33,985,800	45,978,700	57,971,600
Cost per unit			
Package 1	62,972	57,972	55,472
Package 2	65,472	59,638	56,722
Package 3	67,972	61,305	57,972

Revenue $7.5M + (Budgeted variable cost x 1.19)

	500	750	1,000
	36,043,102	50,314,653	64,586,204

Profit ($)

Package	500	750	1,000
1	4,557,302	6,835,953	9,114,604
2	3,307,302	5,585,953	7,864,604
3	2,057,302	4,335,953	6,614,604

Expected profit

Package	500	750	1,000	Total
1	3,873,707	683,595	455,730	5,013,032
2	826,826	2,792,977	1,966,151	5,585,953
3	411,460	2,167,977	1,984,381	4,563,818

2 (a) The branch information appears to be inadequate on a number of levels to appraise the shop manager's performance. The manager should only be held responsible for those areas of performance that they can control.

The branch manager should be appraised on a realistic sales budget. The overall market fall of 12% suggests that the original budget of no change on previous year was not realistic. It is possible to analyse this by calculating planning and operational variances as follows:

	$	
Revised budgeted sales given market fall	234,080	
Budgeted gross margin	60%	
Revised budgeted gross margin	140,448	
Original budgeted gross margin	159,600	
Planning variance	19,152	A
Actual sales	237,100	
Revised budgeted sales	234,080	
	3,020	F
Budgeted gross margin	60%	
Operational variance	1,812	F

The operational variance reflects more accurately the manager's work and from this we can see the manager has done well by limiting the fall in gross profit by $1,812.

This analysis could be extended to other areas of the performance report. For example, if the breakdown of sales prices and volumes for individual product lines were given together with details of market volumes and price movements then the sales price variance could be broken down into operational and planning elements to reflect the manager's use of the limited discounting power that she has. Overall at the Tunny branch, the gross margin has remained constant (at 60%) which indicates that the manager may not have made use of the sales price discounting authority.

There are a number of other non-controllable costs in the branch information. It is unlikely that the branch manager can affect the price variance of heating and lighting costs as the prices are set through central purchasing although they will have some control over usage. The rental cost will reflect head office property management and is not controllable. The manager's own wages are not controllable although the staff costs will reflect the fact that the manager can choose to work longer hours and so save on part-time staff, therefore a labour efficiency variance would be appropriate.

A revised report would split the costs into two groups (controllable and on-controllable) so that a controllable profit would be shown as well as the overall shop profit. This would be the basic measure of performance of the store. A more detailed understanding of responsibility for the variances would be given by a breakdown of the operational (controllable) and planning (non-controllable) elements of each variance.

It might look like this:

Revised performance report
Albacore Chess Stores
Tunny branch   Year to Sept 2011

	Budget $	Actual $	Planning Variance $	Operational Variance $	Variance $
Sales	266,000	237,100	-28,900		
Cost of sales	106,400	94,840	11,560		
Gross profit	159,600	142,260	-17,340	-19,152	1,812
Controllable costs:					
Marketing	12,000	11,500			500
Staff costs Part-time staff	38,000	34,000			4,000
Controllable profit	109,600	96,760			-12,840
Non-controllable costs:					
Staff costs manager	27,000	27,000			0
Property costs	26,600	26,600			0
Shop profit	56,000	43,160			-12,840

Notes:
Property costs includes heating, lighting and rental.
Positive variances are favourable.

Summary
The manager's performance has been good in difficult general economic circumstances since if we exclude the gross margin planning variance ($19,152A) and allow that the part-time staff costs and marketing costs are controllable then we see that there is a favourable variance in controllable profit of $6,312 ($19,152-$12,840).

As indicated, additional variances that could be reported include operational and planning price variances for sales; part-time labour efficiency variances in operational variances; part-time labour rate variances in planning variances; and some price and usage variances for property costs. There is insufficient data to calculate examples of these variances here.

(b) The management style at Albacore is highly budget-constrained (Hopwood). It is driven by financial performance to meet the needs of the venture capitalist owners who have probably highly geared the business at the time of purchase. The cost control attitude is illustrated by the focus on achieving budget in the reward system and the enforcement of staff pay rates. This management style leads to stress for employees and difficult working relationships – as illustrated by the unhappiness of the shop managers. It also can motivate manipulation of performance reports although given the centralised nature of Albacore this appears unlikely at the shop level. It does however focus attention on achieving budget. This could be desirable in difficult economic circumstances.

Alternative styles are:
- profit-conscious where the performance is evaluated on longer-term effectiveness of the business unit in question (plausible here given Albacore's aim of profit maximisation)
- non-accounting where the budget is of low importance in performance evaluation

The performance appraisal system at Albacore reflects this cost-conscious, budget constrained approach. The shop managers are instructed as to their objectives and there appears to be no discussion of this target between the appraiser and the shop manager. For the branch given, it is striking that the failure to make budgeted profit (by $12,840) has lead to no bonus being paid although the shop made an operating profit of $43,160 and the operating margin of the shop has held up at 18% compared to 21% per the budget.

The branch information needs to reflect the areas that the manager can control as mentioned in part (a) to this answer. Using the analysis of revised controllable profit, we have seen that the manager has returned a good performance $6,312 ahead of budget. The increased use of operational and planning variances should help to motivate the managers and reduce the friction with senior staff.

The current contract between the manager and Albacore could be described as coercive as it is imposed. The budget should be agreed between the manager and their appraiser using the detailed knowledge of both parties to improve the budget estimates. Although for Albacore, the likely budget will reflect the expectations of the senior management in order to achieve the business' overall financial objectives.

The reward system could move to a more calculative basis where the manager is paid a percentage of the profit above a certain level, usually this bonus is capped to a maximum as in the current system. The senior management will need to assess the trigger level based on head office costs (administrative support and financing costs). Therefore, the operational director's assessment would become more objective and this could remove lack of clarity in how performance is assessed.

Performance appraisal could also recognise longer-term and non-financial factors in the manager's performance such as innovative marketing ideas and customer feedback on their shopping experience. Additionally, as the branch manager handles the shop's staff development, recognition could be given for branch staff who progress from part-time to shop manager.

3 (a) Evaluation of proposed performance measures

The financial perspective has not been altered from the existing measures of strategic performance. These are appropriate to address the objectives of enhancing shareholder wealth although it has been argued that measures such as economic value added or shareholder value added are better long long-term measures of this topic. Also, it is more common to use share price and dividend per share to reflect total shareholder return. Additionally, measures of survival (cashflows) and growth (in eps) could also be considered.

The customer perspective mainly seems to address the patient (end user) viewpoint. However, it should also reflect the concerns of those paying for the products (the government and insurers). Therefore, measures of cost in comparison to competitors would be appropriate.

The internal process perspective reflects appropriate measures of manufacturing excellence and efficiency in the testing process. This directly addresses the second of the board's objectives.

The learning and growth perspective would appear to be an obvious area to address the third objective on innovation. Again, the ranking of the measures is unclear and it would be surprising if training days were considered the principal measure. From the learning perspective of learning, it would be the improvement in the time to market from product to product that would better indicate learning and the improvement in percentage of drugs finally approved that would indicate learning. It may be appropriate to benchmark these measures against industry competitors as well as internally.

It is not clear if the points in the proposed scorecard are already prioritised and it may be appropriate to reconsider the order of measures, for example, in the internal perspective, the measure of time to gain approval seems to be more directly relevant to the objective of efficiency of the development process.

The suggested scorecard does not consider the difficulty of collecting data on some of the non-financial measures. For example, the measurement of above-industry standard design and testing is likely to be subjective unless the company undergoes a regular quality audit which can be scored.

(b) **Stakeholders and their influence**
The key stakeholders of BDR are the government, the drug companies being tested, the healthcare providers and their funders, and the patients.

A measure of influence of different stakeholders could be obtained by considering the degree to which they have power to affect decisions in the company and the likelihood that they would exercise their power (their degree of interest in the decisions). (Mendelow's matrix would be a suitable technique to perform this analysis.)

The government is an influential stakeholder on this basis as they have power over senior appointments and the funding of BDR. They are unlikely to use this power having delegated authority to the trustees, unless they are provoked by some financial or medical scandal.

The drug companies will be highly interested in the day-to-day workings of BDR as it sets the testing environment without which the drug companies will not have products. However, they will have little influence in the decisions within BDR as BDR must be seen to be independent of them. Nevertheless, it is in BDR's interest to have a successful drug development industry in order to achieve its goal of encouraging new drug development.

The healthcare providers will have interest principally in the quality of the approval process so they can have confidence about the cures that they dispense. They will have limited influence mainly through the pressure that they can bring to bear through the government.

The patients will be concerned that there is innovation as new cures are quickly and safely brought to market. They have limited secondary influence on decisions decision-making in BDR, as for the healthcare providers. Their influence will mainly be felt by affecting the actions of the government.

(c) **Differences in the application of the balanced scorecard**
The objectives at BDR are less obviously financial than at PT. The use of the balanced scorecard approach will be of great use to BDR as it emphasises non-financial performance which fits with BDR's objectives relating to quality of drugs and the relationship with key stakeholders. This can lead to difficulty in setting quantifiable measures due to the soft issues involved, e.g. measuring the level of user understanding of the risk/benefit profile of products. There is also the danger of setting quantifiable measures which are then obsessively pursued without regard to the softer aim of the organisation. An example could be the need to encourage drug innovation at the expense of making sure that each new product was a material improvement on existing drug products.

BDR will have a more complex balanced scorecard than PT due to the diverse nature of important stakeholders. As a public service organisation, the customer perspective may be more significant. The principal stakeholder is the government and so there will be a complex, political dimension to measuring performance.

The primary objective at PT is financial while at BDR there are several key objectives among which there is no clear ranking. Stakeholders may have conflicting objectives, for example, patients want effective drugs but the same individuals as taxpayers/insurance premium payers may not be willing to foot the bill if the price is too high. This will lead to difficulties in setting priorities among the various measures identified on the balanced scorecard.

4 (a) **Environmental cost categories**
PLX will need to identify existing and new cost information that is relevant to understanding its environmental impact.

There are conventional costs such as raw material costs and energy costs which should be broadened to include the cost of waste through inefficiency. These and other conventional costs (such as regulatory fines) are often hidden within overheads and therefore will not be a high priority for management control unless they are separately reported.

There are contingent costs such as the cost of cleaning industrial sites when these are decommissioned. These are often large sums that can have significant impact on the shareholder value generated by a project. As these costs often occur at the end of the project life, they can be given low priority by a management that is driven by short-term financial measures (e.g. annual profit) and make large cash demands that must be planned at the outset of the project.

There are relational costs such as the production of environmental information for public reporting. This reporting will be used by environmental pressure groups and the regulator and it will demonstrate to the public at large the importance that PLX attaches to environmental issues.

Finally, there are reputational costs associated with failing to address environmental issues when consumer boycotts and adverse publicity lose sales revenue.

(b) **Explanation and evaluation of techniques**
A lifecycle view consists of considering the costs and revenues of a product over the whole life of the product rather that one accounting period. For an oil refinery, this might be taken to be the useful life of the refinery. A lifecycle view may take profit or discounted cashflow as the principal measure of performance. This is particularly relevant for PLX given the planned redevelopment programme at the refinery which will highlight the decommissioning costs of such plant. This will aid future long-term investment planning at PLX.

Activity-based Costing (ABC) is a method of detailed cost allocation that when applied to environmental costs distinguishes between environment-related costs and environment-driven costs. At PLX, related costs would include those specifically attributed to an environmental cost centre such as a waste filtration plant while driven costs are those that are generally hidden in overheads but relate to environmental drivers such as additional staff costs or the shorter working life of equipment (in order to avoid excess pollution in the later years of its working life). This will assist PLX in identifying and controlling environmental costs.

Input/output analysis (sometimes called mass balance) considers the physical quantities input into a business process and compares these with the output quantities with the difference being identified as either stored or wasted in the process. These physical quantities can be translated into monetary quantities at the end of the tracking process. Flow cost accounting is associated with this analysis as it reflects the movement of physical quantities through a process and will highlight priorities for efficiency improvements.

These techniques are not mutually exclusive and all can assist PLX in improving performance. However, cost/benefit analysis will need to be undertaken for each of the systems. This will be difficult, as benefit estimates will prove vague given the unknown nature of the possible improvements that may accrue from using the techniques. The non-financial benefits will include a better public image and reduced chance of protest by environmental groups and an improved relationship with the government who is likely to be a key supplier of crude oil to the business. Additionally, ABC and input/output analysis will require significant increases in the information that the management accounting systems collect and so incur increased costs. As a result, the decision to use these techniques is likely to be based on the balance between known costs and estimated strategic benefits of non-financial factors.

(c) **Impact of input/output analysis on information systems**

Input/output analysis will require the information systems to collect not just monetary but also physical measurements of the materials being processed through the refinery. This may require additional records and costly changes to company's existing database structures. Systems will have to be put in place to monitor physical volumes of raw materials, waste and recycled material within the refinery's processes. The collection and use of such information may present a challenge to PLX with its culture of focussing on financial performance measures. The information that will be generated will help to identify efficiency improvements and so drive the profit margin and earnings of the company.

(d) **Lifecycle costing**

A traditional analysis of the costs of Kayplas might yield the product profit given in the original data. However, this ignores capital costs, environmental costs and the cost of decommissioning. A lifecycle analysis aims to capture the costs over the whole lifecycle of the product and it would show

Costs
Production costs	82.3
Marketing costs	17
Development costs	8.6
	107.9

Environmental costs
Waste filtration	8.1
Carbon dioxide exhaust extraction	5.3
	13.4

Other costs
Decommissioning costs	18
Total costs	139.3

This should be compared to revenues of $149.4m and leaves only a small overall return on investment (surplus of $10.1m). It should be noted that the decommissioning costs are estimated at $18m in 5five years. It is likely that given the difficulty in dealing with specialised equipment and the fact that environmental legislation may get stricter, this could easily be a significant underestimate. This could destroy all of the added value of the product.

The value of lifecycle costing often lies in the visibility it gives to costs that are determined in the early stages of the design of the product and in this case, it emphasises the need to minimise the cost of decommissioning. This should be done in the design phase of the refinery extension.

The traditional product profit analysis shows a surplus of $41.5m over the life of the product failing as it does to capture the environmental and decommissioning costs.

Additionally, if volumes of production can be ascertained then a cost per unit of Kayplas could be calculated and this would assist in price setting.

Pilot Paper P5
Advanced Performance Management

Marking Scheme

			Marks
1	(i)	Appropriate metrics	1
		Risk appetites 3 x 0.5	1.5
		Identify key stakeholders and risks	3
		Risk appetite	3
		Demand risk	1
		Cost overrun risk	2
		Other 1 mark per point made	
		Maximum	**9**
	(ii)	Comment on metric used: profit v DCF	1
		Variable cost per unit	1
		Total cost under each package	2
		Cost per unit contract check	2
		Revenue	1
		Profit total table	2
		Maximax calculation	1
		Conclusion	0.5
		Maximin calculation	1
		Conclusion	0.5
		Minimax regret calculation	2
		Conclusion	0.5
		Expected value calculation	1.5
		Conclusion	0.5
		(Working rounded to thousands is acceptable.)	
		Describe different methods 4 x 0.5	2
		Evaluate methods	4
		Maximum	**19**
	(iii)	Recommend method	2
		Final recommendation on contract	1
		Other risk reduction comments	1
		Maximum	**3**
	(iv)	New information system impacts	
		Operation information gathering up to 3 marks	
		Strategic decision-making	
		Benefits	up to 4
		Problems	up to 3
		Maximum	**8**
	(v)	Comments on TSR	Up to 2
		Comments on ROCE	Up to 3
		Comments on EVATM	Up to 3
		Maximum	**7**
		Up to 4 professional marks.	
Total			**50**

2 (a) Variances

Calculations:		
Flexed budget		1
Operation and planning (1 mark per point up to 4)		4
Controllable profit		1
Revised performance report	up to	8
Comments:		
Structure		1
Revenue budget unrealistic		1
Controllable costs		3
(general 1 specific justifications 2)		
Controllable profit		1
Other variances	up to	5
Maximum		**13**

(b)

Management styles (1 mark per point up to 6)	6
Performance appraisal system (1 mark per point up to 6)	6
Improvements (1 mark per point up to 3)	3
Maximum	**12**
Total	**25**

3 (a) 1 mark per point. There is a wide range of good answer points to be made. Points should be made about the measures suggested (whether they cover the perspective intended) and also, if there are other suitable measures. Other marks are for linking the measures to the stated company objectives, commenting on the difficulty of collecting appropriate data and ranking the measures. Maximum of 10 marks.

(b) Up to 2 marks on method of analysis. Up to 2 marks on each stakeholder. Answers must display a consideration of both the power and the likelihood of exercising it in order to score full marks. Maximum of 8 marks.

(c) 1 mark per point. In order to score highly, a candidate must give examples that are relevant to the scenario. Maximum of 7 marks.

(25 marks)

4 (a) Up to 2 marks per cost area discussed. Points must include examples of relevance to the scenario to score full marks. Maximum of 6 marks.

(b) Up to 2 marks per technique – an explanation and its link to environmental performance. 3 marks for an evaluation of the techniques. Maximum of 9 marks.

(c) 1 mark on need for more non-financial information (physical units). 2 marks for comments on sources and difficulties of collecting such information. Maximum of 3 marks.

(d) 2 marks for calculation of lifecycle costs. Up to 2 marks for calculating the product profits of the two approaches. Up to 4 marks for discussion of improvements and issues identified by lifecycle costing. Maximum of 7 marks.

(25 marks)